ESSENTIALS
OF
SHINTO

ESSENTIALS OF SHINTO

AN ANALYTICAL GUIDE TO PRINCIPAL TEACHINGS

Stuart D.B. Picken

Resources in Asian Philosophy
and Religion
Charles Wei-hsun Fu,
Series Editor

GREENWOOD PRESS
WESTPORT, CONNECTICUT • LONDON

Library of Congress Cataloging-in-Publication Data

Picken, Stuart D.B.
    Essentials of Shinto : an analytical guide to principal teachings
/ Stuart D.B. Picken.
        p.   cm.—(Resources in Asian philosophy and religion, ISSN
1073–1156)
    Includes bibliographical references.
    ISBN 0–313–26431–7 (alk. paper)
    1. Shinto. I. Title. II. Series.
BL2220.P47   1994
299'.5612—dc20   93–40619

British Library Cataloguing in Publication Data is available.

Library of Congress Catalog Card Number: 93–40619
ISBN: 0–313–26431–7
ISSN: 1073–1156

First published in 1994

Greenwood Press, 88 Post Road West, Westport, CT 06881
An imprint of Greenwood Publishing Group, Inc.

Printed in the United States of America

The paper used in this book complies with the
Permanent Paper Standard issued by the National
Information Standards Organization (Z39.48–1984).

10 9 8 7 6 5 4 3 2 1

Copyright Acknowledgments

The author and publisher gratefully acknowledge permission for use of the following material:

The Death Poems of Nogi Maresuke, quoted in *Six Lives Six Deaths*, ed. Robert J. Lifton. Yale University Press, 1979. Copyright © Yale University Press. Used by permission.

Text and diagrams from Yamamoto Yukitaka, *Kami no Michi*. Tsubaki Grand Shrine, 1985. Reprinted by permission of Tsubaki Grand Shrine.

Maps from Nagai Shinichi, *Gods of Kumano*. Kodansha International, 1968. Reprinted by permission of Kodansha International.

Every reasonable effort has been made to trace the owners of copyright materials in this book, but in some instances this has proven impossible. The author and publisher will be glad to receive information leading to more complete acknowledgments in subsequent printings of the book and in the meantime extend their apologies for any omissions.

To the 96th High Priest of the Tsubaki Grand Shrine,
THE REVEREND DOCTOR YUKITAKA YAMAMOTO,
the first Shinto Priest to receive an honorary doctorate in theology from
an American university in acknowledgment of his efforts to build
bridges of spiritual and cultural understanding across the Pacific Ocean,
this work is dedicated as my personal offering of
respect for his international achievements
and in appreciation of
the inspiring spiritual comradeship it has been my privilege to share.

Contents

Guide to the Romanization of Japanese Words, Expressions, Forms, and Styles

ROMANIZATION

Romanization follows the Kenyusha *New-Japanese English Dictionary* (1974), which uses a modification of the Hepburn system. The following exceptions to that system bring the text into line with the Kodansha *Encyclopedia of Japan*.

1. *m* instead of *n* is used before *p, b,* or *m,* as in *shimbun, kampaku,* or *Kemmu*.

2. *n* is retained where there is need to hyphenate a word, such as *Gen-pon* (instead of *Genpon*) or *han-batsu* (instead of *hambatsu*).

3. The final syllable *n* is distinguished with an apostrophe when it comes before a vowel or *y*, as in *San'in* or *San'yo*.

4. Macrons are used to indicate the long vowels *a, u,* and *o* except for the following:

   (1) the seven place names, *Tokyo, Kyoto, Osaka, Kobe, Kyushu, Honshu,* and *Hokkaido*.

   (b) in the case of Japanese words that have come into English usage (e.g., *Shinto, daimyo,* or *shogun*).

   (c) where established forms of romanization exist (e.g., Motoori Norinaga).

JAPANESE PROPER NAMES

1. General Names:

   (a) Italicization is used only where the entire name is in Japanese (e.g., *Inari Jinja*). Where the title is half in English, the italicization is dropped (e.g., Hachiman Shrine). The former style is preferred because the purpose is to familiarize readers with Japanese expressions. The Kodansha *Encyclopedia of Japan* preferred the latter because it was intended to be for more general use.

(b) In the names of Japanese *kami*, only the first letter is capitalized (e.g., *Ame-uzume-no-mikoto*).

(c) In the names of the *kami* and in technical expressions, hyphens are included to indicate Chinese characters where this is considered helpful (e.g., *Honji-suijaku-setsu*).

2. Personal Names

(1) For transliteration of Japanese names, the Library of Congress catalog cards are the standard reference. Where no reference exists, the most common form in use is listed.

(b) The order of names is as in Japanese, family name first and given name second (e.g., Hirata Atsutane).

(c) Where there may be more than one form or simply two or more names, both may be listed: for example, En no Gyoja (also known as En no Shokaku).

PLACE NAMES

1. These are romanized as described under "General Names" and capitalized as in English (e.g., Urawa City)

2. English generic terms such as *lake* or *mountain* are capitalized when used as part of a proper name (e.g., Mt. Fuji, but not Mt. Fujisan).

3. Where including English unnecessarily fragments the Japanese name, the Japanese is retained in full (e.g., *Dewa Sanzan* or *Kumano Junrei*). Because they are technical terms as well as place names, they are also italicized.

4. Older place names may be identified by a modern name: for example, Edo (present-day Tokyo).

PRONUNCIATION OF ISE SHRINE NAMES

The written Japanese names of the Inner and Outer Shrines at Ise may be read as Naigu (Inner Shrine) and Gegu (Outer Shrine). Older people of the Ise region have traditionally used Naigu and Geku (softening the *g* to *k* for ease in pronunciation in the case of the Outer Shrine). Another reason for the change is *kotodama*, or the theory that more pleasant-sounding words please the *kami*. Kodaijingu is pronounced Kotaijingu, and *betsu-gu* becomes *betsu-ku* for the same reason. Recent English language publications romanize the Inner Shrine as Naiku in keeping with the Outer Shrine as Geku. Beyond the desire for standardization, there is no other apparent reason for this.

DATES

1. Western dates may be followed by Japanese dating: 1945 (*Shōwa* 20).

2. Solar dates are generally identified for dates before 1873.

Preface

Shinto appears at long last to be receiving a little of the attention and respect to which I believe it is entitled, since it is a religion of one of the world's great civilizations. It has languished under the shadow of the State Shinto era and has been made to bear responsibility for a war in the process. As the victim of wartime propaganda it became the object of academic hostility. Its inclusion in this series on Asian religion and philosophy indicates that it has now been recognized anew as an authentic part of the Asian tradition, unique in that it belongs almost exclusively to Japan's history and culture.

My own first attempt at reinterpreting Shinto in social and religious terms was entitled *Shinto: Japan's Spiritual Roots* (Kodansha International, 1980). Among the reviews following publication was a most kind one by Professor Wilbur Fridell, who pointed out a few merits as well as some limitations of my approach. He concluded his review by suggesting that subsequent general studies of Shinto should begin from it. I hope that those who are interested in this book will complement it by reading the other. It presents a profile of Shinto as a living religion against the background of contemporary Japanese society in a manner that a strictly academic work can never achieve.

The present work, designed primarily as a work of reference, goes beyond empirical description to basic documentation. The format includes an initial historical overview of key aspects of Shinto to provide a general framework of understanding. Then it addresses the Japanese myths, their content, and controversies about interpretation, including the sensitive issue of the relationship between mythology and politics in modern Japan. Part I concludes with a discussion of Imperial Household Shinto rites as they are still performed, the most recent major ones being the accession rites of the present Emperor Heisei in 1991 and the wedding rites of Crown Prince Naruhito in 1993.

Part II examines Shrine Shinto, the Shinto of local shrine life, festivals, and the priesthood. To expand the content of the text as a work of reference, I have constructed a typology of Shinto divinities and related them to the architectural styles of buildings and gateways that are essential to their identity and recognition. Because Shrine Shinto and its life centers on festivals, there is a chapter devoted to the structure of the festival, to the *norito* (the liturgical invocations used at rituals) to the priesthood, and to certain shrine artifacts that are used at festivals and other occasions. Shinto survives more in ritual than in thought, and without reference to these it remains inaccessible and mysterious.

Part III addresses the various types of Sect Shinto. It deals with several forms of folk Shinto and identifies the thirteen recognized sects of Kyoha Shinto, namely, the sects and cults that grew out of orthodox Shrine Shinto but separated and developed independent identities at various periods. Following this is a discussion of certain Shinto-based new religions that have emerged in the twentieth century, some before and some after the Pacific War. There are many more than there is space to discuss. A comprehensive list is included for reference, but only sizeable and influential groups are discussed.

Part IV offers a reference base on Shinto thought. The unique symbiosis of Buddhism and Shinto that flourished during the Heian period is the starting point; from there, the development of different phases and styles of Shinto thought is discussed. Particular attention is devoted to the academic Shinto movement of the Edo period, when Japanese thinkers, following the defined hermeneutical methods, tried to separate within the Japanese mythology those elements borrowed from China from elements that were distinctively Japanese.

I conclude the book with several personal observations of comparison and contrast with Western thought. These may be of interest to philosophically inclined readers and may serve as datum points in Western thought from which to gain an enhanced interpretation of Shinto. My observations may not find universal acceptance, but the discussion may at least provide a starting point for the debate on how to interpret the many phenomena found in the world of Shinto.

I have consistently tried to present Shinto in terms of itself. For example, I have resisted the use of Western terms like *Shintoist* that are untranslatable or become meaningless if rendered into Japanese. Western models of religiosity or commitment to religious organizations have little relevance to Shinto or Japan. I have also preferred the word *shrine* in English as the translation of *jinja* in Japanese. Older works in English speak of *Shinto temples*, which I feel can lead to confusion. According to Webster, the word *shrine* may refer to any sacred place, which seems to be close to the meaning of *jinja*. *Temple*, by contrast, usually refers to a building. Buildings erected within shrine precincts in Japan have separate names and are designated as *shaden*, shrine buildings. However, the shrine is not to be equated with the buildings. I have also avoided translating *kami* as *god* to avoid confusion between different concepts of the divine. If this text succeeds in its aims, what Shinto means by *kami* should become clear.

The general objectives are dictated by the goals of the entire series, with which I happily comply—namely, to produce an English-language reference work on Shinto. I have tried to consult as much basic Japanese material as possible and as much as I could of more recent work by both Japanese and non-Japanese researchers on aspects of Shinto and related subjects based on the following general assumptions.

First, the study of Shinto is worth the effort because it carries tremendous rewards both in itself and because of what it reveals about Japanese history and civilization. Second, Shinto is a remarkably complex and elusive phenomenon to which Western categories about religion do not readily apply without doing violence to its distinctive character. Third, serious study of Shinto can only proceed from a basic grasp of the Japanese language and from broad experience of shrines, their life, and their activities. Fourth, the study of Shinto requires sensitivity because it touches upon some of the most precious and sacred elements of the Japanese tradition. Finally, the study of Shinto demonstrates that it is alive and well, not the dead or dying primitive religion of the critics but a vital form of natural religion that has its place in the pantheon of world religions. It makes its contribution along with the other religions to what Ninan Smart called (in a Judaeo-Christian metaphor) the *Long Journey*, but which I would prefer to describe (in terms more appropriate to Shinto) as the human pilgrimage to the peaks of spirituality, the ascent from *homo sapiens* to *homo excellens*.

Because this is a reference work in English, I have tried where possible to point to available secondary English-language sources. This should make research easier and enable those who do not seek to study the Japanese language to acquire a broad understanding of the essentials of Shinto.

I anticipate inevitable criticism by three self-confessed limitations. First, I acknowledge that there are omissions. The book is intended to present the *essentials* but not *everything* about Shinto. Second, claims to originality must lie, if anywhere, in the overall perspective into which Shinto is cast and the form into which the material is organized. Finally, this is a book written by a non-Japanese primarily for a non-Japanese audience. That fact conditions the style of presentation and influences the manner of explanation.

Acknowledgments could be endless, but I must single out a few to whom I would like to express deep and special thanks. To my good friend the late Professor Toshihito Gamo of Kokugakuin University, I bow my head in respect. His encouragement in the writing of my earlier work gave me the appetite to continue my probings. To my contemporary colleague and supporter, who has offered much about Shinto but most of all who made it all visible in himself, the Reverend Doctor Yukitaka Yamamoto, 96th High Priest of the Tsubaki Grand Shrine in Mie Prefecture, I consider no words of appreciation adequate. He may justifiably be considered one of the most luminous and charismatic priests within the contemporary world of Shinto, and he is very deeply committed to inter-religious understanding and dialogue. It goes without saying that I have been received with courtesy and patience at every shrine I ever visited. I have always received good counsel at the Association of Shrines and its international affairs division. Kokugakuin University has always been open, helpful, and very friendly, as have the two directors of the Japan Culture Institute I have been privileged to know, the late Professor Motoku Anzu and Professor Ueda Kenji. Several individuals looked at parts of this text in different forms and made helpful comments at various stages—Dr. J. Edward Kidder, Jr., formerly of International Christian University; Dr. Delmer Brown, formerly of U.C. Berkeley; Professor Fukuda of ICU; and Professor Asoya of Kokugakuin University, to name but a few. Research assistance has come from many sources and many conversations about Shinto over the years. Also, the efforts and patience of Dr. George Butler, Acquisitions Editor in Philosophy and Religion, and the editorial staff of Greenwood Press are due my hearty thanks, as they are to Professor Charles Wei-hsun Fu of the Series for the opportunity to assemble this work in the first place.

Introduction

MISUNDERSTANDINGS ABOUT SHINTO

It could be said that Shinto has been the subject of misrepresentation more than any other religion. Wide-ranging opinions about Shinto still exist among foreign scholars. The most negative are based largely upon superficial understanding or inadequate experience. This is especially true of early writers. Englebert Kaempfer (1651–1716), who first set foot in Japan in 1690,[1] referred to the three religions of Japan and declared that Shinto was the "old religion of idol worship." The British diplomat W. G. Aston concluded his nineteenth-century study of Shinto by saying that "As a national religion, Shinto is almost extinct. But it will long continue to survive in folklore and custom, and in that lively sensibility to the divine in its simpler and more material aspects which characterizes the people of Japan."[2]

These judgments seem unsatisfactory and inadequate because the same "extinct religion" has been held responsible by other schools of critics for the Pacific War. Clearly, there is room and requirement for improved understanding not only of Shinto as a religion but of what kind of religion it is and how it is related to Japanese culture and Japanese national life.

THE NAME "SHINTO"

The term *Shinto* in English comes from two Japanese words, *shin* (which can also be read as *kami*) and *tō*, or more commonly *dō*, meaning "way." Shinto therefore means the way of the *kami*, or the divine as understood in Japanese culture. The oldest recorded usage of *Shin-dō* is in the *Nihon-Shoki* dating to the Emperor Yomei (r. 586–587), who is said to have believed in the law of Buddhism and revered the way of the *kami*.[3] Consider the two elements separately.

Kami[4] is often translated as "god" with a small "g." This is usually taken as grounds for claiming that the religious culture of the Japanese is polytheistic. However, in the Japanese language, singular and plural are not distinguished as they are in Indo-European languages; and although there may be many *kami*, they all share the same character. *Kami* thus refers to the essence of many phenomena that the Japanese believed were endowed with an aura of divinity. Rocks, rivers, animals, trees, places, and even people can be said to possess the nature of *kami*. Anything that can inspire a sense of wonder and awe in the beholder, in a way that testifies to the divinity of its origin or being, can be called *kami*. What the German phenomenologist of religion Rudolf Otto described as the *mysterium tremendum et fascinans* would qualify as an intelligible definition of *kami*.[5]

Dō has three interesting background elements. First, it is a very important term of Chinese philosophy. The *Tao* of Chinese *Taoism* (as expounded in Lao Tzu's *Tao-Te-Ching*) is the same character, meaning "the teaching of the way."[6] Second, *dō* is used in Japanese as a suffix to several compounds that indicate ways, rituals, or disciplines. For example, there is *ken-dō*, the way of the sword (Japanese swordfencing); *ai-ki-dō*, the way of meeting of *ki*, or spirit (a Japanese self-defense art); *cha-dō*, the way of tea (the art of the tea ceremony, also known as *sadō*); and *sho-dō*; the way of or art of calligraphy. The number could be expanded considerably because Japanese culture makes use of *dō* to identify patterns of practice or discipline. The third meaning of *dō* is simply "way" or "road." In this aspect it is read as *michi*. Why was Shinto named as a *dō*?

Until the sixth century, it seems to have had no name. The gradual rise of Buddhism forced the indigenous cult to distinguish itself from *Butsu-dō*, the way of the Buddha. Hence the term *Shin-dō* (later *Shin-tō*), the way of the *kami*, was coined. Buddhism came to be called *Bukkyō*, the teaching of Buddha (in parallel with Christianity, which is called *Kirisutokyō*). However, Shinto remains a "way" because unlike either Buddhism or Christianity it has no historical founder. It is the natural expression of the spiritual feelings of the Japanese people, which grew and evolved with the development of Japanese history and society. The earliest indication of its importance was the establishment of the Office of Shinto Worship (*Jingikan*) around the time of the Taika Reform of 645 C.E. The Taihō Code of 701 C.E. stated that the highest government office was the Council of State (*Dajō-kan*) and that the Office of Shinto Worship was equal to it. Although its relationship with Buddhism over the centuries was complicated and it sometimes found itself at a disadvantage beside the complex doctrines and quasi-magic rituals of the sects of Buddhism, Shinto was never displaced as the local religion of agricultural communities and the supralocal cult of the families who were eventually to unify the nation.

THE TERM "JINJA"

Japanese religious sentiments were first connected with natural settings and were so deeply embedded in the Japanese perception of nature and its processes that there was no separate word to describe "nature" until the era of modernization, when the term *shizen*[7] was invented. In modern Japanese religious parlance, the term "Great Nature" (*daishizen*) is used with a cosmic or metaphysical flavor to describe the total context of human physical and spiritual life and that of the world itself.

The significance of this point can be seen in the meaning of the term *jinja*, which is translated in this text as "shrine." There are roughly 100,000 *jinja* in Japan, to be distinguished from Buddhist temples, or *tera*. These emerged in different parts of the country alongside the expansion of the communities for which they served as guardians. *Jinja* is a compound of two characters: *jin*, which in this case reads *kami*; and *sha* or *ja*, which means "place." Thus, *jinja* means literally "place of the *kami*." A shrine is a sacred area on which buildings or *shaden* are erected to revere the *kami* of that area.

THE CONCEPT OF KANNAGARA

An expression used in Shinto to refer to the divine essence of the processes and the law of the natural order is *kannagara*,[8] which also can mean "way of the *kami*." Here we see Shinto as a way. It grew and developed around certain impulses, sentiments, and feelings associated with an awareness of the sacred in combination with beliefs and rituals thought to have efficacy in the world of agriculture. It gave birth to a sense of the mysterious but unformulated set of influences, causes, and effects that surround and absorb everything and that bear life on its way. It is from this sense of *michi* that the values of Shinto are derived. People who follow the way are people who know the divine, the human, and how people should live. *Kannagara* is the sense of the term *michi* that marks those who recognize the way of the *kami* in all life.

The discussion of *michi* also introduces the topic of ethics in Shinto. It is frequently asserted that Shinto has no ethics.[9] It may not have formalized rules that guide people's conduct through life, but it is not unaware of a moral sense and it has a distinctive set of values derived from it. Values such as sincerity (*makoto*) or honesty (*tadashii*) have a particular meaning that relates to the overall Shinto view of life. The idea of purification in Shinto also carried ethical overtones.

ATTEMPTED DEFINITIONS OF SHINTO

Among the many descriptions of Shinto found in the writings of Japan's great scholars throughout the ages, the most influential come mainly from the eighteenth century. Ise Teijo (1714–1784) and Amano Nobukage (1660–1733) spoke of it as the Way to celebrate the *kami* of heaven and earth. Hayashi Razan (1582–1657) and Yoshimi Yukikazu (1672–1762) described it as the Way of government or the rule of right and justice, the Way by which the Emperor governs the country. Yoshikawa Koretari (1616–1694), Motoori Norinaga (1730–1801), and Hirata Atsutane (1774–1842) saw it as the Way to govern the country given by the Divine Ancestress *Amaterasu Ōmikami*. Confucian-Shinto scholars considered it to be the everyday Way or the right path of duty that should be followed by all human beings. It was the Way existing between lord and subject, man and wife, parents and children, brothers and sisters, and among friends. Festivities at shrines were of course important, but it was considered improper to regard only these as Shinto.

The view associated with State Shinto declared it to be the national religion that has been transmitted from the age of the *kami* (*kami-yo*). They claimed that it maintained the national constitution and was the moral basis of the nation. Other names for Shinto are *kami no michi* (Way of the Kami), *kannagara no michi* (Way of the Divine transmitted from time immemorial), *Kodō* (the Ancient Way), *Daidō* (The Great Way), or *Teidō* (The Imperial Way). Some of these terms are still in use. Definitions old and modern can be divided into those that affirm Shinto as a religion and those that deny it.

IS SHINTO A RELIGION OR NOT?

A not uncommon viewpoint put forward in Japanese is: "Shinto is not a religion, it is a folk way" (*Shinto wa shūkyō dewai nai, michi desu*). Reasons for this position should be carefully examined. Some Japanese believe that because Christianity or Buddhism have historical founders, they are therefore religions in the formal sense. Shinto simply grew and evolved and therefore should not be classified with them. There is a certain humility in this that should be respected, although I suggest that it may be a little misguided. If it is related to the definition of the term *shū-kyō* (religion) in Japanese (a compound of two terms meaning literally "sect-teaching"), and if religion is defined in terms of the teachings or beliefs of a sect, Shinto in a general way would be hard to classify as a religion. If, on the other hand, the Western etymology of "religion" is considered (that religion is a binding force within society), then the idea of Shinto as a Way would imply that it also is a religion in the fullest sense of the term.

A separate approach claiming that Shinto is not a religion stems from a totally ulterior motive and should not be regarded so generously. It comes from those who claim that if Shinto is not a religion but simply a form of tradition or folk culture, then it cannot clash with any religion. This is in parallel with the State Shinto advocates of prewar days who insisted that

Shinto could be a required practice for all members of the State. In the postwar era, those arguments are advanced to claim that were the Government to assume financial responsibility for the Yasukuni Shrine,[10] such an action would not constitute a violation of the constitutional separation of State and religion, because, by definition, "Shinto is not a religion." This argument is neither humble nor honest. According to some observers, it is a calculated attempt to circumvent the terms of the Constitution and begin the revival of the State Shinto.[11]

During the prewar years, all the various branches of the main religions of Japan, Christianity and Buddhism, were supervised by the Ministry of Education. Shinto was a *dō* (a folk way), and therefore it was supervised by the Ministry of the Interior (the *Naimushō*). A crucial impasse was reached in 1945, before the end of the war, when the Ministry of Education called in the heads of the United Church of Christ in Japan (the *Nippon Kirisutokyō Kyōdan*, a forced amalgam of all Christian groups) to inform them that all references to the Lordship in creation of God (which by implication belittled the Emperor) had to be removed from their literature. The Bible and the Hymnbook required rewriting! If State Shinto were not a religion, it would not have been sensitive to such claims. The truth of the case was given away by that very anxiety. Only the end of the war prevented that collision of ideas from becoming an open conflict.

Shinto can be justifiably described as the indigenous religion of Japan. It would require a peculiar definition of religion to exclude it from the realm of world religions. It should also be noted that if Shinto were not a religion and if Japanese religion were not as powerful as it is, it would not be so difficult for other religions to enter Japan and attract Japanese followers. Buddhism took six centuries to come to terms with Shinto. It is doubtful if such a length of time would have been required had Shinto not been a religion.

OBSTACLES TO GRASPING THE ESSENTIALS OF SHINTO

These arise mostly from the peculiar character of Japanese religion. It makes it impervious to standard forms of Western analysis and categorization and the typical Western assumptions about religion, which are extremely misleading if they are applied to Shinto without qualification.

Consider first the two aspects of Shinto that make the scholar's work very difficult. First, there is the perennial problem that meaning is lost in translation. Terms such as *purity* or *sincerity* can sound too naive to have deep meaning. The depth of the ideas does not come across in verbal equations. When they are written in Chinese characters, they are infinitely more suggestive of meaning and they function differently in the Japanese mind. *Harai* means more than the English word *purification*, and *chōwa* means more than merely *harmony*. In English the metaphor for harmony is musical, but *chōwa* does not mean simply a symphonic harmony of congruous sounds. It implies something more like wholeness or completeness and is also a social ideal, not simply a state of affairs within human relations.

Second, Shinto has no written scriptures and no formally enunciated set of beliefs. The strength of Shinto lies in its survival in ritual. Ritual has the power to keep thought alive. Ritual and its significance keep Shinto before people's minds. The cycle of nature and the life of agriculture lie in the background; however, not only have these recurring events been reflected in the rituals of Shinto, but the cycle of life of the Japanese people has found its rhythm through their influence. In commencing the study of Japanese religion in general and Shinto in particular, this is a vital point to understand. Shinto has been preserved most effectively not through doctrines but rituals and attitudes. Consequently, in the study of Shinto it is more important to pay attention to what people do rather than to seek formal statements of belief.

Beyond these points are several areas of contrast wherein differences create genuine obstacles to understanding. First, because Western religion (generally speaking) is often held most deeply at the personal level, the element of personal faith is assumed to be universal, which is not necessarily the case. Religion in Japan is community- and family-based far more than individually based, and community religions have great powers to survive because the self-understanding of the community is closely tied to them. For example, the central act of Shinto worship, the festival, is in essence a community celebration of life and its blessings. Families are usually registered at temples and come under the protection of shrines. This does not mean that the Japanese do not have individual beliefs. They do, of course. Nevertheless, the emphasis is upon the family. Not infrequently, for example, people who have been Christian throughout their lives will be buried according to Buddhist rituals in the family temple with no regard given to personal beliefs. The old system of temple support known as *danka-dera* (required temple registration) was law during the Tokugawa era; it required that families register at a local temple. Although for some the relation between the people and the temples and shrines may have been one of devotion, undoubtedly for many it was simply a matter of legal requirement. Consequently, not a great deal can be drawn from the meaning of temple or shrine associations in terms of the relationship of individuals to them.

This problem is complicated by confusion over the meaning of *mu-shūkyō* in Japanese.[12] When Japanese are asked about their religion, they frequently answer "*mu-shūkyō*," which means literally "no-sect doctrine" but which usually comes out as "no religion" in loose translation. The reasons why the idea and the form of words is used lie in Japanese history. During the Edo period, when Christianity was prohibited, people were required once a year (usually on New Year's Day) to visit their registered temple and stand on a brass plaque depicting a crucifix. To refuse to do so was to arouse the suspicions of government agents, who in the early years of Edo pursued known Christian families for up to four generations until there was reason to conclude that the Christian ideas had died out. The system of compulsory registration at a temple had the effect of disillusioning many people about organized religion. It had the additional effect of persuading people to conceal any religious ideas or feelings they may have had. Indeed, it was not until the early nineteenth century that any new religious movements began to emerge. Those developments coincided significantly with the more obvious signs of decline in the power of the Tokugawa government. These new movements became Sect Shinto (*Kyōha Shinto*), recognized as such by the Meiji government after the transfer of power in 1868. They possessed, relatively speaking, specific doctrines in contrast to the less structured beliefs associated with followers of Shrine Shinro (*Jinja Shinto*).

Mu-shūkyō therefore really means that the individual has no specific doctrinal preferences or is not too concerned about sects or cults. It does not mean that he or she has no interest in religion or has no religious beliefs whatsoever. Indeed, the individual may well have religious feelings—associated particularly with sacred places, those that have a special aura about them. Surveys on Japanese religiosity have shown that religious feelings are expressed mostly in relation to these.[13] Consequently, Japanese religion tends to be based on feelings rather than ideas, on experiences rather than doctrines. *Mu-shūkyō* must be understood in that context and as a natural barrier to receiving exact doctrinal ideas from anyone who may belong to a religious movement. For the average person who has no specific affiliation, *mu-shūkyō* serves to keep unnecessary inquiry at a distance.

These two points are directly related to a third, namely, that Japanese religion exists much more at the subconscious level than does Western religion. The religious traditions of Japan, particularly Shinto, remain alive in habits of thought and behavior rather than in a formal way. People visit shrines at times like New Year and on special occasions within the cycle of life's events. There is less general discussion of religious ideas and a minimal history of religious controversy as compared to the West.

Because the concept of nature and reverence for ancestors is basic, in both cases the key concept of dependence and its related notion of thanksgiving are central. These are expressed in many actions throughout life but may be seldom articulated. For example, there is no special meaning behind the simple term for gratitude (*kansha*) in Japanese. Western investigations often mistakenly focus on what people explicitly claim to believe as though it could not be possible for people to follow a religion unless they are able to explain in detail what they believe, as opposed to simply believing by following those around them to express their relationship to community life. Any study of Japanese religion must take full account of these three points of contrast.

A further hindrance to the academic understanding of Japanese religion in general is that Japanese thought tends to be eclectic; consequently, consistency of ideas or practice is not a prerequisite for credibility. There is indeed a notable lack of interest in formal consistency of beliefs or ideas. Shinto is not easy to understand in terms of ideas, and it does not offer solutions to keep questions like the theodicy. This characteristic has encouraged some Western scholars to dismiss Shinto as "primitive," unworthy of the attention of intellectuals. The fact that most Japanese (often including Shinto priests) cannot give a coherent, let alone consistent, account of Shinto has led these critics to imagine that Shinto can be ignored or that it plays no important role in religious or social life. But on what basis is it argued that lack of intellectual content disqualifies a religion from having an important place in society and life? Furthermore, if the average Western person with a similar loose relationship to Christianity was asked to give an exposition of his or her beliefs, what view of Christianity would emerge? How intelligible would it be, and would that disqualify it from being taken seriously?

This particular difficulty is enhanced by the fact that Western civilization is heavily dependent upon the verbal and that the role of language in Western religion is different from its role in Japan. The Hebrew term *dabar* implied power and energy beyond the human. The *dabar*, the "Word of God," was the agent of creation in the Hebrew mythology (Genesis 1:1). The New Testament (John 1:1), using the Greek term *logos* (also translatable as "word"), impresses the idea of Christ as the Word and uses the concept of *dabar* again. Greek tradition stressed the role and importance of words and language; thought came to be best expressed in language,[14] and thereafter in other forms such as rituals. The practice of verbalizing everything became the dominant style of Western thinking, with philosophy and literature accordingly using accurate and specific forms of expression.

The definition of Christian beliefs was the work of Christian councils of theologians and theological lawyers who used categories of Greek philosophy in the Latin language to try to express the nature of the Divine, of God, Jesus Christ, and the Holy Spirit. These exercises in verbalization gave rise to the statement for Christians in the form of a creed (*credo*, "I believe") stated in a set of propositions. The Apostles' Creed, the Nicene Creed, and the later Confessions of Faith of the sixteenth century are monumental illustrations of the tradition. There is no counterpart in Japanese religion to this approach, not even within Buddhism.

Western religions are predominantly religions of revelation with defined beliefs. Perhaps most decisive of all is the degree to which Western religion with its emphasis upon revelation has rejected and devalued natural religion or religions of nature. In the view of the nineteenth-century approach to "primitive religion"—to any religion that had a regard for nature or that saw religion as "natural" to human beings—revelation was considered superior. The Christian revelation was made the standard of all religions. Anything that differed was downgraded or condemned. This explains the existence of some of the views of Shinto noted earlier in this introduction. The "superiority" approach, along with the peremptory dismissal of mythology that it entailed, was challenged by Mircea Eliade, who claimed that such out-of-hand rejection of what he called *archaic ontology* had not only robbed the human intellectual task of many potential insights but at the same time had left a negative legacy within the development of Western thought.[15]

Religion, folk customs, and superstition are firmly distinguished from religion in the Western tradition, which has tried to place religion and reason in high prominence and to dispel ideas of a universe in which there is anything but Divine Providence. However, under influence from China, Japanese religion also accepted and used the Oriental Zodiac and did not reject fortune-telling. The fortune-teller in Japan has a long history, going back to the earlier times, and he still exists. The preference for auspicious days in the calendar, the avoidance of unlucky days, and seeking the advice of a fortune-teller regarding when to travel, marry, to have children are still very common. Intelligent and successful business people are not immune either. Before moving the desk in an office, some still have the fortune-teller come and give advice. This is in sharp contrast to the West, where such actions are associated with the occult or semi-occult and therefore are not approved by official religion. To people who live in a totally demythologized universe, it is all nonsense. The same cannot be said of Japan.

The monothesim versus polytheism typology is another potential framework of misunderstanding. The *kami* of Japan tended early on to be geographically limited in their spheres of influence; therefore, concepts of universality or the power of a *kami* outside a certain area were late in developing. If *kami* is equated with "god," the case for Shinto being classified as polytheistic seems closed. But the *kami* of Japan all share the nature of *kami* even though they have many manifestations. Polytheism and monotheism are Western terms that were designed to contrast phenomena from totally different religious worlds. Furthermore, there is within Western religion the standing claim of Islam that Christianity is polytheistic. Buddhism is not even theistic, yet in Japan the Buddhas and the *kami* are sufficiently close to make the case that Japanese Buddhism might be considered a form of polytheism!

The rituals surrounding the death of Emperor Hirohito and the accession of Emperor Akihito drew attention to another mistaken Western assumption, namely, that sacral societies are part of past civilization, or that their existence is incompatible with modern industrialization. One principal reason why the Imperial system, the *tennōsei*, is not satisfactorily discussed in the West, especially in the press and in magazines, it that the models on which thinking is built fail to recognize that Japanese society is still in some regards a sacral society, one in which sacral kingship is exercised by the Emperor. The importance of this, and the rituals, is simply not grasped; until it is, questions and problems surrounding the Imperial system will remain nebulous in the extreme. In the famous movie about Japan's final moments before surrender, *Nihon no Ichiban Nagai Hi* (Japan's Longest Day), in anticipating the surrender and its implications one politician makes the observation that "So long as the *Tennōsei* survives and the rituals are followed, Japan will continue to exist." It is doubtful if the modern Western mind is equipped to grasp that kind of "archaic" logic. Emperor Hirohito's denial of divinity should be understood against this background. First, he was never regarded as divine in the Western sense of the "divinity of Christ." Second, as later commentators have remarked, the outward form changed little because he continued to perform the roles that were his duty before the "change of status."

Western models can be unhelpful at best and decisively misleading at worst. Because of their dominant historical consciousness, Western religions tend to stress exclusivity. In contrast to this, consider the fascinating situation in Japan whereby people can belong to more than one religious group at any one time. In the New Religions, this comes out very clearly. In being invited to join one or another of these groups at different times, I was assured that I could retain whatever other religion I had. The new one would simply add depth to what I possessed already. For example, the idea of being baptized a Protestant and dying a Roman Catholic would be considered equivalent to soliciting a passport to hell in some conservative evangelical quarters. "No man can serve two masters" is often quoted as justification for this. Søren Kierkegaard used the title *Either/Or* for one of his writings that makes precisely this point, the need to make a decision to believe and to be committed to that belief. The nature of commitment in some religions may ultimately call for or demand a degree of exclusiveness. This, of course, can also have a darker side. The mutual lack of tolerance within and between Islam, Judaism, and Christianity has been a regrettable source of many religious conflicts throughout Western history. But are commitment and exclusiveness logically entailed states of mind? Tolerance (*kanyō*) is a feature of Japanese religion that the Westerner often misinterprets as lack of commitment or lack of seriousness. The truth is far from this. The Japanese see religion in such a way that it would not be a matter over which they would go to war. It should enhance life, not destroy it. What religion can justify killing another human being because he defines "God" in a different way? What kind of god would approve of this?

Japanese religion is free from the ideological taints that make Western religions sources of potential violence as well as grace. It was the crude display of such a lack of *kanyō* (tolerance) that led to the expulsion of Christianity from Japan in the sixteenth century. The Franciscan missionaries from the Philippines attacked Japanese religion with aggressiveness and hostility, burning shrines and temples and simultaneously giving the government a great deal of concern about what kind of society would be created if Roman Catholic Christianity were permitted to expand.[16]

Finally, in the Western mind there remains for some the problem of the lingering image of State Shinto. Alongside the development of Shinto as a folk way, there was an input from the government that climaxed in the late nineteenth century.[17] From the Meiji period onward, in spite of protests from many Shinto leaders the government used Shinto as a unifying national ideology. This occurred along the lines of the fabricated blood and soil ideologies that served the causes of national unification in nineteenth-century Europe. This aspect of Shinto was most readily identified in the West as the source of Japan's wartime militarism. Even a cursory look at Japanese society will show that Japan had all the makings of a military society long before State Shinto came on the scene. After 1946 Shinto returned to its former status, although it has continued to bear the stigma of its abused past. It is also a fact that during the era of State Shinto (*Kokka Shinto*) many shrines were forcibly merged against the will of local communities; and not a few of these, enjoying postwar liberation, were restored by those who thought their shrines had been improperly treated by the government. Also, some Shinto priests took a dim view of both State Shinto and the Pacific War.

SHINTO IN CONTEMPORARY JAPAN

Shinto today comprises a loose agglomeration of approximately 80,000 shrines. Among these are 200 that are central shrines of various *kami*, cults, or districts; and over 2,000 that could be called major shrines.[18] They can be classified according to their historical standing, location, or the particular *kami* that are enshrined in them. Although in certain regards they are different in their function from Western churches, shrines contribute to the survival of "Shinto" in the abstract, as the structure of beliefs and ideas that undergird the fabric of Japanese life and society in private as well as in public.

The general support for Shinto and for Shinto shrines is more readily observed at some times of the year than others. Festivals are still central events of community life, as they have been for centuries. It is in these that the heart of old Japan can most easily be seen, beating with strong rhythmic intoxication to the flute and the drums. Fields and farmhouses as well as factories and firms still acknowledge the way of the *kami*. The strategic location of shrines makes it obvious that they fulfill a role in the national way of thinking that would take more than a government edict to obliterate. The worldview of Shinto remains the *Weltbild* or *Weltanschauung* of the Japanese, the principal source of self-understanding within the Japanese way of life. Shinto is indeed a religion that is "caught" rather than "taught," its insights "perceived" before they are "believed," its basic concepts "felt" rather than "thought." As one eminent Japanese of an earlier generation observed, Shinto is interested not in *credenda* but in *agenda*, not in things that should be believed but in things that should be done.[19]

The finest possible introduction to Shinto, which underlines how much it is a religion of experience, is to take part in a festival, to help carry the portable shrine (*omikoshi*) or pull one of the great wagons through the streets. For the truly adventurous, I suggest making the journey to a mountain shrine to plunge into an ice cold waterfall at midnight with crisp, frozen snow on the ground. In *misogi shuhō*, purification under a free-standing waterfall, the cosmic, the mysterious, and the energizing life of the waterfall meet and explain more eloquently than any number of words why Shinto, with neither scriptures nor saints, has survived as the basis of Japanese religion and culture and why it will continue to remain the living spiritual roots of Japanese culture.

NOTES

1. Englebert Kaempfer, *History of Japan*, 2 volumes (London 1727)), tr. by J. G. Scheuchzer.

2. W. G. Aston, *Shinto: The Way of the Gods* (Longmans, London, 1905), p. 377.

3. *Nihon Shoki*, Book XXI.

4. The etymology of *kami* is complicated by the fact that the term was in use in Japanese before the written script was introduced from China. Hirata Atsutane (1776–1843) thought it was derived from *kabimoye*, meaning "to grow and germinate." Yamazaki Ansai (1618–1682) said it was an abbreviation of *kagami*, "mirror." Another suggestion was an abbreviation of *kashi-komi*, "reverential awe." Hori Hidenari (1819–1897) suggested a reference to the dual aspects of the divine: *ka*, meaning "something concealed," and *mi*, meaning "something visible." *Ka*, meaning "strange," and *mi*, meaning "a person," was another explanation. The dictionary lists several words pronounced as *kami* but having different Chinese characters assigned to them. The principal ones are (1) top or upper part (of a district), (2) seasoning, (3) feudal lord, (4) housewife, (5) paper, and (6) hair. Numbers 5 and 6 are pronounced a little differently, with the tone falling on the second syllable. The study of Shinto words and their origin is a basic form of research, particularly in the study of *Kotodama*, the spiritual meaning of words in the *norito*.

5. Rudolf Otto, *Das Heilige*, 1917 (*The Idea of the Holy*, Pelican, London, 1959).

6. *Tao* is almost as versatile in Chinese as *logos* (word) was in classical Greek. *Tao* is used in the New Testament to translate *logos* (John 1:1).

7. The etymology of *shizen* is a combination of *ji*, meaning "self," and *zen*,

meaning "to decree": "That which moves by its own decree," rather different from *natura* in Latin.

8. Yamamoto Yukitaka, *Kannagara to Shinto* (Shinryusha, Tokyo, 1971) pp. 13–18.

9. See Chapter 10 for a fuller discussion of this issue.

10. The government, inspired by the Liberal Democratic Party, has unsuccessfully initiated five bills to this effect in the National Diet since 1946. See Helen Hardacre, *Shinto and the State* (Princeton University Press, 1989), pp. 145–157.

11. Dr. Ernest Lokowandt of the East Asia Society House in Tokyo made such claims in a paper read to a joint meeting with the Asiatic Society of Japan in 1982.

12. Stuart D. B. Picken, "Religiosity and Irreligiosity in Japan: Aspects of *mushūkyō*," *Japanese Religions* 11 (December 1979): 51–67.

13. Joseph Spae, *Japanese Religiosity* (Tokyo, Oriens Institute for Religious Research, 1971), pp. 218–219. The data are based on pre-1970 research.

14. Ernst Fuchs, *Gesammelte Aufstäze Zur Frage nach dem historischen Jesus* (J.C.B. Mohr, Tübingen, 1960), pp. 143–167, 219–430.

15. Mircea Eliade, *Le Mythe de l'éternel retour: archétypes et répétition* (NRF Paris, Library Gallimard, 1949). The first English version was *The Myth of the Eternal Return, or Cosmos and History* (Princeton University Press, 1954).

16. Immaneul Kant, in his *Essay on Perpetual Peace* (Library of the Liberal Arts Edition, Bobbs Merrill Press, New York, 1957, pp. 22–23), positively applauded the action of the Edo government in expelling Roman Catholic missionaries because they were perceived as a subversive threat to an ordered society.

17. Japan was merely following the international trend toward self-defining forms of nationalism. Whereas Prussia and Italy created these in the interests of national unity, Japan's isolation had engendered greater cultural homogeneity than was possible in Europe. This may be one reason why Japan's nationalism took such radical and extreme forms.

18. For names, addresses, and telephone numbers, see *Sourcebook of Shinto* (Greenwood Press, Westport, CT, forthcoming).

19. Nitobe Inazo, *Bushidō: The Moral Ideal of Japan* (Heinemann, London, 1924), p. 24.

Part I

HISTORY AND MYTHOLOGY

Chapter 1

Historical Aspects of the Development of Shinto

HISTORIOGRAPHY, JAPANESE HISTORY, AND SHINTO

The writing of history is more than a matter of reading documents, gathering information, and drawing conclusions. History, the past, is inaccessible directly to the present precisely because it is the past, witnessed only by those alive at the time. Without the exercise of what R. G. Collingwood called the a priori historical imagination,[1] no reconstruction of history is possible at all. This is evidenced by the way in which archaeological research calls for such imagination to interpret the use of utensils, for example, in recreating the life of a past civilization within the mind of the researcher. In the case of shinto, immediate experience of its artifacts and rituals as well as the study of documents become means of gaining access to the secrets of the past. The researcher may then produce interpretations that are actually judgments on what has been observed. This does not imply that historical research is arbitrary, but it means that the organization of information and its subsequent evaluation is selective and is based upon insights the researcher has gained by sifting through the materials of the past. Consequently, different theories have been formulated about the historical origins and development of Shinto. In examining these, two important points should be borne in mind.

First, the historical development of Shinto cannot be separated from the entire history of Japanese religion, including that of Buddhism, Confucianism, and other continental influences that have interacted for centuries. The fate of Shinto has been intertwined with the fate of Emperor's courts in different eras, with the rise and fall of powerful Buddhist groups, and with the overall destiny of the nation. This makes it difficult to speak of Shinto as having an independent history as a religion. Nevertheless, an identifiable strand of tradition can be isolated for discussion and called the development of Shinto in Japan. However, we must recognize that when the term *Shinto* is used, the denotation might be similar but the connotation in different eras may vary considerably.

Second, although there is Shinto with a capital "S"—the religion, the cults, the shrines, and the rituals—there is also shinto with a small "s." The latter exists not only in rituals and acts of reverence but more so in the attitudes that find expression in many actions of daily life, like taking baths at night or washing the porch of the house every morning. These attitudes are both derived from and embedded in mindsets and linguistic forms that function like an implicit metaphysic, guiding thought and behavior firmly but almost imperceptibly.[2] Throughout the text, the distinction between the two has been carefully maintained. However, the distinction is easier to draw than to apply, owing to the fact that various shrines and priests within the tradition (Shinto with a capital "S") have developed their own forms of shinto (with a small "s") because they also became the popular beliefs of masses of people. There is a further distinction to be noted: a distinction between cults that have their roots in the written Japanese mythology, and cults that came into existence at a later date or through folk traditions.

Shinto: Cult of the People or the State?

This question is raised because Shinto has been described as the source of Japan's creative spirit[3] on the one hand, and as an incorrigible source of militaristic nationalism[4] on the other. Although the roles need not be incompatible, the question draws attention to two faces of Shinto. There are folk origins as well as cults encouraged by governments, and these have not always coexisted harmoniously. There have been times of conflict and times of peaceful growth. In the creation of State Shinto, the conflict is seen at its height. The Meiji period government, in the interests of manipulating Shinto as a state ideology, was prepared to sacrifice the entire popular spirituality of Shinto to the extent of suppressing shrines and removing *kami* from communities. This underlines the dual origins of Shinto and the ways in which local and national interests have not always been harmonized. Sect Shinto (of the late Edo period) and the New Religions (of the twentieth century) show striking parallels in their development. They are windows that enable the outside observer to see into the popular religious mind. The august status of the Grand Shrines of Ise and the veneration with which they are regarded illustrate the awesome respect in which the Imperial tradition is held, along with its primal *kami*, Amaterasu, the *kami* of the sun.

The chart in Diagram 1[5] is arranged in parallel columns. It presents a historical diagram of the era of Japanese history and the various cults and traditions that developed within them. It distinguishes the two sets of origins: those that can be assigned to the work of non-institutional religious leaders, mountain holymen, and local folk religious culture; and those that the government chose to encourage, support, or manipulate for the purpose of greater political and social control. The creation of State Shinto in the early years of Meiji brings these lines together. The diagram closes with the establishment of the Voluntary Association of Shinto Shrines (the *Jinja Honchō*) in the postwar era.

The Problem of Sources

Shinto is highly visible in Japan, but not so readily accessible to historical investigation. It survives primarily in rituals. If you look at ancient drawings of the removal of the *kami* of the Grand Shrines of Ise to a renewed building every twenty years (*Shikinen Sengū*) and at a modern photograph, the angle of carrying the canopies has probably not changed since the Heian age or before. The rituals have to be studied, their significance stated, and their meaning interpreted by drawing out the implications of the symbolism involved.

Documents do exist from individual shrines or eras, but most date from the introduction of the writing system from China. The Japanese mythology and the various codes that exist in written form all postdate the arrival of Buddhism. Later texts like the *Engishiki* assemble and collate already existing formulas and forms but give no indication of their age. As Japanese history progresses, documents in the form of government records and the records of individual shrines begin to accumulate and a composite picture begins to emerge. In the early phases, however, the archeologist must be given pre-eminence as the principal researcher of Japan's pre-Buddhist heritage.

Chart of the Development of Shinto

Era	Folk Tradition (Popular Origin)	Government-Acknowledged (Political Origin)
Jōmon	Primitive Religion (1) Animism (2) Nature Worship	
Yayoi	(3) Ancestral Reverence (4) Shamanism (5) Agricultural Rites	

Kofun	Primitive Shrines	Buddhism, Confucianism, and Tao-
	Ujigami of clans	ism are recognized by the Court
Taika Re-	Jinja Shinto	Imperial Shinto
form 645–650		Nakatomi clan chieftains as priests
Nara 711–794		Rise of Hachiman kami
Heian 794–1185	Shimbutsu shūgō kei	Honji-suijaku-setsu
	Jinja combined	(Assimilation Principle)
	shrines and temples	Sannō-Ichijitsu Shinto (Tendai-shū)
	Rise of Jingū-ji	Ryōbu-Shinto (Shingon-shū)
Kamakura	Hokke-Shinto (Lotus	Ise Shinto formalized
1185–1333	Shinto)	Yoshida Shinto (Yoshida Kanetomo
	(Nichiren)	1435–1511)
	Shugendō and Mik-	Yuiitsu Gempon Sōgen Shinto
	kyō	Urabe Shinto
Muroma-	Yashikigami	Gakuha Shinto
chi 1333–1600		Yoshikawa Shinto
		Watarai Shinto (Watarai Nobuyoshi 1615–1691)
		Suiga Shinto (Yamazaki Anzai 1618–1682)
Edo 1600–1868	Minkan Shinto	Restoration Shinto
	Inari Shinko	Kokugaku
	Kyōha Shinto	Motoori Norinaga (1730–1801)
	Tenri-kyō	Hirata Atsutane (1776–1843)
	Kurozumi-kyō	Expansion of Jingū-ji
	Konkō-kyō	
Meiji Restora-		Separation of Buddhism and Shinto
tion 1868		Shimbutsu-bunri

KOKKA SHINTO
(STATE SHINTO)
Jinja Honchō
Post-1945

PRE- AND PROTO-HISTORIC ROOTS
(B.C. 7000–552 C.E.)

The ancient Japanese probably began to form a civilization around the eighth century B.C., although no exact dates can be given.[6] Archaeologists identify the following periods.

Jōmon (Neolithic): B.C. 7000–250

This era is identified by Stone Age clay pottery with distinctive *jōmon* rope markings made by pit-dwellers of obscure origins who lived by hunting and fishing. Japan's oldest pottery dates to before 10,000 B.C., which is early by world standards. The relationship between religious rites or practices that existed then and what later became Shinto can only be a matter of speculation. For example, figures have been discovered in Ehime Prefecture etched on small stones and clearly depicting the female form, perhaps anticipating the fact that the primal divinity of the Japanese of later days would be female. Some have been found set up on other stones, almost like an altar, although most are in fact broken.

Burial methods included folding the body, which is thought by some scholars to imply the fetal position and therefore a belief in life after death. In common with ancient peoples of other cultures, large cemeteries have been found. These tell very little about religious belief but indicate that some social hierarchy had begun to develop and that there was a clear desire to isolate the dead from the living. Burial jars have been found in addition to burial pits and stone graves.

At Ōyu in Akita Prefecture, there is an artifact in the middle of a field consisting of two sets of circles made of flat stones, each with an upright stone to the northwest of the center. This is known as the *Nonaka-do*. It appears to have been a place for communal religious observance. Beneath some of these are pits for graves containing various artifacts typical of the Stone Age. In this regard Japan shows the same impetus to ritual and symbol as is found in other primitive civilizations at a comparable stage of development.

Yayoi (Bronze-Iron): B.C. 250–c. 100 C.E.

Yayoi is a Tokyo district that gave its name to pots found in 1884 that identified a culture between the neolithic and proto-historic eras. Evidence exists of a sedentary rice-culture and metalwork in the form of spears, a few swords, and mirrors in bronze. These appear to have been used for religious rituals. Settled community life led to people associating themselves with particular places.

Items belonging to this era include *dōtaku* (metallic bell-like artifacts) along with the bones of deer that may have been used in fortune-telling. Some of these are quite large, being one meter or more in height. They are often found buried and may have been used in religious rituals rather than funerary ones. Burial methods included cists, jar burials, and clustered pots in pits. The *dōtaku* are restricted to the Yayoi era and vanish with the coming of the *kofun* type of burial mound.

The Japanese classics, the *Kojiki* and the *Nihongi*, although later in composition, document the sense of awe with which the ancients viewed certain aspects of nature. These impressive realities they called *kami*, and it is here that the origins of *kami* worship can be detected. Some of the earliest terms and concepts of Shinto began to be coined, such as spirit (*tama*) or sacred object (*mono*). The beginnings of the Japanese festival (*matsuri*) can be traced to the oldest and most primitive form of worship of such *kami* in the emerging Japanese society of that age.

Kofun (Proto-Historic): 2nd Century–552 C.E.

This was the era of large burial mounds for Japan's early leaders. The tomb of Emperor Nintoku in Osaka occupies eighty acres. This indicated the growth of social differentiation and the rise to political power of a few families with the emergence of the Yamato court.[7] The earliest signs of the development of the Japanese state can be traced to the growth of the Yamato clan's cult and its rising power. The massive burial mounds were known as *kofun*, of which there were several types.[8]

Numerous mountain religious sites have been found dating to this era, but none have any apparent link with the burial mounds. Isonokami and Mt. Miwa in Nara Prefecture are two such places. To this era also date many of the interesting items found on the islands of Okinoshima, off the shore of Fukuoka Prefecture, which traditionally marked the ocean boundary between Japan and Korea. Because of its location as well as its awe-inspiring appearance, it has been revered as a *kami* for centuries and contains a wealth of artifacts from early eras that speak of the cultic practices of the fourth and fifth centuries in which beads, mirrors, and horse-related items were used. These rituals were probably among the earliest of which remnants and evidence remain. In west Japan, sites on which similar rituals were held became the earliest shrines of succeeding eras. The use of mirrors prefigures the later use of mirrors as symbols of the divine (*goshintai*). The divine beings revered in these early ages seems to have been the *kami* of the mountains and the oceans, as they came to be known more formally when Shinto developed. What kind of rituals were performed or what kind of emotions they evoked we can only imagine, but certainly divine beings were revered and offerings were made to them. To these were added eventually divine beings of the land itself and specially sacred spaces. All of these are still recognizable aspects of Shinto.

Roots of the Tradition

From general descriptions of these early periods, plus a reading of Japan's oldest written texts, six fundamental roots an be identified and defined. Although they are not unique to Japan or Shinto, their significance in the context of Japan's natural environment as well as the influence of Chinese culture makes the growth of Shinto as a Japanese religion more readily intelligible.

Animism. This belief sees life and divinity in all the phenomena of Nature from lightning to the winds and rain. The ancient Japanese gave these names and called them *kami.* Animism is simply a way of recognizing and responding to an encompassing sense of life in all its forms. In the festival, Shinto celebrates the vitality of life and its power to endure. The oldest Japanese cult was probably the belief that ancestral spirits resided in nearby mountains, coming down in spring to assist the community through harvest and returning after the fall. This is known as *Sangaku Shinkō.*[9]

Nature Worship. Closely linked to animism, nature worship is the general Japanese reverence for nature and the origin of shrines in places of great natural beauty. Shinto in this sense may be described as both natural (rather than revealed) religion in its most basic sense and as a religion of nature. Shrine buildings were located in places that were considered sacred, and natural objects that overtly manifested a sense of divinity were marked with a sacred rope called a *shimenawa.* These may be found over the tops of waterfalls, around trees at the entrance to shrines, and in many other places.

Ancestral Reverence. This is found in Japan as in most Asian nations. A late nineteenth-century resident of Japan, Lafcadio Hearn, called it Japan's ultimate religion, meaning that any religion coming into Japan either had to come to terms with it or risk not finding a place in Japanese society. Buddhism was required to alter fundamentally many of its doctrines, notably reincarnation, because they were not consistent with ancestral reverence. Modern Japanese are no less meticulous in matters pertaining to funerals and ancestors than were those in previous eras. Most recent research shows that it continues to be a powerful social and political force.[10]

Shamanism. This belief has a long history in Japan.[11] Most probably, the early Empresses were shamanists, a role that is not inconsistent with the kind of power they wielded. A Chinese document[12] records eighty years of civil war preceding the installation of shaman "queen" Himiko, who died around 247 C.E. Another civil war broke out when a male succeeded her, and only after a thirteen-year-old girl had been made "queen" did peace return. The training of youths to be shamans for the divining of harvest prospects continues in modern Japan, particularly in the Tokohu region.[13] Famous also are the blind women shamans at Osorezan. They claim to have direct contact with the dead, and people resort to them for communication with their deceased relatives and friends. The fortune-teller and the shaman combine and are still found active, even in the modern city.

Agricultural Rites. Thee appear in references to the *kami* of the stars breaking down divisions between rice-fields. The principal shrine festivals coincide with sowing, harvesting, and the cycle of rice cultivation, as do the related Imperial Household rituals, showing how profoundly Shinto is related to the agricultural year. Modern life still receives its framework from the Shinto calendar. New graduates are employed by companies in spring, from April 1, when the school year also commences. Police and schools seasonally change uniforms, and department stores do the same with their staff liveries. Seasonal awareness has always seemed important in Japan, perhaps because the four seasons are more clearly distinguished there than they are in some other countries.

Lustration. Bathing in rivers to be rid of pollution has long been associated with Japanese culture. The Chinese Wei Dynasty records noted that the Japanese bathed in rivers after a funeral. This predates the composition of the mythical narrative of Izanagi washing himself in the river after visiting the kingdom of impurity and darkness (*Yomi no kuni*) in search of his dead wife, Izanami. Purification is one of the most distinctive ideas of Shinto that lies at the root of Shinto's most central and common ritual. Priests may be seen waving a wand of paper streamers on building sites, at weddings, over an automobile for road safety, or even over politicians prior to elections in the public act of purification (*oharai*). Other forms of ritual purification can and do involve water. The ocean, lakes, rivers, and waterfalls are all used. It has been suggested that the Japanese fondness for the bath may be traced to the idea of lustration as a central religious concept. It is certainly connected with the desire to keep everything clean and fresh, from the taxi cab to the entranceway into a company or a restaurant. The sparkle of fresh water adds more than a welcome. It shows respect to those who will enter. It would be hard to find a concept that better expresses the basic outlook of Shinto. Shinto is obviously much more than that, even in its broad origins; but as a uniting theme, purification (*harai*) is a useful explanatory concept.

CONTROVERSY OVER THE ORIGINS OF SHINTO

The question of the origins of Shinto is a controversial topic, especially among scholars in Asia, notably Chinese and Korean specialists. Tsunoda et al.[14] argue that Shinto was not the indigenous religion of the "Japanese," because they were not the first inhabitants of the islands and because the religions found in Japan came from elsewhere. Similar types of religious culture may be seen in other parts of Northeast Asia, especially Korea. Tsunoda also argues that the idea of referring to Shinto as the "National Faith of Japan" was very much the work of nineteenth-century Western scholars trying to discover Japan after the country's long isolation. He maintains that Shinto was an amalgam of diverse cults that later received strengthening from Han Dynasty Confucianism, Esoteric Buddhism, Neo-Confucianism, and Christianity.

This line of argument, popular among those who wish to trace the origins of Japanese culture to roots outside of Japan, raises a number of questions on methodology and objectives. Regarding methodology, at a more general level there is the issue of the degree to which identification of origins can be used to weaken the validity of claims about unique aspects of development. Some historians present phylogenetic arguments, as though identifying origins in some way determines how the development should be interpreted. How and in what way origins and validity are related requires clarification. To claim, on ontogenetic grounds, that X cannot make adult decisions because he began his life as a child is hardly convincing! Discussions about the origins of Shinto should be separated clearly from what Shinto came to be within the evolution of Japanese civilization and its distinctive significance for Japanese self-understanding. Once developed, Shinto did become unique to Japan. Shinto as such did not develop anywhere else.

This point applies not only to Shinto but to a number of arguments of both Western and Asian scholars concerning the origins of the Japanese race and the Imperial family. These range from the emotional at best to the purely polemic at worst. Both Korean and Chinese scholars have made claims that are tantamount to saying that everything that developed in Japan came from China or Korea. Because the exact migration patterns of ancient peoples is not known, there is doubtless more truth in such claims that some Japanese scholars would like to recognize. The origins of Japanese culture are nonetheless complex and were probably eclectic. Unitary lines of explanation of the origins of a culture are to be suspected as concealing (pro or contra) an ulterior racist theme. From time to time, the Japanese Ministry of Education is accused by other Asian nations of trying to rewrite the history of the Pacific War. Their distress is understandable. But neither these nations nor their scholars are themselves entirely models of reasonableness. Anyone making an academic presentation on Shinto to an audience of local scholars in Asia will be fascinated (or frightened) by some of the reactions to even the most seemingly innocuous statements!

Returning to Tsunoda et al.'s arguments, it is possible to accept the points made but to reject the framework of understanding within which they are cast. Before Western scholars tried to excavate the roots of Japanese culture, Motoori Norinaga and the National Learning (*kokugaku*) movement tried to distinguish what was essentially Japanese from the Chinese overlay of culture by means of textual analysis of the Japanese classics. Among other things, it was concluded that the basis of Japanese religious thought was the doctrine of Amaterasu, in other words, a solar myth. Japanese culture may well have drawn elements from Northeast Asia, because metalwork—and later Buddhism—came through Korea. However, it should not be forgotten that Korea was an occupied nation at the time. Furthermore, the styles of architecture (e.g., the Grand Shrines at Ise) resemble Southeast Asian rice storehouses, or the storehouses of ancient South coastal China, built on stilts. Their designs probably originated there.

Such ontogenetic studies of Shinto may continue to reveal a complicated mass of diverse ideas and practices. Nevertheless, these factors do not preclude the possibility of designating the borrowed items as Japanese, because it was the emerging Japanese culture that integrated them into a worldview that later became part of Japan's cultural identity. The view of life embodied in the Japanese classics, although set forth in Chinese language, is quite different from any other views of life found in Asia. Arguments about diverse origins do not determine the identity of what their amalgamated form may in time become. In its history, Japan has borrowed so many elements from outside that it would be easy to claim that there is nothing "Japanese." However, under the mold of local influences these can become distinctively Japanese.

Critics of Shinto might point out that "State Shinto" was a fabrication of nineteenth-century ideology. I have no quarrel with this claim. I do, however, question any attempt to reduce all of Shinto to borrowed strands of culture. This would be to falsify history and to render unintelligible the early conflicts between Buddhism and Shinto that took place in their first encounters inside the Japanese court.

Arguments that Shinto and popular Chinese Taoism share common origins may be addressed in the same way. Asian folk religion has common elements, not least in ancestral worship and shamanism. Practices found in more traditional parts of Japan may be similar to what can be seen in Taiwan, for example, or in China. However, the place that these came to occupy in culture need not be the same—and in fact was not the same. The case of Okinawa, the former republic located between Taiwan and Japan, underlines the point. Although Okinawa is now a prefecture of Japan, Shinto really does not exist in Okinawa; and Okinawan folk religion is merely a distant cousin of Shinto. Arguments about identical origins would sound ridiculous. How, then, can we discuss the origins of Shinto in terms of Shinto and Japan itself? Apart from archaeological evidence, the Japanese classics offer a description of ancient Japanese life; from them we can inductively build a composite picture of the Yamato country of the time. In the narratives dealing with Amaterasu and Susano-o-no-mikoto, for example, there are references to rice cultivation, fences between fields, a palace, weavers, an iron industry, and the manufacture of mirrors and jewels.

Therefore did the eight hundred myriad Deities assemble in a divine assembly in the bed of the Tranquil River of Heaven . . . assembling the long-singing birds of eternal night . . . taking the hard rocks of Heaven from the river-bed of the Tranquil River of Heaven . . . and taking iron from the Heavenly Metal-Mountains, calling in the smith . . . charging Her Augustness Ishikoridome to make a mirror, and charging His Augustness Jewel-Ancestor to make an augustly complete string of curved jewels.[15]

To this list might be added the existence of ceremonial harvest rites, domestic animals, and the art of weaving from the passage in which Su-sano-o-no-mikoto drops the skin of a spotted horse into the palace through a hole in the roof, which results in the death of a weaver working at the loom. From these accounts, it has been argued that the origins of the family or clan heads (*uji no kami*) can be traced to the development of consanguineous family life. Deceased leaders eventually came to be worshipped as protective *kami* of the living, combining the Japanese sense of awe with mainland Asian ancestral reverence. The honorary title *mikoto* probably derives its origin here, and later the simple term *kami* was used of them. Although little more can be said of a specific nature, certain characteristic attitudes and practices that are associated with Shinto can be seen, at least in generic form, both within the Japanese classics and in external references to Japan of the ancient period. To me, this is a fruitful and scholastically sound approach to origins, which will display nothing if nothing is there to be displayed. It does not treat the classics as an authority. It looks at them in an almost hermeneutic way and seeks to interpret origins. Much can be inferred about Japan from the types of descriptions given, although problems do remain—such as the meaning of the reference to an alligator,[16] hardly a native of Japanese waters.

ASUKA AND NARA PERIODS (552–794)

Asuka (552–710)

The emergence of Japanese society and the origins of the Imperial Family and the Yamato State are normally dated to this period, although mythological accounts of Japan's origins date the Imperial Family to about 660 B.C. It is probably safe to claim that the imperial institution was established in Yamato as a sacral kingship concerned with the combined duties of *kami* worship and government (*matsuri-goto*). The hegemony of the clan was far from beyond doubt in the early days, although the unquestioned authority of the Yamato clan had probably been established by the early Nara period at the latest. It remains the world's oldest hereditary office and has never been usurped by revolution throughout the history of its officially claimed 125 incumbents.[17] In the very early stages of its development, the term *Shinto* as such was not widely used. *Kami* worship was practiced, but the term *Shinto* later came to distinguish the older indigenous cult from Buddhism. Over the centuries Buddhism grew in power and influence; and because of the illustrious and colorful complexity of Chinese culture, Shinto became obscured. Although Shinto was not able initially to compete with Buddhism, it never ceased to be important and it was only a matter of time before its cultural power was steadily revived. In the *Nihon Shoki* account of Emperor Sūjin it is recorded that he instituted the distinction between the *kami* of heaven and earth and identified lands and estates for their worship.[18] This can be dated with relative confidence to either 258 or 318 C.E. based on glosses in the text.

It was almost as a response to Buddhism that Shinto began to formalize itself and establish more permanent symbols of its character. With the building of Buddhist temples, for example, shrines began to appear in more permanent form instead of the older, loosely identified sacred spaces (*himorogi*) or places where a *kami* was worshipped in the open, usually surrounded by stones (*iwasaka*), both of which delineated sacred locations. The organization and classification of the various *kami* was probably the result of mainland influences and the distinction between heavenly and earthly *kami*. During the Asuka era, a code of laws was drawn up and Buddhism from China and Korea, which probably had been filtering in from mainland Asia with immigrants from generations before, finally received recognition in the Imperial Court. To mark this, the Horyu-ji was erected in Nara Prefecture. Prince Shōtoku (574–622), the famous Imperial regent, used Buddhist and Confucian ideas as the basis of his seventeen-clause[19] set of guidelines for national life, ways of life and thought that were intended to bring about national prosperity and harmony.

The Taika Reform (Taika no Kaishin, 645–646)

This was an early attempt at organizing the emerging nation hierarchically. A system of provincial districts was organized during the governmental restructuring known as the Great Reform (*Taika*). The two districts of Taki and Watarai in the province of Ise were gifted to the Grand Shrine of Ise as divine estates and thereafter similar land endowments were made to shrines such as *Izumo Taisha* and *Kashima Jingū*. During the reign of Emperor Tenmu (672–686),[20] the sacred office of the highest priestess (*itsuki no hime miko*) at Ise, also known as the *saiō*,[21] was again filled. The last occupant had been Sukate-hime-no-hime-miko, who died in the 29th year of the reign of Empress Suiko. The office of *saiguryō*, the government official at Ise responsible for the *saiō*, was also created. In addition, the practice of removing the Ise shrines to alternate sites (*shikinen sengū*) was decreed by the Emperor, a tradition that has continued in almost unbroken cycles of twenty years.[22] The annual cycle of festivals and other *gyōji*, or events, for major shrines was stylized and implemented on a nationwide scale. The identity and pattern of Shinto activities dates largely to the era of Emperor Temmu, the Hakuho period (645–710).

The ancient clan histories were corrected at this time to conform to "official" history. These histories included texts such as the *Teiki* and the *Kyuji* (neither of which now exist). This provided the formal basis for the traditions of the nation, both legend and myth as well as history, to be recorded and made publicly available.

Taihō Code (Taihō Ritsuryo)

The Code of the Taihō period was promulgated in 701[23] and entailed further restructuring of government, including major provisions for both Buddhism and Shinto. It set up a Council of State known as the *Dajōkan* and an office of Shinto affairs known as the *Jingikan* (office of *kami*). The authorization was contained in the *Jingiryō*, the part of the code that dealt with all matters relating to Shinto. Its chief official had the responsibility of ensuring that the *kami* were properly worshipped. His work also included the supervision of priestly families (*hafuri*) and the divine estates (*kanbe*), which had been given to very privileged shrines.

The *Jingiryō* classified shrine festivals into three ranks. First were major festivals (*Taishi*). This title was given exclusively to the *Oname Matsuri*, which is also known as the *Daijōsai*, the first celebration of the harvest festival by a new Emperor.[24] Second were middle-ranked festivals (*Chūshi*), which included the *Toshigoi* (the Spring Festival), *Tsukinami* (acts of thanksgiving performed on appointed days), and the *Kanname* or *Niiname* (Autumn Festival). Third were minor festivals (*Shōshi*), which included all remaining festivals anywhere throughout the country. All shrines nationwide were officially ranked and records of the important ones were kept in registers (*Kanshachō*), which were to be the responsibility of the office of the *kami* (*Jingikan*). The *Jingikan* also presented offerings to these shrines on the occasion of the *Toshigoi* and *Niiname* festivals. The establishment of regular rituals under government supervision, as well as the erection of buildings to house them, gave Shinto much of its ordered and nationwide character and led to the ranking and regulating of these facilities. Thus, Shinto grew in close relationship with the government and its supervision of national life while maintaining good relations with Buddhist institutions.

Nara Period Shinto (710–794)

Japan's second "capital," Nara, was designed and constructed on the grid model of a Chinese city, as was Kyoto in a later age. Some early Buddhist texts and sects appeared then, and for the first time the indigenous faith faced the danger of being eclipsed by the immigrant cult. The Japanese *kami* did not seem to be on a par with the grandeur surrounding the Buddhas and the awesome power of Chinese civilization. However, the Shinto *kami* were not in fact eclipsed; indeed, they became very much a part of the new civilization of Nara. Nara Buddhism grew under the influence of Emperor Shōmu (701–756), who was also the first Japanese Emperor to become a Buddhist priest; but it became a Buddhism designed to ensure the protection and prosperity of the State. The establishment of provincial temples called *kokubunji* (with convents called *kokubunniji*) was one aspect of this policy, as was the building of the great bronze Buddha to protect the nation. The *Shoku Nihongi* records many problems that occurred at the casting of the Buddha and indicates that the *kami* Hachiman was invoked for protection. An oracle reportedly delivered the promise, "I will lead the *kami* of heaven and earth and without fail see to the completion of the Great Buddha."[25]

The germ of the later idea of assimilation can be seen by the way in which the *kami* Hachiman was involved in protecting the construction of the Tōdai-ji. Following this precedent, Japanese *kami* were invoked in the building of temples and monasteries and Buddhist sutras were read before them in shrines as an act of appreciation. The building of the Tōdai-ji was justified by various arguments, but mainly because of the words of the *kami* of the sun who appeared in a dream experienced by Emperor Shomu on 11 November in the 14th year of Tempyo (742). "This land is the country of the *kami*. The people should worship them, but the wheel of the sun is *Dainichi Nyorai*. The true nature (*honji*) is Vairocana. If sentient beings understand this logic, they should convert to Buddhism."[26]

The Nara period saw the development of Buddhism and the beginning of the unique relationship between Shinto and Buddhism that remains a distinctive feature of Japanese religious history. The favor with which Buddhism was received at the Imperial Court had much to do with its development. The origins of the rapprochement are traced by Kitagawa to two sources. First, there was a sociological factor. Although Buddhism was developing, in 737 there were over 3,000 recorded Shinto shrines, and temple owners found that people derived their sense of identity from their local *kami* and Shinto cults. They thought that if shrines were erected on their premises, they would be protected. Hence, the need for a *kami* to protect Buddhist establishments. This also led to the identification in 783 of Hachiman as a *bosatsu*, a bodhisattva.

The second point of meeting between Buddhism and Shinto came through the existence of the shamanistic Buddhist, the *ubasoku-zenji*. The ascetic, magician, healer, and medium functioned as a bridge between Shinto and Buddhism. Although not recognized by orthodoxy, these individuals roamed the countryside exerting their spiritual powers to achieve results that made people stand in awe of them, while their syncretistic ideas appealed to the ordinary religious consciousness. One early example was En-no-Shokaku (known by various names, including En no Gyōja),[27] who, among other things, claimed to have been an original disciple of Buddha and an Emperor of Japan in his previous existences. He was associated with Mt. Katsuragi and is credited with having acquired supernatural powers through ascetic practice. His popularity among the populace troubled the government and the Buddhist aristocracy; eventually, by order of Emperor Mommu, he was banished to the island of Izu at the beginning of the eighth century. The popularity of the *ubasoku* lay in the way they mediated a kind of Buddhism that fitted Japan's traditional religious way of thinking. The Buddha was depicted as a *marebito*, a *kami* who visits a community at special times to confer blessings, which strengthened the appeal of that type of religion.

Second, the religious institutions themselves were dominated by the aristocracy. Only aristocratic families could consider the religious life in terms of profession; consequently, like the *ubasoku*, lay religion was open for development. Third, the ordinary people of the Nara and later Heian period benefitted little from the splendor of the court. Their lives were filled with suffering, and the existence of such a healer and comforter gave them strength and hope in the face of adversity. The conflict between institutional Buddhism and the *ubasoku* was, as Kitagawa has aptly interpreted it, a conflict between a soteriological understanding of charisma (the official one whereby the ecclesiastical voice is officially transmitted and the charisma is handed on in that way) and an eschatological understanding of charisma in terms of a creative spirituality and immanental eschaton of healing and hope.[28] This might also be considered one root of the dual-source view of Shinto, the government-sponsored as opposed to the folk origins of the tradition.

Reconciliation between the two required the maximum effort at cooperation by Emperor Shomu and Gyōgi Bosatsu (670–749).[29] Gyōgi was disliked by the orthodox priests, who rejected his teachings as superstition. He was arrested in 717 for teaching a doctrine of meritorious works among the peasants. He taught that the way of the holy man (*hijiri*) was the way to salvation. To ordinary people he was a *bosatsu*. He was eventually appointed by the Emperor as the leading ecclasiastic in the court, and it was with his cooperation that the great Buddha of Nara was finally put in place.

In spite of the growth of Buddhist power, one incident showed that the *kami* still retained their ancient authority. A Buddhist monk, Dōkyō,[30] tried to usurp the throne because of his favor with Empress Shotoku; but he was foiled by an oracle from the Usa Hachiman Shrine of Kyushu declaring him to be unacceptable and barring him from further office. It is surprising that in the midst of a heavily Buddhist ecclesia, a shrine oracle should have so much authority. Yet it did, and it underlies the complexity of the relationship between Buddha and *kami* in the Nara period. Buddhism was introduced primarily in the interests of modernizing Japan and bringing its culture into line with the great civilization of China. The purpose was not the salvation of people's souls but the protection of the State.[31] The earliest Buddhist sutras were read to bring on rain for rice-growing; and even by the end of the Nara period, Buddhism remained very much the property of the court and the government. Hence the conflict with people such as Gyōgi. By the end of the Nara period, the rapport between Emperor Shōmu and an unorthodox figure like Gyōgi had pointed the way toward a future symbiosis of the traditions, although no matter how closely integrated they became, basic differences remained. The gap between the official and orthodox tradition and the *ubasoku*, the holy man of the people, was considerably narrowed. This provided the background to the Heian age, which took these developments one stage further. Nevertheless, the fortune-teller, the popular shaman, the healer, and the charismatic remains very much at the core of popular Japanese religion. He has never been displaced.

HEIAN PERIOD SHINTO (794–1185)

Although Chinese influence remained, the removal of the capital to Kyoto encouraged the flourishing of distinctive styles of Japanese art and literature. The Heian period was a time of relative stability and cultural flowering, which still lives in the artifacts and atmosphere of the city of Kyoto. The world's first novel, the *Tale of Genji*, was written by Lady Murasaki. Esoteric Buddhism (*Shingon*) was introduced from China by Kūkai (774–835), later known as *Kōbō Daishi*, and semi-esoteric Buddhism (*Tendai*) by Saichō (767–822), later known as *Dengyō Daishi*. The Pure Land sects, *Jōdo* and *Shin*, emerged under the local leadership of Hōnen (1133–1212) and Shinran (1173–1262); they represent the reduction of Mahayana Buddhism to a very simple form of belief and rituals more in keeping with Japanese tastes. Within Shinto, various developments were also taking place. Some were concerned with the government organization and systematic ordering of shrines and worship; others were concerned with Shinto's relationship with Buddhism.

Government Systematization of Shinto

Suppression of Taoism. If an ordinance of 791 relating to rituals is considered as evidence, suppression of Taoism and a general anti-Chinese sentiment seemed to be growing. The *Shoku Nihongi* (November 787)[32] records that four years earlier Emperor Kammu had performed worship of the heavenly *kami* at Katano following what seemed to be a Taoist ritual. A small circular hill was set up on the day of the winter solstice on which sacrifices were offered to heavenly beings. All this was to be terminated. The edict also forbade farmers in specifically named provinces (including Ise and Omi, Echizen and Kii) to slaughter animals as sacrifices to (Chinese) Taoist deities.

The Practice of Chinkon: Pacification Rites. These began in the Heian court, a place of intrigue and scandal where malicious gossip could lead to the sudden rise and fall of courtiers and politicians. When they died (as they often did) in exile or from an assassin's knife, subsequent natural disasters were frequently attributed to their vengeful spirits. The idea of *chinkon*, of pacifying these vengeful spirits by reverencing them, led to worship known as *goryōe*. The first recorded instance took place in 863, when a service was held at the Shinsen-en gardens in Kyoto to calm the distressed spirits of Emperor Sudo, Prince Iyo, Fujiwara Fujin, Tachibana no Hayanari, and Bunya no Miyatamaro. The most famous case was that of Sugawara Michizane, who died in exile in 903. Local Shinto cults grew out of some of these cases.

The Records of Ise. These began to be collected in 804, when two important documents were lodged with the *Jingikan* from the shrines at Ise: the *Kotai-Jingū Gishiki-chō* and the *Toyōke-gū Gishiki-chō*.[33] These were books of rituals and ceremonies along with other important information concerning the two shrines, including the explanation of their origins, foundation, and the details of priestly dress, the divine treatises, the system of shrine removal, the subordinate shrines, the divine lands, and the annual cycle of rituals. They are basic works of reference for the traditions of Ise, and they provide evidence of an organized system of Shinto that is intelligible in modern terms.

Shrine Endowment. This was approved in a document of 806[34] (included in the *Shin-Shokyaku-cho-kofu-sho*), which records that 4,870 agricultural households had been assigned to Shinto shrines, or *shinpo* (or *kanbe*, as noted earlier), showing that concern existed for the nationwide endowment and financial stability of shrines. In addition, the Imperial Princess was sent as *saiō* to the Grand Shrines of Ise, and another was sent to the Kamo Shrines in Kyoto as *saiin* (High Priestess to the shrines of Kamo). This occurred in 810 during the reign of Emperor Saga.[35]

Compilation of the Engishiki. The completed system of *kami* and rituals was finally drawn up and issued in 927.[36] The text is undoubtedly a watershed in the history of Shinto. It set into order things as they were at the time and thereafter exercised a formative influence upon all future developments. It includes many detailed rules and regulations governing everything from ritual practice and liturgy to priestly duties. Worship was detailed for specific occasions and times. There were regulations regarding the *Ise Daijinū*, the saigu-ryō, the *saiinshi* (*Jingikan* handling the business of the office of *saiin*), and the proper performance of the *Senso-daijōsai*. The liturgies (*norito*) were also written down or composed, and lists were compiled of the 2,861 shrines (along with the 3,132 enshrined *kami*) that were acknowledged by the *Jingikan* and designated as qualified to receive offerings. A system of ranks was introduced for the special shrines collectively referred to as *kansha*. Powerful shrines came under the management of the government, and a period of intense state control began.

The Twenty-Two Shrines: Ni-jū-ni sha. As time progressed, the sending of offerings to all the shrines on the list[37] was amended to the sending of Imperial envoys only to certain powerful shrines around the Kyoto area. The number of such shrines was initially fourteen, but in 1081 it was increased to twenty-two, the Twenty-Two Shrines. These included Ise, Iwashimizu, Upper and Lower Kamo Shrines, Matsuo, Hirano, Inari, the Upper Seven Kasuga Shrines, Ōharano, Ōmiwa, Iso no Kami, Ōyamato, Hirose, Tatsuta, the Middle-Seven Sumiyoshi shrines, Hie, Ume no Miya, Yoshida,

Hirota, Gion, Kitano, Niu, and the Lower Eight Kifune Shrines. This special ranking of twenty-two shrines remained in force until the mid-Muromachi era and functioned as a guideline for both the government and the common people, whose devotion centered around them.

The District First Shrines: Ichi-no-Miya. Certain important locally revered old shrines[38] came to be known as *Ichi-no-miya* (first shrines). The first reference to this system appears in the *Konjaku Monogatari*, where the term was applied to the *kami* known as Suo-no-kuni-tama-no-ya-Daimyōjin. The "first shrine" title was applied in each province to the shrine that drew the most widespread worship of the ordinary people. Many shrines still carry these titles, usually stated in the form of, for example, *Ise-no-ichi-no-miya* followed by the name of the shrine. *Ni-no-miya* and *san-no-miya*, second and third shrines, are also found. This shows that in addition to the national and government-backed shrines, recognition was given to local shrines derived probably from tutelary and clan *kami* (both *chinju* and *ujigami*), which were closely related to the daily lives of many ordinary people. These were given special attention and respect by government and common people alike.

Joint Shrines: Sosha. One noteworthy development regarding shrines of the Heian age was the establishment of *sosha*, or joint shrines, at which the worship of numerous *kami* could take place.[39] The *kami* of an entire province would be "invited" to a single provincial *sosha* and joint worship would be offered. In the same way, a large family would "invite" all the *kami* with which they had a relationship to a single clan *sosha* for special ceremonies.

Other developments within the Heian age belong to the assimilation of Buddhism and Shinto and the complex relationship that was slowly growing between them.

Relations between Buddhism and Shinto

The Creation of Shrine/Temples: Jingū-ji. Assimilation between Buddhism and Shinto, which could be seen germinally from the Nara period, began to express itself more concretely during the early Heian period. One significant development was the construction of *jingū-ji*, or shrine/temples. A document of the *Tado-Jingū-ji* records that in 763 the *kami* known as *Tado-no-kami* (of the *Tado Jinja in Tado-machi*, Kuwana, Mie Prefecture) issued an oracle on this. "It is my fate to have been born a *kami* but I wish straightaway to practice the Buddhist oath, shed my *kami*-body and became a Buddha. But I am troubled, without the ability to receive the necessary (good) karma. For this reason I desire that a place of (Buddhist) practice be established."[40] In response, a hall was erected for the purpose of training the *kami* in Buddhism. This was the origin of the *jingū-ji*, the most well known of which were *Tado-jingū-ji*, the *Kehi-jingū-ji* in Echizen (Fukui

Prefecture), the *Nangu-jingū-ji* in Mino (Gifu Prefecture), the *Atsuta-jingū-ji* (Nagoya city), and the *Kashima-jingū-ji* in Hitachi province (Ibaraki Prefecture).

Even the construction of the great esoteric temples such as the Kongobu-ji on Mt. Koya and the Enryaku-ji on Mt. Hiei required the cooperation and good will of the *kami* of these mountains. The ranking of Buddhas, *kami*, and men seemed to be accepted, although the relationship was more complicated in practice. For ordinary people, Shinto remained closest to their community life, because Buddhism retained the image of an aristocratic and courtly religion. The rapport between Buddhism and Shinto in the Heian period continued at the popular level with the introduction of many superstitious practices, some of which were eventually condemned and forbidden. However, it was the introduction of the two schools of Buddhism mentioned earlier, Tendai and Shingon, that made possible further developments of the relationship between Buddhism and Shinto. Both used rituals and ceremonies that must have been very impressive to the people of the Heian era, particularly the *goma* or fire rite.

Harmonization of Kami and Buddha: Shimbutsu Shūgō. This was one form of the system of ideas used to maintain harmony between Shinto and Buddhism. It can be traced to as early as 698, when the *Taki Daijingū* was moved. This is recorded in the *Zoku Nihongi*[41] as having taken place during the second year of the reign of Emperor Mommu. It is probably safe to say that it was a policy that had been in existence since the earliest encounter between Buddhism and Shinto, as a way of avoiding conflict and effecting harmony over the years.[42]

The concept of *honji-suijaku* (literally, "original essence, descended manifestation") can be viewed in a general way as the natural outcome of the process of *shimbutsu shūgō*, the close identification of interests between Buddhism and Shinto. The Buddhism of India was thought to be the *honji*, and the Japanese *kami* portrayed the *suijaku*. The *Iwashimizu Hachiman-gū Monjo* records that the government center in Dazaifu in Kyushu permitted one thousand copies of the Lotus Sutra to be placed in the *Hakozaki Jinja*.

Original Essence, Descended Manifestation: Honji-Suijaku. Developments led to the close identification of Buddhas and *kami* in the concept of *honji-suijaku*, which implied that the *kami* and Buddhas were one and the same. Actual listings in many cases were drawn up to show how the identification was to be understood. In 1175, the *kami* of the Kasuga *Taisha* were listed as follows:

Suijaku: Shinto		Honji: Buddha
Ichinomiya	Kashima-takemikazu-chino-kami	Fukūkenjaku Kannon
Ninomiya	Katori-iwai-nushi-no-mikoto	Yakushi Nyorai

Sannomiya	Hiraoka-amakoyane-no-mikoto	Jizō Bosatsu
Shinomiya	Aido-no-hime-no-kami	Jūichimen Kannon
Wakamiya		Monjushiri

The notion of *honji-suijaku* is first found in the Lotus Sutra, which is probably one reason why its role in Japanese religious thought has been so important. It was the idea that the understanding of Shinto *kami* and Buddhist deities could be in some way combined; it was first used (according to Matsunaga[43]) in the *Sandai-jitsuroku* (Chronological Description of the Three Generations of Emperors) written during the first years of Engi (901) and dated August 28 of the first years of Jogan (859). Eryō, of the Enryakuji, was granted two priests whom he requested to expound sutras for the *kami* at the Kamo and Kasuga shrines. At that time he stated: "When the Buddha leads existence he sometimes uses *jitsu* (truth) or *gom* (manifestation). The Nyorai reveals *jaku* (*suijaku*) and sometimes becomes a king or *kami*. Therefore when the noble king governs the nation, surely he will rely upon the help of the *kami*."[44]

The dating of its rise to the Heian period accords historically with the shift of the court from Nara (where Hinayana and semi-Mahayana types of Buddhism were introduced to Japan) to the Heian period, when Japanese religious thinkers such as Saichō and Kūkai took the initiative in combining the traditions. Esoteric Buddhism was more readily able to express the integration; this enabled Buddhism to come into contact with ordinary people, thus making it possible for popular forms to develop. *Honji-suijaku* is better understood not so much as a doctrine formulated by one person at a particular time but as a phenomenon brought about spontaneously by a great number of reasons that resulted in the creation of a new type of Buddhism and a new relationship between Buddhism and Shinto. It was with the two esoteric types of Buddhism that the first manifestations of the synthesis are seen, in *Ryōbu Shinto* in the Shingon tradition and in *Sannō Ichijitsu Shinto* in the Tendai tradition.

Shinto of the Two Parts: Ryōbu Shinto. This phase of development carried the principle of *honji-suijaku* further to the stage of actual unity between branches of Buddhism and Shinto. Kūkai took as his starting point the Shingon mystical concepts of the Diamond Realm and the Womb Realm, which were depicted on two Esoteric Buddhist *mandalas* (sacred cosmograms). There was the *Kongōkai Mandala*, known as the Diamond Mandala, and the *Taizōkai Mandala*, known as the Womb Mandala. The two parts were the two mandalas.

In this Dual Shinto, the *Naikū* of Ise was associated with the *Dainichi Nyorai* (Mahavairocana) of the Womb Realm and the *Gegū* was considered the equivalent to *Dainichi Nyorai* of the Diamond Realm. *Ryōbu Shinto* also made use of *mudras* (secret hand signs), *dharani* (mystical incantations), *yoga* (concentration), as well as *mandalas*, all of which found their way into aspects of Shinto rituals. The secret rituals were one way to achieve Buddhahood in the flesh and, consequently, to attain superior powers through spiritual exercises. Although it is neo-magical, this aspect has had great appeal. Heian-age priests performed *kaji-kito*, a ritual for the healing of the sick, exorcising ghosts, and safe delivery at childbirth. Traces of these are found in extant groups of Sect Shinto and in the Shinto-based New Religions.

Tendai Shinto. In this version of Shinto, which originated through the influence of Saicho, the *kami* known as Oyamakui no kami (who was worshipped at the *Hie Jinja* on Mt. Hiei) came to be known as *Sannō Gongen* (Mountain King avatar), a practice that followed a similar model in Tang China. The *honji* of this *kami* was considered to be Yakushi and the *honji* of Ōmiwa no kami was identified with Shaka, the historical Buddha. These relationships were explained through the Tendai concept of *isshin sangan* (one mind, three insights). The name *Sannō-Ichijitsu* means "Mountain King: One Truth."

Kumano Shinto. Around this period, the cults of the Kumano region began to develop. The appearance of mountain ascetics known as *shugenja* may be dated much earlier, but it was during the Heian period that the beginnings of cults that came to flower during the Kamakura period could be traced. During the latter part of the Heian age, the idea of the final age of the Buddhist Dharma law become widely influential under the concept of *Mappo*, and the Pure Land faith became popularly associated with the bodhisattva *Kannon*. This also developed in the Kumano area because Kumano was to the south of the capital and Kannon's place of dwelling was to the south as well. Three religious centers developed in Kumano, the *Hongu*, *Shingu*, and *Nachi*; these were known as the Kumano *Sanja*. Pilgrimages to Kumano became so popular that later literature referred to the "pilgrimage of ants to Kumano" led by retired Emperor Shirakawa, who made the first of twenty-three pilgrimages here in 1091. Kumano had long been known as the land of the *kami* and still attracts many visitors and pilgrims. Most famous of the Shinto/Buddhist relics of the age is the Kumano Mandala, a systematically assembled piece of syncretistic cosmological art.

Shinto at the Close of the Heian Period

Shinto had undergone dramatic change and transformation under the influence of Chinese culture. Externally, shrines came to be more colorful, typified by the *Kasuga Taisha* painted in bright vermilion, with dancers using ancient Chinese costumes. People continued to venerate the *kami*, but the *kami* were identified with Buddhas and even with *goryō*, the unhappy spirits. Buddhist priests and Shinto priests as well as those of other cults offered the *goryō-e* to pacify these souls. *Hijiri*, holy men, continued to work incantations on the people, but doctrines of assimilation had become powerful. It is interesting, however, that both Saichō and Kūkai chose mountains as holy places for their temples, Saichō choosing Mt. Hie near Kyoto and Kūkai choosing Mt. Kōya in Wakayama. The natural appeal of mountains as places of spiritual encounter had not been displaced by the immigrant cult. It has been argued by some scholars that Japan became a truly Buddhist culture during that time because Shinto gave way to Buddhist influences. But is it so simple? It has been argued, on the other hand, that Buddhism compromised its essential character, its belief in reincarnation, and its moral principles in order to achieve that position. Kitagawa formulates the crucial question thus: "is is not equally true that Buddhism surrendered to the ethos of that nebulus religion of Japan, which lay deeper than the visible religious structure, commonly referred to as Shinto?"[45]

SHINTO IN THE KAMAKURA PERIOD (1185–1333)

The Rise of Minamoto

In 1192, the last cloistered ruler (*inezi*), retired Emperor Go-Shirakawa, died and Minamoto Yoritomo established his military government (*bakufu*) in Kamakura, in effect moving the nation's capital to that city. The Imperial Court remained in Kyoto until the Meiji Restoration. This sequence of events began the Kamakura period. Minamoto no Yoritomo's earlier life was quite dramatic. He was captured after the Heiji uprising (*Heiji no ran* of 1160) and was sent in exile to Izu, where he spent twenty years until he was thirty-four years of age; at that time he began raising troops for a challenge to the government of the day. He seems to have developed a personal devotional faith in *Kannon* through those years. After 1180, when he began raising an army proper, he turned his devotions to *Hachiman kami* worshipping, particularly at the Tsurugaoka shrine in Kamakura. The Hachiman cult consequently grew widely due to its popularity with Yoritomo. However, he also maintained a reverential attitude toward the Grand Shrines of Ise. As a mark of respect, he donated estates known as *mikuriya* to shrines along with land-ownership rights called *ando*. There is a reference in a text known as the *Gyokuyo*[46] to Yoritomo presenting a general report to the Emperor in 1183 that referred to the promotion of shrines and temples in the *shinkoku*, the land of the *kami*. He actively cultivated this theme (taken from the *Nihon Shoki*) among popular ideas of the period. It was one part of his legacy that survived long after him.

Popular Religion and the Imperial Regalia

Various events took place during the Kamakura age that centered around the Imperial Regalia: the mirror, jewel, and sword. At the battle of Danno-

ura in 1185, the closing confrontation of the war between Taira and Minamoto, Emperor Antoku was drowned and the Imperial sword was lost as
the Taira clan was routed. In 1183, when Antoku was with the Taira clan
in west Japan, retired Emperor Go-Shirakawa presided over the accession
rites of Emperor Go-Toba without any of the Imperial Regalia. The result
of these events was dramatic and the significance of the Imperial Regalia
came to be taken very seriously.

From the point of view of Buddhists of the time, the chaos was evidence
of the coming end of the world, the era of *mappō*. The emerging power of
Yoritomo seemed to offer hope. His reverence for the traditional Japanese
kami seemed to qualify him for leading the nation into the future. His
devotion to Hachiman was particularly beneficial to the growth of the cult.
Yoritomo's reverence for the Imperial Regalia is recorded as impressive.
Doubtless, he was using the Imperial system to legitimize himself as shogun,
although it is unlikely that any Emperor would have been able to refuse
him—especially because Antoku had been on the Taira side, which Yoritomo totally destroyed.

It remains an open question whether Yoritomo (or the Tokugawas four
centuries later) genuinely revered the Imperial Household and the Imperial
Regalia or whether a large degree of self-serving cynicism was the ultimate
motivating factor. At any rate, the result was clear. Yoritomo was the unquestioned master. After peace had been restored (and here history may
provide grounds for thinking that Yoritomo was sincere to some extent),
he later quarreled with his brother Yoshitsune after the battle of Danno-
ura, partly because he had permitted the young Emperor to die and partly
because the Imperial sword had been lost as a result of lack of attentiveness
to what was happening. In response, the Council of State drew up a series
of regulations as the basis of social order. These were known as the *Goseibai shikimoku* or the *Joei* law, drafted by the Council of State in 1232
under the leadership of Hojo Yasutoki. The first lines read: "Shrines are to
be maintained in good order and used dedicated to worship."[47]

The Grand Shrines of Ise began a major expansion of the cult at that
time, emphasizing their own pre-eminence as the prime shrine of the *kami
no kuni*, the land of the *kami*. It is to this time that the reverence of the
masses for the Grand Shrines of Ise can be dated. Pilgrimages there also
date from this period, and these began to supersede those made in the past
to Kumano. The growth of the ideas of Ise Shinto began around this time.

The Emergence of Nichiren

Other developments that marked the age included the life of Nichiren
(1222–1282), who appeared as a radical figure in Japanese Buddhism with
his aggressive emphasis upon the Lotus Sutra. Zen arrived from China. The
Mongols under Kublai Khan failed twice to invade, as Japan was saved by

the weather and the divine winds (the *kami-kaze*, as Nichiren designated them). However, Nichiren's name shows that the images of Shinto are never far from sight. The first character of his name means "sun" and the second means "lotus." His own enlightenment took place at sunrise, and he clearly had a deep sense of the *kami* of Japan as well as of the Buddha. From the tradition he established, *Hokke* (Lotus) *Shinto* developed.

Shugendō: The Way of Spiritual Power

Shugendō and Shinto in the Kamakura age were closely integrating to produce some of the unique features of Japanese religion. During the Heian age the tentative links began to flourish, but it was during the Kamakura age that the most significant developments took place. With the growth of ascetic religious practice in Esoteric Buddhism under the influence of both Saichō and Kūkai, many Buddhist temples came to be built in mountains, some in areas where shrines as far back as the ninth century had already been established. The two key terms, *shugen* (meaning to acquire spiritual powers through special discipline) and *shugenja* (someone who is in the process of acquiring or has acquired such powers), were introduced to describe these ascetics. They were also called *yamabushi* (literally, "those who lie down and sleep in the mountains") because they lived there for long periods of time. The goals of *Shugendō* were apparently to try to find ways of drawing spiritual energy from sacred places.[48] The roots of the popularity of these mountain cults were strengthened by the natural reverence the Japanese had for mountains. In addition, shrines of ancient origin could be found in many mountain areas that were thought to possess such power spots. Because of the prestige and the mystical imagery of Esoteric Buddhism in all its exotic manifestations, some of these developed as centers of mountain ascetic activities between the Nara and the Kamakura ages; and in spite of reversals of fortune they have managed to continue the tradition down to the present. Not a few of these claim a lineage in *Shugenō* practices that can be traced to a visit (real or alleged) by Kukai, who was said to have initiated those present into the secrets of esoteric practices during the Heian age.

The Yamabushi-chō: the Yamabushi Register

During the thirteenth century, a register was compiled of the people and activities of the *yamabushi* who practiced their cults in the Kumano region. Earlier scholars presumed that they wandered through the mountains from Yoshino to Kumano (now a national park). This view has been shown to be erroneous, probably the result of a desire to play down the significance of the independent cults. In fact, as the register shows, they were highly organized and engaged in a complex variety of rituals and activities. They worked from specific locations, and codes of dress and behavior regulated community life. Clearly, the mountain cults and the *shugenja* played a more important part within the history of Japanese religion than at first might seem the case. This is particularly important when the role of charismatic individuals is considered. The *Kumano Junrei*, a mountain pilgrimage practiced by the Kumano *shugenja*, has been revived in the twentieth century[49] as further testimony to the tenacious vitality of the mountain tradition in Japan. Apart from these professional or semi-professional courses, between Buddhism and Shinto, Japanese religion still can boast of over 400 traditional pilgrimages that have been pursued on a regular basis into modern times.

Shugenja and Ninja

Among other activities of the *shugenja* was their work as spies and mountain commandos. They would bless horses and troops and perform rituals for camp sites. They passed information and could send it over long distances at great speed. They also became involved with the great *Ninja* masters of the martial arts; so good were the *shugenja* at disappearing and re-appearing that they were likened to the *tengu*, legendary "demonic" creatures who haunted mountain regions. *Shugenja* were often used as soldiers; not infrequently, vanquished lords escaped disguised as *shugenja*. Yoshitsune escaped in this way from Yoritomo, and later, Prince Morinaga did the same. But their military exploits also led to their destruction in some cases, when they became too much feared. The decline in *Shugendō* can be accounted for in part by its political involvement and in part by the changes in religious tastes during the Edo and Meiji periods. For their revival in modern times, they had to wait until the twentieth century and the liberation of religion after the Pacific War.[50]

MUROMACHI (1333–1568) AND AZUCHI-MOMOYAMA (1568–1615) SHINTO

Rise of the Ashikaga Shogunate

The capital returned to Kyoto in 1334 and a new military government took control of national affairs, though not to the same extent as the Kamakura government. The Ashikaga warriors for the most part lived in a district of Kyoto called Muromachi, hence the name of the era. The Muromachi *bakufu* was more restricted in its area of authority and consequently could pursue policies only as far as its power extended. Among cultural developments of the period, *Noh* drama began to grow out of shrine ceremonies, and the tea ceremony and black and white painting developed under Zen patronage. Some of the famous Zen temples of Kyoto, the Nanzen-ji, Daitoku-ji, Daikaku-ji,and Ryoan-ji, date from this era. In 1549 Francis Xavier, a Jesuit missionary, began the introduction of Christianity to Japan. Civil wars divided the land, but unification was gradually achieved: first through Oda Nobunaga (1534–1582), who destroyed Buddhist power; Toyotomi Hideyoshi (1536–1598); and finally Tokugawa Ieyasu (1542–1616), who founded the Tokugawa Shogunate. The Muromachi *bakufu*, within its own limitations, continued the policy of the Kamakura government toward Shinto and appointed a commissioner of temples and shrines known as the *jisha bugyō*, charged with the task of ensuring that the ownership of shrine lands was protected and the shrine buildings were periodically renewed.

The Imperial Court had mixed fortunes during this period, and on account of economic restraints, even the *Oname-sai* was postponed. Offerings to the twenty-two major shrines could not be continued. Only the Grand Shrines of Ise received offerings from the *Jingikan*. National and local finances were such that the rebuilding of the shrines at Ise (*shikinen sengū*) was discontinued for over a century. From 1462 to 1585 the Inner Shrine was not rebuilt, and the Outer Shrine was untouched from 1434 to 1563. The continuing civil war made it impossible to dispatch the high priestesses (*saiō*) from the Imperial Household. This dates to the reign of Emperor Go-Daigo (1318–1339), and the practice was never re-instituted.[51]

The Beginnings of Urabe Shinto

Although government policy could not protect shrines as it desired, popular attachment to the local cults continued and various new syncretistic types of belief emerged, typified by writings such as the *Shinto-Shū* (The Shinto Collection). It was during this period that the traditions of *Ise Shinto* found a new champion in Urabe Kanetomo (1435–1511), who began advancing theories of the uniqueness of Japan along with the rejection of the Buddhist/Shinto syncretism represented by *honji suijaku*. Kanetomo belonged to the Urabe family, one of the official hereditary houses within the *Jingikan*. During the Heian period, the Urabe family had served as priests of the Matsuo Shrine and later at Hirano, *Ume no Miya*, and the Yoshida Shrines. During the Kamakura period Urabe Kanekata had written the *Shaku Nihongi*, which gave the family a reputation not only for preserving the Shinto classics but also for possessing sound scholarship and profound thought. Kanetomo was also known as Yoshida Kanetomo, because that was the branch of the Urabe family to which he belonged. He put forward a theory of Shinto called *Yuiitsu Genpon Sōgen Shinto* ("the one and only original essence Shinto"), also called *Yuiitsu Shinto* or *Yoshida Shinto*. This movement had a remarkable influence upon shrines and the entire culture of Shinto.

The range of theological ideas that Kanetomo developed are reflected in the titles of the books he wrote, some of which he claimed had been written by a family ancestor and some of which he wrote under his own name.[52] He defined three types of Shinto: *Honjaku Engi Shinto*, Shinto of "true essence and manifestation"; *Taishi-Ryū Shinto*, also known as *Shotoku Taishi Shinto*, or *Ryōbu Shūgō Shinto*; and finally his own *Genpon Sōgen Shinto*. Kanetomo claimed that this form of Shinto drew its authority from the *kami* known as Ame-no-koyane-no-mikoto, and that this was the true source of Japan's unique Shinto. Buddhism and Confucianism were considered to be the flowers and fruits of the true root, which was Shinto. He defined *kami* as the absolute existence proceeding from Heaven and Earth and responsible for forming them. In Heaven this is called *kami*, its objects are called *rei* (spirit), and in humans it is called *kokoro* (mind).[53] Shinto was the way to protect the mind. Thus, a person must exert himself to internal and external purity in order to follow the way of the *kami*.

Although he rejected Buddhism, Kanetomo permitted purification by fire (*goma*) and invocations (*kaji*) and permitted a rite of initiation into Shinto borrowed from Esoteric Buddhism. Although he had clear concepts of Shinto to present, he permitted the popular appeal of Esoteric Buddhism to remain in the background and within certain rituals and ceremonies of purified Shinto. Politically shrewd, he claimed for himself the title of Supreme Official of the *Jingikan* and created a system of Writs of Authorization of Shrines, which remained in effect until the beginning of the Meiji era. He claimed jurisdiction over four areas, namely, transmission of Shinto practices (forms of ceremonies for worship, offerings, and related rituals); priestly status, titles, and ranks; priestly dress (the *kazaore*, *eboshi*, *jōe*, *hashaku*, and other items of dress recognizable to the present); and the *kanjō* (invitation) and enshrinement of the *goshintai* (symbols of the *kami*) in any new shrines to be created in the future. He also created within the Yoshida shrines what he claimed was the supreme national ritual site. He built a hall of eight *kami* that was to serve as the central place for the proper administration of ceremonials in their honor. The Imperial Court received lectures on the *Nihon Shoki*, which has been discontinued since the Heian period, and Kanetomo himself lectured on the *Nakatomi-no-Ōbarae* to enrich the religious life of the Court. He circulated popular tracts such as the *Sanja Takusen* in order to expand the influence of his ideas.[54]

Other Developments in Shinto during the Period

With the disappearance of the southern court at Yoshino, the fortunes of the Ise cult began to decline. This left room for other traditions to develop or regain lost ground. The growth in importance of the Hirano cult can be traced to this era. The Hirano tradition devoted the years of the *Sengoku Jidai* (1467–1568) to transcribing the classics and maintaining its own traditions. The *Sanno* cult of Mt. Hiei and Lotus Sūtra (*Hokke*) Shinto developed freely. Sociologically, within the life of the cults changes also occurred. The Shinto community became transformed from *uji-bito* (clansmen) to *uji-ko* (children of the *kami*). The traditional structure of the community had been based upon the relationship between clan and *uji-kami*. The idea of regional *kami* grew stronger than the kinship idea of *kami*, and this became the new basis of Shinto within the developed nation. This was at a time when the basis of society was shifting from the clan to the household, the *ie*. The *za* (trade guilds) and *miya-za* (groups appointed to look after shrines) also came into being, and shrine organization became more systematic. This new approach was an early step toward the great developments in Shinto thought that took place during the Edo period.

The religious attitudes of the three generalissimos of the era present a confusing tapestry. Oda Nobunaga held Tendai and Shinshu Buddhism in great suspicion because they tended to side with his political foes. He destroyed some shrines that seemed menacing, but he rebuilt the dilapidated Grand Shrines of Ise and the Atsuta Shrine in Nagoya. Hideyoshi, although a very superstitious individual, greatly feared any religious interference in the work of government. He insisted that he be enshrined after his death, but whether this was done out of sincerity or for the sake of his ego, we may never know. On the record is a remark he made to a Portuguese diplomat: "To know Shinto is to know Buddhism as well as Confucianism."[55] It may not reveal a lot, but perhaps it catches the syncretic tendency of national leaders to control the state through weakening any independent tendencies in its religious life. This was the background to the emergence of Japan's most powerful Shogun Tokugawa Ieyasu, and his fourteen successors who held power until 1868.

EDO PERIOD SHINTO (1615–1868)

The Character of the Edo Period

After the defeat of the last of Hideyoshi's supporters at the battle of Sekigahara, the power of Tokugawa Ieyasu was unquestioned and a new era began. He government moved to Edo, whose population grew to over 1 million people. Christianity was suppressed, all foreigners were expelled, and the country was technically closed and remained so for over two centuries. Neo-Confucian thought was applied to establish uniformity and maintain control, while revived study of the Japanese classics by the Kokugaku scholars led to new movements in Shinto. The rice-based economy eventually began to stagnate and was in critical decline when Commodore Perry arrived off the shores of Japan in 1853. This set in motion the long chain of events that ushered in the Meiji period in 1868 and Japan's entry into the modern world. The development of Shinto thought during the period is most easily grasped by reviewing the principal thinkers of the era.

Although the institutions underwent various developments, the most important movements were academic, ultimately providing a religious and ideological backdrop to the Meiji Restoration.

Tokugawa Ieyasu and Religion

Ieyasu devoted considerable time and energy to the study of Japanese religions and to the creation of the policy to control them. He studied the doctrines of the Tendai, Jodō, and Zen sects of Buddhism. He also received instruction in Shinto teachings and ideas by Yoshida Kanemi's younger brother. He entrusted his will to his closest advisors, including the regional lord (*daimyo*), Honda Masazumi; its provisions included the instruction to give him a Shinto funeral and to inter his remains in Mt. Kuno. He requested a Buddhist ritual funeral at the Zōjō-ji in Edo (near the modern Tokyo Tower) and instructed that a memorial be placed in the Taiju-ji in Mikawa (his birthplace). He also ordered that after the first annual memorial service following his death, a shrine was to be built at Nikko and his spirit revered as a *kami*. This became the famous *Tōshō-gū*, where he is enshrined as the *Tōshō-Dai-Gongen* (Great Avatar Light of the East). The shrine belongs to the *Tendai Shinto* tradition.

Ieyasu's instruction in Shinto included information about a mountain shrine called *Danzan Jinja*, where Fujiawara Kamatari (614–669, the genius of the Taika Reform) is enshrined, and about the *Kitano Tenmangū*, where Sugawara Michizane is enshrined. In both cases there had been a time lapse before their enshrinement. Ieyasu, astute as ever on the topic of power and influence, and clearly hoping to rule the social order from the grave, chose to be enshrined following the precedent of his two role models. Toyotomi Hideyoshi had been enshrined for about a year after his death in a similar way. Ieyasu also decided that he would become the protective *kami* for the eight provinces east of the *Sekisho* (checkpoint) at Hakone (which still stands and houses a museum). During the Edo period, the Imperial Court sent offerings only to the Grand Shrines of Ise and to the *Tōshō-Gū* at Nikko. As a result of the expulsion of Christianity to eliminate one possible source of disharmony, and after the power of all rival political and religious groups had been broken, a relatively stable and peaceful society permitted the cultivation of the arts and some technology, such as printing. Shinto studies began to develop in various regional and private academies of learning.

Yoshikawa Confucian Shinto

Confucian learning prior to the Edo period had been associated closely with Zen Buddhism and studied especially at five famous Zen temples known as the *Gozan* (Five Mountains). Confucian studies then detached themselves from Buddhism, becoming independent. Some Confucian scholars became uncomfortable with Buddhism and were attracted to Shinto instead. This led to a hybrid Confucian-Shinto defined first by Fujiwara Seika and developed later by Hayashi Razan. Scholars of this rejected not only the concept of *honji-suijaku* but also the concepts of *Yuiitsu Shinto*, because a number of Buddhist theories were included within it. Yoshikawa Koretari, although initiated into *Yuiitsu Shinto*, rejected its Buddhist elements, bringing together Shinto and the Confucian cosmology of Chu Hsi (1132–1200), which was known as *Rigaku* (the Study of Rational Principles). Chu Hsi's social thought became the basis of the Tokugawa social order; and with some changes, it also became the foundation of Yoshikawa Shinto (*Rigaku Shinto*).

Seikyō Shinto

"Teaching of the sages" (i.e., Confucianism) was used to describe Shinto by Yamaga Sokō (1622–1685), who insisted that Imperial reverence was the basis of Shinto. It was partly the influence of Chinese Confucianism during the Edo period that led to the development of Shinto thought along ideological lines, with heavy emphasis upon the duties of individuals within the sociopolitical system. Despite the later movements that undertook to establish the content of pure Shinto, the Confucian assumptions remained in the background although they were never overtly discussed. This line of development also contributed to the deliberate creation of State Shinto as a national unifying ideology after the Meiji Restoration.

Ise Shinto during the Edo Period

Ise had undergone reversals in fortune; indeed, along with the imperial institution during the long periods of civil war, it has been threatened with the prospect of extinction due to lack of revenue. The relative peacefulness of the Edo period permitted a renaissance, largely the work of a descendant of the Watarai family, Nobuyoshi (1615–1690), who revived the thought of the *Gekū*, the Outer Shrine. He formally rejected any synthesis with Buddhism and Confucianism and proposed instead a return to the simpler forms of the Shinto of Ise. Although strong Confucian influences remained in his ethical and political thinking, the revival of Shinto from Ise had commenced and in pursuing scholarly research Watarai formulated original concepts of his own. He also began serious documentation work and collected the extant documents of the Grand Shrine, establishing the *Toyomiyazaki Bunkō*, a library and school for priests of the Outer Shrine. He researched and revised the classic texts of Shinto and tried vigorously to revive the branch shrines of Ise, many of which had been destroyed and their locations lost during the civil wars. Ise pilgrimages started to become popular after 1650, occurring throughout the year. There were also the famous *okagemairi* (thanksgiving shrine visits), which took place every sixty years. Hundreds of thousands of worshippers joined in these events.

Suiga Shinto

The "Shinto of Divine Revelation and Blessing," known as *Suiga Shinto*, was perhaps the most aggressive form of anti-Buddhist Shinto. Having studied the ideas of Yoshikawa and Watarai, Yamazaki Ansai (1618–1682) claimed there was but one Way, that of *Ōhirumemuchi* (Amaterasu, the *kami* of the sun). There was only one Teaching, that of *Sarutahiko-no-mikoto*, who had guided the heavenly grandson from the Plain of Heaven to the land of Japan. The term *Shinto* meant the study of the sun-virtue (*nittoku*) of Amaterasu, whom he claimed was united with the sun in the heavens, *amatsuhi*. He added the concept of the absolute sovereignty of the Emperor as direct descendant of Amaterasu. The greatest power on earth is united with the greatest celestial power of the heavens. Later disciples of Ansai, such as Ogimachi Kinmichi and Izumoji Keichoku, provided more solid academic support for the Imperial loyalists and anti-*bakufu* movements of the late Edo period.

Kokugaku Shinto: National Learning Shinto

Beginning from different premises, a group of scholars began searching the Japanese classics to identify what was distinctively Japanese in the eras before the influence of Buddhism and Confucianism. The movement was called *Kokugaku*, the National Learning movement. Although there were others before him the principal figure of the movement was Motoori Norinaga (1730–1801). He claimed that the pure Shinto he had identified as the doctrine of the sun *kami* was the fundamental root of the Japanese nation. It was not simply the worship of *kami* but also the origin of government, ethics, and everything under the sun. The concept of *saisei itchi* (unity of worship and government) was the proper development of national life. The influence of Motoori Norinaga and the *Kokugaku* movement also contributed indirectly to the strengthening of the loyalist movement prior to the final collapse of the feudal government. Its line of transmission was through the succeeding generation of scholars who took it in a more specific and ideological direction.

Fukko Shinto: Restoration Shinto

The religious nature of Shinto based on the principle of the unity of worship in government came to be known as *Fukko Shinto*, or Restoration Shinto. It was largely the work of Hirata Atsutane (1776–1843), whose thought exercised great influence on the declining samurai class and drew many of them toward the Imperial cause. It left an indelible impression upon the political thought of the Meiji government and upon the concepts of the nature of Shinto and *kokutai,* the body politic, which came to be defined as the Emperor along with the people. Among other influences, these gave Japanese nationalism its unique flavor once the ideology of the Meiji period had been generated.

Popular Religion of the Edo Period

Shrines that had suffered during the civil wars and those that had lost prestige came to gradual restoration during the Edo age. During the time of the fourth Shogun, Ietsuna (1641–1680), 985 shrines were given special grants known as *shuin-ryō* (vermilion seal money). The amount of endowment equaled 151,925 *koku* of rice.[56] Local lords could also donate to shrines under their *kokuin* (black seal). Although not unsizable, the amount was still too little to restore the prestige the shrines had enjoyed during the earlier periods. Consequently, the shrines began to forge stronger links with communities and with ordinary people. Among the shrines that grew in popularity were the *Fushimi Inari,* the *Kitano Tenmangū,* and the *Gion Jinja* in Kyoto; the *Konpira Jinja* at Sanuki; the *Itsukushima Jinja* in Aki; the *Taga Jinja* in Omi; the *Tsushima Jinja* in Owari; the *Sanno Jinja* and the *Kanda Myōjin* in Edo; and the *Suwa Jinja* in Nagasaki. Most still retain great popular appeal.

The cult of *Inari* began to spread throughout the country, and the familiar red rows of *torii* standing like a covered avenue of approach became common with the cult's special appeal to merchants.

Kyōha Shinto: Sect Shinto

New cults also began to develop. Alongside the shrine and their activities grew up local movements under charismatic leaderships that later became recognized as *Kyōha Shinto,* or Sect Shinto. All were popular movements, formally approved and classified by the Meiji government, although their origins were mostly in the Edo period. Some have had varied fortunes. A number are now almost extinct; but the best known ones, *Tenri-kyō, Konkō-kyō,* and *Kurozumi-kyō,* remain active and successful and still have many thousands of followers.

Shrine Organization and Administration

Depending upon how shrine affairs were administered, five categories can be identified during the latter Edo period. (1) Those managed by trained Shinto priests: these were normally under the hereditary control of major Shinto families, such as Watarai or Urabe. They might also serve as village shrines, but their management was totally in the hands of the shrine family.[57] (2) Those controlled by temples: these dated to the time when temples and shrines were closely related, and some shrines were built by temples for protection. The close link between shrine and temple is still seen in the pattern of the *Toyokawa Inari* Shrines (as distinct from the *Fushimi Inari* group). (3) Village Shrines: many of these had no permanent priests of their own but would call upon the services of a priest from a larger shrine to conduct festivals and rituals. The village headmen (*shoya*) were responsible for running the shrines, assisted by district representatives within the villages. (4) Those managed by a *za*: these were primarily parish shrines that related only to a district within a larger area. The *za* was a type of trade guilt based upon product interest (rather than profession, as in the West) that met to commune with the *kami* and be concerned about a shrine throughout the year. Priests might be invited from outside or from the group (the *tōya* system). However, general management was in the hands of the membership of the *za*. (5) Shrines of individuals located on private land for worship and private family use: these were controlled either by the individuals or the family. They ranged from *yashikigami*—occasionally elaborate shrines to protect the land, buildings, and the *ie*, the house itself—to shrines erected to revere a local individual who performed some great feat for the community. Some communities declared such persons *daimyōjin*, gracious *kami*, and revered them while they were still alive.[58]

MEIJI (1868–1912), TAISHŌ (1912–1926), AND SHŌWA (1926–1989) PERIODS

The Meiji Isshin: The Meiji Restoration

In 1867 the fifteenth shogun, Tokugawa Yoshinobu, recognizing that he could no longer maintain viable government, yielded to a group of young *samurai* who invaded the Imperial Palace in Kyoto proclaiming the young Emperor Mutsuhito restored as ruler as well as sovereign. The nation then began a process of modernization that crushed the *samurai* and created a modern state. The ultimate driving force of history, change through technological innovation, was seen at work when the presence of the U.S. navy in 1853 shocked the government and the *samurai* into an awareness that Japan had fallen behind in technology and consequently was in danger of invasion. The external threat and the general ineptness of the latter Tokugawa governments, especially their inadequate rice policy combined with their general inflexibility, set people searching for original solutions. The intellectual movements within Shinto provided focal points for the clarification of these issues, and the combination of influences finally led to groups of lower-ranked *samurai* from the outer domains successfully sweeping away the three-centuries-old government of the Tokugawas. The political theory of the new leadership and eventually of the new government was deeply infused with the thought of *Fukko Shinto*.

Kokka Shinto: State Shinto

The reconstitution of Shinto as an independent tradition began between 1868 and 1871.[59] It was marked by the Emperor's proclamation of the *Taikyō Senpu* to further the teachings of the Great Way and to revive the earlier notion of *saisei-itchi*, the unity of government and reverence. State Shinto was not formally instituted until after the establishment of shrines for the dead of the Meiji Restoration and those who died in Japan's first military campaigns abroad (Russia, 1894–1895, and China, 1904–1905). Administration of Shinto in the early Meiji era was a matter of considerable confusion and reflected the lack of consistent policy on the part of the Meiji government. The first stage was the separation of Buddhism from Shinto (*shimbutsu-bunri*) to allow for a return to "pure Shinto." In 1869 the *Jingikan* of the Nara period was re-established and put in charge of Shinto rituals. The head was made *Dajokansei*, a member of the Council of State, to ensure respect for Shinto and reverence for the Emperor. A system of propagandists (*senkyōshi*) was set up to educate the people in the policies of the new government and to cultivate Shinto. An Imperial Edict of January 1870 proclaimed the enshrinement of the *kami* of Heaven and Earth, the eight central *kami*, and the Imperial Ancestors by the *Jingikan*.

In October 1870 a system of Imperial and national shrines was instituted, with each category being divided into three classes based on size. A shrine ranking system was established along with a listing of rituals to be performed, and a system of ranking for priests was formalized. Local governments were ordered to compile records of shrines in their area. These were steps to bring all shrines throughout the nation under government control. In 1871 shrines were declared national institutions and the system of hereditary priesthood was formally abolished, although many families and their shrines could not be so easily separated. Consequently, the creation and enforcement of State Shinto was not something unequivocally welcomed by people or by shrines.

However, Japan was seeking to create institutions that resembled at least outwardly those of the nations with which it would have to live and compete. In August 1871 the *Jinkigan* was abolished in response to criticism and was replaced by a new Ministry of Shinto Affairs, the *Jingishō*, immediately below the Council of State. Between 1870 and 1882 the favored position of Shinto was challenged; in reply, an idea was circulated by the government that Shinto was not a religion. Buddhism resisted this claim strongly under the influence of Shimazu Mokurai; and with pressure from the *Jōdo-Shinshū* sect, the government was forced to form the *Kyōbushō*

(Minister of Religious Instruction) in 1872 to replace the *Jingishō*, whose functions were transferred there. The *senkyōshi* were mostly ultra-nationalist Shinto priests who often launched unreasonable attacks on Buddhism, ignoring both local feelings and the needs of Japan in a changing world. Under heavy criticism from Buddhists and independent intellectuals, the system was abolished in April 1872.

A new system of instructors, called *kyōdōshoku*, was created that consisted of both Buddhist and Shinto priests. It worked effectively until 1884, when it too was abolished. The power of Restoration Shinto had begun to decline partly because of these problems and partly because it was advocating a return to the past, which, whether mythical or otherwise, was certainly not going to help Japan emerge as a powerful modern nation. Earlier, in 1877, the *Kyōbushō* had also been abolished and the administration of shrines had been transferred to the *Shakikyoku*, which was part of the Ministry of the Interior.

From 1882 the separation of religion and politics (*seikyō-bunri*) became a major issue, because it appeared that many religious instructors were actually promoting their own teachings or those of cults that were unrelated to the objectives of the government. An edict was passed forbidding religious instructors to be priests of any group at all; this led the Meiji government to recognize the rights of independent groups, many of which had developed during the Edo age. These received status as the thirteen sects of *Kyōha Shinto*. They were split off from Shinto and classified with other religious groups and Buddhist sects, and therefore not with the nation's shrines.

Shrine Statistics and Ranks within the Kokka Shinto System

The Council of State (*Dajōkan*) issued a proclamation on 14 May 1871 according to which all shrines were ranked in a new comprehensive system, which is outlined in the following list.[60]

Imperial Shrines

Kansha (The Grand Shrines of Ise)

  (a) *kampeisha*: Government shrines

  (b) *koku-heisha*: National shrines

  (c) *kankoku-heisha*: Government and national shrines

Minsha Fuken ika sha (Shrines of Prefectural Rank and Below)

  (a) *fukensha*: Prefectural shrines

  (b) *gōsha*: District shrines

  (c) *sonsha*: Village shrines

Unranked Shrines Small local shrines, sacred groves, trees, and stones. Statistics for 1880.

Kansha	kampeisha	55
	koku-heisha	68
Minsha	fukensha	369
	gōsha	3,272
	sonsha	52,754
Ungraded Shrines		130,293
Total Number of Shrines		186,811

The 1889 Constitution recognized Shinto, Buddhism, and Christianity as official religions. This was the first step toward a special status for Shinto. In 1894 many of the former government ranks were restored to the people's shrines (*minsha*), which had been removed as the government drew back from full state control of Shinto. The government began giving official civil servant status to all priests, even of unranked village shrines. After the 1894 ranks were issued, government control went with it, because all those appointed under the new system received prefectural authorization from the governor. This was the key to establishing State Shinto. Once it was denied that Shinto was a religion, every citizen could be compelled to visit shrines and show respect.

In 1900 the *Jinjakyoku* was set up within the Ministry of the Interior to handle Shinto affairs separately from the Bureau of Religion, which dealt with Buddhism, Christianity, and the Shinto sects. The logic was that there should be a ministry teaching enrichment of the entire body politic based on Shinto to encourage the following of the national way, the traditional way of the Emperor.

After the wars against China and Russia, which had been fought at enormous cost to the developing economy, there was great social and political unrest, clear symptoms of the breakdown of national order and the socio-political structure. This, amongst other factors, promoted a series of government measures to address the situation and to strengthen national vision and goals. There was the *Boshin* Rescript on Thrift and Diligence (1908), the revision of school textbooks (1910), the *Hōtoku* movement (government-supported after 1906), the formation of the *Teikoku Zaigō Gunjin-Kai* (Imperial Rural Military Association, 1910), and the *Chihō Kairyō Undō* (Local District Improvement Movement, 1909). These were designed to generate social stability, to recreate national values, and to add weight to the national ideology.

In 1913 the Bureau of Religion was moved to the Ministry of Education, so that all non-Shinto groups would be supervised by the Ministry of Education. Shinto affairs were left in the hands of the *Shinto Honkyoku*, a department of the Ministry of the Interior, which existed until the end of the Pacific War.

The Shrine Merger (Jinja-Gappei) Movement

When the shrine merger movement began,[61] the number of shrines was gradually reduced from over 170,000 to fewer than 70,000. It began in 1900 when the Bureau of Shinto Affairs raised the status of shrines dramatically and emphasized that Shinto was simply a patriotic institution. From 1906 the government itself began to escalate *minsha* improvement programs, and here the question of merging shrines was raised. The objective was to make the shrines impressively fewer, easier to control, and better instruments of government policy. A set of standards was issued that had to be met if a shrine was to be recognized. The conditions were not easy to meet, and consequently many shrines lost recognition. It was a small matter to send inspectors to check on shrines and to report that some were not worthy of the name and should be eliminated. This led to the closure and abolition of many, with their *kami* being removed to new locations. The movement was variously called *gōshi* (joint enshrinement), *jinja gappei* (shrine merger), *jinja seiri* (shrine consolidation). The latter was the official term, which concealed the extreme nature of the actions involved. *Gappei* meant not that shrines were united but that the physical presence had been removed and the *kami* transferred to another shrine. Village shrines were thus consolidated into one and traces of local shrines were mostly removed. The name of the consolidated shrine would reflect the community or town, and this would strengthen the unity of Shinto and State. The results were effective, if statistics are reliable. The number of *minsha* between 1879 and 1947 were reported as 176,722 in 1879; 195,072 in 1905; 111,699 in 1929; 110,077 in 1941; and 87,369 in 1947.

Between 1903 and 1920 the total number of shrines was reduced by 77,899. The movement created great resistance, peaking in 1911 until 1920, after which it was not nearly so vigorous. In fact, between 1903 and 1920 it was primarily unranked shrines that were merged (from 136,947 to 66,069). In effect, approximately 41 percent of village unranked shrines were simply abolished, creating strong reactions in many communities. Shrines that were declared to have no recorded historical lineage (*yuisho*) were considered subjects for merger. There were strong opponents to the movement on the grounds that it was weakening links between people, their communities, and shrines, not making them stronger. Filial piety was being ignored and the essence of the nation's life and history was being damaged in the process. It was claimed that the mergers were damaging to patriotic feeling. Indeed, it was argued that the interference with the folk tradition might be damaging to the entire nation. The people themselves frequently felt desolated and deprived with the departure of their protective *kami*, who were now being served by strange people in strange shrines. Gradually it came to be realized that as far as shrines were concerned, feelings came first rather than beliefs or thoughts. The loss of local festivals was one tangible result, and it is recorded that many villages were hung with gloom at traditional festival times. Some areas refused to cooperate; others were put under extremes of pressure. By the beginning of the *Taishō* period (after 1912), shrine mergers were not demanded but prohibitions remained on their reconstitution. However, after the defeat of Japan in 1945 and the subsequent liberalization policy, many shrines were in fact reconstituted.

Shinto and the Japanese Empire

With Japan's overseas expansion during the early years of the century and the eventual proclamation of the *Dai Nippon Teikoku*, the Empire of Great Japan, occasions for the creation of new shrines became possible. Perhaps the best known of the overseas shrines was the *Taiwan Jinja*, which enshrined Kitashirakawa no Miya, Yoshihisa Shinno. Born in 1847, he became a soldier in the Imperial Army and was dispatched to Taiwan in 1896, where he died after a successful engagement at Tainan on October 28 of the same year. His remains were returned to Tokyo for a state funeral. From 1897 local efforts were made in Taiwan to establish a shrine. General Nogi, Governor General at the time, led a committee that chose a site. Baron Kodama, his successor, persuaded the government in Tokyo to give its approval to establish *Taiwan Jinja* (1901). It was to be ranked as a government great shrine (*kampeisha taisha*) to enshrine Okuni-tama-no-mikoto, Onamuji-no-mikoto, and Sakunihikona-no-mikoto as well as Yoshihisa Shinno. Until the end of the Japanese occupation, various other shrines were added to the oldest, *Kaisan Jinja* (1898); *Taiwan Jinja* itself brought the final total to over thirty throughout the island. Shrines were also erected in Korea and in other occupied areas to gain recognition for the Empire. These were dismantled after the close of the Pacific War.

Shokonsha, shrines for the war dead, were also established. None were ever erected in Korea, although the Japanese armies were in occupation. However, a festival for the souls of the dead (*iresai*) was held annually as long as a Japanese division was present. Manchuria had several, including Tailen and other centers. The *Kenko Jinja* was established in Taiwan in 1929 to enshrine 15,350 *kami* who were not simply military personnel but every Japanese citizen who had died while working for the welfare of Taiwan within the Japanese Empire. All these shrines had annual festivals, and they continued where practicable until the retreat of Japan from its Empire and the final collapse in 1945.

The inter-war period was one of liberal trends often known as the Taishō democracy. Its benefits were quickly suppressed as the political power of the military grew. Tokyo was also destroyed during this period by the great earthquake of 1923. The Manchurian Incident of 1931 and Japan's departure from the League of Nations indicated a change of mood. Extremists took control of the government and Japan moved toward war with the United Kingdom, the Netherlands, and the United States. During the early Shōwa period, nationalism was actively promoted through the use of Shinto rituals; in 1940 the *Jingiin* (College of Kami) was established within the Ministry of the Interior. The year 1940 also marked the legendary accession of the Emperor Jimmu 2,600 years earlier. To commemorate the event various activities were undertaken, including the expansion of the *Kashihara Jinja* in Nara Prefecture and the construction of the *Omi Jinja* in Shiga Prefecture. With the outbreak of war, shrine festival events such as the competition between *mikoshi* (portable shrines) and *dashi* (large wagons) were further restricted and Shinto was promulgated as a form of national ethics and nothing else. The significant question remains whether the government succeeded in its goals of making shrines more impressive in order to strengthen the value system of family and emperor. Patriotism was stimulated, but as much—it seems—by the education system as by shrine mergers. The damage to the feelings of the communities, however, loosened the ties of millions to their local shrines forever. The government, like the army, was pledged to promote Japan; and by the end of the war both had almost succeeded in destroying the very things they held most sacred.

The Allied Occupation and Shinto

General Douglas MacArthur, Japan's first foreign "shogun," was Supreme Commander of the Allied Powers from August 1945 until the Treaty of San Francisco restored Japan's independence in 1952. After long suppression from the Meiji period, the separation of religion and state enabled repressed movements to find new life, older traditions such as pilgrimages to be re-established, and many prohibited practices to be revived. Shinto began the difficult movement away from being a system of government-inspired moral education to being a natural religion. All these provisions were covered in the Shinto Directive of December 1945, which insisted that shrines be disestablished from the state, that Shrine Shinto was not to receive any national support and was not to be under any kind of state control. Shinto was thereafter to remain a recognized religion for the individual Japanese citizen to practice or not at personal discretion.

Jinja Honchō: Association of Shinto Shrines

When the Occupation abolished the *Jingiin*, leaders from the three major private groups, the *Dai Nihon Jingikai* (The Great Japan Association for the *kami*), the *Kōten Kokyū-sho* (Center for Research on Imperial Rites), and the *Jingū-Hōsai-kai* (The Grand Shrine Service Association), met for consultation. In February 1946 they formed the *Jinja Honchō* (Association of Shinto Shrines), which oversees the nation's shrines and acts as a central communication point within the complicated system. Its basis was voluntary, however, and depended, as it still does, upon subscriptions from member shrines. From time to time, differences have occurred and some shrines have left. However, it is the only coordinating body for Shinto in Japan and the only organ (other than individual shrines) by which Shinto can be formally represented at a broad administrative level. The *Jinja Honchō* continued to supervise the administration of the network of shrines, and after many years of being located in Shibuya near Kokugakuin University it moved to a new site near *Meiji Jingū* in 1988.

The Modernization of Jinja Shinto (Shrine Shinto) since 1946

After the Shinto Directive to abolish State Shinto, Shrine Shinto was faced with a new problem. Although it was now free to pursue its own life, it had spent almost three-quarters of a century under government control and, more particularly, had benefitted from government support. It was now in the same plight as Buddhism in the Kamakura period, bereft of patronage. It had to seek private support and develop ways and means of surviving into the new age of democracy, not a small undertaking.

Such necessities brought about a number of natural changes that have worked toward greater participation by the community in shrine life. For example, under State Shinto new shrine buildings, *shaden*, had to be constructed according to government specifications. The worship hall (*haiden*) was made quite small so that only priests, designated officials, and community (*ujiko*) representatives could enter. This kept the shrines at a distance from the general populace. In the postwar era, worship halls were enlarged to accommodate large numbers of people upon whom the shrines depend for income. Teaching became a necessity and general office facilities were enlarged to include meeting rooms and lecture halls. *Meiji Jingū* makes use of its Memorial Hall for film screenings and various meetings. *Atsuta Jingū* uses its *Bunka-den*, its Culture Hall, to store ancient treasures, to hold lecture meetings, and to house a library on Shinto. *Kasuga Taisha* has a well-known Botanical Garden that attracts visitors, as does the *Hitomaru Jinja* in Yamaguchi. Another innovation in the postwar era was the introduction of kindergartens and nurseries. Between 1945 and 1965, the first twenty years after the war, approximately 200 kindergartens and nurseries were organized, catering to the needs of over 20,000 children. In the same period eighty or so Boy Scout troops were organized, catering for the needs of almost 2,500 boys. Most significant was the growth of women's organizations, about 370 in all with a membership of over 100,000. The

Jinja Honchō became active in disseminating information through publications and lectures. At local *jinja-chō* in various areas there are almost 2,000 lecturers and what might be called missionary teachers *(kyōka)* engaged in educational activities. Lecturers who visit prison inmates have been appointed. In ways like these, shrine priests have come to take more of a pastoral role in community and regional life than they had been permitted since the Meiji era. It should be remembered that one appeal of Sect Shinto was that it could freely pursue such goals. Shrine Shinto had to learn this; doubtless it was partly a return to old ways and partly an emulation of Christian Church models. The shrine wedding was another major development that has given Shinto not only substantial income but a gentler image than it had previously.

THE CONSTITUTIONAL SEPARATION OF STATE AND RELIGION

The 1947 Constitution continued the aforementioned principles, and Shinto was listed as one of the other religious bodies in Japan. Individual shrines became incorporated religious legal persons *(shūkyō hōjin)*. Although these provisions were fairly straightforward, they were not without difficulties. Four principal topics emerged since 1946, and they remain as continuing and unsettled controversies.

The Use of Shinto Rituals for Local Events

When a village or a city plans a new road or building, it is traditional to have a Shinto priest perform the ceremony of *oharai* and to perform *jichin-sai*, rituals to calm the *kami* of the area who might be disturbed. Many Japanese do this when they build a new house, as do companies when they erect new facilities. As long as these are paid for by private individuals or companies, there is no violation of the Constitution. However, local authorities often carry out such rituals, and in many instances since 1945 cases have been taken to court on the grounds that these acts are unconstitutional.

The Yasukuni Shrine Problem

This problem is not easy to grasp because of the emotional delicacy and political complexity associated with the shrine. The shrine cannot be compared to the various international war memorials, such as the one in Arlington in the United States or the Cenotaph in London. They came later. The concept embodied in the Yasukuni Shrine lies deep in Japanese culture and must be viewed in that regard. Reverence for the dead is promoted in Japan in unique and extreme ways. The need for such a shrine was first expressed in 1868 as a place to house the spirits of the 3,588 soldiers who fell during the Meiji Restoration struggles on behalf of the Imperial cause. The original site at Kudanshita in Tokyo, near the old castle of Edo that had become the Imperial Palace, was secured in 1870 and the shrine was erected in 1871. In 1880 it was designated a *Bekkaku-Kampeisha*, having the highest rank of shrine wherein the *kami* are subjects of the Emperor; at the same time, Emperor Meiji named it *Yasukuni* (Peaceful Country) *Jinja*. The Ministry of the Interior was responsible for the administration, finances, and appointments to the shrine staff, and thus it remained until the disestablishment of State Shinto in 1945.

The period from1894 to 1905 was marked by the steady rise of patriotic feeling, associated in large part with shrines where prayers for national success were offered. The wars against China and Russia provided stimulus for the strengthening of patriotic fervor, and it was here that the practice began of praying at a shrine as soon as a son went to war. If the son died he was given the privileged status of national *kami*, which at that time must have been a great honor. The Emperor himself on set occasions would visit the Yasukuni Shrine to show respect. These actions did a great deal to place the shrines and their unconscious symbols deep in the sentiments and imagination of the masses of rural people from whose ranks most of the infantry was drawn.

By 1911, over 105 *Shokonsha* (shrines for the war dead) were in existence all over the country. These were special places of devotion for those who had lost sons during Japan's era of military adventures. (From the perspective of the Meiji Restoration, twenty-two of these are in Yamaguchi, the home of the Choshu clan, and fifteen in Kagoshima, the home of the Satsuma clan.) Some *Shokonsha* pre-dated the Meiji Restoration, but they were all integrated into the system and helped to bolster local community commitment to the Imperial System and the State.

After the Pacific War, the Yasukuni Shrine became a privately incorporated religious and legal person (*shūkyō hōjin*), but controversy was not long in gathering. The issue is whether or not financial responsibility for the shrine should be taken over by the State. Those who favor this argue that the State has an obligation to maintain the memorial of the war dead. The government draws much support and money from the various associations of "bereaved families." The *eirei*, the "glorious war dead," is a subject that cannot be raised without risking dramatic emotional backlash. It is the result of calculated Meiji government manipulation of natural Japanese sentiments, but it has remained a significant political resource throughout the entire postwar era and shows little sign of diminishing.

Opponents of the government proposal charge (quite correctly) that it would be against the Constitution. Therefore the question of constitutional revision is closely linked with the Yasukuni problem. The governments of Korea and China, whose peoples experienced savage treatment under the

Japanese Imperial Army before the war, as well as opposition parties and religious groups in Japan, are vigilant in commenting on any signs of Yasukuni being specially honored, because to them shrines for the war dead are symbols of militarism and the indignities they had to endure. Their comments are similar, that Japan's war dead should not be honored because they were simply predators in Asia who committed outrageous crimes against humanity.

Clearly, there has been a move toward seeking government support for the shrine. However, public and international reaction seems to have impeded its expected development. Two events are worthy of note, however. First was the enshrinement of the fourteen Class-A war criminals designated at the Tokyo War Crimes Trials, including General Tojo, the original war leader. Although it is understandable in Japanese terms that they should be enshrined along with all the others who died, the enshrinement shocked many people in Japan and outraged the governments of China and Korea. Western presses used the occasion for raking up Japan's wartime past. To these dangers, Japanese governments seem always oblivious. This took place in the fall of 1979. Among the enshrined is former Foreign Minister Matsuoka Yosuke, one of the architects of the Berlin-Rome-Tokyo Axis. The situation becomes ironic when it is remembered that Matsuoka was Christian (a Presbyterian) and that controversy has arisen over enshrining a member of the Self Defence Forces whose wife was Christian in the *Gokoku Jinja* in Yamaguchi.

The other controversial act occurred when Prime Minister Nakasone visited the Yasukuni Shrine with several cabinet members, an event that takes place annually. Until Nakasone's visit, previous Prime Ministers had signed the book as ordinary citizens and donated from their own pockets. Nakasone signed "Prime Minister (*Sori Daijin*) Nakasone Yasuhiro," making the visit official and stirring up considerable controversy. His successor, Mr. Takeshita, avoided the issue by deciding not to make the visit for one year. Like those arguing for the revision of school textbooks to soften Japan's image as an aggressor, protagonists claim that these are domestic matters. The distinction between domestic and international cannot be so easily or exclusively drawn in the age of international business and finance.

In dealing with an appeal by the right-wing Iwate Prefectural Assembly against a Sendai High Court decision that it had acted unconstitutionally, the Supreme Court in Tokyo ruled on 25 September 1991 that official visits by either the Emperor or Prime Minister to the Yasukuni Shrine violate the Constitution's separation of government and religion according to the terms of Article 20. On the one hand, this ruling seems to be fairly conclusive and should be welcomed as clarifying the situation. On the other hand, it may simply fuel the fires of demand in certain quarters for constitutional revision. Time alone will tell which consequence prevails.

Newly inaugurated cabinets always visit the Grand Shrines of Ise, as do members of the Imperial Family at important times. No one has objected to this, surprisingly, when it is considered that these are the central shrines of the Imperial System (*Tennōsei*). But the Yasukuni Shrine remains an emotional issue. As close as Okinawa, now a prefecture of Japan, there are still unhappy memories of the Japanese military. There was little joy there when Emperor Akihito visited Okinawa as Crown Prince in his father's stead to read a letter of sympathy. Of the 224,000 who died, approximately 160,000 were civilians and not military personnel. Most died at the hands of the Japanese army, which by that time was totally out of control and compelling people to commit suicide with it.[62]

The Funeral of Emperor Shōwa in 1989

When Emperor Hirohito died in January 1989, the question of religion and state came up again. Who should pay for the funeral? What kind of funeral should take place? The *Taiso no Rei* was held on 24 February 1989 in Shinjuku *Gyoen*, and the late Emperor was interred at the site of the Imperial Mausoleum in Hachioji. Controversy centered on the erection of a white *torii*, the gate to a shrine in front of the pavilion where the rites were conducted according to the Shinto tradition. The argument was whether the Imperial Household, the *Tennōke*, should use Shinto rituals as their own personal right, or whether the national funeral should be free of religious ritual. In fact, the appearance was confusing and although the *torii* was removed, controversy ensued. However, the controversies that followed over the alleged war responsibility of the Emperor far outshadowed the debate about the funeral.[63] With the beginning of a new era, Shinto may find peace to be itself without government or other interference.

The Accession Ceremonies of Emperor Akihito

In the accession of the new Emperor, the government was faced with the same problem it encountered in the funeral of Emperor Shōwa; how to provide for the rites at public expense without violating Article 39 of the Constitution. The *Sokui-no-Rei* was declared to be a state matter and would be funded by the government. The *Daijōsai* was declared to be a Shinto rite that was the prerogative of the Imperial Family; as such it was considered to be an Imperial Household rite, which the State would fund because it is also of national interest. On matters of budget, the funding for the *Daijōsai* was taken from the *kyutei* budget for the Imperial Court for public affairs as distinct from the *naitei*, which is the Court budget for private use by members of the Imperial Family. It could also be argued that because the Constitution permits freedom of religion, the Imperial Family is merely expressing its preference for Shinto rites to mark the formal accession of Emperor Akihito. Those against government funding of the rites continue to question the Imperial system; others on the right wing insist that the government's way of handling the issue was weak, compromising, and inadequate.

The Association of Shinto Shrines produced a brochure to explain the *Daijōsai* to the public. It described the role of the Emperor as revering the *kami* on behalf of the people and suggested nothing about special status of the Emperor, as the doctrine was expounded in the Meiji period. Rather, it pointed in a different direction. It closed with a sentiment that is appropriate to Japan's place in the modern world: "A new era has begun. The Emperor together with his people will work for the well-being of the nation and for the peace of the world."[64] The *Daijōsai* in effect inaugurates this new age.

SHINTO, THE HEISEI ERA, AND JAPAN'S INTERNATIONALIZATION

When Crown Prince Akihito became Emperor on 24 January 1989, a new era of Japanese history began. The naming of Imperial Eras (*Gengo*) has a long tradition. The year 1989 began the era of *Heisei* which loosely means "Peace and Development," the new age of Emperor Akihito.

Outside the former Japanese Empire proper, only two other areas have shrines, both built voluntarily by Japanese immigrants of the Meiji period and having nothing to do with State Shinto. The islands of Hawaii have several shrines as well as a number of Buddhist temples, as does Brazil, where many Japanese settled. California, which had a large immigrant Japanese population, boasts numerous temples going back to the Meiji period, but for some reason no shrines. The first branch shrine (*bunsha*) created outside of Japan since 1945 was set up in Stockton, California, in 1985 as a point of intercultural meeting.

How will Shinto fare in the foreseeable future? The Association of Shinto Shrines seems to recognize that the religious dimension of Shinto is significant for the Japanese people and for religions abroad that wish to communicate. Consequently, it has set up an international exchange division that tries to explain Shinto abroad and conduct dialogue with other faiths. Shinto cannot easily internationalize itself and should not be expected to do so in the way that banking and commerce can be internationalized. Culture is different. However, two points can be made. First, Shinto will again begin to absorb other influences as it travels around the world. It may even begin to develop a new image of itself. Second, in the process of exchange it will transfer some of its precious insights and ideas to enrich other religions and cultures. The rate of change in the modern world—and in Japan itself—suggests that these developments might occur with greater speed than observers expect. As long as mutual spiritual enrichment and better understanding result, such developments can only be for the best.

NOTES

1. R. G. Collingwood, *The Idea of History* (Oxford University Press Paperbacks, London, 1961), pp. 231–249.

2. Japanese language is more closely related to Japanese culture than a language like English, for example, which is used in many cultural settings.

3. Joseph W. T. Mason, *The Meaning of Shinto: The Primeval Foundation of the Creative Spirit in Modern Japan* (Dutton, New York, 1935), 252; *The Spirit of Shinto Mythology* (Fuzambo, Tokyo, 1939), pp. xiii, 285.

4. Robert J. Ballou, *Shinto: The Unconquered Enemy* (Viking Press, New York, 1945).

5. The idea of the diagram is borrowed from Murakami Shigeyoshi, *Kokka Shinto* (Iwanami Shinshō, Tokyo, 1970), p. 17.

6. J. E. Kidder, Jr., *Japan before Buddhism* (Thames & Hudson, London, 1958).

7. The location of the ancient state of Yamato remains controversial. Both names *Yamato* and *Yamatai* are found in ancient documents. Some scholars have considered them to be identical. In contrast, Sansom and Reischauer have held that Yamatai was a separate kingdom in northern Kyushu. See Joseph M. Kitagawa, *Religion in Japanese History* (Columbia University Press, New York, 1966), pp. 5–6, for a fuller discussion.

8. Kidder, *Japan before Buddhism.*

9. The *Nihon Minzoku Eizo Kenkyūjo* (Center for Japanese Ethnological Visual Documentation in Shinjuku, Tokyo) has filmed rituals entailing *Sangaku Shinkō* beliefs over a period of seven years in Hiroshima Prefecture.

10. Robert J. Smith, *Ancestor Worship in Contemporary Japan* (Stanford University Press, California, 1974).

11. Carmen Blacker, *The Catalpa Bow: A Study of Shamanistic Practices in Japan* (George Allen & Unwin, London, 1975), p. 326.

12. Tsunoda Ryusaku et al., *Japan in the Chinese Dynastic Histories*, ed. L. Carrington (Goodrich, South Pasadena, 1951), pp. 23–26.

13. Ishizu Teruji, *Exorcism and Shamanistic Patterns in Tohoku Districts of Japan* (Proceedings of the VIIIth International Congress of Anthropological and Ethnological Sciences, Tokyo and Kyoto, 1968), pp. 126–128.

14. Tsunoda et al., *Japan in the Chinese Dynastic Histories.*

15. *Kojiki,* Vol. I, Section 16 (Tuttle, 1982, Chamberlain's translation), p. 63.

16. *Kojiki,* Vol. I, Section 21 (Tuttle, 1982, Chamberlain's translation), p. 81.

17. See *Sourcebook of Shinto* (Greenwood Press, forthcoming) for a complete list.

18. *Nihongi* (Tuttle, 1972, Aston's translation), p. 154.

19. The first clause declares harmony as the basic social ideal to be followed.

20. It has been suggested that the first formal claims to the divine lineage of the Emperor were made during the reign of Emperor Tenmu.

21. *Saiō* has also been read as *saikū.*

22. In the postwar era, the years of *shikinen-sengu* have been 1953, 1973, and 1993. The cost in 1973 was approximately U.S. $20 million.

23. The reforms were undertaken by order of Emperor Kotoku between 645 and 649.

24. This dates to the time of Emperor Tenmu (r. 672–686).

25. Hachiman is recorded as having come in the form of a priestess to visit the Tōdai-ji in Nara. The reference is in the *Zoku-Nihongi, Kokushi Taikeii*, Vol. II (Yoshikawa Kobunkan, Tokyo, 1935), p. 206.

26. Emperor Shōmu (r. 724–748) tried to implement a program of Buddhist expansion, which (according to Professor Antonio Forte) was the result of a drive from China under Quan Xiancheng (651–692) to establish an international *pax buddhica* centered on Luoyang, where a *mingtang* (comprising a Hall of Government with a five-storied pagoda) and a giant clock were built to standardize in a symbolic way the ideals of nations participating in the Chinese dream. Shōmu called for a seven-storied pagoda in each province of Japan. Antonio Forte, "Some Characteristics of Buddhism in East Asia," *East Asia Culture and Korean Culture* (Papers from Institute of Korean Humanistic Sciences International Cultural Symposium, 1986), pp. 46–61.

27. A biography of En no Gyōja, also known as En no Ubasoku (Sanskrit: *Upasaka*) was compiled by Gigen in 724. Tradition dates his birth to 634. See Byron Earhart, "Shugendō, the Traditions of En no Gyōja and *Mikkyō* Influence," *Studies in Esoteric Buddhism and Tantrism* (Koyasan University, 1965), pp. 297–317.

28. Kitagawa, *Religion in Japanese History*, pp. 40–41.

29. Gyōgi (670–749) was a Hosso sect priest who received the title *Bosatsu* from the Emperor after his death.

30. Ross Bender, "The Hachiman Cult and the Dōkyō Incident," *Monumenta Nipponica* 34, no. 2 (Summer 1979): 125–153, gives an account of the origins of Hachiman and the political background to the Dokyo incident.

31. Nakamura Hajime, *Ways of Thinking of Eastern Peoples* (East-West Press, Honolulu, 1973), pp. 455–457, noted that the Japanese were not converted to Buddhism but that Buddhism was converted to Japanese tribalism. For a discussion of sutras in use in Japan of the seventh and eighth centuries, compare M. W. De Visser, *Ancient Buddhism in Japan* (Brill, Leiden, 1935) and Jacques Kamstra, *Syncreticism or Encounter* (Brill, Leiden, 1975).

32. *Shoku Nihongi*, by J. B. Snellen, "*Shoku Nihongi*: Chronicles of Japan Continued from 697–791," *Transactions of the Asiatic Society of Japan* 11 (1934): 151–239 and 14 (1937): 209–279.

33. The two texts contained the rituals of the two shrines, inner and outer.

34. The record is to be found in the *Shin Shōkyaku-cho-kofu-shō*.

35. Saga (r. 809–823).

36. The importance of the *Engishiki* cannot be overestimated as a guide to form. Only parts are rendered in English, including the *Ōbarae norito* and parts of the *Daijōsai*.

37. The *Engishiki* formally designates the list.

38. The existence of these shrines strengthens the case for the antiquity of *Jinja Shinto* over politicized Shinto. The *Ichi-no-Miya* founded their own association in 1991.

39. The practice of multiple enshrinements can probably be traced to this period, prior to which probably only local *kami* would have been enshrined.

40. From the *Tado Jingū-ji Garan Engi Shizai-cho*, which dates to around 801.

41. *Zoku Nihongi*, see previous note 25.

42. A fuller discussion can be found in Alicia Matsunaga, *The Buddhist Philosophy of Assimilation* (Sophia, Tuttle, Tokyo, 1969), Chapter 5.

43. Ibid., pp. 231–232.

44. Ibid., pp. 227–228.

45. Kitagawa, *Religion in Japanese History*, p. 85.

46. The diary of Kujo Kanezane (1149–1207, a Kamamura age courtier), which was known as *Gyokuo* or *Gyokukai*, remains a valuable source for historical research.

47. *Joei shikimoku* or *Goseibai shikimoku* was promulgated to regulate vassals of the Kamakura shogunate. It became the basis of the warrior house law (Bukehō).

48. This tradition belongs firmly to the folk side of Japanese religion and was viewed with great suspicion by officially sanctioned groups.

49. H. Byron Earhart, *A Religious Study of the Mount Haguro Sect of Shegundō* (Sophia University, Tokyo, 1970) is a most valuable study.

50. Paul L. Swanson, "*Shugendō* and the Yoshino-Kumano Pilgrimage," *Monumenta Nipponica* 36, no. 1 (Spring 1981): 55–84 is a study of the pilgrimage in modern times. A detailed Japanese account can be found in Gorai Shigeru, *Yama no Shūkyō* (Tankosha, Kyoto, 1970).

51. The last *saiin* is recorded as having been a daughter of Emperor Go Toba, and the last *saiō* was a daughter of Go-Daigo. Lack of funds prevented even the *Daijōsai* from being held. Only the *kagura* (sacred dance) of the *Kashikodokoro* was held without interruption.

52. *Yuiitsu Shinto Myō Bō Yōshū* and *Shinto Yurai-ki* were attributed to an ancestor; *Shinto Taii* was written under his own name.

53. This important distinction became a basic element of Shinto anthropology and is still used in modern religious movements.

54. See Miyachi Naokazu, *Shinto-shi*, Vol. 3 (Yuzankaku Publishing Co., Toyko, 1964).

55. Akiyama Kenzo, *Nisshi Kosho-shi Kenkyū*, Studies in Sino-Japanese Diplomatic History (Iwanami Shoten, Tokyo, 1939), p. 663.

56. One *koku* was a little over five bushels. The 250 (or so) *daimyo* received stipends ranging from the minimum of 10,000 to the maximum of 50,000.

57. Some claim long heritages and descent from the *kami* enshrined there. *Izumo Taisha* claims ninety-five generations, the *Tsubaki Dai Jinja* in Mie Prefecture claims ninety-six, and the *Aso Jinja* claims eighty. They survived State Shinto because the Japanese military police were sensitive toward shrines whose *kami* were identified in the mythology.

58. Kato Genchi delivered a now famous defense of the existence of *ikigami* to the 17th International Congress of Orientalists at Oxford in 1928.

59. For sources, see Wilhelmus H. M. Creemers, *Shrine Shinto after World War II* (E. J. Brill, Leiden, 1968), pp. 1–35; Helen Hardacre, *Shinto and the State: 1868–1989* (Princeton University Press, 1989); D. C. Holtom, *Modern Japan and Shinto Nationalism* (University of Chicago Press, 1943).

60. Data and statistics are taken from the sources listed in note 59.

61. The authoritative work in English is Wilbur M. Fridell, *Japanese Shrine Mergers 1906–12* (Sophia University, Tokyo, 1973). Basic Japanese accounts include the following: Morioka Kiyomi, "*Meiji makki ni okeru shuraku jinja no seiri*" (Shrine Consolidation in Late Meiji), *Toyo Bunka* (University of Tokyo Publication), no. 40 (March 1966): 1–50; Nishikawa Masatani, "*Jinja seiri mondai no shiteki kosatsu*" (Historical Investigation into the Problem of Shrine Consolidation), *Shinto Kenkyū* 3, no. 4 (October 1942): 47–65; *Mie-ken Jinja-shi* (A History of Shrines in Mie Prefecture) (Prefectural Publications); Toki Shokum, "*Meiji iko ni okeru jinja seiri no mondai: jinja hōrei o chusin to shita sono keika ni tsuite*" (The Problem of Shrine Consolidation from Meiji—Its Development as Centered on Shrine Laws), *Shinto Shūkyō* (Tokyo), no. 17 (August 1958): 36–47.

62. Historian Ienaga Saburo's proposed school text, which deals with the war, remains unpublished because the Ministry of Education, using its system of *ketei* (screening), changed what Ienaga had written. He has sued the government three times since 1965 for trying to falsify history. The Supreme Court in Tokyo ruled against him on March 16, 1993, declaring that the system was constitutional. The debate nevertheless continues.

63. The subsequent shooting of the Mayor of Nagasaki in August 1988 by a fanatical rightist because he had expressed the opinion that the late Emperor did share some guilt for the war underlies the intensity of feeling that still exists in Japan on the subject.

64. *Jinja Honcho*, Opinion Series 3, *Daijosai* (*Heisei 1*, 1989).

Chapter 2

Mythology

THE CONTEMPORARY QUESTION OF INTERPRETING MYTHOLOGY

How to understand mythology has been an important and recurrent topic of debate among scholars of religion in the nineteenth and twentieth centuries. Approaches have varied dramatically. Max Muller dismissed them all as the result of diseases of language in the same manner that Plato referred to the Greek myths as noble lies. Among twentieth-century scholars, on the one hand there stands Rudolf Bultmann's *entmythologisierung* program to demythologize the Judaeo-Christian tradition. He thought to rid it of its clumsy and misleading myths in order to release its true and saving message.[1] On the other hand there stands the approach taken by Mircea Eliade in his *Myth of the Eternal Return*.[2] Far from wishing to discard myths, he claimed to recognize in them an "archaic ontology." He made an intriguing comment concerning certain unhealthy tendencies of Western thought:

Western philosophy is in danger of "provincializing" itself (if the expression be permitted): first by jealously isolating itself in its own tradition and ignoring, for example, the problems and solutions of Oriental thought; second by its obstinate refusal to recognize any "situations" except those of the man of the historical civilizations, in defiance of the "primitive man," of man as a member of the traditional societies.[3]

He went so far as to claim that the "cardinal problems of metaphysics could be renewed through a knowledge of archaic ontology. In several previous works, especially in our *Patterns of Comparative Religion*, we attempted to present the principles of this archaic ontology, without claiming, of course, to have succeeded in giving a coherent, still less an exhaustive exposition of it."[4]

One of Eliade's contentions in that Judaeo-Christian thought has substituted existence in the Cosmos for a relation with history. The Cosmos too has a history, and through its "myths" that history is conveyed to those who live within it.[5] The Cosmos and society can be renewed periodically through participation in the meaning of these myths. This could add, for example, a new dimension of meaning to the celebration in Japan of the New Year (oshōgatsu) or the first sunrise of the New Year (hatsu-hi-nōde). Eliade is recognizing that the archaic ontology, as he calls it, has meaning that can be reflected upon and studied. Japanese mythology is probably the outstanding surviving example of the cosmically sensitive archaic ontology that generated rituals and a society dependent upon them for meaning and periodic regeneration.[6]

Other approaches to myth could be mentioned, but I think the approach taken by Eliade is particularly useful in the present context in that it asks the student of the myths to read them in their own terms, as the product of a cosmic awareness, as a version of archaic ontology, of human awareness in traditional society before historical consciousness developed. This is very much in keeping with what I have suggested about not imposing Western mindsets upon the raw data of Shinto. This, as we shall see, becomes a most acute and complicated problem in dealing with the Japanese mythology.

PROBLEMS OF INTERPRETING THE JAPANESE MYTHOLOGY

There is one additional complication regarding the mythology. Shinto has no official holy writings[7] because its survival has been guaranteed almost entirely by the preservation and perpetuation of its rituals. Nevertheless, the origins of Shinto, although not directly documented, are recorded in a compilation of Japanese mythology that dates to around 682 C.E. This is the Kojiki, the records of ancient matters. It was submitted to the Imperial Court around 712 C.E. and was received as the official account of the origins of the Japanese people, the Japanese archipelago, and what is known as the "age of the kami." Another version of essentially the same material, known as the Nihongi (or Nihon Shōki), dates to around 720 C.E. Both texts are basic resources for the historian once the narrative has entered the fifth century. Prior to that, they give an account of Japan's mythological origins.

These texts are the raw materials that must form the basis of discussion and interpretation. It should be remembered that they were written in a Chinese style of writing that is extremely difficult to read. Allowances must be made for the influence of Chinese forms of expression, although most of the key terms are so-called *Yamato-kotoba*, original Japanese words whose use predates the introduction of the Chinese writing system and the Chinese characters. Professor Jean Herbert, an eminent French Orientalist close to the spirit of Eliade, said that after prolonged study he had "come to believe that the cosmogony outlined in the Shinto scriptures is the product neither of the fanciful imagination of poets, nor of the intellectual fumblings of a primitive people, as has been almost uniformly alleged by western scholars. Like those found in other authentic scriptures of different religions, it is a faithful description of truths which great sages, in close touch with the laws of nature, have seen and understood."[8]

Although I may not share such a pious approach, I would not deny that the Japanese mythology possesses unique qualities that I have not encountered elsewhere in quite the same style. I include Herbert's interpretation as one guide to the mythology along with the remarks of certain Japanese scholars who have had reservations about this approach, to indicate how quickly controversy can surround any attempts at interpreting the mythology.

These pages on the mythology are little more than a guide to a journey of exploration that each researcher must undertake alone. The most basic way to begin the study is to read the *Nihongi* (Books I–II) and the *Kojiki* (Volume I). To assist, I offer a parallel synopsis of these sections. Follow this by reading Herbert's analysis, then read the texts again and consider the various responses made by Japanese scholars. Some have pointed out the political nature of the myths and regarded his views as "beating the air." Some did consider that he provided a vehicle of understanding, showing, for example, that mythology and science do not conflict. Others have felt that myth was beyond the bounds of science. One interesting comment praised him for the spiritual purity of his approach but qualified any praise in these terms: "But I cannot help feeling that it is a product of the West-European intelligence, which should not be understood as a compliment!"[9] Herbert devoted the succeeding seven chapters of his book to an amplification of the mythology along the lines presented here. Although I am in sympathy with his approach, I feel nevertheless that he became somewhat carried away with his ideas to the detriment of his study, falling into precisely the pitfall he sought to avoid, that of imposing Western forms. The archaic ontology does not yield so simply to the analytic techniques of the mind of historical civilization.

PARALLEL SYNOPSIS OF THE KOJIKI AND THE NIHONGI[10]

Kojiki	*Nihongi*	
Volume I	Book I	Contents
Section 1	I:1–3	Separation of Heaven and Earth.

Section 2	I:4	The generations of the *kami*.
Section 3	I:5	The jeweled spear of heaven and the island of Onogoro.
Section 4	I:5–6	Izanami and Izanagi procreate.
Section 5	I:7–9	Izanami and Izanagi procreate again.
Section 6	I:10–11	They give birth to various islands.
Section 7	I:12–14	They give birth to various *kami* and Izanami dies.
Section 8	I:15–17	Izanagi kills the fire *kami* and other *kami* appear.
Section 9[11]	I:18	Izanagi visits Yomi no Kuni.
Section 10	I:19–20	Izanagi escapes and divorces Izanami.
Section 11	I:21	He purifies himself in a river and Amaterasu is born.
Section 12	I:22	He hands on his task to the three noble *kami*.
Section 13	I:29	Susano-o-no-mikoto misbehaves and is expelled.
Section 14	I:30	He visits Amaterasu to bid her farewell.
Section 15	I:31	They bear more *kami*.
Section 16	I:32	He offends Amaterasu.
Section 17	I:37–49	She hides in the Ame no Iwato (the Heavenly Rock Dwelling). Ame-Uzume-no-mikoto entices her out.
Section 18	I:50–51	The eight-tailed serpent.
Section 19	I:52–58	The Palace of Suga.
Section 20	I:59	Ancestors of Okuni-nushi-no-mikoto.
Section 21		Okuni-nushi-no-mikoto and the white rabbit of Inaba.
Section 22		The plot against Okuni-nushi-no-mikoto.
Section 23		Okuni-nushi-no-mikoto saved by a mouse.
Section 24		Okuni-nushi-no-mikoto overcomes his eighty brothers.
Section 25		Okuni-nushi-no-mikoto woos and sings to Nuna-kaha-hime.
Section 26		Nuna-kaha-hime replies in song.
Section 27		Okuni-nushi-no-mikoto sings farewell to Suseri-hime.
Section 28		Okuni-nushi-no-mikoto is persuaded not to leave.
Section 29		The descendants of Okuni-nushi-no-mikoto.
Section 30		Sakuna-hiko appears to help in creating the land.

Section 31		Genealogy of various *kami*.
Section 32		Ame-no-ho-hiko is sent to pacify the land.
Section 33		Ame-no-waka-hiko is sent but does not return.
Section 34		The funeral of Ame-no-waka-hiko.
Section 35		The sons of Okuni-nushi-no-mikoto surrender the land.
Section 36		The second son of Okuni-nushi-no-mikoto surrenders.
Section 37		Okuni-nushi-no-mikoto is worshipped at Izumo.
	Book II	
Section 38	II:17	Saruta-hiko-no-mikoto and Ame-Uzume-no-mikoto.
Section 39	II:18	The descent of Ninigi-no-mikoto.
Section 40	II:	Saruta-hiko-no-mikoto and the shellfish (Chamb. 36).
Section 41	II:24	Marriage of Ninigi-no-mikoto.
Section 42	II:42	The lost fishhook.
Section 43	II:34–35	The palace of the *kami* of the sea.
Section 44	II:33–34	The *kami* of the sea lends the crocodile.
Section 45	II:48–49	Toyo-tama-hime gives birth.
Section 46	II:50	The children of Toyo-tama-hime-no-mikoto.

The two texts are not entirely identical or completely parallel, but the form in which the narrative is cast is similar. This provides the basis of the various interpretations discussed.

THE KAMI-YO: THE AGE OF THE KAMI

The first outline of the *kami-yo* is based on the work of a reputable prewar scholar who tried to set down a chronology of the *kami*. Thereafter, for the purposes of contrast, two Western summaries of the *kami-yo* are presented.

Akiyama's Outline of the Age of the *Kami* (the *Kami-Yo or Jin-Dai*)

Ame-no-Minakanushi-no-kami	*Kami* of the High Plain of Heaven
Takami-musubi-no-kami	*Kami* of Creativity
Kami-musubi-no-kami	*Kami* of Creation
Umashi-Ashikabihiko-no-kami	*Kami* of Creation

Ame-no-tokotachi-no-kami	*Kami* of Heaven
Kuni-no-tokotachi-no-kami	*Kami* of Earth
Toyokumonu-no-kami	"Mercury"
Ujini-no-kami	"Saturn"
Suijini-no-kami	
Tsunugui-no-kami	"Jupiter"
Ikigui-no-kami	
Otonoji-no-kami	"Mars"
Otonobe-no-kami	
Omodaru-no-kami	"Venus"
Ayakashikone-no-kami	
Izanagi-no-mikoto	
Izanami-no-mikoto	
Amaterasu-Okami	*Kami* of the Sun: primal *kami* of Japan
Ame-no-oshihomimi-no-mikoto	Son of Amaterasu
Ninigi-no-mikoto	Grandson of Amaterasu
Hikohohodemi-no-mikoto	Great-Grandson of Amaterasu
Ugaya-Fukiaezu-no-mikoto	Great-Great-Grandson of Amaterasu
Iwarehiko-no-mikoto, also known as Jimmu Tennō	Fourth son of Ugaya-Fukiaezu-no-mikoto, the first Emperor of Japan

The name for the Japanese archipelago was *Toyoashihara* (Fertile Land of Reed Plains), to which Amaterasu bade her grandson descend and govern for ages eternal. The sacred Regalia—the Mirror, Jewel, and Sword—were given to him. He descended upon the peak of Mt. Takachiho in Kyushu and married the *kami* known as Konohana-Sakuyahime. Their fourth grandson became the first Emperor.[12]

Herbert's Analysis of the Kami-Yo

Herbert summarizes the age of the *kami* by dividing it into seven successive stages:

1. *The appearance of differentiated non-material principles.* From an undefined and probably monistic pre-existence proceed in perfectly logical order the successive constituent principles which will permit the creation of the world. They are represented by the first seventeen *kami* listed in the *Kojiki*.

2. *The appearance of solid matter.* The original pair of actual Creators gradually brings the Earth out of the primeval Ocean, and gives birth to the individual *kami* representing the forces required to support the material world.

3. *The beginnings of mortal life.* Death . . . makes its appearance, and since it is a

basic imperfection and requires a purifying process, there also appears the possibility of purification, represented by a number of *kami.*

4. *The establishment of separate rulers for heaven and earth.* The three parts of the universe are organized and a distribution of duties is effected between their respective rulers. But since earth cannot subsist or prosper without the protection, blessing and co-operation of the heavenly forces, the latter are made to exercise the required influence.

5. *The consolidation of the earth by the heavenly powers.* The *kami* who are specifically in charge of the earth make and consolidate the land.

6. *The conquest of the earth by the heavenly powers.* The Heavenly *kami* feel that the earth being now organized but not yet divinized, the time has come for them to take charge of it. They make a number of successive and unconclusive attempts and finally succeed. The Heavenly *kami* now entrusted with the ruling of the earth takes charge of it.

7. The Heavenly *kami* effect complete intimate union with the powers of the land and of the sea, and finally with the earthly *kami* themselves.[13]

Wheeler's Version of the Kami-Yo

Another interesting attempt at analyzing the mythology into a chronological structure was produced by a former U.S. diplomat in Tokyo, Post Wheeler. His book was written primarily to attribute Japan's militarism to the idea of Divine Descent (he uses the capital letters). Although the original goal might have been polemic, he drew heavily upon Japanese scholarship of the day and presented the mythology in a form not dissimilar to that of Herbert. It provides further material for contrastive purposes to read alongside the originals.

Chaos	The Separation of the Sky and the Earth
The Sky	The Appearance of the Primal Deities
	The Appearance of the Lesser Deities
	The Appearance of the Creative Deity-Pair
The Earth	The Formation of the first Land by the Creative Pair
	The first House (architecture)
	The first Marriage (ceremony)
	Cohabitation
	Trial Birth (unsuccessful)
	The Birth of Lands
	The Birth of Elemental Deities (food, trees, mountains, rivers)
	The Birth of the Fire-Deity
	The first Death
	The first Murder
The Underworld	The first Divorce
	The Creation of Phallic Deities (thunder, disease, etc.)

The Earth	The Creation of the Three Ruling-Deities
	The Sun-Deity (good)
	The Moon Deity
	The Rebellious Deity (evil)
	The Distribution among these of the All-Rule
	The Withdrawal of the Earlier Creator
	The Murder of the Food-Deity
	Creation of grains, silk, and beasts of burden
The Sky	The Struggle between the Good Deity and the Rebellious Deity
	Weaving (the loom)
	The Self-Sequestration of the Good Deity
	The Sky and Earth Eclipsed
	The Return of the Good Deity Invoked (divination)
	Invention of Sculpture
	Metal-working (forge)
	Feminine Adornment
	Music (wind- and string-instruments)
	Liturgy
	Dance
	Song (incantation)
	The Return of the Good Deity
	The Birth of the Sky-Ancestor of the Imperial Line
	The Expulsion of the Rebellious Deity
	Reigious Purification
The Earth	The Peopling of the Earth by the Rebellious Deity
	Distribution of trees and seeds
	Cultivation of the land
	The Slaying of the Earth-serpent
	Poetry (the first poem)
	Multiplication of Earth-Deities
	The Birth of the Land-Master
	The Withdrawal of the Rebellious Deity to the Underworld
	The Persecution of the Land-Master by his Brethren
The Underworld	The Rape of the Rebellious Deity's Daughter and Property by the Land-Master
The Earth	The Land-Master Vanquishes his Brethren
	Improvement of the Land
	The Coming of the Southern Over-Sea Deity
	His Assistance
	Medicine
	The Hot-Bath
	His Departure
The Sky	The Decision of the Good Deity to assume Earth-Rule
	The First Embassies to Earth (unsuccessful)
The Earth	The Land-Master Submits to the Sky-Ancestor
	The first Temple (ritual)

The Sky	His Abdication Confirmed by the Good Deity
	The Descent of the Deity-Ancestor
The Earth	The First Earthly Emperor
	His Conquest of the Realm[14]

One reason for including these two accounts is to provide models based on Western-style analysis. Of the two, Wheeler is the more "Western" in his approach, yet he reproduces more of the complexity of the narrative. Herbert is more metaphysical. Neither one addresses the problem of why the primal *kami* of the mythology appears so late. Amaterasu is the ancestor of the Imperial House, yet she makes her appearance after Izanagi and Izanami. The *zōka-sanshin* (the three central creative *kami*) are not treated satisfactorily in either of the accounts. Wheeler tries to find significance in the words rather than in the atmosphere or impressions that the mythology creates. He identifies the final separation of Izanami and Izanagi as the first divorce. Indeed, he pronounces the formula of divorce, but by that time she is already dead!

Questions like these strongly suggest that the content of the narratives of this archaic ontology is not readily accessible to the Western inclination to simplify and impose a rational structure upon mythology. There is no doubt that the study of the classics in general and the mythology in particular is basic to a developed and balanced view of Shinto. This each individual can achieve only by himself or herself.

THE MYTHOLOGY OF CREATION

According to both texts, when heaven and earth came into being there were five *kami* who were born in the High Plain of Heaven, Takamahara. The next level is Takamanohara. It was from the Floating Bridge of Heaven, Ame-no-Ukihashi, that the two creative *kami* discovered the island of Onogoro-jima, which has been taken traditionally to mean the Japanese islands. The *kami* were led by the Master of the August Center of Heaven (Ame-no-minakushi), the *kami* of absolute beginnings, the very first *kami*. There were also the August Producing *kami* (Takami-musubi-no-kami), and the Divine Producing Wondrous *kami* (Kami-musubi-no-kami). The concept of *musubi* means "biding together or bonding." Along with these three *zōka-sanshin* (the three central creative *kami*) were the Pleasant Reed Shoot Prince elderly *kami* (Umashi-ashikabi-hikoji-no-kami) and the Heavenly Eternal Standing *kami* (Ame-no-tokotachi-no-kami). The world came into being through the work of the *kami* and their union. The idea of uniting (i.e., balancing or harmonizing) is also a part of the idea of creation. The universe gradually becomes defined through the union of pairs of *kami* who represent opposite extremes. After these, ten more *kami* of heaven are born; following them are the Male-Who-Invites (Izanagi-no-mikoto) and the Female-Who-Invites (Izanami-no-mikoto).

After receiving a jeweled spear from heaven and standing on the Floating Bridge, they thrust the spear down and stir. As they lift the spear from the ocean beneath, drops of brine harden and form the island of Onogoro. Izanagi and Izanami descend to the land they have found and created; and discovering their sexual identities, they make love.[15] (The description of the act of love was considered by Chamberlain to be too much for the gentle eyes of Victorian readers, so he rendered Section IV into Latin! The same section makes reference to the erection of a hall of eight fathoms, which has been considered by some scholars to refer to *Izumo Taisha*, although there is no final agreement on this.) Section 5 narrates the return of the pair to discuss the matter with the Heavenly *kami*, who in turn order them back to their work of love. They produce fourteen more islands and thereafter a succession of *kami*, last of whom is the *kami* of fire.

Izanami becomes ill after this last birth. As she lies dying, *kami* spring from her vomit, feces, and urine. Before her death, fourteen islands and thirty-five *kami* have come into being. From an anthropological point of view, Izanami's death after giving birth to the *kami* of fire presumably refers to the stage of civilization in which the utility of fire as well as its dangers came to be understood. Izanagi grieves for Izanami in a touching way, and he follows her to the underworld (Yomi-no-kuni), where he is ordered not to look at her. He disobeys and sees her decomposing form covered with maggots.[16]

The ugly hags of the underworld are set upon him and he flees to the border of the land of Yomi-no-kuni. He draws up a "thousand-draught rock," and in the closing scene they finally part, with Izanami threatening to kill one thousand people every day if he returns. He in turn insists that he can cause fifteen hundred to be born, which has been taken as a affirmation of the power of life over death, a strong and consistent theme in Shinto thought. The awareness of death as natural, but the polluting effect of the physical aspect of death, remain motifs of Japanese culture.

Izanagi then proceeds to a river mouth where he washes and purifies himself completely, thereby providing the origin of the practice of purification to remove *tsumi*, impurity. Before entering the Tachibana River, he throws off his jewelry and clothing and from each object a *kami* is born. He then plunges into the middle of the river, enacting the generic form of the later ritual of *misogi*. As he washes his face, three final *kami* appear: the *kami* of the stars, Susano-no-mikoto; the *kami* of the moon, Tsuki-yomi-no-mikoto; and the primal *kami* of the sun, Amaterasu-o-kami.

The *kami* of the stars, Susano-no-mikoto, was inclined to be impetuous and to perform acts that affronted the other *kami*. After a series of misdeeds, the sun *kami* hides in the Rock-Dwelling known as Ame-no-Iwato. The world is plunged into darkness; and the *kami*, using a *sakaki* branch (found in most Shinto rituals), try to induce her to return. At this point Ame-uzume-no-mikoto performs a ribald dance that makes the other *kami* laugh. On hearing the noise, the *kami* of the sun, Amaterasu, emerges. The other *kami* quickly throw a rope over the mouth of the cave to stop her returning, and the world again has light.[17]

Thereafter occurs the descent of the grandchild of the *kami* of the sun, Ninigi-no-mikoto.[18] The appearance of a massive *kami* called Sarutahiko-ō-kami, at the point where heaven and earth meet, causes fear in the heavenly *kami*. Ame-uzume-no-mikoto, whose trick had brought out the sun *kami*, is asked to go and meet this huge Earthly *kami*. She meets him and they settle on the earth, with Sarutahiko-ō-kami becoming the head of the earthly *kami* and his wife, Ame-uzume-no-mikoto, becoming the principal *kami* of entertainment, marriage, and defense. Thereafter, the grandson of the sun *kami* descends and the culture of rice is begun. From the descent of the August Grandson the Imperial Family has claimed its lineage with Jimmu Tennō being the first Emperor.[19]

DISTINCTIVE ASPECTS OF THE MYTHOLOGY

Certain features of the mythology illustrate how fundamentally different it is from Indo-European mythology and how difficult it is to interpret in an analogous manner.[20] Although the academic desire to conduct exercises in comparative mythology is justified, most of the meaningful parallels are drawn almost entirely from within traditional culture sharing some common heritage. It should not be surprising that the Japanese myths do not fit into categories devised for myths from different types of archaic society.[21]

The Relationship between Kami and Humanity

Humanity is descended from the *kami*, not created by them. This fact puts the Japanese mythology into a unique category and demonstrates how different it is from the Judaeo-Christian myths, for example. It is not a mythology of creation in the Western sense. The ancient *kami* are born and they too die.[22] *Kami* even have graves, in some instances. There are *kami* with a creative role, but their relationship to the creative process is extremely complicated and inconsistent, as a cursory reading of the narrative shows. It is more like a theory of the evolution of humanity from the *kami*, symbolized supremely by the *kami* origins of the Imperial House.

The Problematic Nature of Kami

This is a notorious issue to which I wish simply to draw attention. If a list is drawn up of all the beings that are identified as *kami*, and if the manner of their birth and death is recorded, what do they have in common that makes them *kami*? This question may be inspired by Plato's search for universals, but it is not wholly unreasonable. I noted several definitions in the Introduction to this book, but the one I prefer is based upon what are designated *kami* in the world around us in addition to the *kami* of the mythology. Yet in terms of the mythology alone, what indeed is a *kami*?

The Late Appearance of the Primal Kami

The sequence places the *kami* of the sun as late in appearing. This makes the mythology an unusual solar myth. Western critics have widely assumed that Shinto is based on a solar myth expressed in the legend of the sun *kami*. The Imperial Regalia of the Mirror, Jewel, and Sword identify well with the sun, moon, and lightning. However, to read these solely in a political way ignores the role of the sun, moon, and lightning in the process of maturing rice.

Lack of Interest in Formal Consistency

It is a strange metaphysics or religion from a Western (especially a classical Greek) point of view that could speak of a god dying. The gods by nature are immortal, and the idea of a man in later ages becoming a god is also difficult to express. The narrative goes back and forth over certain themes even when something impossible is being said, such as the "divorce" of Izanagi from his dead wife. The same point has been made about Japanese thought in general, namely, that it exhibits little interest in formal consistency.[23]

The Manner of Transition from Mythology to History

With no seeming sense of gap, the narrative flows quite freely from the *kami-yo* to the islands of Japan, from the timeless era of the *kami* to the historical Japan. Perhaps this is the result of the tremendous influence of Chinese culture at the time of the composition of the *Kojiki* and *Nihongi*. The idea of Divine Descent becomes all the easier to discuss, although it does raise certain metaphysical questions. These are of no interest to the narrative, however, which continues to weave myth and history together even as the historical eras begin to dawn.

JAPANESE INTERPRETATIONS OF THE MYTHOLOGY

Various schools of interpretation exist in Japan, but the beginning of the study of the classics in modern times dates to the work of the *Kokugaku* (National Learning) school of Shinto Studies.[24]

Kokugaku Interpretations

Japanese scholars over the centuries have written expositions of the *Kojiki* in particular and Japanese mythology in general. Leaders among them were Kamo no Mabuchi (1697–1769); Hirata Atsutane (1776–1843), who developed the political meaning of the mythology; and, supremely, Motoori Norinaga (1730–1801).[25] His work was analogous to that of the late nineteenth and early twentieth-century German *Formgeshichte* (form criticism) school, which was concerned with the origin and formation of the New Testament. Just as these scholars tried to separate the content of primitive Christianity from its Hellenistic overlays, Motoori Norinaga tried to identify what was pure Japanese mythology and to separate it from the influence of Chinese style and thought. He concluded that the doctrine of Amaterasu, the *kami* of the sun, was the principal theme of the mythology. Regardless of the validity of his conclusions, his work stands as an early Japanese attempt at textual analysis in order to probe primitive roots. It is also the starting point for almost all modern work on the *Kojiki*.

Political Interpretations

Tsuda Sokichi was the earliest among modern scholars to express a clearly political view of the ancient texts. He argued in a Marxist manner in a series of works on the *Kojiki* that it was composed as neither history nor as myth, but as a document to legitimize the rule of the Imperial House. He propounded this theory first in 1913; understandably, its radical nature led to considerable controversy. However, his influence was established and remains dominant, with most later work being simply the development and amplification of his thought.[26] Anesaki Masaharu, close to the spirit of this, declared that

Whatever the mythical significance or historical value of these stories may be, the Yamato race always believed in its descent from Heaven and worshiped the Sun-goddess as the ancestress of the ruling family, if not of all the people. They also endeavored to force this belief on the subjugated peoples, and partly succeeded in impressing them with that and other associated ideas. These legends and beliefs, together with the accompanying religious practices, make up the original religion of the Yamato race, now known as Shinto.[27]

Literary Views

Watsuji Tetsuro, famous for his work on the role of climate in the philosophy of culture, published a major work in reaction to Tsuda's. He favored a literary appreciation of the *Kojiki*, claiming that this gave it inner coherence.[28] This was taken a stage further by Kurano Kenji,[29] who suggested that the *Kojiki* may best be compared with epic literature of the West and that it should be so regarded, much in the way that *Beowulf* is read now as an epic of the Anglo-Saxon world. The most thorough recent study of the structure of the text was undertaken by Takeda Yukichi, whose work covers the middle years of the century.[30] More recently, the unique role of imagination in Japanese myth has been discussed by Nakanishi Susumu.[31]

Sociological and Folklore Interpretations

Some scholars argue that the role of Japan's rice culture was decisive in the growth of its social self-awareness. The sense of divinity within life precedes these, and ultimately that idea is enshrined within the forms of the mythology. Like the mythology of the ancient Hebrews, which was borrowed from Babylon and elsewhere, it is not the form of the borrowed that is important nor even its original message, but what the borrower wished to communicate through it. In the case of the Japanese, the objective was to express a self-understanding about the world and the place of the *kami* and the Japanese people within it.

It is generally agreed by scholars that although material culture of Japan was quickly enriched by contact with China, the social and religious culture of Japan was more sophisticated than was first thought by early Western critics. Comparisons with pagan nature worship in the West are consequently misleading. Western nature worship, and later Christianity, fostered a sense of fear and the need to atone for evil and deformity. Shinto seems inspired by a religious mood of love and gratitude for natural beauty. Therein lies the key that explains the contrast between the two worldviews. All these points emerge in the great studies of Japanese folklore and their meaning. The most famous scholars in this area were the folkorist Yanigata Kunio[32] and a student of mythology, Matsumura Takeo.[33]

Modern Liberal Interpretations

In more recent times, some thinkers have tried to universalize the meaning of the mythology. For example, in the earliest stages when heaven and earth came into being, there were five *kami* born in the high plain of heaven. This can be radically reinterpreted.[34] Takamahara, the High Plain of Heaven, can be taken to mean the cosmos. The next level, Takamanohara, can be taken to mean the solar system. From the floating bridge of heaven, Ame-no-Ukihashi, the two creative *kami* discovered the island of Onogoro-jima. This could mean the Japanese islands, but from its etymology (literally, "self-condensing") it could also refer to the planet Earth.

The concept of *musubi*, which means "binding together or bonding," can also carry the nuance of "creativity." Along with the three Divine Creators (the *zoka-no-san-shin*) were the Pleasant Reed Shoot Prince elderly *kami* (Umashi-ashikabi-hikoji-no-kami) and the Heavenly Eternal Standing *kami* (Ame-no-tokotachi-no-kami). The world comes into being through the work of all these *kami* and their union. The idea of uniting (i.e., balancing or harmonizing) is also part of the idea of creation. The universe is designed to reflect the balance and harmony that their uniting achieves. As a result, conflict becomes understood as unnatural. After these, ten more *kami* of heaven are born as well as the Male-Who-Invites (Izanagi-no-mikoto) and th Female-Who-Invites (Izanami-no-mikoto). The universe becomes further formed and expanded by the union of these two *kami* of opposites. By command of the first *kami* everything is ordered according to the guidance of truth, reason, and principle. This kind of interpretation can be carried right through to the close of the *kami-yo*. Its purpose is to expound the universal significance of the narratives.

These ideas have been praised by some thinkers and condemned by others. Whether or not Japanese mythology can be universalized is not an old question. It represents an attempt to break out of the Meiji period State Shinto orthodoxy and away from conventional thinking toward more spontaneous and meaningful ways of speaking about the mythology, not just to the outside world but to the Japanese people themselves.

RESIDUAL INFLUENCES IN JAPANESE CULTURE

The myths of the *Kojiki* and the *Nihongi*, despite their antiquity, continue to exert indirect influences on modern Japanese culture much in the same way that Western myths affect the cultures they helped to create. Myth leaves its mark upon society. From this we can learn more about the myth and society as well as how they relate. The following sections review six significant areas of continuing influence that have been identified and discussed by various critics, including Namakura Hajime, the reknowned scholar of Buddhism and Japanese intellectual history.

The Idea of Spontaneous Creativity

This concept differs from the Western idea of a Creator God by whose sole agency the world comes into being.[35] The Japanese myths identify the collective activity of many *kami* whose action and interaction bring into being the world as we know it. The idea of *musubi* is central to this role. The Japanese inclination to rely on the result of spontaneous collective effort without trying to predetermine the outcome too strictly seems to have survived in aspects of modern decision-making processes in which widespread participation to achieve a harmonious conclusion is the objective.

Confidence in the Power of Life

Motoori Norinaga pointed to the great sense of power of life in the mythology. In modern times this may be reflected partially in the often-repeated affirmation that Japan's only real natural resource is its people and specifically in the Matsushita Corporation philosophy of "Human Resource Management." The Japanese festival as a celebration of life for its own sake is one way in which the principle is expressed in community life.

The Desire for All-Inclusiveness

A preference for all-inclusiveness and the reconciliation of differences may be attributed to the idea that pairs of *kami* representing opposites brought the world into being. These *kami*, in their harmony, become creative and are caught up in each other's efforts. Thus, a world comes into being that expresses the principle harmony as a natural ideal. Such ideals seems to imbue many Japanese workplaces with a distinctive atmosphere. Great scrolls bearing the characters for harmony (*chōwa*) may often be seen.

Styles of Artistic Expression

These are heavily influenced by Shinto ideals concerning nature, beauty, and goodness. Buddhist statuary in Japan was given greater benignity in its facial lines in keeping with the general good-naturedness of the Japanese *kami*. Gardens were designed to reflect the best of nature's seasons. Houses came to be made of natural wood like the oldest shrines, and the relationship of both to their surroundings came to be a complete art form. Tea houses provide outstanding examples of this concept. Aesthetic quality grew to be a value in Japan, whereas it has always been viewed with some suspicion in the West, whose primary non-ethical value norm is the "scientific" in the broadest sense.

The Inclination to Nationalism and Ethnocentrism

Narrow interpretation of the mythology, especially during the early nineteenth century, led to the growth of an ethnocentrism that served the interests of nationalism during the time of Japan's modernization when national self-awareness was necessary. However, it was manipulated and eventually transformed into a doctrine of racial superiority and the basis of a militaristic ideology. Although this has receded into history, there is no doubt that Japanese governments still think in ethnocentric terms with regard to the other peoples of Asia and consider nationalism to be a virtue, regardless of its potentially dangerous implications.

In his introduction to *Shinto: Japan's Spiritual Roots*, Ewdin O. Reischauer perceptively observed that it is difficult to imagine Japan without Shinto or Shinto anywhere except in Japan. Historically that is the case. However, Shinto mythology is capable of broader interpretation than it has received from certain commentators. It is not devoid of universal elements. These are now being sought so that Shinto, through reflection upon its own mythology, can engage in a dialogue with world religions.

MYTH IN MODERN JAPANESE SOCIETY

There are grounds for arguing that the power of myth is far from dead in modern Japan, even the Japan of the postwar era. Japan began the process of modernization and industrialization in 1868, so one would expect developments in Japan to follow the patterns of modernization found elsewhere. This was certainly the expectation of the Modernization School of the 1960s. Japan's modernization has incorporated more of the traditional society than would be expected on the basis of Western models.[36] This has been asserted by numerous Japanese, and it is now receiving even greater credibility by one leading Western sociologist who has retracted his earlier position.[37]

Kokutai Thought from Meiji to Shōwa (1868–1989)

The term *kokutai* (literally, "national body" or body politic) in Japanese consists of two characters. One represents the idea of "country" and the other of "body." The term *kokutai* belongs to Meiji period political philosophy. Another considerably older term,[38] *kunigara*, carries essentially the same meaning. It consists of the same character for country, read here as *kuni*, and the ending *gara*, whose roots mean "pattern" or "character." For example, *iegara* identifies social standing or the pedigree of a house lineage. *Hitogara* describes moral elegance in an individual. *Aidagara* refers to the "between" aspect of relationships. *Kunigara* is therefore the quality of national character (or virtue in the Confucian sense).

The Meiji definition of *kokutai* was "Emperor plus people." *Kunigara* seems to have a cultural rather than political nuance. The distinction is similar to that between government-sponsored Shinto cults and those that grew from popular roots. Likewise, the two sets of ideas may be set side-by-side in a table of contrasts between different ways of appreciating the national tradition.

The diagram is merely a guide designed to suggest that there is more than one line of thought about the nature of the body politic. There is a narrow one around which gathered the political ideals of Meiji Japan, such as *fukoku-kyōhei* (prosperous country, strong army) or *wakon-yōsai* (Western techniques, Japanese spirit). There is also a broader and more cultural one, which seems to be reflected in the postwar Imperial Edict for the reconstitution of the State given on 1 January 1946. The *Manyōshū*[39] term *kunigara* existed prior to the modern state; like the *Manyōshū* itself, it gives a different picture of Japan from that of the rigid feudal society of Edo, which was quickly transformed into the narrow-minded nationalistic state of the Meiji period. The emphasis of postwar to Heisei Japan seems to be more upon the cultural and political ideals.

Kokutai Thought: Understanding the Meaning of the National Tradition

kokutai As an appreciation of the basic role of the State and the Emperor	*kunigara* As an appreciation of the Japanese tradition in the broad sense—a spiritual understanding of *kokutai*
kokutai (Political) About the constitutional nature of the body politic	*kunigara* (Religious) (This half can be read alongside the diagram on the development of Shinto)

kokutai The official history of the land of Yamato and the origins of the Imperial House	*kokutai* The mythology of the *Kojiki* and the *Nihon Shoki*	*kunigara* Reverence for *kami*, reverence for the dead, reverence for nature, love of life
Sai-sei-itchi Unity of worship and government—legal and constitutional principles	*kokutai* *Sai-sei itchi* *Matsuri-goto* *Yamato-damashi*	*kunigara* Appreciation of the excellence of the Japanese tradition of diligence, etc.
kokutai Ideals of the Imperial Rescript on Education	*kokutai* *Kokka Shinto*	*kunigara* Appreciation of natural beauty, historical culture, sense of humanity

Kigensetsu and Kenkokusai

The influence of the Meiji ideals has proved difficult to dislodge. For example, the early Meiji government declared the birthday of Emperor Meiji and the accession day of the first Emperor, Jimmu Tennō, to be national holidays.[40] This was decreed in 1873. The term *Kingensetsu* referred to the mythological national founding day in 660 B.C. Nationalists began a campaign to reinstate it as soon as the San Francisco Treaty had been signed. The February 11 debate was resolved when the holiday was formally included in the calendar of national holidays in 1966. It was named the *Kenkokusai* festival to mark the national founding day. It subsequently became an occasion for ultra-nationalists to organize rallies to decry the postwar Constitution and demand a new and militaristic constitution befitting the modern Japan.

The Separation of Mythology and Politics

The constitutional separation of State and Shinto that took place after the war has been discussed earlier in this book. It is stated in the Constitution and therefore is part of the law of the land. The separation of *mythology* and *politics* in Japan has proven to be more difficult to effect. I cite several reasons for this with minimum comment because they are factors that must be recognized and addressed openly and frankly, regardless of individual opinions.

First, religion and politics cannot be readily separated. The United States might have explicit constitutional provisions, yet there is such a thing in the United States as "civic religion." The U.S. dollar proclaims "In God We Trust." British monarchs receive the crown from the Archbishop of Canterbury. Islamic nations have made Islamic values the basis of law as well as morality. Buddhist cultures have done likewise. In spite of hunger in India, the cow remains sacred. Examples could continue indefinitely. Separation of Church and State, meaning that a government will not financially support any specific religious institution, is about the most that can be guaranteed. Religion and mythology in the broader sense of ideas and values cannot be separated from political life any more than language can be separated from the culture to which it gives expression.

Second, unlike many nations in Asia, Japan was not colonized in the nineteenth century and therefore was able to develop independently of colonial influences. A national way of thinking was established by the Meiji government that survived into the modern period, because it offered a sense of security and identity in a world that was changing with dramatic speed. It also helped to restore stability in the nation after the disastrous Pacific War and has not been absent from the era of economic development. New elements may be added to the Japanese tradition, but what is already in place cannot be changed—or so the common sense has it. Japan's dynamics of social change function according to their own laws.

Finally, it is more than reasonable to argue that Japan is a modern nation that differs from modernized Western nations in that its government has preserved (intentionally or not) much more of its past than other nations have, not least of all its roots in the mythology of a sacral society. This cannot be made to disappear. It is like a tree whose branches may be broken from time to time but whose roots are strong and healthy and too deep to be completely dislodged.

NOTES

1. Rudolf Bultmann, *Jesus Christ and Mythology* (SCM Press, London, 1958). The post-Bultmann theological discussion of secularization can be traced to Ronald Gregor Smith, *The New Man* (SCM Press, London, 1955) and his subsequent work, *Secular Christianity* (Collins, Glasgow, 1970).

2. Mircea Eliade, *The Myth of the Eternal Return* (Princeton University Press, 1974).

3. Ibid., p. x.

4. Ibid.

5. Ibid., pp. xiii-xiv.

6. The interesting question remains of how Japan can operate so successfully within the historical structures created by Western thought and yet retain such a grip on the archaic ontology. Japan's perennial problem of adjusting to the outside world may arise from the lack of a sense of what Eliade called the "terrors of history."

A valuable and related study of the literary roots of the Shinto tradition is Herbert Plutschow, *Chaos and Cosmos: Ritual in Early and Medieval Japanese Literature* (E. J. Brill, Leiden, 1990).

7. Western commentators frequently but misleadingly refer to the *Nihongi* and the *Kojiki* as Japan's sacred scriptures. Although they contain mythology and some early history, they have no spiritual significance on a par with the Bible or the Koran, or even with any of the sūtras popular in Japanese Buddhism. They are not guides for life and they are not used in any religious rituals, although the names of *kami* appear within them.

8. Jean Herbert, *Shinto: At the Fountainhead of Japan* (George Allen & Unwin, London, 1967), p. 228. His work was based primarily on interviews with priests and scholars. It is a remarkable achievement in terms of the limited method of research.

9. This comment appeared in a 1962 issue of the *Kodo-Ishin* (a magazine for Shinto priests). See Herbert, *Shinto: At the Fountainhead*, pp. 229ff. The comments show just how divergent views are in Japan concerning the mythology.

10. English versions of the *Kojiki* and the *Nihongi* quoted are W. G. Aston's translation, *Nihongi* (1896, Tuttle edition of 1972); Basil Hall Chamberlain's translation, *Kojiki* (1919, Tuttle edition of 1982); and Donald Philippi's new translation, *Kojiki* (University of Tokyo Press, 1968), which differs from Chamberlain's chapter divisions. The diagram follows the divisions in Philippi's translation. The *Nihongi* column is blank where the narratives of the *Kojiki* are not found.

11. The major differences in chapter divisions begin from Philippi's division of Section 9 into two parts and continue thereafter. *Mikoto* means "lord" or "prince."

12. Akiyama Aisaburo, *Shinto and Its Architecture* (Kyoto Welcome Society, Kyoto, 1936).

13. Herbert, *Shinto: At the Fountainhead*, p. 231.

14. Post Wheeler, *The Sacred Scriptures of the Japanese* (Schuman, New York, 1952), pp. xliv-xlvi.

15. *Kojiki*, Vol. I, Sections 3-4.

16. Ibid., Section 9.

17. Ibid., Section 16.

18. Ibid., Section 23.

19. I have also verified the understanding of these sequences by referring to a rare text in my possession entitled *Kannagara no Michi*, which was prepared within the Imperial Household for use in instructing Empress Taishō in the history and origins of the Imperial Family.

20. Wheeler, *Sacred Scriptures*, p. 389, suggests parallels with other mythologies, particularly those of Babylon and Egypt. In view of my contentions here, I have reservations about pursuing these. See also Joseph Campbell, *The Mythic Image* (Princeton University Press, 1974).

21. Anesaki Masaharu, *Mythology of All Races*, Vol. 8 (Marshall Jones, New York, 1928; Cooper Square Publishers, New York, 1964), p. 221, draws attention to the differences in styles of mythology.

22. The grave of *Sarutahiko-no-mikoto* is found within the precincts of the Tsubaki Grand Shrine. No human graves are located in shrines because of the impurity entailed.

23. Nakamura Hajime, *Ways of Thinking of Eastern Peoples* (East-West Center Press, Honolulu, 1964), pp. 345–576.

24. See Chapter 9 of this book.

25. Motoori Norinaga, *Kojiki-den* (completed in 1798, first published in 1822).

26. Tsuda Sokichi, *Nihon Koten no Kenkyū*, 2 vols. (Iwanami Shoten, Tokyo, 1948–1950). These volumes contain basic exegetical ideas and his text-criticism.

27. Anesaki, *Mythology*, p. 212.

28. Watsuji Tetsuro, *Fūdoron* (Iwanami Shoten, Tokyo, 1920).

29. *Kurano Kenji, Kojiki no Shin-Kenkyū* (Shibundo, Tokyo, 1927).

30. Takeda Yukichi, *Kojiki Kenkyū*, Vol. 1: *Teikiko* (Seijisha, Tokyo, 1944); *Kojiki Setsuwagun no Kenkyū* (Meiji Shoin, Tokyo, 1954); *Kiki Kayoshu Zenko* (Meiji Shoin, Tokyo, 1956).

31. Nakanishi Susumu, *Amastukami no Sekiai, Kojiki o Yomu*, Vol. 1 (Kadokawa, Tokyo, 1986).

32. Yanigata Kunio (1875–1962) was the founder of *minzokugaku* (folklore studies). See Nakamura Akira, *Yanagita Kunio Shisō* (Hosei University, Tokyo, 1968) and Kamashima Jiro, *Yamagita Kunio Kenkyū* (Tokyo, 1973).

33. Matsumura Takeo, *Nihon Shinwa no Kenkyū* (Baifukan, Tokyo, 1954–1958).

34. Yamamoto Yukitaka, *Kami no Michi* (Tsubaki Grand Shrine of America Publications, Stockton, Cal., 1984).

35. Anesaki, *Mythology*, p. 221.

36. Isaiah Ben-Dasan, *The Japanese and the Jews* (Kinseido, Tokyo, 1973). The case he has made about there being as much continuity in Japan as change seems now quite well founded. The same point is made with regard to Japan's business development.

See also Stuart D. B. Picken, "The Role of Traditional Values in Japanese Society," *Shell International Conference on Continuity and Innovation*, University of Stirling Centre for Japanese Studies, Discussion Paper 3, 1984.

37. One of the principal exponents of the school, S. N. Eisenstadt, revisited Tokyo in 1984 and gave a lecture at the International House of Japan. At this time he took a large step back from the theory of the convergence of cultures he had promulgated earlier in view of the developments in Japan he subsequently witnessed. Although Japan appears to bear many resemblances to the West, the inner core has changed much less than many observers (Japanese and non-Japanese) realize or recognize. Robert Bellah now takes a similar position.

38. Ono Sokyo handled this topic in a different way in his various writings. He argued that the combination of characters may be read in Chinese in three separate

ways, two of which are relevant here. One reading is *kokutai* itself, which he claims has a clear political nuance. The other is *kunigara*, which carries more a moral nuance of virtue. For the idea of the diagram I am indebted to him, although I have restructured it in accordance with my own understanding of the phases of tradition. See Ono Sokyo, *Jinja Shinto Shingaku Nyūmon* (Introduction to the Theology of Shrine Shinto) (Jinja Shimpo, Tokyo, 1953); *"Jinjahō to Shūkyō Hōjinjhō Kaisei"* (Shrine Law and the Revision of the Religious Juridical Persons Law), *Jinja Shimpo Senshu* (June 1957): 216–217. He also published in English *The Kami Way* (Tuttle, Tokyo, 1959).

39. *Manyōshū* poem. 220.

40. This practice has continued. The birthday of Emperor Shōwa was designated a national holiday after his death in 1989 and is now known as Green Day, a tribute to his lifelong study of biology.

Chapter 3

Imperial Household Shinto

THE IMPERIAL HOUSEHOLD AND SHINTO

The Imperial House of Japan has been the subject of substantial research within the fields of history, politics, and religion. This chapter introduces some of the rituals and ceremonies performed by the Emperor or within the Imperial Household or Imperial Palace throughout the year. These have continued off and on at least since the Heian age. The vast majority cannot be seen by the general public; indeed, to the average Japanese their existence is little known, if at all. However, the passing away of Emperor Shōwa (known better by his personal name, Hirohito), which received massive media coverage in Japan, brought again to light the complex relationship between Shinto, the Imperial Family, and the 1946 Japanese Constitution that separates Religion and State. The Constitution follows the basic principles of the Constitution of the United States, which was designed to prevent the institution of a State religion. It is the logical creation of a pluralistic society. However, Japan is not a pluralistic society in the American sense of the term, although Japanese society may not be as homogeneous as is frequently claimed. Its homogeneity is implied as an unspoken premise of action by the Liberal Democratic Party, the government, and the bureaucracy. From that point of view, the holding of Shinto rites is not seen as a violation of individual Japanese rights. Many elderly members of the ruling party were brought up to believe that being a Japanese citizen and observing Shinto rituals were one and the same thing. This view has not totally disappeared. The entire debate about whether or not Shinto rites are religious was revived quite controversially over the funeral observances for the late Emperor Shōwa.

The attitude toward and atmosphere surrounding these events created by the government shows a marked contrast to transitional periods in Western monarchies that follow the principle "The King is dead, God save the King!" There is usually a State Funeral followed by a massive celebration on the coronation of the new monarch. The Emperor Shōwa died on 4 January 1989 in the early hours of the morning. Television was blacked out, except for government reports on the change of the name of the era to Heisei from Shōwa. Thereafter, the new Emperor, Akihito, received the Imperial Regalia and formally became Emperor. His seal authorized the name of the new era in accordance with the Constitution. The funeral ceremonies, attended by approximately 160 dignitaries of foreign governments, took place over one month later.

The month was a period of national mourning during which all celebratory events were cancelled. In fact, when it became known that the Emperor was suffering from a terminal cancer, the government declared a state of *jishiku*, a period of self-restraint. It was considered inappropriate to hold end-of-year parties, New Year parties, weddings, or any special events. Public celebrations virtually ceased from October 1988 until early March 1989, a state of affairs that caused great hardship to businesses such as hotels, restaurants, and wedding halls. Because red is normally a celebratory color, red items were almost universally removed from the marketplace, including red soy beans. The funeral rituals were finally completed on 24 February 1989, when the enshrinement of the late Emperor took place at the Imperial Mausoleum. The mourning period within the Imperial Court continued for a full year; consequently, the government announced that the formal accession rites would take place in November 1990, almost two years after the death of the previous Emperor.

Throughout this time, key administrative decisions relating to the accession were made by the *Kunaichō*, the Imperial Household Agency funded by the State. It follows the recorded dictates of tradition, although it must receive authorization as well as funds from the government in accordance with the Constitution. The present situation is not very different from what existed before the Meiji Restoration.[1] The only major difference is the manner in which the Imperial Household was manipulated.

The Tokugawa government retained the Imperial Household in low profile and in the traditional Imperial Palace in Kyoto to function as the imprimatur of its status. The Meiji leadership, whose new government was described as a restoration of direct Imperial rule, brought the young Emperor to the city renamed Tokyo (literally, "east capital") to live in the Tokugawa Castle, which was restyled as the Imperial Palace. It was, in reality, no more than a calculated political move to boost the prestige and power of the new government, which claimed to be administering the nation's affairs in the name of the Emperor. During the preceding Edo period, there were times when Imperial accession rites could not be held because of lack of finances. All rituals had to be limited because of expense. However, Japan's post–World War II economic growth made it possible for the nation to spend billions of dollars on the funeral of the Emperor Shōwa. Many domestic critics of the Japanese government labeled it politically motivated, with the purpose of adding prestige to the Imperial System, the *Tennōsei*, in their view the most manipulated monarchy in human history. Japan, like all Asian countries, has had its warlords. Only in earliest times did these include Emperors, and then only a tiny handful. The warlords and the Imperial Household have always gone their separate ways. Emperors have been more like High Priests than monarchs, and warlords have received authorization from the Emperor. It may be difficult to conceive, but history suggests that the Imperial Household and the Imperial System have always displayed the paradox of being simultaneously Japan's most prestigious institution but one of its weakest and most passive.

"God stops at the traffic lights" was the headline of an article in a British newspaper[2] about the less formal style of Emperor Akihito, whose car stops at traffic lights when he is conducting private business. The article underscored the change in status undergone by the Emperor and the Imperial Household after the death of the Emperor Shōwa. The divine status of the Emperor was formally denied by the late Emperor Shōwa in 1946; and although he worked hard at his new role of *Ningen Tennō* (human Emperor), much of the past remained. Japanese Emperors are considered to be direct descendants of Ninigi-no-Mikoto, grandson of Amaterasu, the *kami* of the sun. Therefore, not only is he Emperor but, being descended from a *kami*, he was in the past understood to participate in the nature of *kami*. This placed him apart. It is important to note that there are other families that claim descent from *kami*,[3] just as, on various occasions, human beings have been declared to be *kami* and have been enshrined and revered during their lifetimes.[4] The demarcation between human and divine in Japanese thought can be rather vague, as the mythology shows, and certainly quite different from what is understood in Western thought.

There is no doubt that in the interests of strengthening its own authority, the Meiji government manipulated the symbol of the Emperor. Ito Hirobumi, an important figure in the preparation of the Meiji Constitution, spoke in a dramatic and exaggerated way of the emperor as an object of reverence. He may well bear responsibility for stimulating the cult of Emperor worship in modern times when he declared that "The Sacred Throne was established at the time when the heavens and the earth became separated. The Emperor is Heaven-descended, divine and sacred; He is preeminent above all his subjects. He must be reverenced and is inviolable."[5]

Many such quotations could be listed from the Meiji era right through to the end of the Pacific War. Typical of the scholarly view is the following, which indicates how thoroughly the belief was being instilled: "The Emperor is regarded as a living *kami*, loved and revered by the country above everything else on earth. The Emperor himself loves and protects the people who are considered sons of the *kami-nagara* (the way of the *kami*) and who are entrusted to his care by the *kami*. Shinto is therefore to be equated with the doctrine of the Emperor."[6]

School textbooks carried similar propagandist materials as part of what was later judged by liberal thinkers to be a politically undesirable program of moral education. The most extreme—and, ironically, the last—statement of this position was contained in the *Kokutai-no-Hongi*. It was issued by the Bureau of Thought Control in the Ministry of Education as a guide to teachers responsible for moral education. Its tone is well summarized in the following lines from the introduction: "on the one hand, the Emperor worships the spirits of the Imperial Ancestors and on the other as a deity incarnate (*akitsu-mi-kami*) leads the people."[7] The language of the document was effulgent and emotional but it also contains expressions that distantly echo the terminology of nineteenth-century German Idealist philosophy. The monistic metaphysics of Hegelian thought was particularly appealing to Meiji period thinkers, not least of all to Ito. He went to Europe in search of a framework of ideas for the Constitution, where he fell under the spell of right-wing European thinkers such as von Gneist.[8] There is also, in my view, good reason to suggest that the form in which the Imperial doctrine was cast was as much derived from Western thought as from traditional Japanese sources.[9]

Whatever the origins of the modern doctrine, it was formally renounced on 1 January 1946 when the Emperor declared that his relationship with the people was based not upon myths and legends nor upon false doctrines of racial superiority, but upon mutual trust and affection. The death of Emperor Shōwa closed out the era that began with the Meiji Restoration. Although lingering traces of the old sentiments can be found, it must be said that a majority of the population (according to opinion polls conducted around the time of the Emperor Shōwa's death) is rather distant from these concerns.

Future Emperors will doubtless continue to perform Shinto rituals within the Imperial Palace and, according to the Constitution, will do so as private individuals. In principle, the problem seems solved. However, in the accession ceremonies, which are considered a State occasion, the principal event is in fact a central ritual of Shinto. It is performed essentially by the Emperor himself. No crown is placed upon his head on behalf of the people or the State. It is a self-affirming act in which he receives confirmation from the *kami*. This seems, in the view of some critics, not quite consistent with his Constitutional status. The sacral society in that sense is not so readily dismissed by a clause in a modern constitution. The link between mythology and politics may not be so easily broken. The enigma remains—although, fortunately, it is not charged with the emotional fervor of the early years of Meiji or the fanaticism of the mid-years of Shōwa.

IMPERIAL HOUSEHOLD CEREMONIES: KŌSHITSU SAISHI

The Imperial Household[10] performs a set program of rituals within the palace grounds throughout the year. Some of these relate to rice cultivation—one reason, incidentally, why the very word *rice* becomes an emotional issue in Japan. It is both a religious symbol and the nation's staple diet. Rice is offered on Shinto altars along with rice wine (*sake*), and all rice harvests are reported to the *kami*. The Emperor performs the rituals on behalf of the nation, acting as High Priest as well as a symbol of the State. Other rituals are performed according to a traditional cycle throughout the year. They follow forms laid out in the *Kōshitsu Saishierei*, the Ordinance of Imperial Household Ceremonies (1908). Although this has been superseded by the Imperial Household Law enacted after the Pacific War, the power of precedent remains strong.

The Kyūchū Sanden

There are three main shrines in the palace grounds. The most important is the *Kashikodokoro*, where the sacred mirror is enshrined. It contains the guardian *kami* of the Imperial Palace, including the five *musubi-no-kami*: Kami-musubi-no-kami, Takami-musubi-no-kami, Tamatsume-musubi-no-kami, Ikumusubi-no-kami, and Tarumusubi-no-kami. There is the *Kōrei-den* in which the spirits of all past Emperors are enshrined. The third shrine is called the *Shinden*, the hall of the *kami* of Heaven and Earth. The three shrines play a central role in the various year-round rituals performed in the Imperial Household by the Emperor.

Festivals and Gyōji

Imperial Household officials called the *Shotenshoku* are in charge of all ceremonies. Dr. Delmer Brown, in his Preface to the second edition of Holtom's famous work on the enthronement ceremonies, recorded that the Grand Master of the Ceremonies of the Imperial Household informed him "that the Emperor, even though now defined by the constitution as a 'symbol of the state,' still conducts—personally and privately—more than thirty ceremonies a year at one or other of the three Imperial Court Shrines."[11] Some of these are known in detail only to the Imperial Household. Principal among them are the following:

1. The *Saitansai* is performed on New Year's Day. This festival is intended to acknowledge the New Year and was regarded as a minor festival.
2. The *Genshisai*, the festival of origins, is performed on January 3. It is one of

the major ceremonies in the Imperial Household and was a prewar national holiday.

3. The *Shunki Shindensai* (classified as a great festival) is the major festival of spring. It is a former national holiday. Classified likewise is the *Shunki Kōreisai* (the festival of the spring equinox). The *Toshigoi no Matsuri* (spring festival) is a simple ritual to ensure a good harvest. It was classified as a lesser ceremony.

4. *Shūki Kōreisai*. In autumn are the festivals of the *Shūki Kōreisai* (a prewar national holiday) and the great festival of the *Shūki Shindensai*.

5. *Daisai*. Festivals exclusive to the Imperial Household alone include the *Daisai*, the festival on the day of the death of the preceding Emperor instituted in the Meiji Imperial Ceremonies Article 21 (Meiji 41, 1909), and the *Reisai*, the festival for the spirits of the three preceding Emperors. There are others relating to particular Emperors, of which some were national holidays before the Pacific War but which now have no public significance.

6. *Kannamesei* and *Niinamesai*. The *Kannamesai* (festival of the new rice, October 17) and *Niinamesai* (harvest festival, November 23) were major festivals. The first complete *Niinamesai* of a new Imperial reign becomes the *Daijōsai*, which must be discussed separately.

These rituals, among others, are part of the life cycle of the Imperial Household. Which of these will be continued in their present form is a decision of the reigning Emperor. However, in 1989 in an article in the newspaper of the Associaton of Shinto Shrines, Emperor Akihito indicated that he wished to continue the traditions of his father. From this it may be concluded that most of the festivals listed will be continued, either in their present form or as modified to match the needs of the period in the style of the Imperial declaration of enthronement, whereby the Emperor declared he had acceded to the throne in accordance with the Constitution.

THE GRAND SHRINES OF ISE

The tradition remains that all acts and major events in the life of the Imperial Household should be reported to the *kami* of the sun at Ise. Newly inaugurated cabinets led by the Prime Minister go there to announce their appointment. The highest ranked *Sumo* wrestlers and the heads of the Sumo Association (on their provincial tours) pay a formal visit to the Grand Shrines of Ise, because *Sumo* is the Imperial Sport.[12] The special status afforded the Grand Shrines of Ise dates to an early period of Japanese history, although the shrines themselves may not be as old as some other shrines, which also have a lineage that can be traced to the *kami* of the mythology. Their status grew with the status of the Imperial Family, although there were long periods when the importance of shrines was eclipsed. However, they retain their special status and unique place in the religious affections of the Japanese people. Most Japanese try to visit Ise at least once in their lifetime.

The Grand Shrines are architecturally unique among the world's religious buildings and are rebuilt in identical form every twenty years on adjacent sites (*shikinen-sengū*). Emperor Temmu decreed that they be eternally new, and the task is performed according to traditional specifications with traditional methods of construction that does not involve the use of nails. Since the end of the Pacific War, the twentieth century has seen rebuildings in 1953, 1973, and 1993. The rituals begin with *Kimotosai*, the cutting of the first trees for the rebuilding. Other links between the Shrines and the Imperial Household include the tradition of the High Priestess at Ise (*saiō*), who was from the Imperial Household; and the *Chokushi*, the Imperial messengers dispatched to various festivals throughout the nation.

IMPERIAL FUNERAL RITUALS AND MISASAGI (MAUSOLEA) OR GORYŌ

When Emperor Hirohito died, the pattern followed was basically that of the passing of Emperor Taishō seventy years before.[13] It was the most readily available model. These in turn have followed patterns going back to the Heian period, when many of the present-day ritual forms were determined. They may have included Buddhistic elements in the past, which probably were purged during the Meiji period when Buddhism and Shinto were separated by the government. The procession format, however, remained modeled upon court scrolls from the Heian age. In referring to the death of the Emperor, the normal word *shinu* (die) is not used in formal statements, nor is the euphemism *naku-nareru*. The term *hōgyo* is used, which in traditional texts means the death of a *kami*. The funeral followed five distinct stages:

1. *Rensō-tōjitsu-hinkyusai-no-gi* (ceremony of farewell): a private ceremony of the Imperial Household held on the day of the funeral and entombment.

2. *Jisha-hatsuin-no-gi* (ceremony to transport the Imperial hearse from the Imperial Palace to the funeral site): this was also private. The *Reikyu* (the Imperial coffin) was brought to the place where the ceremony was to be held.

3. *Sōjōden-no-gi* (ceremony at the Funeral Hall): a Shinto ritual involving the new Emperor and several Shinto priests. The *Sōjōden* was a hall erected for the purpose of conducting the ceremonies. By this time, the *Reikyu* had been placed upon the *Sōkaren*, a palanquin weighing 1.5 tons.

4. *Taiso-nō-rei* (the State Funeral): the Emperor was host and the Prime Minister was Chairman of the State Funeral Committee. This was public, involved the visiting heads of state, and was considered a secular ritual. At the funeral of Emperor Shōwa, the *Torii* was removed between the two rituals to emphasize

the distinction between the private rituals of the Imperial Household and the public State Funeral.[14]

5. *Ryōshō-no-gi* (ceremony of entombment at the Imperial Mausoleum): the *Sō-karen* was carried to the place of interment by fifty members of the Imperial Household Guard[15] wearing special robes called *Sōfuku*. In the case of both Emperor Taishō and Emperor Shōwa, this was the Imperial Mausoleum at Hachioji. On the occasion of the funeral of the Emperor Shōwa, the rituals lasted approximately five hours. This part was televised only to the stage at which the bier disappeared into the compound. To complete events, the *Mitamashiro*, containing the *tamashī* of the late Emperor, is finally brought to the *Kashikodokoro* of the Imperial Palace, where the ancestral Imperial souls reside. This took place one year after the date of death of the Emperor. It lay during the interim period in the *Gonden*. Thereafter, the new Emperor visited it as an act of reverence and later to announce the date of his formal accession rites.

The funeral rites of Emperor Meiji were an emotional event, and the famous General Nogi committed *seppuku* (ritual suicide) along with his wife on the day of the funeral. His funeral poems reflected the feelings of those who had grown up with the new Emperor and the Japan of the Meiji era.[16] The funeral of Emperor Taishō drew over a million people to central Tokyo. The cortege of Emperor Shōwa drew only 200,000 mourners but had a TV audience of more than half the nation.

IMPERIAL ACCESSION RITUALS

The term *coronation*, which appeared in many foreign newspapers to refer to the accession rites of Emperor Akihito, is a misnomer. It not only conceals but also misleads those who are not familiar with the distinctive way in which Japanese Emperors ascend the Chrysanthemum Throne.[17]

Coronations in the West trace their heritage to the victor's crown received after battle. The process evolved into a peaceful ceremony by means of which the crown is placed upon the royal head by a representative of the people, usually from the Church. Because there is no crown in Japan, the word *coronation* is inappropriate. The new Emperor ascends the throne with the approval of his august ancestors and he then stands in the great lineage. The title *Emperor* in English, employed during the Meiji period, was used to reinforce the image of authority, although the Japanese title *Tennō*, Heavenly Son, simply denotes his descent from the *kami* of the sun. Extravagant language was used to describe the accession of Emperor Hirohito, which followed almost identically the rituals surrounding the accession of Emperor Meiji. These followed traditional patterns yet included a number of changes. For one, it was customary for the Emperor to name his Consort out of several candidates after the *Sokui-no-Rei*. The Meiji Constitution limited the Emperor to one Consort, and thus the format of the *Sokui-no-Rei* changed. Other changes reflected the new era and the evolving perception of the status of the imperial institution. The abundance of military uniforms seen at the Shōwa accession were of course not present in the accession of Emperor Akihito.

Descriptions of the accession of Emperor Shōwa suggest a silent and reverent populace, not the cheering crowds that greet Western coronations or presidential inaugurations. The 1990 accession rites[18] were celebrated in a relatively solemn manner, although many felt they should have been performed in a lighter manner befitting the steady modernization of the nation's central institution. An open car ride from the *Sokui-no-Rei* to Akasaka was the main concession to modernity. The accession rituals comprise five stages:

1. *Senso.* In the presence of members of the Imperial Family and the government, the Emperor symbolically receives the Imperial Regalia and formally accedes to the title. This usually takes place immediately following the death of the previous Emperor. In 1989 it was televised live for the entire nation to witness. The ceremony took less than four minutes.

2. *Sokui-no-Rei.* The ceremony of ascending the throne took place on 11 November 1990. The Emperor's accession is proclaimed before the nation, the government, foreign dignitaries, the *kami*, and the Imperial Ancestors. His address drew attention to his role as defined by the Constitution.[19]

3. *Daijōsai.* This is the Great Food Festival, which took place on 22 and 23 November 1990 because it was necessary to have a rice crop cut after the proper ceremony of planting. The performance of the *Daijōsai* required the building of the *Daijokyu*, a set of buildings in the East Garden of the Imperial Palace grounds. The *Jokan-Gishiki* of the ninth century details the manner of construction. Two ancient rituals are performed. The *Yuki-Den-Kyosen-no-Gi* is held in the *Yuki-Den*, and the *Suki-Den-Kyosen-no-Gi* is held in the *Suki-Den*. There is also the *Kairyu-Den* wherein the Emperor and Empress perform purification rituals and change clothes prior to the various ceremonies. The *Daijōsai* requires further separate discussion because of the controversy surrounding it.

4. *Daikyō-no-Gi.* This is the formal banquet to celebrate the completion of the accession rites. Three main banquets are held after all the rites have been completed. Various leading people along with those involved in the *Daijōsai* take part.

5. *Goshinetsu.* The Emperor completes the entire program of rituals with a visit to the Grand Shrines of Ise to report the successful completion of the accession rites, in particular to the four preceding Emperors. In the case of Emperor Akihito, they would be Emperors Komei (1846–1867), Meiji (1867–1912), Taishō (1912–1926), and Shōwa (1926–1989). Earlier records note that Imperial messengers were dispatched to the Grand Shrines of Ise to report all these matters on the Emperor's behalf. The first Emperor on record as having made the trip himself was Emperor Taishō, and this has been continued in the accession of Emperor Akihito.

INTERPRETATIONS OF THE DAIJŌSAI

The Daijōsai[20] is of great interest because it is the central and most important of all the ceremonies surrounding the accession. It is the most purely Japanese part of the accession rituals, unlike the *Sokui-no-Rei*, which is more Chinese in origin. The *Daijōsai* is interesting also because it is the rare use of a harvest ritual as the central feature of an accession ceremony. But beyond these points, the *Daijōsai* holds a unique fascination because it is the most controversial of the accession rites and because its real meaning is remarkably obscure. Its importance places the Emperor at the apex of the hierarchy of the entire half of the Shinto tradition that has been government-supported or government-inspired. It leans heavily upon the doctrine of Amaterasu and the idea of Imperial descent and traditionally has been understood in a general way as the ritual that brings to completion the status of the new Emperor. Emperors who did not celebrate the *Daijōsai* for various reasons are on occasions referred to as *han-tei* (half-Emperors), implying that their status was incomplete in certain respects. This draws attention to the importance attached to the *Daijōsai*.

Phases of Development

The *Daijōsai* is usually traced to a decree of Emperor Temmu (r. 672–686) that each new reign should commence with its celebration. The Heian period probably saw its fullest early development, which included a Buddhist ritual of accession ordination known as the *Sokui Kanjō*. During eras of civil war, because of rival courts and lack of funds the *Daijōsai* was abandoned for over 200 years, between 1466 and 1687. During the Edo period, permission was given by the Tokugawa government for its performance, but changes were made that forbade the Emperor to perform related preparatory rituals in public. So it became a private ceremony in its entirety.

The Meiji Restoration saw the *Daijōsai* undergo further major changes. First, it was purged of all Buddhist and non-Japanese elements. Second, it was used to add mystique to the Imperial image. Third, it was incorporated as a basic element of the Imperial System in its public role as the center of national ideology. The accession rites of Emperors Taishō and Shōwa followed the pattern of that of Emperor Meiji. It was during the early years of Shōwa that the overt connection between the Imperial House and the rising tide of nationalism was forged in every conceivable way, generating the fanaticism that eventually propelled Japan into a war that could well have resulted in the destruction of the Imperial line.

Character of the Daijōsai

The *Daijōsai* is the offering of the first cuttings of rice to the Imperial Ancestress by the new Emperor. The rice is planted and harvested with great care and is eaten in a manner prescribed in the book of rituals accompanied by purification rites and appropriate liturgies (*norito*). Its origin was the festival of the new rice crop, and the connection remains. The areas where the rice is grown are chosen by divination. One is called *Yuki* and the other *Suki*. Corresponding to these are two buildings erected in the palace grounds known as the *Yuki-Den* and the *Suki-Den* in which the *Daijōsai* takes place.

The Emperor performs purification rituals and a sequence of rites in the *Yuki-Den* that last until around midnight on the appointed day, and he then repeats the same sequence in the *Suki-Den* beginning at two in the morning. The halls are barely furnished except for the mysterious seat of the *kami* (*shinza*), which is in the center of the hall. The procedures followed by Emperor Akihito were those performed by his father and grandfather, which is one reason for the controversy about the meaning of the *Daijōsai*.[21]

Meaning of the Daijōsai

The question of the meaning of the *Daijōsai* is extremely controversial. None of the accounts of the rituals surrounding the *Daijōsai* nor any records of the past offer interpretations of the event. As to how far back we can trace the idea that the *Daijōsai* transforms the Emperor into a living human *kami* (*aruhitogami*), there is no clear evidence.

One theory claims that because it begins with the selection, planting, and harvesting of rice, it represents the celebration of the rice *kami*. In the *Daijōsai*, the Emperor in a sense travels back in time to become unified with the sacred *kami*; thereafter the welfare of state and people is embodied in his unique person. In his high priestly role, he represents them before the *kami* of Heaven and Earth for provision of their basic needs, namely rice.

According to other theories, the numerous purification rites are designed to separate the Emperor from the power of death. The *Yuki-Den* is the hall in which the spirit of the deceased Emperor resides. The *Suki-Den* is the residence of the new Emperor. The clear distinction between life and death, basic to Shinto, is used in this theory. The Emperor receives the power of the ancestral spirits and their *kami* nature, and his role can thus be fulfilled.

The most ultra-nationalistic interpretation of the twentieth century was that of Origuchi Shinobu (1887–1953),[22] who argued that one eternal Imperial soul is magically transmitted from the previous Emperor to the new one. Less dramatic is the claim that a *bunrei* (a branch spirit) of Amaterasu is conferred upon the new Emperor. In truth, however, none of these can claim to be "orthodox" because no formal interpretation has ever been issued by the Imperial Household. The Imperial Household Agency prepared a statement entitled "The Daijosai" that simply recited the sequence of events. The question of meaning simply was not addressed. The issue of its quasi-religious character has appeared in numerous press briefings and reports, but no clear concepts emerge. Having reviewed a vast amount of the literature surrounding the *Daijōsai*, including fierce attacks on it by some Christian and other groups, I can only feel confused as to why so much heat could be generated over a ritual whose meaning is nowhere authoritatively defined. I have never researched such an unsatisfactory and ill-focused debate.

THE SANSHU-NO-JINGI: THE THREE DIVINE IMPERIAL REGALIA

Central to the accession rites is the sacred regalia, the Mirror, Jewel (*magatama*), and Sword. They first make their appearance in the Japanese myths when the fourteenth Emperor, Chuai (192–200), meets a man called Itote in Tsukushi. According to the narrative, the man presents the Emperor with a mirror, a jewel, and a sword, along with an admonition:

As to these things which thy servant dares to offer, mayst thou govern the universe with subtlety tortuous as the curvings of the Yasaka jewels (*Yasakani*); may thy glance survey mountain, stream, and sea-plain bright as the mirror of white copper (*yata no kagami*); mayst thou, wielding this ten-span sword (*kusanagi no ken*), maintain peace in the Empire.[23]

This origin suggests a great deal more about the origins of the Japanese people and the Japanese State than there is room to discuss in this book. The Regalia appears to have been regarded in ancient times as a set of protective charms. Witness the anxiety on the part of Yoritomo when the sword was lost at sea. However, through different eras their image gradually evolved. Kitabatake Chikafusa (1293–1354) wrote of them in quite different terms:

The mirror reflects from its bright surface every object as it really is, irrespective of goodness or badness, beauty or the reverse. This is the very nature of the Mirror which faithfully symbolizes truthfulness. . . . The Jewel signifies soft-heartedness and obedience, so that it becomes a symbol of benevolence. The Sword represents the virtue of strong decision, i.e., wisdom. Without the combined strength of these three fundamental virtues, peace in the realm cannot be expected.[24]

This kind of allegorical account of the Regalia became popular after the rise of Ise Shinto. Ichijō Kaneyoshi (1402–1482), a nobleman of the Muromachi era, wrote in a similar vein:

The Three Divine Imperial Regalia are the essence of Shinto tenets and the fundamental principle of the Imperial rule; the final fusion with Confucianism and Buddhism, thus interpreted, is not entirely alien to the Japanese mind. The essential elements of Confucianism, Buddhism and Shinto have their existence in our mind: there is no Truth apart from our minds; we cannot find Truth outside them. The mind is Divinity, Truth is the Way. The three teachings are after all one and the same thing. The selfsame One is manifested in a threefold way. Thus considered, the Three Divine Imperial Regalia symbolize one and the same mind.[25]

Perhaps under the influence of Chinese culture the Japanese became fond of allegorical explanations, which, if not embellishing upon history, add a new dimension of meaning to it and its artifacts. The Imperial Regalia currently are in the custodianship of *Atsuta Jingū* in Nagoya City.

NOTES

1. Japan's military governments of the past always appeared to consider the Imperial Family as necessary to legitimize their status, although they could easily have dispensed with it. In this sense the modern constitutional status of the Emperor differs little from his Imperial status after the Heian period.
   English-language materials on the Imperial tradition are scant. Some useful but sycophantic papers by R.A.B. Ponsonby Fane were collected and published by the Ponsonby Memorial Society (Kyoto) under the titles *The Imperial House of Japan* (1959) and *Sovereign and Subject* (1962).
2. "Survey on Japan," *Financial Times* (London), July 10, 1989, p. xiv.
3. The *Shinsen Shojiroku* (Newly Compiled Record of Surnames), compiled between 799 and 815 by Prince Manda (788–830, son of Emperor Kammu), claimed that 402 clans were descended from *kami*, the Imperial Family was descended from Amaterasu, and others from *shimbetsu* (other *kami*), or *bambetsu* (foreign origins).

1. Kami	Clan	Descended Clans
Tsuhaya-musubi	Fujiwara	41
Kogoto-musubi-no-mikoto	Fujiwara	10
Takami-musubi-no-mikoto	Otomo	30
Kamimusubi-no-mikoto	Agatainukai	40
Tsunugoro-musubi-no-mikoto	Oginomuraji	6
Furi-musubi	Kisunomuraji	4
Isu-musubi-no-mikoto	none	
2. Hi-no-kami		
Nigihaya-no-mikoto	Monobemuraji	104
Ho-akari-no-mikoto	Owari	46
Hosurori-no-mikoto	none	
Hinohayahi-no-mikoto	none	
3. Others		121
	Total	**402**

4. The status of *ikigami*, "living human *kami*," has long been conferred upon special individuals. In the case of the Imperial sport of *Sumo*, the *tsuna*, or special attire of the *Yokozuna*, the highest ranking (Grand Champion), denotes sacral status.
5. Ito Hirobumi, *Commentaries on the Constitution of the Empire of Japan* (Toyko, 1889).

6. Kume Kunitake, *Nippon Kodai shi to Shinto no Kankei* (The Relation of Shinto to Classical Japanese History) (Sohensha, Tokyo, 1907), p. 194.

7. *Kokutai-no-Hongi* (Cardinal Principles of the National Entity of Japan), tr. by John Owen Gauntlet, ed. Robert King Hall 1949). Included are expressions such as *Hakko Ichiu* (the eight corners of the world under one roof) and other nationalistic slogans.

8. Richard Storry, *A Short History of Modern Japan* (Penguin, London, 1960), p. 115.

9. The influence of Hegel's political and social thought in Japanese universities began after the early flirtations with British and American liberalism were abandoned in favor of the German metaphysical approach to ethics. See Stuart Picken, "Philosophy and Ideology in the Meiji Era," *Proceedings of the Tōhō Gakkai*, June 16, 1978.

10. Sources consulted include the following: S. Murakami, *Tennō no Saishi* (Iwanami, Tokyo, 1977); K. Hoshino, *Nihon no Saishi* (Tokyo, 1987); D. C. Holtom, *The Japanese Enthronement Ceremonies* (Kyobunkan, Tokyo, 1928; 2d ed. with Preface by Delmer Brown, Sophia Press, Tokyo, 1972); Robert S. Ellwood, *The Feast of Kingship: Accession Ceremonies in Ancient Japan* (Sophia University, Tokyo, 1973); John R. Piggot, "Sacral Kingship and Confederacy in Early Izumo," *Monumenta Nipponica* 44, no. 1 (Spring 1989); Felicia Bock, *Engi-Shiki*, Books VI–X (Sophia University, Tokyo, 1972).

11. Brown, Preface to Holtom, *Japanese Enthronement Ceremonies*.

12. *Sumo* wrestling is steeped in Shinto tradition. It has been traced to a form of harvest divining in ancient times. The top ranks in the sport are assigned on the basis of the "presence and quality" (*hinkaku*) of the person as well as technique, winning skills, and a good record of victories. Other aspects of Shinto may be seen in the canopy that stands above the ring or in the way *Sumo* wrestlers throw handfuls of salt each time they come face-to-face with each other in the center of the *dohyō*. *Sumo* tournaments in Tokyo for many years have been dedicated to Emperor Meiji. Consequently, all promotions to *Yokuzuna* are reported to the spirit of Emperor Meiji. New Grand Champions perform their first *Yokuzuna* ritual, known as the *dezu iri*, at the *Meiji Jingu*, where they receive their documentations. *Sumo* is also performed at the Yasukuni Shrine.

13. Material for this and the ensuing section was collected from Japanese newspapers, magazines, Association of Shinto Shrines publications, and government documents, as well as from historical accounts of the funeral and accession of Emperor Taishō.

14. This act failed to satisfy either the right wing, who thought the ceremony should be completely Shinto, or those constitutional critics who argued that the rituals could have been planned differently to eliminate all appearance of Shinto rites.

15. On the matter of who should bear the Imperial bier, an interesting controversy arose in 1988 when the residents of Yase in Kyoto's Sakyo Ward claimed the right because of a fourteenth-century incident. They had protected Emperor Go-Daigo (1288–1349) when he was being pursued by the members of the Ashikaga clan. Successive Emperors exempted the villagers from taxes and had conferred upon them the role of Imperial Palanquin bearers. They bore the coffin of Emperor Taisho and that of his widow, the Empress Dowager Teimei, who died in 1951. Their representatives were in fact invited as observers but were relieved of their

traditional privilege in view of the logistics of the cortege's movements. Emperor Taisho was transported by an oxcart and accompanied by 115 youths from the village of Yase. The tradition ended there. It may only be a footnote to history, but it underlines how seriously such traditions are regarded.

16. The two death poems of Nogi Maresuke:

> The light of the *kami* shines no longer,
> The Great Lord's memory is revered all the more.

> The *kami* departs from this world,
> The Great Lord's memory I know and follow.

17. Sources include the following: Kurabayashi Masatsugu, *Tennō no Matsuri: Daijōsai Shinron* (Daishi-houki Suppan, Tokyo, 1984); Mayumi Tsunetada, *Nihon no Matsuri to Daijōsai* (Shuro Shobo, Osaka, 1990); Takamori Akinori, *Tennō to Tami no Daijōsai* (Tentensha, Tokyo, 1990).

18. Sources for the *Daijōsai* in 1990 included an Imperial Household Agency paper, *The Daijōsai*; press briefings by Yamamoto Shichihei, Sata Kinko, and Ishihara Nobu prepared by the Foreign Press Center of Japan; documents from the *Jinja Honchō*; and Japanese press reports in English and Japanese, *Mainichi Graphik, Heisei Sokui no Rei*, December 1 1990.

19. The official text of the Emperor's accession address was as follows:

Having previously succeeded to the Imperial Throne in accordance with the provisions of the Constitution of Japan and the Imperial House Law, I now perform the Ceremony of the Enthronement at the Seiden and proclaim my enthronement to those at home and abroad.

On this occasion, I pledge anew that I shall observe the Constitution of Japan and discharge my duties as symbol of the State and of the unity of the people, always wishing for the well-being of the people, in the same spirit as my father, Emperor Shōwa, who during his reign spanning more than sixty years, shared joys and sorrows with the people at all times, and ardently hope that our country, through the wisdom and unceasing effort of the people, will achieve further development and contribute to friendship and peace in the international community and the well-being and prosperity of mankind.

20. Controversial and critical articles in English include the following: "The Emperor System and Religion in Japan," *Journal of Japanese Religions* 17, nos. 2–3 (June–September 1990), which contains eight substantial papers; *Japan Christian Quarterly*, Summer (Vol. 56, no. 3) and Fall (Vol. 56, no. 4) 1990, which contain articles on the *Daijōsai* as well as sources for further study.

21. One critic made the point in these terms: "Why, if the Emperor is not and does not regard himself as a divine descendant of the Shinto deity Amaterasu, should he participate in ceremonies which at least some believe will transform him into a living deity?" Kurihara Akira, *"Niho monzoku shūkyō to shite no Tennōsei: Nichijo ishiki no naka no Tennōsei no monjuru,"* Sekei 526, no. 4 (1989): 92–108.

22. Origuchi Shinobu, *The True Meaning of the Daijōsai, Complete Works*, 3 vols (Chuo Koron-sha, Tokyo, 1928).

23. *Nihongi*, VIII: 7 (Aston translation, p. 221).

24. Kitabatake Chikafusa, *Jinnō Shōtōki* (Chronicles of the Direct Descent of the Divine Ruler), Vol. I p. 20.

25. Ichijo Kaneyoshi, *Nihonshoki-Sanso* (Notes and Fragments on the *Nihonshoki*), Vol II p. 42.

Part II

JINJA SHINTO

Chapter 4

Shrines and Kami

JINJA SHINTO

Jinja Shinto (Shrine Shinto) refers to the shrines and cults that emerged as the historical core of the mainline Shinto tradition. It is the Shinto of the central shrines that, although not necessarily originating through government initiative, passed under its supervision once the *Jingikan* was first established. Chapters 4–6 deal with Shrine Shinto, to be distinguished from both Imperial Household Shinto and the Shinto of the sects, new and old. The cults discussed in this section are the norms of the tradition. They make use of the liturgies, observe the festivals, and are supervised by the regular priesthood described in Chapter 6. The artifacts described in Chapter 5 relate only to these "orthodox shrines" and cults and are included for discussion as essential parts of their identity.

To completely describe Shrine Shinto as it exists in modern Japan would require a detailed history of every shrine, its buildings, and *kami,* clearly a task beyond the scope of one book. It would in fact become a 70,000-volume series![1] So diverse is the variety of rituals and ideas that generalizations invariably break down. Therefore, I have tried to identify some of the principal *kami* most commonly encountered in shrines and describe a little of their background and origins. One or two are discussed in greater detail to illustrate the tremendous problems surrounding such research. The discussion also illustrates the complex and independent manner in which various cults and *kami* emerged as important in different eras and why it is difficult to speak of standard beliefs and practices. The *Jingikan* was created to bring about a degree of order and control, and the Association of Shinto Shrines continues that traditional task—which has proved to be most difficult. Much is inconsistent, confused, or vague. Another interesting but complicating factor is that lateral communication among shrines is limited. High-ranking priests of the major shrines do have some acquaintance with each other through the Association of Shinto Shrines and other agencies, and shrines within the same group such as *Inari* or *Hikawa* may have some contact. Beyond that, shrines function on their own and priests of one tradition may know very little in depth about the workings of other groups beyond their names.[2]

It is helpful to classify the *kami* into categories for the purpose of making of a structured presentation. This could be done in numerous ways. I have elected to follow my own categorization:

1. *Kami* of the Japanese mythology:
   Amatsu-no-kami: the *kami* of Heaven
   Kunitsu-no-kami: the *kami* of Earth

2. *Kami* not named in the mythology:
   Those associated with natural phenomena
   Those derived from historical personalities
   Those traceable to political origins
   Those associated with commerce and prosperity

It should be noted that the first distinction between Heavenly and Earthly *kami* does not appear within the early mythology. It arises in the later narrative as an attempt to set the *kami* into a hierarchy with the *kami* of the sun at the pinnacle. However, the *kami* of the sun is derived from other *kami* (as we observed in the discussion of the mythology) and her primacy seems to have come later, being one consequence of the ascendency of the fortunes of the Grand Shrines of Ise.

It is no less difficult to deal with *kami* not found in the mythology. Tracing their origins usually leads into grey areas, many of which are sensitive or controversial and impinge upon the delicate issue of the origins of the Imperial Family and some of Japan's oldest clans.

It should also be noted that the pattern is seldom simply that of one *kami* to one *jinja*. Frequently there are several enshrined *kami*; and, of course, many *kami* are enshrined as major *kami* in some shrines and as merely additional *kami* in others. Hachiman, for example, is enshrined in approximately 30,000 different places.[3]

KAMI OF THE JAPANESE MYTHOLOGY

The *kami* of the Japanese mythology are not all identified individually at their own shrines. They have been divided into two categories, the Heavenly and the Earthly *kami*. Only the principal ones have their own shrines. The rest are collectively identified in the *norito* under the three categories

Amatsu-kami, Kunitsu-Kami, and *Yao-yorozu-no-kami* or they are enshrined jointly (*gosho*) with other *kami.*[4]

Amatsu-no-kami: The Kami of Heaven

Principal of these is Amaterasu, who is revered at the Grand Shrines of Ise. Many *kami* of the mythology have independent shrines. Okuni-nushi-no-mikoto is revered at the *Izumo Taisha,* which is famous for its enormous *shimenawa* and is referred to in the mythology as an "eight-fathomed palace." *Kasuga Taisha* enshrines Takemi-kazuchi-no-mikoto, Futsunushi-no-mikoto, and Ame-no-Koyane-no-mikoto, along with some lesser *kami. Kasuga Jinja* was accorded the title *Taisha* (Great Shrine) in 1946. The *Atsuta Jingu* in the city of Nagoya enshrines Amaterasu, Susano-o-no-mikoto, and Yamato-Takeru-no-mikoto. The *Hikawa Jinja* in Omiya City in Saitama Prefecture enshrines Susano-o-no-mikoto, Onamuchi-no-mikoto, and Idahime-no-mikoto. Hikawa (the Hi River in Izumo) is identified in the *Kojiki*[5] with the descent of Susano-o-no-mikoto as the river where he slew a great eight-headed dragon. The shrine was established in the Musashi province during the reign of Emperor Kosho, the fifth Emperor. The *Hikawa Jinja* has at least 160 branch shrines in Saitama Prefecture alone and several hundred in the Kanto region. Similar patterns of development can be seen within other groups of shrines, often centering on the alleged activities of a single figure.

Yamato-Takeru-no-mikoto, for example, described by Ivan Morris[6] as the tragic hero of Japanese mythology, was engaged in a campaign in the province of Musashi during the reign of Emperor Keiko (r. 71–130). He visited the *Hikawa Jinja,* which was subsequently named an *ichi-no-miya* during the Heian period. This is a good example of the political promotion that characterizes the right-hand column of the historical guide to the development of Shinto in Diagram I. Yamato-Takeru traveled extensively throughout the realm and is consequently enshrined in many places. A massive statue of him stands in the grounds of the *Mitsumine Jinja* in Saitama Prefecture. Just a few miles away at *Hodo-san Jinja,* located at a corner inside the fence surrounding the *honden,* there is a small natural spring in which he is said to have performed the *misogi* purification ritual during his travels. Generally speaking, the *kami* of Heaven are usually found at fairly old and prestigious shrines, invariably in connection with feats performed in the vicinity or a significant mythological occurrence.

Kunitsu-no-kami: The Kami of Earth

The earthly *kami* are enshrined in different places along the same lines as the heavenly *kami.* Just as there is a head of the heavenly *kami,* Amaterasu, there is a head of the earthly *kami,* Saruta-hiko-no-mikoto, who stood at the crossroads of Earth and Heaven when the Heavenly Grandson was to descend to the Land of Reed Plains.[7]

Ame-Uzume-no-mikoto was sent down to charm him, and eventually they married and settled in that location. The central shrine of Saruta-hiko is the *Tsubaki Dai-Jinja* in Suzuka City in Mie Prefecture.[8] There is also a side shrine to Ame-Uzume-no-mikoto, who serves as the guardian *kami* of entertainers. The figure of Saruta-hiko may have carried phallic (fertility) overtones in the past but is primarily associated with pioneering and the cultivation of rice in modern times.

Famed also as a guide is the *kami* known as Yatagarasu, another interesting case study in obscure but clearly ancient origins. Emperor Jimmu Tenno, the first Emperor, was guided through one stage of his campaign by a three-legged crow.[9] The name *yatagarasu* means "eight-hand-crow," suggesting that it was a large bird. Some scholars claim that this was in fact Taketsunumi-no-mikoto, which would make the crow a *kami* of Heaven by descent. But the famous shrine of Taketsunumi-no-mikoto, the *Kamo Mioya Jinja*, bears no trace of the worship of Yatagarasu. On the other hand, there is a separate Yatagarasu shrine; and Yatagarasu rites are conducted at the *Nachi Jinja* in Kumano, where priests wearing crow-like hats perform esoteric rituals using fire and the water from the falls.[10] In the liturgies used at *Nachi Jinja* there is some identification of the two. Such fascinating enigmas will continue to provide researchers with perplexing questions for generations to come.

THE NI-JŪ-NI-SHA: THE TWENTY-TWO SHRINES

The twenty-two shrines listed in the *Engishiki*[11] of the Heian age offer a historical basis for identification of the older and more prestigious shrines recognized by the government. They also serve as a historical link between the *kami* of the mythology and those of later origins. The list, in three categories, is as follows:

1. *Jo* (upper seven): *Ise Daijingū, Iwashimizu Hachiman-gū, Kamo Jinja* (upper and lower), *Matsuo Jinja, Hirano Jinja, Inari Jinja, Kasuga Taisha.*
2. *Chu* (middle seven): *Ōharano Jinja, Ōmiwa Jinja, Isonokami Jingū, Ōyamato, Hirose Jinja, Tatsuta Jinja, Sumiyoshi Taisha.*
3. *Ge* (lower eight): *Umeno Jinja, Yoshida Jinja, Gion Jinja, Kitano Jinja, Hirota Jinja, Hiyoshi Jinja, Niu Kawakami Jinja, Kifune Jinja.*

It is not possible to examine all of these individually. Almost every one has been the subject of extensive writing. I will discuss only one or two as models. Some are discussed under different headings in the succeeding sections, specifically *Hachiman, Inari,* and the *Kitano Tenmangū.* The chapter on shrine buildings also provides more details about some of these famous shrines.

Kamo Jinja

Location and Origins. The upper (*Kamigamo Jinja*) and lower (Shimo-gamo Jinja) shrines are located in the northern suburbs of Kyoto. The first evidence of buildings on the site dates to approximately 678 A.D. There is some suggestion that it was moved from Takakamo in Yamato to Kyoto during the reign of Emperor Temmu, further indicating its probable ancient importance.

Enshrined Kami. The primary one is Tamayori-hime-no-mikoto, whose name means "maiden devoted to the service of the *kami.*" There is also evidence of the worship of Taketsunumi-no-mikoto, the great-great-grandson of Kami-musubi-no-kami, which brings the shrine into the category of those derived from the mythology.

Historical Importance. The *Aoi Matsuri* (Hollyhock Festival) is celebrated here every year on May 15, visited by a *chokushi,* an Imperial Messenger. The pattern of procession is that found in the shrine's Heian period documents and scrolls. Records of its veneration by the Imperial Court date to the eighth century.

Isonokami Jingū

Location and Origins. The shrine stands in what was formerly Yamato province, south of the modern city of Nara and a little north of Tenri, the headquarters city of the *Tenri-kyō* Shinto sect close to the Meihan expressway. Its foundation is claimed to date as far back as the Mononobe clan.

Enshrined Kami. The *kami* of *Isonokami*[12] is mentioned in the classics. As well as the Futsu-no-mitama-no-Tsurugi, there is the Furu-Mitama-no-Okami, who is associated with recovery from illness and with good health and longevity.

Historical Importance. The shrine has the title *jingū,* reserved normally for shrines with an Imperial connection. The shrine is guardian of the sacred sword known as the *Futsu-no-mitama-no-Tsurugi,* which has been understood at different times to be the *arimitama* of Takemikazuchi-no-mikoto and later of Amaterasu herself. It was patronized by Emperor Shirakawa (r. 1072–1086), who as retired Emperor visited it in 1092 and bestowed special privileges upon its priests.

Tatsuta Jinja

Location and Origins. The shrine is located in Tatsuta City in the modern Aichi Prefecture near Tsushima. The oldest reference is to nineteen acts of worship conducted there during the reign of Emperor Temmu. The notices were recorded in 676.

Enshrined Kami. The *kami* of the winds are found here, according to the *Nihongi*.[13] Its reverence for the *kami* can be traced to the time of Emperor Sujin, the tenth Emperor, who was perplexed about bad harvests until an oracle told him that worship to the *kami* of the winds should be offered at Tatsuta.[14] This he did, and not only did the the cereals grow but a series of natural devastations stopped.

Historical Importance. The shrine is close to *Hirose Jinja* and is related to it in that the combined *kami* of both shrines are considered to be the *kami* of the harvest. *Hirose Jinja* enshrines Wakaugame-no-mikoto, the *kami* of food, known also in the *Gekū* of *Ise Jingū* as Toyokehime-no-Kami.

Sumiyoshi Taisha

Location and Origins. *Sumiyoshi Taisha* is located in the modern city of Osaka. Legends date it to the time of Empress Jingu, who was in Naniwa en route to Korea. Her ship would not leave the harbor; she received instructions that the *arimitama* of Amaterasu wished to be at *Hirota Jinja* and that certain other *kami* had preferences about where they wished to be enshrined. As a result, all the *kami* of Sumiyoshi were enshrined as they are now. The original site may have been at Nagato, but the present site is claimed to date to around 470 or before.[15]

Enshrined Kami. In the main shrine (*Dai-ichi-hon-gū*) is Soko-tsutsu-no-o-no-mikoto. In the second main shrine (*Dai-ni-hon-gū*) is Naka-tsutsu-no-o-no-mikoto, and in the third main shrine (*Dai-san-hon-gū*) is Uwa-tsutsu-no-o-no-mikoto. Empress Jingu herself is enshrined in the fourth under the name Oki-naga-tarashi-hime-no-mikoto.

Historical Importance. The shrines received recognition from the Imperial Court and have long been associated with the protection of shipping. The buildings preserve a number of important documents, Shinto statuary, and some of the oldest seals ever made in Japan. There is a collection of Imperial Rescripts that postdate the Kamakura period. There is also a bronze bell, which tradition says was presented by Empress Jingu. It has been certified as from the early stages of the Koma dynasty and is therefore probably approximately 1,900 years old. The older reading of *Sumiyoshi* was *Suminoe*.

These brief descriptions do little more than suggest how much time could be spent on one shrine alone. It is impossible to elaborate on the scholarly debates about the meaning of names, historical origins, identities of the *kami* enshrined, and historical importance of each shrine. Needless to say, the political importance of the *ni-jū-ni-sha* contributed to the deepening of the ideal of *sai-sei-itchi* (unity of worship and government) which goes back to the roots both of Shinto and of Japan's culture.

KAMI NOT NAMED IN THE JAPANESE MYTHOLOGY

Many of Japan's *kami* do not belong to the official mythology, although many main shrines celebrate *kami* from that origin or have included them with their original or local *kami*. We now consider some principal ones, each of which comes from a unique set of associations.

Kami Associated with Natural Phenomena

Although some of these can be found in the mythology, many others are derived directly from Shinto's animistic roots. Here again classification becomes difficult. Some of the *kami* associated with nature are earthly *kami*—such as Kukunochi, the master *kami* of the spirits of trees; or Kayanohime, *kami* of grass; or Totohehime-no-mikoto, *kami* of rice plants. We have already noted that the *kami* or *Tatsuta Jinja* are the *kami* of the winds. Inazuma is the lightning that makes the rice grow.

However, apart from these are many shrines that revere aspects of nature or animals, some of which are regarded as *kami* because they are servants of the *kami*. The deer is the messenger of the *kami* at Kasuga; the monkey serves the *kami* of Mt. Mie; the pigeon serves Hachiman; the fox serves Inari. The tortoise is associated with Matsuno, and the crow is associated with Kumano. *Mistumine Jinja* reveres the wolf, which is referred to as *o-inu-sama* (honorable dog) or *okuchi-no-kami*, the *kami* with the large open mouth. Statues of the wolf can be found all over the mountain, and the weathered look of some indicates the many centuries they have been revered.

Kanasana Jinja (in Saitama Prefecture) has no main building because the mountain behind it is both *kami* and *honden*. The most famous mountain *kami* is Oyama-tsu-mi, according to the mythology a child of Izanami and Izanagi. The number of sacred mountains in Japan gives an indication of the degree to which reverence for mountains (*sangaku shinko*) was part of ancient Japanese religion, probably stemming from the awesomeness of Japan's many active volcanoes.[16] The entire island of Okinoshima off the coast of Kochi in southern Shikoku is considered to be a protective *kami* of seafarers. It is approximately 2.5 miles in perimeter and rises straight out of the sea to a height of over 700 feet. Only priests may visit the island, and they must first perform *misogi* in the sea before setting foot upon its sacred soil.

Local *kami* of rivers, the sea, rocks, trees, and other phenomena of nature are widely revered. There are *kami* of the road (*michi-no-kami*); *kami* of the field (*ta-no-kami*); *kami* of the river and of the waterfall; and *kami* of the house, including even a *kami* of the toilet. *Kami* of nature named in the mythology were most likely included for political reasons or because of important geographical locations associated with them. Those that did not find their way into the mythology are testimony to the extent of the animistic roots of Shinto and the way in which some elements of the divine were elevated above others. In one way or another the entire pantheon of nature is glorified in Shinto, including even male and female genitalia in rock formations.

Kami Derived from Historical Personalities

The enshrinement of famous people is normal in Japan. This includes at least twelve past Emperors. Holtom, in *National Faith of Japan* (p. 6), labeled this "anthropolatry." Numerous individuals also are enshrined because of their special deeds. Others trace their lineage back to the *kami*. Among non-Imperial human personalities, the most famous is the *kami* of learning Tenjin.

Tenjin. Enshrined at the *Kitano Tenmangū* in Kyoto, this *kami* has origins that go back to Sugawara Michizane (845–903). He was a brilliant Confucian scholar of the Heian period who was elevated to the life of the Court at a time when most positions were reserved for members of the great families, the Fujiwara, the Minamoto, and the Taira. At around age fifty he was appointed *Chunagon* by Emperor Uda, who, unfortunately for Sugawara, abdicated in 897. Emperor Daigo ascended the throne at the age of fourteen. His principal minister was Fujiwara no Tokihira, a man only twenty-seven years old, with Sugawara next below him. Sugawara's outstanding ability and the young Emperor's near reverence for him caused great anxiety among the Fujiwara. Finally, a plot was created to discredit him. One of his daughters had married the Emperor's younger brother; this, it was claimed, implied that he planned to usurp the throne in favor of his son-in-law. He was exiled to Dazaifu in 901, where he died in disgrace two years later, stripped of his rank. His only remaining pleasure in life was reverentially bowing toward Kyoto and the Emperor from a nearby mountain. Shortly after his death various disasters struck the city: plague, fires, floods, and unexpected deaths. Fujiwara no Sugane, Fujiwara no Tokihira, and Minamoto no Akira all died suddenly while still young. Yasuakira, an Imperial prince, died shortly afterwards. A fiery comet added drama to these omens, which continued unabated until gradually the *arimitama* of Sugawara was judged to be the cause. The wrongs he had received had led his spirit to seek expiation.

Sugawara and the legends surrounding him were the product of a deeply superstitious culture. His life itself magnified these tendencies. Stories about him and his relationship with bovines are legion. He was born in the year of the ox, and his coming of age at fifteen was celebrated on the day of the ox. That very night he dreamed of a violent storm uprooting some pine trees, which fell and killed a white cow. Taking this as a warning he made a picture of a cow, which he thereafter revered. For the remainder of his life he treated every twelfth day as a day of mourning. He once took a stray white cow home with him because it looked at him in an appealing way and because it reminded him of the incident when Confucius met a winged creature while walking in the hills. There is also a record of him falling into an ambush when he had only one retainer with him. A bull appeared and killed the leader of the assassins, permitting Sugawara to escape. When Sugawara died, his remains were placed on an ox-drawn cart to be borne to the place of his burial. When the animal got to the place that is now the site of the *Daizafu Tenmangū,* it refused to go any further and apparently went crazy. This was taken as meaning that Sugawara should be buried there. Doubtless, many of these stories grew up long after his death. However, they are typical of the Heian belief in the need to pacify unhappy souls to avoid misfortune. The case of Sugawara remains the best known and best documented of all.[17]

Emperor Daigo lifted the ban of exile in 923 and restored Sugawara's court rank. He probably felt guilty about the treatment of Sugawara, from whom he had received his basic education. However, the process leading to enshrinement seems to have begun with the townspeople to whom the *arimitama* made itself known. Taijihi no Ayako, the daughter of a poor family, was the first to hear the voice of Sugawara. She built a small shrine near her house and named it *Tenmangū.* The seven-year-old son of a Shinto priest next heard the spirit tell him that it should be offered reverence in the *Ukon-no-baba.* His father went to speak to a priest of the Asahi-dera, who knew the story of Ayako. Out of incidents like these, the idea of a shrine to Sugawara developed. There were also Sugawara estates in southwest Kyoto, where the *Kisshoin Tenmangū* now stands.

Another legend has it that Emperor Suzaku carved a statue of Sugawara with his own hands and had it placed in the *Kisshoin* as a *go-shintai.* Tradition also states that the statue still exists and is in fact the *go-shintai* of the main *Tenmangū.* It may well have been that he was revered there first, after which the Kyoto shrine came into being. Regardless of how it developed, it is an astonishing tale, beginning with Sugawara's death in disgrace in 903, through the appearance of a tiny shrine built by a poor girl in 943, and climaxing in full enshrinement within fifty years (in 959) on the initiative of the Fujiwara clan that had destroyed him. To complete the recognition, the Court celebrated a festival there in 987 and its name came to be listed among the nineteen central shrines by 990. In 1005 the Emperor himself visited the shrine, just over a hundred years after Sugawara's death.

The origin of the name *Tenmangū* or *Tenjin Tenmangū* in relation to Sugawara is quite obscure, and it has been the subject of great speculation.

It has been attributed to an Imperial Edict that called him *Tenjin* (heavenly *kami*), although the oral tradition of an oracle survived alongside that version. *Tenjin* can also be read as *Amatsu-kami, kami* of Heaven. He was certainly not so in the sense of the mythology, but the title indicates the degree of reverence accorded him. There may also have been some influence of Buddhism, which, in Heian style, tied him to an incarnation. The architecture of the building has the *gongen*-style roof over the *haiden* found most commonly in shrines that were in some way syncretistic, because it is also the standard roof form of Buddhist temples. Doubtless, many elements went into the making of the legend.

Tenjin was established thereafter as the *kami* of learning, perhaps in appreciation of Sugawara's scholarship. The *Yushima Tenjin* shrine in Tokyo hosts thousands of pilgrims and worshippers each year prior to university and high school entrance examinations. They write their prayers on wooden tablets and pray for the inspiration of the *kami* of learning in order to pass their examinations successfully and win a place in a good school or college. Thus, *Tenjin* continues to be revered in the present.

National Heroes and Military Leaders. Among Japan's military leaders, Minamoto Yoritomo (1147–1199) is enshrined in the *Shirahata-Jinja* in Kamakura, and Tokugawa Ieyasu (1542–1616) in the *Nikkō Tōshō-gū*. Oda Nobunaga (1534–1582) is enshrined in at least two places. Toyotomi Hideyoshi (1536–1598) is the *kami* of a number of shrines. In the *Kuno-san Tōshō-gū*, a branch of the *Nikkō Tōshō-gū*, Ieyasu is enshrined along with Nobunaga and Hideyoshi as *aido-no-kami*. Of the main figures of the Meiji Restoration, Takamori Saigo (1827–1877) is enshrined in the *Nan-shu-Jinja*.

General Nogi, enshrined in *Nogi Jinja* in the Roppongi district of central Tokyo, is a somewhat dramatic case from the twentieth century. He was a controversial military figure of the early Meiji period whose career as a soldier was one of mixed fortunes. Throughout his life he carried a sense of guilt for having lost the Imperial Color during a battle in his youth, and he laid out the Imperial pardon alongside his death poems. His ritual suicide (*seppuku*) on the day of the funeral of Emperor Meiji made him famous, and he was thereafter enshrined by the government as a symbol of the martial spirit it was fostering.[18] In addition to military leaders, all who fought for the success of the Meiji Restoration are enshrined in the *Saku-rayama Jinja*.

Men of Culture. As in the case of Sugawara, the statesman and scholar, other men of letters are variously enshrined. The *Nagano-Jinja* enshrines the four great religious thinkers of the academic Shinto movement. Motoori Norinaga is enshrined in *Motoori Jinja*; Hirata Atsutane in *Yakata Jinja*; Kamo no Mabuchi in *Agatai Jinja*; and Kada no Azumamaro in *Azuma-maro Jinja*.

Living Human Kami. Emperor Meiji was enshrined in several places while he was alive. The famous *Meiji Jingū* in Tokyo, established after his death, is devoted exclusively to him. The concept of *ikigami* (living human *kami*) or *aru-hito-gami* has been discussed in this book under Imperial Household Shinto. The enshrinement of human beings in their lifetime is well documented and extends to judges, tradespeople, and even village headmen who have performed special service to the community. Not all *ikigami* were created for political reasons.

Modern Kami. The postwar era has seen relatively little activity on account of Shinto's controversial status and the Shinto Directive. However, it is significant that discussions quickly started for some form of enshrinement of the founder of Matsushita Electronics (National Panasonic), Matsushita Konosuke, after his death in 1989 at the age of ninety-three. Likewise, discussion about a shrine to Emperor Shōwa commenced informally early in 1990.

Kami Traceable to Political Origins

The principal *kami* that fits this heading is Hachiman, although it could include any *kami* enshrined to protect the nation.

Hachiman. The prominence of Hachiman was first highlighted in the infamous case of Dōkyō, a Buddhist priest who successfully gained the affections of the retired Empress Kōken and who by 768 had established himself as the most powerful person in the state. He began to aspire to the Imperial title and claimed an oracle from Hachiman in Kyushu declared that if he ascended the throne, there would be peace. Wake no Kiyomaro, a minister of state, was sent by Kōken (after she had been instructed in a dream) to Kyushu to find out the true will of Hachiman. The oracle with which he returned condemned Dōkyō and almost cost him his life: "Since the establishment of our state, the distinction between lord and subject has been fixed. Never has there been an occasion when a subject was made lord. The throne of the Heavenly Sun Succession shall be given to one of the imperial lineage; wicked persons should immediately be swept away."[19]

The significance of the incident is enormous because (1) Kōken became the last female to occupy the throne without an Emperor, and (2) it is from then that the cult of Hachiman takes on special importance. Why was an oracle from a *kami* in an obscure part of Kyushu required to judge issues at the Imperial court in Nara? How did Hachiman later become the guardian *kami* of the entire Kanto plain?

Origins of Hachiman. The *Shoku Nihongi* contains the earliest reference to Hachiman: offerings were sent in Tempyo 9 (737 C.E.) to five shrines on the occasion of conflict with the kingdom of Silla in Korea. It is also stated that the *kami* is enshrined at Usa in Buzen province in northeast Kyushu. Within three decades of that reference, Hachiman had risen to such prominence that an oracle could determine the foundation of the shrine. Much research has been done on the origins of Hachiman, but little is conclusive.

One legend, recorded by the governor of Buzen in 844, concerns a blacksmith who lived beside a lake below Mt. Ōmoto in Usa. The blacksmith was visited by a holy man named Ōmiwa, who lodged with him for three years and devoted his time to prayer and meditation. In the thirty-seventh year of the reign of Kimmei, a golden hawk appeared in front of Ōmiwa. The hawk became a dove and then transformed itself into a young boy who announced that he was "the sixteenth human emperor, Homuda Tennō (Ōjin), the broad-bannered Hachiman-maro." The legend is rejected by Japanese scholars because of inadequate evidence for the connection between Ōjin and the Hachiman cult. However, the images of the blacksmith and the boy possessed by a *kami* do suggest strong shamanistic influences.

The most credible of modern Japanese accounts of the Hachiman cult is that of Nakano Hatayoshi,[20] who believes that the history of Shinto cannot be separated from the *shizoku* social structure that formed local beliefs. Consequently, he has concentrated upon the clans (*uji*) known to have been connected with Hachiman as far back as the ninth century. He traces the origins of Hachiman to the family cults of the Usa, Karajima, and Ōmiwa clans. The Usa clan was a union of smaller clans including the Ama, whose *kami* was a dragon, widely revered along the Kyushu coast. They also revered three large sacred stones on the Maki peak of Mt. Ōmoto and a female *kami* who protected shipping. According to Nakano, the Karajima clan may be considered Korean in origin on account of their bronze weaponry and use of shamanistic *miko* as mediums. This would also explain the association between Hachiman and the copper mines of the area. The Ōmiwa clan was from Yamato and may have been involved in assisting the Yamato to maintain local control during the Soga-Mononobe conflict. Thus, the Ōmiwa clan's links with the Ōjin cult may have introduced it to Kyushu. The syncretistic linking of the cults is consistent with Japanese practice and also explains the diversity of powers and roles of Hachiman. This is all speculation; the link between Ōjin and Hachiman remains a mystery. One radical explanation is that Ōjin was part of a fourth-century invasion of Japan from Korea and that he founded the imperial institution. The *Shoku Nihongi* contains no reference to the Ōjin-Hachiman link, so responsible scholarship must either explain the omission or begin from there.

Professor Herbert, to whom reference has been made in the discussion of mythology, researched Hachiman mainly through visiting Hachiman shrines and asking senior priests their about the origin of the cult.[21] His work revealed a strong tendency on the part of Hachiman priests to associate Ōjin and Hachiman, sometimes even suggesting that the existence of Hachiman prior to that era is either unimportant or unknown. The desire to exalt Hachiman's roots is understandable, but this leaves too many questions unanswered. The father of Ōjin was Chuai, who was a son of Yamato-Takeru-no-mikoto. His mother, the Empress Jingu, was famous for her invasion of Korea. From this illustrious line Ōjin appeared. In numerous Hachiman shrines the enshrined *kami* are Emperor Ōjin, Jingu Kogo, and Hime-gami. Most frequently the three *kami* are enshrined together. In branch shrines, where Hachiman alone is identified, distinctions are ignored and all three together are considered to be Hachiman. Documents that directly connect Ōjin with Hachiman date from no further than the Heian period.

The Meaning of the Name Hachiman. The ancient Japanese pronunciation of *Hachiman* was probably *ya-wata* (literally, "eight-banners"). This was the reading that Motoori Norinaga[22] gave in his transcriptions of the edicts of the *Shoku Nihongi*. A late legend has it that when the Usa shrine was founded, eight banners floated down from heaven and stood on the roof of the building. The banners could refer to the Chinese military practice of carrying flags; because eight in Chinese can mean a large number, the military link could have come from that incident. Other scholars choose an agricultural connotation. Nakano suggests that due to the union of the Karajima and Usa clans, the regions of Yama and Toyo in Kyushu were linked. The consequent union of *Ujigami* led to the name *Yama-toyo,* which became *yawata,* and in due course *Hachiman.* The very possibility of the existence of a name like *Yamatoyo* takes the issue back to the question of Yamato power and, of course, to the Ōjin-Hachiman link. If the local maritime and feminine cults had been overcome by a shamanistic cult from Korea, Hachiman could have become associated with the conquest (of one clan by another) and thereby acquired a military connotation. This view seems corroborated by another, later legend about the origin of Hachiman. In the *Kojiki* there is the narrative of the "Fire-Shine" and "Fire-Fade," according to which Hikohodohemi represented the Imperial ancestral clan in Kyushu and the Dragon *kami* of the Sea symbolized the Watatsumi clan, coastal seafaring people. Hikohodohemi married Toyo-tamahime, the daughter of the Dragon *kami*; the resulting *kami* was Hachiman, whose powers include the very elements listed by Nakano.

Growth of the Hachiman Cult. How was the Hachiman cult able to advance so rapidly to such prominence in such a relatively short time? Various aspects of the history, geography, and culture of the Usa region constitute one part of the explanation. It is referred to in the *Nihongi* in connection with Emperor Jimmu's military expansion to the east. He was entertained by local clan chieftains; by Imperial command, in appreciation of the support a local princess of the region was married to the Imperial attendant minister. It was from this union that the Nakatomi descended. Usa itself was also equipped with a good harbor and was a natural point of entry for continental ideas, information, and practices.

The local religious cults, particularly the *miko* of Buzen, were regarded as superior to the *miko* elsewhere in Japan because of their unusual abilities, which apparently resulted from the combination of Korean, Buddhist, and local beliefs. The Nara Court apparently held them in awe as possessing unique powers. In addition, by the period in question Kyushu had become significantly integrated into national political life as a result of the steady policy of centralization of the Taika and Taihō reforms. Taihō created the post of *Dazai Sochi* (Governor General) in Kyushu, which could rise to the third rank at Court, just below *Chunagon*. The significance of the post is evidenced by the importance attached to its acquisition by the Fujiwara clan in 732. One of Fujiwara Fuhito's sons, Muchimaro Dainagon, was also appointed *Dazai Sochi,* with responsibilities including the administration of the shrines in Kyushu.

A second group of factors that may account for the rise of the cult relate to the role played by the Hachiman shrines during the Hayato uprisings that disturbed Kyushu from the era of Wadō (708–714) to that of Yōrō (717–723). The *Shoku Nihongi* records a major rebellion in Osumi and in Hyuga in 720 that was suppressed, but no reference is made to Hachiman. Other documents of the Nara Court refer to prayers being offered at the Hachiman shrine and to priests leading an army endowed with divine power to defeat the Hayato. This suggests that people first resorted to Hachiman as a *kami* of great power to deal with crises. It was in this latter capacity that the Nara Court first consulted Hachiman, reporting misdeeds by the ruler of Silla. In Tempyo 12 (740), prayers were offered to Hachiman on the occasion of the rebellion of Fujiwara Hirotsugu, a former governor of Yamato who had been demoted to *Dazai Shoni* (Vice-Governor) of Kyushu on account of court politics. Azumabito was ordered by the Court to pray to Hachiman and to lead an army of 15,000 against Hirotsugu, which successfully captured him after he tried to escape to Silla. These early invocations of the Court to Hachiman for military victory must have strengthened the image of Hachiman as a *kami* of war.

The Tōdai-ji and Hachiman. The Nara Court invoked Hachiman for help in the construction of the Tōdaiji and the Daibutsu during the reign of Emperor Shōmu. This finally brought Hachiman into direct contact with the imperial institution and elevated Hachiman's status from that of regional war *kami* in Usa to that of the most revered *kami* in the entire nation.

Around 735, a plague from Kyushu reached Nara and killed all four sons of Fujiwara Fuhito. This weakened the power of the Fujiwara clan. The Emperor did not fall ill, which was attributed to the care of Gembo, the *Hosso-shū* Buddhist abbot who had studied in China and had succeeded in establishing the post of *Naidojo,* an office modeled on T'ang Dynasty Buddhist priests in the Chinese Imperial Court. This was the first permanent Buddhist office in the Imperial Court.[23]

The simultaneous weakening of the Fujiwara family made this possible. In 728 Emperor Shōmu (whose wife, Empress Kōmyō, was a Fujiwara), following upon the edicts of Emperor Temmu concerning Buddhist images being placed in homes, tried to actualize the idea. He ordered ten scrolls of the *Konkōmyō Sūtra* to be sent to each province and read for the peace of the nation. In 741 he issued an edict that every province had to erect a monastery (*Konkōmyō Shitennō Gokoku no Tera,* or *kokubunji*) and a convent (*Hokke Metsuzai no Tera,* or *kokubunniji*). Each temple was guaranteed land for support of its activities in return for reading the sutras every month for the peace of the people and the protection of the nation. To crown these efforts, in 743 the Emperor issued an order to cast the great bronze image of *Roshana* (*Vairocana*) Buddha at the Todai-ji. The link between Hachiman and copper mining would make sense in this context.

The statue was successfully completed in 752 and a great ceremony held, at which Shōmu, now retired, was present along with the reigning Empress, his daughter Kōken. An edict was read thanking Hachiman for protection during the great task and the *kami* was awarded the highest rank at Court. The form of Hachiman's aid is nowhere stated, but a donation from the Usa shrine would be one possible explanation. In 749, after the promotion of various officials at the Usa shrine had been approved by the Court, Hachiman made a formal visit to Nara. Courtiers and soldiers were added to the procession, and approximately one month after leaving Kyushu, Hachiman began the approach to Nara. Hachiman was enshrined in a newly built hall, and various rituals were celebrated. The *Shoku Nihongi* records the event as follows:

The nun and priestess of the Great Kami Hachiman, Ason Omiwa Morime, worshipped at the Tōdai-ji. His palanquin was of a purple colour, like that of the Imperial palanquin. The empress and retired Emperor and Empress also proceeded to the temple. On this day, great numbers of government officials and various members of the aristocracy all gathered at the temple. Five thousand priests prayed, performed ceremonies of veneration of the Buddha, and read sutras. The music of Great T'ang, Paekche, and Wu and the Gosechi and Kume dances were performed. Then the Great Kami Hachiman was awarded the first rank and *Himegami* the second. *Sadaijin* Tachibana Moroe presented an edict and read it to the *kami*.
"The sovereign Emperor proclaims, saying:
"In a recent year, we worshipped the Roshana Buddha at Chishikiji in the Agata district of Kōchi. Because we desired to construct such an image and yet were unable to do so, we appealed to the Great Kami Hachiman of the Broad Ways who dwells in the Usa district of Buzen province. The *kami* said:

We, leading and inviting
the heavenly *kami* and the earthly *kami*
Shall certainly accomplish this task.
We will turn water into steam for the casting;

We will merge our body with the grass, trees and earth.
It shall be done without hindrance.

"Because of the proclamation of the *kami* we were overjoyed and have been able to accomplish this work. And now, although it is with awe and trepidation, we confer a cap of the first rank."
Omiwa Tamaro was awarded the outer junior fifth rank, lower grade. Four thousand substance households, one hundred male servants, and one hundred female servants were bestowed on the Tōdai-ji. Those involved in building the temple were given ranks according to their labour.[24]

By 750, priestesses of Usa held the fourth court rank, whereas the highest officials at Ise ranked only fifth. This pinnacle of prominence was retained only until about 770, when the last instance of the Nara Court sending offerings to Usa was recorded. However, between the time preceding the building of the *Daibutsu* in Nara and the close of the Nara age, Hachiman's power as arbiter and authenticator of the Imperial tradition was unquestioned. When Dōkyō created a crisis in the matter of Imperial succession, it was the oracle of the *miko* at Usa that enabled the indigenous Japanese tradition to withstand the pressures of Buddhist ideology and remain strong enough to resist a challenge to the imperial institution, even at its weakest.

Ross Bender's research on the Dōkyō incident leads him to conclude that the rise of Hachiman was, in the context of the Court, an attempt to discover a balance between native beliefs and Buddhism. In the native view the Emperor's sovereignty, derives from his divine ancestry, which made him an *akitsukami*. In Buddhist thought it was dependent upon his being a meritorious Buddhist. The implicit threat to the Imperial lineage was visible and called for careful but effective measures to ensure its integrity. The Hachiman cult successfully provided these guarantees. It is indicative also, in Bender's view, that the native cult and its relatively primitive conception of divine rule was capable of surviving "more sophisticated systems of religious and political thought."[25]

Hachiman in the Heian Period. Hachiman lost some of the power of the Nara age, but politics involving Buddhism that were typical of the Nara Court were less frequent within the Heian Court, which was one result of the transfer of the capital. The crisis of legitimacy had been settled and the position of the *kami* was guaranteed.

Hachiman slowly came closer to Buddhism and actually became identified as a bodhisattva (*Dai-Bosatsu*) from 809. The coexistence of Shinto and Buddhism under the principle of *Honji-Suijaki* is in keeping with contemporary developments in Japanese religion and society. But the cult continued to expand. The head of the *Dai-Butsu* fell off sometimes shortly after 850. To facilitate repairs, a messenger went to Usa with apologies and a request for the aid of Hachiman in the work of reconstruction.

Shortly afterward, the *Iwashimizu Hachiman-gū* was established in

Kyoto to enshrine a *bunrei* (branch spirit) of Hachiman. The legend of its origin appears in ninth-century records. The founding is credited to a famous priest of the Daianji called Gyōkyō, who travelled to Usa and spent six months in prayer and devotion at the shrine. He received an oracle from Hachiman that instructed him to go to the capital and pray for the protection of the country. He proceeded to Kyoto and built a retreat at Otokoyama. A bright light was seen on the mountain, and simultaneously the Emperor and Empress had dreams of a cloud coming down from the mountain and resting protectively on the palace. This became divination for the shrine site. Perhaps in spite of the removal of the Court to Nara and the break with Buddhism and its political ambitions, the need was felt to have a Hachiman shrine in the new capital. The fortunes of Hachiman continued in his way to be associated with the Imperial Family.

Hachiman in the Kamakura Period. The links with military prowess were confirmed by Minamoto Yorimoto at the end of the twelfth century. He chose the coastal city of Kamakura at the edge of the Kanto plain as the location for his military government and nominated Hachiman to be the guardian *kami* of the city. The Tsurugaoka Hachiman shrine was established along lines parallel to the creation of the Iwashimizu Hachiman shrine in Kyoto. Although having the powerful Hachiman in Kamakura as a branch of the Kyoto shrine in the Imperial city helped to legitimize his activities, Yoritomo apparently had a particular affection for Hachiman. The development of Hachiman as the guardian *kami* of the entire Kanto region paved the way for the massive expansion of the number of Hachiman shrines, as the communities of succeeding eras began to develop. The modern climax was reached when Hachiman enshrinements reached approximately thirty thousand.

Gokoku Jinja. The idea of *kami* protecting the nation is of ancient origin, as the cult of Hachiman aptly demonstrates. After modernization in the nineteenth century this was given a new twist within the philosophy of State Shinto, when the idea was introduced of enshrining ordinary soldiers as *kami* to protect the nation. These shrines (with *Yasukuni Jinja* at the peak) are the *Gokoku Jinja,* where all of Japan's war dead are enshrined. After the establishment of *Yasukuni Jinja* a network of shrines was constructed to enshrine the dead of Japan's mid-Meiji era military adventures against China and Russia. These shrines were never dismantled after the abolition of State Shinto and remain scattered throughout the country. The dead of World War II are enshrined in them also, and they consequently remain in somewhat controversial status. They are venerated by some of those whose loved ones are enshrined there, yet others bitterly denounce them as the foolish reason why their loved ones had to die. The enshrinements are in the most complete sense "political," having had as their purpose the nationalistic orientation of the people through according special honor to the war dead. This is on a par with the enshrinement of heroes in the past, except that it is the first time in Japanese history that mass enshrinements of ordinary people have taken place.

Kami Associated with Economic Origins

Inari. The shrines of Inari are distinguished by the frequent occurrence of large numbers of red *torii* at their entrance and by the presence of stone statues of foxes.

Origins of Inari. Inari[26] is a well-known, although not very high, mountain at Fushimi, which forms the southern end of the *Higashi Yama* (eastern mountain) range in the south district of Kyoto. The collective name *Inari* refers to the *kami* worshipped there. Numerous theories on the meaning of *Inari* have been advanced; but like explanations of the term *kami,* they are mostly speculation.[27] The earliest associations seem to have been with food. The complex relation between rice and the fox became the central feature of the cult.

Anthropological research on the origins of the Japanese has unearthed incidental information relevant to the study of the Inari cult. For example, the Ainu[28] have a ceremony of salutation to new crops in which older men receive cereal cakes and offer a ritual prayer in a tasting ceremony. This is reminiscent of the *Niinamesai* (and of the *Daijōsai*) and of the idea of food as a *kami*. The Ainu also use the skull of the fox in witchcraft and divination.

Ethnologically related groups provide further interesting parallels that may suggest common origins. Some Siberian tribes[29] share beliefs and practices similar to Shinto, including the idea that the physical aspect of death is impure. A death in a community means that sacred places cannot be visited without purification. Foxes are also considered capable of being divine. One legend tells of a hunter who shoots a fox, which breaks into two. The front half flies to heaven and reports the matter to her father, who comes down and kills the hunter, cutting him in two. The idea that misfortune can result when a fox crosses the path of a human being may come from this.

Malay people[30] practice the cutting of the first sheaf of rice—the "rice child," as it is called—at a special autumn ritual. It is interesting also that white is both a sacred color and the royal color. Within the *Fushimi Inari Jinja,* the *Byakko-sha,* or "White Fox Shrine," is the most popular place of reverence. Both Japanese culture and Shinto thought share numerous features with both north and southeast Asia.

Accounts of the Origin of Inari. In what is probably the principal Shinto account, a rich man called Iroku-no-hata-gimi used *mochi* (rice cakes) as targets for archery practice. The *kami* of rice was indignant, and the man was frightened when it flew in the form of a white bird to the mountains and perched on a tall Japanese cedar. He realized that he had abused a divine gift. To pacify the distressed *kami* and to preserve his fortune, he went to the place where the white bird had alighted and built a shrine to the *kami* of rice. This incident is dated to the reign of Empress Gemmyo (c. February 7, 711 C.E.), which is the official date of the founding of the Inari shrine as recorded by Hirata Atsutane in the *Koshinden*.[31]

There is also a Buddhist version of the founding of the shrine involving Kōbō Daishi. It records his meeting an old man carrying sheaves of rice and calling himself Shiba Mori Shoja Ina-tomi (rice wealth), who lived at the Nikai-bo temple in Kyoto. Kōbō Daishi was told that if he dedicated a shrine to the old man, he would be assisted in propagating his teachings. Kōbō Daishi built a shrine at Inari Mountain and named it *Inari,* using the Chinese characters for "rice," *ina,* and "carry," *ri* (because he was a famous calligrapher). Some years later, a shrine named *Uga-dama-no-mikoto* (food-spirit-*kami*-princess) was dedicated near the Inari shrine and also called Inari. It was then that the entire mountain was given the same name.

There is a tradition of a *mikoshi* that was laid up (*tabisho*) at the Nikai-bo temple containing a tablet written by Kōbō Daishi and bearing the characters *ina-ri*. Kōbō Daishi, although a genius beyond doubt, was in the view of many never liable to have qualms about a little elaboration on the truth for the sake of gaining a point. His skills in manufacturing syncretistic ideas are legendary. For example, when he became abbot of the Toji he wished to best his Tendai rivals on *Hie-san*. Accordingly, he claimed the *Inari kami* as the original protectors of the Toji and enshrined them there. He used Shinto, the old faith, to support his activities in the new. This was the beginning of *Ryōbu* Shinto, when Shinto *kami* were identified with Buddhist *bosatsu*. It remains to be explained how Kōbō Daishi could have been involved in the founding of a shrine that came into being approximately sixty-four years before he was born! Although he could not have had much of a hand in founding the *Inari Jinja,* it is possible that the tradition benefited from his influence at a later date.

The association of Inari with rice, along with superstitions about the fox,[32] can be traced to the folk origins of primitive Shinto, although the actual development of the cult as such came much later. Reverence for nature would lead to reverence for the *kami* of rice as a *kami* that supported human life. This belief permeates all of Shinto. To this, folklore about the fox was added, including the fox's fondness for bean curd. Foxes running wild in rice-fields probably first suggested the idea to farmers, who may have thought they were inspecting the crops. In gratitude, the foxes were offered red rice and fried bean curd. The roots of the generic ideas of the cult probably lie in the combination of these traditions.

Although the fox came to be the messenger of the rice *kami*, it is more likely that in ancient times the fox itself was revered as the *kami* of rice. In later days the spirit of rice was revered as a *kami* by the name of Uga-no-mitama-no-kami (food-augustness-*kami*) and the fox became her messenger. From such beginnings the fox became revered and, because of other folk beliefs, also feared by the agricultural masses. Thus, the naming and ranking of types of fox began to be instituted.[33] Reverence for—and fear of—the fox have a long history and are prominent elements in the background of the Inari cult. Although the folk tradition of the fox may not be pure Shinto, it is (in the manner in which Hachiman serves to illustrate the political roots of some Shinto cults) an example of the complicated animistic roots of other cults. Fox anthropomorphosis, fox possession, possession of fox power, and use of foxes are the four principal forms of folk belief.

Fox Anthropomorphosis. Chinese culture[34] added to Japanese folklore the unique skill of the fox to transform itself into a female form, because it is a night animal that absorbs mostly the *Yin* (female) elements of the universe. In China four methods could compel the fox to return to its original form. One was the use of Taoistic charms. A second involved presenting it with a sacred metallic Buddhist mirror. A third involved a mystic geometric form, and a fourth involved confronting the fox with a stone pillar or tree of the same age.

Stories abound concerning foxes that have transformed themselves into beautiful women who teased or tormented men. The *Konjaku Monogatari*[35] narrates the story of a young *samurai* who copied the Lotus Sutra for the peaceful repose of the soul of a fox. He lived in Kyoto and was passing the Shujaku Gate of the Imperial Palace when he saw a beautiful and well-dressed eighteen-year-old girl. He invited her inside the gate to talk to him. She accepted, and they talked until it became dark. He then asked her to spend the night with him. She declared that if she did so, she would die. The *samurai* could not believe her. She protested that he had merely become infatuated and she wept because she said that she knew she had to die for a man who was emotionally unstable. She agreed finally and they went to a nearby hut to spend the night. At sunrise, the girl declared she was returning home to die but asked him to copy the Lotus Sūtra for the sake of her soul. The *samurai* insisted that she would not die, but he promised nevertheless to do as she asked should anything happen to her. The girl told him to come to the neighborhood of Butoku-den to the west of the Imperial Palace later that morning. She also asked him for his fan as a memento. Then she vanished into the morning mist. The *samurai* duly went to the place where he had been requested to appear and saw an old woman weeping. Being asked why she wept, the woman declared that she was the mother of the girl and that her daughter was indeed dead. When he asked her where the young girl lay, she pointed to the spot. The old woman then vanished, and when the *samurai* went to the place indicated he found a young fox lying dead, covered by an open fan. It was the fan he had given the girl. He was shocked and saddened to realize that the prediction had come true, and he returned home to keep his promise and copy the Lotus Sūtra. Night and day he prayed for the peace of the fox's soul. Approximately six weeks later he had a dream in which the girl appeared as beautiful as before, announcing that he had saved her soul by copying the Lotus Sūtra. He saw her accompanied by celestial music and two maids of honor ascending to paradise and to the Great Buddha, who held copies of the sutra he had made. Although it was a dream, the tale ends by saying that the young *samurai* never abandoned his custom of copying the Lotus Sūtra.

Twentieth-century incidents have been reported by the chief priest of the *Inari Jinja* at Wakayama.[36] A man driving his car up the *Kurumazaka,* which leads to the shrine, was faced by a large car coming directly at him at high speed. A collision was avoided, but the same thing happened a day or two later when he was going down the slope. The same huge car was racing toward him, and a collision seemed inevitable. The driver braced himself for the impact, but there was only a dull thud and the car was gone. When the driver got out he found in front of the car the body of an old dead fox, which had been killed attempting to make him crash. Episodes like this, both ancient and modern, illustrate the character of the fox when it becomes deceitful and menacing. The description of people in Japan as "foxy" carries negative connotations.

Fox Possession: Kitsune-tsuki. In the Japanese mythology, Ame-Uzume-no-mikoto, who danced to entice the *kami* of the sun out of the cave in which she was hiding, was considered to have been "possessed" at the time.[37] According to both the *Kojiki* and the *Nihongi,* Empress Jingu, was possessed when she received instructions to undertake the conquest of Korea. These early instances of female shamanism foreshadow the later belief (as the image of the fox grew in folklore) that just as the fox could change its form, it could also take temporary possession of a human body. This led to more serious ideas concerning the psycho-physical influences of the fox.

In the *Konjaku Monogatari,* a young fox-possessed woman was seen playing with a jewel (tama), used also to symbolize the *tamashii,* or soul. A *samurai* took it from her and she became very distressed, because it was in reality the soul of the fox who was possessing her. When the woman was finally exorcised the jewel was gone, because of course the fox took it with him when he departed.

In Shrine Shinto there is no formal recognition of the religious merits of shamanistic possession, whereas in Sect Shinto, particularly *Shinshu* and *Ontake,* fox possession is recognized. It is interesting to note, however, that in Buddhist sects that recognize possession (Shingon, Tendai, and Nichiren), the Shinto *gohei,* the symbol of the presence of a *kami,* is hung and it is always a *kami* who is considered to descend and take possession.

Fox possession is understood medically as a psychosomatic disorder found mainly in residents of rural Japan. People believe that a fox has entered their chest or under their fingernails and can live its own life inside them. The resulting schizophrenia may involve the fox and the person arguing with each other in different voices. The majority of cases occur in women, although men may be affected. The condition has been attributed to many factors, including brain function or the Japanese aesthetic imagination, but why it remains so common in an industrialized society is still largely unexplained.

Nichiren sect priests traditionally are the most effective in the difficult task of exorcising foxes, although in some cases they have unintentionally killed the victims by administering sulphur to the eyes and nostrils while chanting the *Namu-myō-hō-renge-kyo*. The twang of a bow string (as in the case of the daughter of Emperor Juntoku) is also considered effective, as is the threat of fox-hunting, which Hideyoshi used to exorcise the wife of one of his retainers. The *Busha-sai* (Shooting Festival) of the *Fushimi Inari Jinja* consists of a ritual firing of arrows (which foxes dislike) to chase away misfortune. Arrows may be seen at New Year, at *Setsubun-sai,* and on the last day (*Senshuryaku*) of every *Sumo* tournament, when an arrow is given to the first winner in *Sanyaku.*

Possession of Fox Power: Kitsune-mochi. This form of supernatural power[38] is believed strongly in some parts of the country, especially in Izumo. Families known as fox owners are feared because of their esoteric powers and because they are thought to be protected by seventy-five human foxes known as *Jinko.* These foxes protect family, land, and wealth.

Use of Foxes: Kitsune-tsukai. This type of enchantment was first recorded in the era of the Ashikaga shoguns by Nakahara Yasutomi (1398–1457).[39] Four prominent members of the Court were accused of *kitsune-tsukai,* and the service of priests was required to drive out the foxes from the apartment of the shogun's consort. The men were pronounced guilty and the court physician was exiled for life to Sanuki province. To receive the power of a fox it was necessary to tie three rice balls to the end of a three-meter-long straw rope. Each night a short length had to be taken to the local *Inari Jinja*; this had to be repeated for one hundred nights until a fox came to eat the rice ball. Provided the worshipper was of pure heart, the fox would become a servant, according to popular belief.

Somewhat more mysterious than this is the cult of Izuna-san, known as *Izuna tsukai* according to the methods first practiced on Izuna in the province of Shinano. The teachings of the priests at the two shrines there became known as *Isuna-ho.* A 1742 account of the sect that describes the method of acquiring fox power also offers a model of the integration of Shinto rituals and folklore about the fox:

First they purify themselves by fasting and then go into the mountains to seek for fox holes. If they find a pregnant fox, they politely ask her to make her young their child. Night and day they bring her food and when the little fox is born the mother brings it to them. Then the sorcerer says to the young fox "Henceforth you shall follow me as my shadow." He gives the young animal a name and then the mother and child go away. From that time the fox always appears immediately when the sorcerer calls him by name and tells him all kinds of secret things, the knowledge of which gives him among the people the reputation of being a divine man. But if such a sorcerer becomes in the smallest degree lewd or greedy, he cannot exercise his art any longer, for the fox does not come again.[40]

Nineteenth-century records identify three fox *kami* (*miketsu-no-kami*) as revered in *Izuna Jinja*. *Dagini-Ten* is another name for the rites practiced there and on *Hie-san*. The shrine there is called *Seijo-sha*, shrine of the saintly woman. Another name for *Dagini* is *Kiko-Ten* (Venerable Fox–Heavenly King) or *Fuku-Tenjin* (Happiness–Heavenly *kami*). The real *Dagini* are called *Kanshoku Jinshin* and were introduced (originally from Indian tantrism) by Shingon priests. They were female deities empowered to confer supernatural power and esoteric knowledge upon their worshippers. The teachings of that sect were considered by orthodox Buddhists as *Maho* (demonic teaching) or *Geho* (heretical teaching). It was they who made use of *Osaki kitsune* (pipe foxes), who could confer upon their owners great wealth and honor.

Historical Development of the Inari Cult. When the capital of Japan was moved from Nara to Heian-jo (The City of Peace) Kyoto in 794, the arts and learning of all kinds began to flourish.[41] The shrine on Mt. Inari had been built in 823. In July 852, Imperial messengers asked various shrines to pray for rain. The fact that an Imperial petition was sent to an *Inari Jinja* indicates that the shrine had reached a high level of recognition and respect.

In the twelfth year of Jokwan (870), messengers bearing newly minted coins were sent to various shrines, including Inari shrines. It is interesting that the popular use of coins should be associated early with Inari. There is a reference in 908 to Fujiwara Tokihira having ordered the building of three *Inari Jinja* to honor the *kami* of food and clothes. The influence of Inari had gone far beyond simple agricultural concerns. Even members of the Imperial Family would set aside a small piece of rice from each meal to the *Uga-dama* or food spirit, Inari.

The *Nijūni-sha* included Inari in the most important seven. In 1072 there is the record of an Imperial visit to the *Inari Jinja* when horses were presented. In 1189 the Empress, who had reached the fifth month of pregnancy, donned a maternity girdle and, with proper ceremony, offered prayers to Inari for safe delivery.

The Kamakura age was more intimately connected with the rise of Hachiman through the influence of Shogun Yoritomo. The fortunes of Inari at the national level seem to have been eclipsed by Hachiman. The only significant reference is to a retired Emperor and Empress who went together to *Inari Jinja*. Likewise, in the Namboku-Cho and Muromachi era (1333–

1600) there is little reference to Inari. Indeed, in 1469, during the era of civil turbulence, all the shrines on *Inari-san* were destroyed in the course of a major battle. In 1589, however, Toyotomi Hideyoshi built a large shrine, which suggests that even though Inari may have lost some political power, it was considered sufficiently necessary for a man like Hideyoshi to feel he should replace what had been destroyed.

In the Edo period Inari began to find a new identity and entered a phase of development associated with commerce and popular concerns rather than Imperial matters. The relative stability that the Tokugawa shogunate afforded the country facilitated the gradual expansion of the rice-based economy. This gave birth to the new and rising merchant class. Its power by the end of the Edo period came to exceed that of the warrior class, which had been idle for over two centuries. References to Inari suggest the rise of a new class of followers.

In the twentieth year of Kan-ei (1643), a private ritual was conducted in the palace for the accession of the new Emperor. Inari was one of the shrines chosen to be informed of the accession and to be asked for protection for a trouble-free ceremony. Prayers for the Imperial Court were ordered to be made in various important shrines every month, and again Inari was chosen. Emperor Reige is reported to have visited the Inari shrine on 28 October 1697 and also as having composed a 31-syllable *tanka* poem about Mt. Inari. In 1704 an Imperial Edict declared that because of the great earthquake in Kanto in Genroku 16 (1703), prayers were to be offered at all *Inari Jinja*. A list of what was required for the festival is still extant:[42]

1. Decorations for the shrines and places of purification
2. Implements for the *Ohbarae*
3. Preparations for the sacred dance (*Kagura*) and collecting of musical instruments
4. Great food and drink offerings to the *kami*
5. Preparation for the feasts from the food and drink offerings to the *kami*.

The budget for these items was estimated at 80 *koku* of rice. Also contained in the document is a detailed program of festivals, which were to occupy approximately one week. The priests were to be purified on the first day and thereafter would follow this routine:

Assembly in the early morning of all priests in the *haiden*

They enter the shrine enclosure and take up their positions

The Chief Priest opens the *honden*

The offerings are made

Norito is read

The priests leave their places and enter the *haiden*

The implement for purification is taken up

All are purified (*oharai*)

Norito is read

All enter the precincts of the inner shrine

The instrument of purification is replaced in the inner shrine

All the priests leave the shrine

All enter the place for the preparation of the offerings

They leave and take up their places in the *haiden*

All are again purified

They go to the shrine, bearing offerings

Norito is read

Sacred music and dance

The offerings are removed

The offerings are taken to the *Sairo-oku,* the place where they are prepared and kept when not in use. The ceremony of *Gembuku* (of reaching the age of majority) in the Imperial Palace (which includes receiving the *eboshi*) was to be protected by the seven great shrines, which again included Inari.

Outside of the Imperial Household, among both townspeople (*chōnin*) and merchants (*shōnin*) Inari became popular with those seeking prosperity. Many people erected Inari shrines and Inari *yashiki-gami* on their own land for success, the *shusse Inari*. The characteristic rows of red *torii* gates became well-known and very popular features of Edo life.

Toward the end of the Edo age, in 1834 there is a record of the Emperor's illness being reported to the *Inari Jinja* on February 4 and prayers being offered for his recovery. The last great pre-modern act of the *Inari Jinja* was in 1863, when British warships entered Yokohama harbor. Special prayers were ordered for one week so that the barbarians would be driven away and the sacred soil of Japan would not be defiled by their presence. Prayers for the Emperor and the Empire were also offered.

These constitute most of the great developments of the Inari up to the Meiji Restoration, but Inari did not lose prominence entirely thereafter. In Meiji 2 (1869), all important shrines were instructed to offer special prayers for seven days to ensure the safety of the Emperor's journey to the eastern capital, Tokyo. By June 18, Meiji 4 (1871), the *Inari Jinja* had been raised to the rank of *Kampei Taisha* (Government Shrine). The silver wedding anniversary of the Emperor and Empress Meiji (9 March 1884) was announced to the *kami* at the *Inari Jinja*. Thereafter, all important national or international matters were reported at the *Inari Jinja,* including the treaties that followed the wars against China and Russia. Inari had reached the peak of prominence, the climax of the process begun when an alliance was forged with Shingon Buddhism.

The Kami of Mt. Inari. People performing *seishiki sampai* at a local *Inari Jinja* are probably not aware of the fact that several *kami* are revered under the name *Inari*.[43] *Inari-sama,* if correctly revered, will endow worshippers with peace, happiness, and prosperity. In fact, at *Inari-san* in Fushimi there are five shrines known as the *Inari-gosha* enshrining nine *kami,* the original of whom was Uga-dama, the *kami* of food (associated the names of Saruta-hiko-ō-kami and O-ichi-hime). The abundance of foxes on the mountain suggested the fox as messenger of the *kami,* and it became the practice to offer earthenware foxes to the *kami.* From this the gradual identification of Inari, the *kami* of the mountain and the foxes, came about. The *Inari-gosha* probably evolved as new *kami* were identified by new groups of foxes. The original *kami* of Fushimi is worshipped on the third peak of Inari Mountain at a place called *Mannaka Shimo no Yashiro* (Central Lower Shrine) under a variety of names, all of which relate to food. According to the mythology, Izanagi and Izanami procreated Uka-no-mitama-no-mikoto (food-august-spirit-*kami*). Other versions of the mythology identify a *kami* of food. *Bunri-kami* (branch-*kami*) include the *kami* of grasses and weeds, known as Ya-bune-kuku-no-chi-no-mikoto (house-shell-stem-elder-*kami*), and the *kami* of the home, known as Ya-bune-toyo-uke-hime-no-mikoto (house-shell-abundant-food-princess-*kami*). Inari believers include carpenters and contractors as well as farmers.

The second principal *kami* is Saruta-hiko-no-mikoto,[44] along with Ame-Uzume-no-mikoto. The fourth and fifth *kami,* known together as the Ta-naka-o-kami (rice-field-center-*kami*), are O-na-mochi-no-kami and O-toshi-no-kami. The former is also known as Daikoku, the *kami* of wealth, and the latter is the guardian *kami* of harvest and fields. At the fifth shrine the *Shi-dai-jin* (four-great-*kami*) are revered, and ten additional *kami* are enshrined in different locations on the mountain.

Toyokawa Inari Jinja. After the *Fushuimi Inari Jinja,* the next best known is the *Toyokawa Inari Jinja*[45] in Toyokawa, five miles from Toyohashi. It was completed in March 1930. It is also known as *Toyokawa Bakini Shinten* because it was a Soto Zen temple that dates back to the fifteenth century. The worship of the *Byakko,* or white fox, was allegedly brought from the *Inari Jinja* in Kyoto to Toyokawa. This is an interesting case of syncretistic worship in modern times, as a visit to the *Toyokawa Inari Jinja* on Aoyama-dori in central Tokyo will confirm. Shrine and temple are adjoining, and Inari is served in both.

The continuing and persistent popularity of Inari makes the following remarks of a missionary commentator in 1930 interesting reading: "it seems likely that with the increasing emphasis by the Government on mental and moral training, the gross and superstitious elements of the religion (of Inari) will be eliminated, leaving the strong and worthy features to be absorbed by higher and nobler faiths."[46] This is another case of either wishful thinking or lack of insight into the distinctive character of Japanese religion.

Ebisu. In the words of Herbert, Ebisu is both popular and controversial. The association with trade and commerce is even more explicit than in the case of Inari. Ebisu is depicted in physical form more readily than other *kami* and appears in the well-known shape of a fat bearded figure, smiling happily, holding a fishing line in one hand and a large *tai* (sea bream) in the other.[47] The association of Ebisu is consequently with good fortune and good luck. In this sense, the status of Ebisu is somewhat different from those Shrine Shinto *kami* whose origins are slightly less at the folk level—although as the case of Inari demonstrated, the reality is often far more complex.

Origins of Ebisu. The most likely origin of the cult is that of a *kami* called Ebisu-no-kami who protected fishermen. He was a *kami* of the sea; consequently the oldest *Ebisu Jinja* are near the ocean. In Ishikawa Prefecture, on the Pacific side of the northernmost promontory there is an *Ebisu-zaki* (Cape Ebisu), suggesting a place of refuge in the more fierce northern oceans. The only place name in the country where the identical *kanji* for Ebisu the *kami* are used is a district within the Minato ward of Tokyo.

Development of the Cult of Ebisu. By the twelfth century, reverence for Ebisu became associated with markets. A purification ritual and prayers for prosperity were offered before the market commenced. The cult seems to have flourished on the Pacific side of Japan, from what is now Mie Prefecture toward the island of Shikoku. Ebisu is also found in Kyushu. The principal shrine is in the city of Nishinomiya, between Kobe and Osaka in the Kansai region. In the earliest records, the market *kami* was Ichikishima-no-kami. Twelfth-century records show that in front of the Joraku-ji, a large Buddhist temple in the outskirts of the modern city of Handa in Aichi Prefecture, south of Nagoya City, there was a famous market from ancient times where an *Ebisu Jinja* was established. The same occurred in the case of the large South Market in Nara. Historical evidence suggests the frequent association of Ebisu with markets. Names like Yokkaichi (with markets on days with the number four: 4th, 14th, and 24th), a large city in Mie Prefecture, or Itsukaichi (with markets on days with the number five: 5th, 15th, and 25th) near Tokyo can be traced back to the ancient market day system, a well-known feature of the traditional Japanese economy. It is interesting to note, however, that not one Ebisu shrine is listed among the principal shrines nationwide.

The Identity of Ebisu. Who is Ebisu, and who is enshrined? In the *Imamiya-Ebisu-Jinja* in Osaka, Koto-shiro-nushi-no-mikoto is identified with Ebisu; and in Nishinomiya, Hiru-kuni-no-kami is identified with Ebisu.[48] The identity of Ebisu may have been less formal in earlier days, but after the Meiji Restoration and pressure from the government to eliminate "unworthy" shrines and cults, Ebisu (whose name may not have been considered respectable for a Japanese *kami*) probably became identified with other *kami*. Ebisu is not considered to be among the *kami* who visit Izumo at the *Kami-ai-sai* in October, when the *kami* assemble there from all over the country. Consequently, Ebisu festivals are held in October. It might also be taken to mean that the Japanese could permit all their *kami* to visit Izumo, with the notable exception of the protective *kami* of the market-place and commerce, a possibility that carries its own nuances of meaning. **Ebisu and Daikoku.** There is an association with Daikoku,[49] the *kami* of prosperity, that in turn indirectly links Ebisu with Okuni-nushi-no-mikoto of the *Izumo Taisha*. However, the figure of Daikoku is different from that of Ebisu. Daikoku is normally depicted as a fat and wealthy-looking merchant sitting on two bolls of rice, carrying a sack full of valuable items on his back. He holds the sack on his back with his left hand; in his right he holds a *tsuchi,* a kind of mallet, which could also associate him with carpenters. The amount of construction work undertaken during the Edo age, especially in the city of Edo, would make sense of identifying Ebisu with more than commerce, which was less prominent in the Edo economy than it was in Osaka, for example. The place of Ebisu in rituals preceding commercial ventures seems well established by adequate historical precedent.

Shichi-fuku-jin. In the minds of most Japanese, however, Ebisu and Daikoku are distinguished; and they, plus five other deities of various sorts, constitute the seven *kami* of good fortune. They are not in fact all Shinto *kami* but are noted here because they are known as the seven *kami, Shichi-fuku-jin* (seven good-fortune *kami*).

The others are as follows. Ben-ten is a female derived from an Indian deity, Sarasvati, the patron of music. Bishamon-ten is a warrior in armor with a grotesque face, holding a spear in one hand and a treasure tower in the other. Fuku-roku-ju is said to be derived from the Chinese legend of a Sung Dynasty hermit. This is the *kami* of wealth, prosperity, and long life. Hotei is a fat-bellied Buddhist priest who carries a sack, which—like that of Santa Claus—never empties. He also carries a fan. Jun-ro-jin is often identified with the Southern Polestar but is depicted also as a Chinese-style hermit. He has a large head and carries a long stick to which a book is attached, the book of life, which includes anyone who consults him.

The seven *kami* are often seen sailing in a treasure ship, a *takara-bune,* filled with magical instruments, rich merchandise, a hat that makes people invisible, and a bag of money that never empties. In fact, most of these are of Buddhist origin. Indeed, Daikoku may also be of Indian origin, being identified by some with Mahakala, a domestic Hindu deity associated with cooking. Happiness was later included. There is also an association with Ta-no-kami, the *kami* of the field. In contemporary Japan, people carry money with them each year to have it washed in the sacred waters of Ben-ten so as to enlarge its value through purification. This is certainly in the order of folk religion rathern than pure Shrine Shinto, but it illustrates how one level almost imperceptibly runs into the next. It also underlines the point that in the popular mind (from the Edo age onwards, but probably before) the distinction between *kami* and *hotoke,* between the *kami* and the Buddha, and between popular religion and institutional religion has never been clearly drawn, if at all.

NOTES

1. No exhaustive series of publications on shrines exists because it would be a documenting task of massive proportions. To visit all of Japan's shrines at the rate of one per day would take 290 years! Gakusei-sha, a Tokyo publishing company, began the *Nippon Jinja Series* in 1969 to cover twenty-two main shrines. Over twenty years later, less than half had been published. Individual shrines publish guidebooks based on material from their own archives. The Ponsonby Fane series offers some general studies in English. Data in this and the ensuing sections are verified from the *Shinto Jiten,* ed. Anzu Motohiko of Kokugakuin University (Horii Shoten, Tokyo, 1968).

One method by which the study of Shinto is advancing is through the study of various cults. Recent work on the cult of Kasuga is a good example. There is Royall Tyler's *The Miracles of the Kasuga Deity* (Columbia University Press, 1990) and more recently Susan Tyler's *The Cult of Kasuga Seen Though its Art* (University of Michigan, Ann Arbor, 1992). There is also Allan Grapard's excellent work entitled *The Protocol of the Gods: A Study of the Kasuga Cult in Japanese History* (University of California Press, 1992). The cults of Sumiyoshi, Hikawa and Suwa, to name but three, must be candidates for this kind of treatment.

Grapard is particularly interesting when discussing the possibility of using Kasuga as a structural model for interpreting the multiplex-based aspects of Japanese social and religious history. I have also used the term "multiplex" in a discussion of values in Japan, and I found Grapard's thesis most suggestive and illuminating. ("The Evolution of the Japanese Value System," *Humanities Journal* 17 (International Christian University, Tokyo, 1983, p. 148). A similar insight is found in William R. LaFleur's description of Japanese ethics as moral bricolage. (*Liquid Life: Abortion and Buddhism in Japan,* Princeton University Press, 1992 p. 12).

2. I was made aware of this in the case of Buddhism while attending a funeral in the company of a priest of the Jōdo sect. When the officiating priest began his intonations, I was astonished when he asked if I knew to which sect he belonged. Shrines at least share the same mythology, although it is questionable if many priests know the details of *kami* enshrined in shrines other than their own. The Association of Shinto Shrines has records only for shrines that are affiliated with it; this reflects what Delmer Brown has described as the particularlism of Shinto.

3. Statistics are from the Association of Shinto Shrines.

4. The *kami* of heaven, the *kami* of earth, and the myriad *kami*. "Myriad" is usually explained as "eight millions," a Chinese form of expression for "countless."

5. *Kojiki,* Vol. I, Section 18.

6. Ivan Morris, *The Nobility of Failure* (Meridian Books, New York, 1976), pp. 1–13.

7. *Kojiki,* Vol. I, Section 33.

8. This was determined after extensive research and debate.

9. *Kojiki,* Vol. II, Section 46. The name has also been taken to mean "eight-headed crow" by Motoori Norinaga. Aston claims that it is a reference to a Chinese myth about a three-clawed crow, reddish in color, that lived on the sun (*Nihongi,* Aston translation, p. 168, footnote 2).

10. For a description of this, see the *Nihon Jinja Series* study by Shinohara Shiro of *Kumano Taisha* (Gakuseisha, Tokyo, 1969), pp. 120 ff.

11. Sixteen of the shrines that made up the *Ni-ju-ni-sha* were first identified during the reign of Emperor Murakami (r. 946–967), who had them offer prayers to end a time of floods. He classified them into *Kampeisha,* which received *hei* (Imperial offerings) directly from the Court, and *Kokuheisha,* which received them from the *Kokushi* (Provincial Governor). The completed list of twenty-two was finally drawn up in Choryaku 3 (1038) by Emperor Gosuzaku.

12. *Kojiki,* Vol. II, Section 45.

13. *Nihongi,* Vol. II, Section 33: 37.

14. The story is preserved in the *Engishiki* and is contained within the *norito* of the *Tatsu Kaze no Kami no Matsuri.* An English version of the *norito* by Ernest Satow can be found in *Transactions of the Asiatic Society of Japan* 7, pt. 4, 1879.

15. The *Nihongi* version and the *Kojiki* account of Empress Jingu's conquest of Korea and the subsequent enshrinement of the *Sumiyoshi kami* do not completely agree. Opinions differ over whether the recorded incidents happened before or after the expedition.

16. Hori Ichiro, "Mountains and Their Importance for the Idea of the Other World in Japanese Folk Religion," *Japanese Religions* 6, no. 1 (August 1966): 1–23.

17. For a concise account, see George Sansom, *History of Japan,* Vol. 1 (Tuttle, Tokyo, 1979), pp. 215–216.

18. For sources on the life and death of Nogi Maresuke, see Lifton, Kato, and Reich, *Six Lives, Six Deaths* (Yale University Press, 1979), pp. 29–66.

19. *Shoku Nihongi Jingo Keiun* 3.9.25. Sources on the Hachiman cult include the following: Usa Engi (Records of Rituals of the Usa Hachiman Shrine in Kyushu); Miyaji Naokazu, *Hachimangū no Kenkyū* (Studies in Hachiman) (Risōsha, Tokyo, 1956); *Tsurugaoka Hachimangū* official publications; and records from the *Hachimangū Shamusho.* Ross Bender, "The Hachiman Cult and the Dōkyō Incident," *Monumenta Nipponica* 34, no. 2 (Summer 1970): 125–153, is a useful discussion in English of some of the theories about Hachiman.

20. Nakano Hatayoshi, *Hachiman Shinkoshi no Kenkyū* (Studies in the Hachiman Cult) (Yoshikawa Kobunkan, 1976).

21. Jean Herbert, *Shinto: Foundation of Japan* (George Allen & Unwin, London, 1967): 426–440. Herbert also made reference to the *Hachiman-gū-do-kun,* a Kamakura age document about Hachiman written for children, and Miyaji's work cited in note 19 of this chapter.

22. Motoori Norinaga, *Zenshu* (Complete Works), Vol. 5, (Yoshikawa Kobunkan, Tokyo, 1926–1927), p. 112.

23. Gembo (?–746) represented the highwater mark of Nara Buddhist power in the court of Emperor Shōmu.

24. *Shoku Nihongi* record of *Tempyo,* 1.12.27.

25. Ross Bender, "The Hachiman Cult and the Dōkyō Incident," p. 153.

26. On Inari the following texts were consulted: *Kampei Taisha Inari Jinja Meisei Zusho* (Details of the Government Grand Shrine of Inari) (Inari Shrine Authorities, 1884), Okabu Jo, *Kampei Taisha Inari Jinsha Go-Saijin Ki* (Records of the Kami Celebrated in the Government Grand Shrine of Inari) (Tokyo, 1920); Yoshida Motozaburo, *Fushimi Inari Zen Keinai Meisho Zue* (An Illustrated Introduction to Famous Locations within Fushimi Inari) (Fushimi Inari Shrine, Kyoto, 1925); Hata no Kimihata, *Kami no Yashiro Hata no Kimihata Nikki* (Diaries of Negi Hata of the Upper Inari Shrine) (1821–1827); *Inarisha Kokon Jijitsu Kosko* (Studies on Inari Shrines Ancient and Modern) (c. 1820); *Inari Jinja Kobunsho* (Ancient Papers on Inari Jinja) (author and dates unknown); *Inari Jinja Kokiruoku* (Ancient Records of Inari Jinja) (author and dates unknown); *Shashi Tsukiban Zakki* (Records of Monthly Duties at the Inari Jinja) (1688–1911); *Inari Jinja Shamusho Nisshi* (Daily Record of the Inari Jinja Office) (1868).

English sources are scant. However, the following are useful: Daniel Crump Buchanan, "Inari: Its Origin, Development and Nature," *Transactions of the Asiatic Society of Japan* (Tokyo), December 1935 (a period piece, but a useful starting point); Karen A. Smyers, "Of Foxes, Buddhas and Shinto Kami: The Syncretic Nature of Inari Beliefs," *Japanese Religions* 16, no. 3 (January 1991): 60–75; Nozaki Kiyoshi, *Kitsune: Japan's Fox of Mystery, Romance and Humor* (Hokuseido Press, Tokyo, 1961). Nozaki's book contains a wealth of background information about the fox and can be read alongside the relevant portions of Blacker's *Catalpa Bow*, mentioned earlier in the context of shamanism.

27. *I*, meaning "rice," and *nari*, "form" or "shape," constitute one idea. When rice is poured into a bowl it often takes a conical shape, which would fit *inari yama* (rice-shaped mountain). There is *ine* (rice plant) and *nari* (form), based upon the idea that Inari is the spirit of the rice plant that sometimes appears in human form. This relates to the fox as the messenger of the *kami* and the shamanistic belief in fox possession. *Ine* (rice plant) and *nari* (fertile) would imply that Inari is the *kami* of the flowering rice plant. Ine plus *kari* (cutting) or *ine* plus *iru* (gathering) are also plausible candidates. *Ine* (rice plant), with *ka* read as *ri* (load or burden) are the characters used in the name *Iño* as it is usually written. Japanese explanations often favor etymology that most readily fits the characteristics or qualities they wish to identify or highlight. The result may often be as much supposition as scholarship.

28. John Batchelor, *The Ainu and Their Folk-Lore* (Religious Tract Society of London, 1901); Peng and Geisen, *The Ainu: The Past in the Present* (Bunka Hyoron, Hiroshima, 1977). Batchelor's many studies are still classic.

29. Czaplika, *Aboriginal Siberia* (Clarendon Press, Oxford, 1914); Diōszegi, *Tracing Shamans in Siberia* (Ousterhout, Holland, 1968).

30. William Walter Skeat, *Malay Magic* (Macmillan, London, 1900).

31. Hirata Atsutane, *Koshinden* (Account of Ancient History) (1812).

32. Nozaki, *Kitsune*, Chapter 2.

33. Names and ranks of the fox are listed as follows:

Kitsune	The normal term for the fox.
Byakko	White fox, the *kami* of Inari.
Genko	Black fox; its appearance is a good omen.
Shakko	Red fox, a sign of good fortune.

Kiko	Spirit fox, used by *Yamabushi* in divining.
Kwanko	Pipe fox, also read as *Kuda-gitsune,* a small fox that can be inserted into a pipe and used by *Yamabushi* in divining.
Kūko	Air fox, considered identical to *Tengu* and extremely malevolent.
Jinko	Man fox, the fox in human form.
Reiko	Ghost fox, a powerful demonic fox.
Tenko	Heavenly fox, a fox who flies and may also be a *Tengu.*
Koryō	Haunting fox, who bewitches people.
Yakan	The most powerful and haunting of all foxes.
Kiko Myōjin	Venerable gracious *kami* fox and messenger of Inari.
Chōko	Fox chieftain, also read as *Osa-gitsune,* the king of all foxes in Japan and descendant of *Kiko Myōjin.*
Kyūbi no kitsune	Nine-tailed fox, a sign of good fortune.
Osaki gitsune	Osaki fox, the same as *Kwanko.*
Myōbu	Court lady, a fox revered on Mt. Inari.
Tome	Old Woman, a fox revered in the Byakko Jinja on Mt. Inari.
Tōka	Rice carrying, also read as *Inari,* the *kami* of the mountain.
Kotai	Fox regiment, groups of foxes who appear as soldiers.
Yako	Field fox, the lowest grade of fox.
Yorikata	Assistants, a grade higher than field fox.
Shuryō	Chief, the highest rank of fox.

A listing also appears in Buchanan, "Inari," pp. 34–36.

34. E. T. C. Werner, *Myths and Legends of China* (Bretano, New York, 1922); J. J. M. De Groot, *The Religion of the Chinese* (Macmillan, New York, 1910).

35. Narrated in Nozaki, *Kitsune,* Chapter 4.

36. See Basil Hall Chamberlain, *Things Japanese* (John Murray, London, 1905), for similar incidents. Buchanan vouches for the car incident as coming from a priest of the *Inari Jinja* in Wakayama. See also Nozaki, *Kitsune,* Chapters 13 and 14.

37. Nozaki, *Kitsune,* Chapters 21 and 22. This disorder continues to exist in many rural parts of Japan. Blacker discusses this in *Catalpa Bow,* pp. 238–239, 242, 301.

38. This is usually considered equivalent to sorcery. See Blacker, *Catalpa Bow,* pp. 53–54.

39. *Yasutomi-Ki* (Diaries of Nakahara Yasutomi), 1401–1457, p. 50.

40. Daiyata Misaki, *Ro-on-Cha-wa* (Old Ladies' Tea Chatter).

41. See historical sources listed in note 26 of this chapter.

42. Records exist in the *Inari Jinja Kobunshō* (Ancient Papers of the Inari Shrine). See also Kata Nobutomo, *Goten Azukari Kata Nobutomo Nikki* (Diary of Kata Nobutomo, Priest of the Shrine) (Fushimi Inari); and Sir Ernest M. Satow, "Ancient Japanese Rituals," *Transactions of the Asiatic Society of Japan* 7 (nos. 1, 2, and 4) and 9 (1878 and 1881).

43. On Inari and Phallicism there is clear evidence of the fertility dimension of the Inari cult in the past, when the agricultural mysteries of birth and growth were revered along with the protective *kami* of rice production. Various artifacts and festivals existed throughout the country. These were suppressed during the early years of Meiji and again under the weight of State Shinto when attempts were made to sever the link between Shrine Shinto and folk religion.

44. See the discussion of Saruta-hiko and Ame-uzume-no-mikoto in Chapter 2

of this book. My references are the *Kojiki* (Chamberlain's translation, pp. 130–136) and the *Nihongi,* Vol. I, pp. 77–79.

45. Information was provided from the *Toyokawa Inari Jinja.*

46. Buchanan, "Inari," p. 141. In spite of modern Japanese Christian protests about the *Daijōsai,* there seems little sign of the contemporary *in visa retrospecta* disapproval of both the Emperor system or the Japanese government's moral education program.

47. The Japanese name of sea bream, *tai,* is used in a word play to mean the last part of *omeditai,* a congratulatory wish. Consequently, the *tai* is used at weddings or celebrations, thereby becoming associated with happiness and prosperity.

48. The initial association of these *kami* seems to have been the work of Edo period scholars who wished to give Ebisu a more impressive pedigree than a simple folklore origin. A major research project is needed to trace in detail the origins and development of Ebisu on the same lines as the work on Hachiman and Inari. Paralleling the study of Hachiman, which deals with religion and politics, it could be an interesting preface to the relationship of economics and religion in Japan. The only study listed was Yoshii Yoshihide, *Nishinomiya Ebisugami Kenkyū* (Studies in the Kami Ebisu of Nishinomiya) (Tokyo, 1935).

49. At a dinner to open a British fair in the Mitsukoshi Department Store in Tokyo, as part of the entertainment a lion dance was performed as a religious act to close the evening. The program explained that the lion was Daikokusama, who was also Okuni-nushi-noi-mikoto, the *kami* of *Izumo Taisha,* the guardian shrine of Mitsukoshi. To encourage the blessings of the *kami,* as the lion danced around the *tatami*-matted hall it went first to the President of the store, who placed a 10,000-yen note in its wooden jaws. The British Ambassador was obliged to follow suit. My fellow Scots, with their accustomed sense of thrift, asked me what would be the smallest acceptable donation! The idea of a Shinto rite in that form took almost all the foreign visitors by complete surprise.

Chapter 5

Shrine Buildings (Jinja Shaden)

ORIGINS OF SHRINES AND SHRINE BUILDINGS

Jinja in Japanese refers to a location, not to a building. Shrines began as places of theophanic manifestation, perhaps less dramatic than the burning bush that Moses saw or the place where Jacob dreamed of a ladder stretching up to heaven. But certainly they were no less impressive to the Japanese of old, who felt that those places were the residences of *kami*. Consequently, Japan's oldest and most impressive shrines are located in places of dramatic natural beauty. Early worship centered upon these sacred spaces, the precursor of the *himorogi*, marked off initially by a rope but later fenced by trees, rocks or carefully laid out stones. These were the locations where eventually buildings were raised to house acts of worship. This has continued in modern practices related to the erection of new buildings. When *jichinsai* is performed to pacify a *kami* of the earth, a *himorogi* is marked with branches of *sakaki* and straw-plaited *shimenawa*. The area inside is considered sacred for that time and the ceremony is conducted by a properly purified priest.

The earliest shrines were probably little more than rock piles that marked a sacred spot. Buildings came to be located in front of them or at the foot of the mountain where these spaces were identified. Some *jinja* of very ancient origin have no *honden*, and some even had no buildings whatsoever. The island of Okinoshima[1] was the center of the worship of the *Munakata-o-kami*. The government energetically promoted this cult, which prospered because of Japan's domination of the southern part of the Korean peninsula. *Munakata-o-kami* was the protective *kami* of the ocean waterways. The entire island is dotted with numerous altars. The huge volume of artifacts and treasures found here suggest the vitality of the cult between the fourth and seventh centuries, yet there is no evidence whatsoever of any building having been erected there.

It is from such simple beginnings that the modern shrine developed. It was indeed the "place of the *kami*," a *yorishiro*; because the space was perceived as sacred, *himorogi* and *iwasaka* developed. Some shrines continue to have no main buildings. The *Omiya* (great shrine) near Nara has Mt. Miwa as its *honden* and its *kami*. It is topped by a large rock that serves as a *yorishiro*. The *Isonokami Jinja* in Kyoto and the upper *Suwa Jinja* in Nagano had no *honden* until the Meiji era.

Once buildings began to appear, probably around the fifth century, *Jinja shaden* (shrine buildings) came to provide another example of Shinto's tendency to identify *kami* with particular places. Not only are *kami* worshipped in specific localities, but they are also worshipped in specific types of buildings whose form is associated with them. It would be incongruous to see the worship of Hachiman taking place inside buildings that looked like an Inari shrine, for example.

It is quite possible to have *massha* (subordinate shrines) to another *kami* inside shrine precincts. *Inari massha* are found in many shrines of other *kami*. Although there are historical reasons for the differences of design, these designs have become identifying marks of the *kami*.[2] This in part relates to the fact that the locations of *jinja* and buildings is the choice of the *kami* rather than the worshippers. For example, the need to have a particular *kami* might be felt by a community or a family, which would be taken as a sign from that *kami*. The location would be determined by divination in various ways[3] to choose a propitious site. The location then becomes sacred, and shrines or their buildings are seldom relocated unless under the most exceptional circumstances.[4] The individual details of shrines extend beyond buildings to the types of *torii* (gateway) and the kinds of *shinsen* (food offerings) that the various *kami* prefer. There are approximately sixteen main styles of architecture of varied historical origins and over twenty types of *torii* associated with different *kami* and locations. These I will describe with the names of principal exemplary shrines and *kami*.

It has been claimed on the basis of mythology that the first shrine building was erected by Okuninishi-no-mikoto to revere his own *kushi-mitama* (soul of mysterious virtue). Shortly thereafter, Nininigi-no-mikoto, grandson of Amaterasu, is said to have erected a shrine modeled on his palace to honor Okuninishi-no-mikoto at Obama in Izumo. This became the famous *Izumo Taisha*. Also according to legend, in February 657 B.C. Emperor Jimmu enshrined the spirit (*tamashii*) of Amaterasu on Mt. Tomiyama in Yamato although no buildings were erected. In 92 B.C. the sacred mirror (formerly kept in the Imperial Palace) was enshrined by Emperor Sujin at Kasanui in Yamato. In another legend Emperor Suinin constructed *Ise Jingū* in 5 B.C. for the sacred mirror, and from that date shrine buildings came to be erected. Of course, this is mere legend, because the dating is beyond verification. Much of this mythology was embodied in the teachings of State Shinto after the Meiji Restoration.

Alongside the politically inspired legends of shrine origins,[5] many old shrines have independent folk origins. There are shrines for the *kami* of Earth and other shrines that predate politicization. No Imperial approval was given to these shrines, which merely reflected the spiritual aspirations of an agricultural people to have their own places of veneration.[6] Many old shrine buildings around the countryside local to a community belong to this category. Most have no names and would have been part of the 100,000 eliminated by government ordinance during the era of State Shinto, when the wholesale destruction of local folk shrines was undertaken in order to strengthen government-authorized shrines.[7]

The earliest buildings were extremely simple, constructed—as in the case of *Ise Jingū*—of plain Japanese cypress[8] with no decoration and using few if any nails, to stand in stark beauty and simplicity. Polynesian rice stores are thought to be the nearest similar buildings. The shrines draw architects from all over the world to study their design, construction, and functions. Later shrines came to reflect Chinese and other influences in the use of vermilion and in the addition of color in general. The various styles of architecture that emerged reflect the different ages of Shinto and the periods through which the development of its traditions passed. The use of curved lines did not appear until after the eighth century, which was about the time that Chinese and Korean architectural influences began to appear in Japan.

Shrines reflect two deep traits of the Japanese character: the love of purity and the love of newness. The periodic rebuilding of shrines (usually replicating the existing form) expresses the spirit of endless renewal that seems to lie at the root of the culture along with the desire for purity and brightness. The *kami* should not be revered in buildings that are decrepit, dirty, and neglected. They should be fresh, clean, and well kept.

The capital has been moved from time to time for the same reason. Emperor Kwammu moved it from Nara to Kyoto in 794, ushering in not only a new period of Japanese history but also new styles in building, manners, and dress. From that time on, the styles of shrines began to change, matching the mood of the ages. Nevertheless, the ideals expressed in the simple, graceful form of the Grand Shrines of Ise, for example, remain the classical product of the Japanese spirit.

DEVELOPMENT OF SHRINES AND SHRINE ARCHITECTURE

The simplest method of classifying shrines is according to the *kami* enshrined. This affects the shape of the *torii* (which mark the entrance to the sacred site) and the architectural style (*zukuri*) of the buildings.[9] There are normally at least two buildings, one exclusively for the *kami* and another for use by worshippers.

The original purpose of erecting buildings was to provide a place in which the *kami* could descend and where both *kami* and worshippers could be together. Once shrine buildings have been erected and the *kami* has descended, the ground is sacred. *Tatari*, misfortune, threatens any who violate that sanctity by removing the shrine or damaging the grounds.[10]

PRIMITIVE SHRINE STYLES

Tenchi-Gongen

The name "Heaven-Earth origin" implies the basic distinction of *kami* into the Heavenly *kami* and the Earthly *kami* and suggests that it is a point where heaven and earth can meet. The diagram[11] is largely conjecture, but it combines anthropological and archaeological ideas about the residence of ancient anthropoids. Two posts are firmly embedded in the

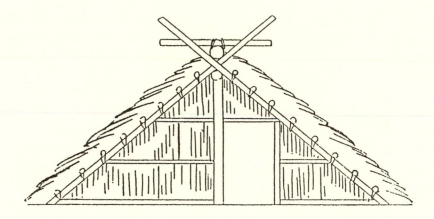

ground, and two slanted poles are tied front and rear to make a frame. Thin bamboos are added and thatch is placed on top of these. The only limitation of this design is that it would be flooded in the rainy season, unless the lower parts of the roof could be raised. This style seems closer to the North American Indian tepee whose lower covers could be opened for ventilation.

Tenchi-Gongen may also have been used as coverings for pit dwellings used by Japan's earliest inhabitants. Beside the *tate-ana* site in Toro, Shizuoka Prefecture, there is a restored raised house. In New Guinea, the *Tenchi-Gongen* style can be seen with two distinctions: it is round like the Indian tepee, and it has an upper floor for sleeping. Regardless of origin, the roof silhouette of shrines probably begins with the *Tenchi-Gongen* style.[12]

Takakuya

This "high house" style seems a more likely original form, although it
has been argued that it is a later development. It is elevated to avoid flood-
ing and has a staircase. The diagram is based on drawings on pottery and
on ancient mirrors found during excavations. It fits the pattern of Southeast
Asian houses in New Guinea, Sumatra, or Palao, where carved models are
sold as tourist souvenirs. The style can be traced, at least in form, as far

back as the Yayoi period. Models of raised-floor buildings are among the
funerary offerings made of baked clay known as *Haniwa* that date to the
fifth century C.E. Similar buildings may be found particularly on outlying
islands, such as Hachijo, Kyushu, and Okinawa. Some are constructed with
a system of interlocking joints at corners for extra strength (known as *ta-
azekura*), an extremely ancient method of construction still seen in the *Ar-
amatsuri Jinja,* a branch shrine (*betsu-gu*) of *Ise Jingū.*

In the Yamato Court, designated storehouses of the government were
known as *Okura* (great treasure house). There were three types. (1) *Imikura*
were storage houses for ceremonial regalia of various kinds. These were
supervised by the Imbe clan. (2) *Kura* were general storage places for

state property supervised by the Hata clan. (3) The *Okura* was the national treasury, which was supervised by the Yamato no Aya clan. *Isonokami Jinja,* near the Kyoto Imperial Palace, was used as an arsenal under Mononobe control. In this way, the religio-political role of the buildings grew with the evolving Yamato society. This would also explain why *Ise Jingū* had only one building surrounded by sacred fences: its sole function was the enshrinement of *kami. Ise Jingū* was thought to be a natural development from *Imikura* of the earlier period, built originally and controlled by the Imbe clan (who were also hereditary directors of the *Jingi-kan*). The turning point appears to be during the sixth century, when the *takakuya* were superseded by improved building techniques.

It was at this point that the Imbe made a point of stressing the uniqueness of the *Imikura* by retaining the archaic architectural style while other building styles changed. In this way *Ise Jingū* acquired its distinctive style. Raised building did not totally disappear; one other outstanding example is the *Shoso-in* in Nara, which dates to the eighth century. It is an example of the large-style *Okura*. The prototype for this appears to be Chinese. Han Dynasty (206 B.C.– 220 C.E.) tombs contain tiles on which such buildings are depicted. The style seems to have been in use in China at an earlier date, although this does not have significant implications for the religious use to which the Japanese adapted their buildings. Once they developed, they became an integral part of the Shinto tradition and have remained so ever since.

ROOF DESIGNS AND ORNAMENTS ON SHRINES

Chigi

Chigi are sets of timbers standing vertically and sitting crosswise at the upper end of the roof ridge. The oldest buildings were erected from two intersecting timbers raised and crossed as shown. They eventually became

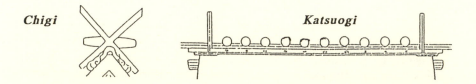

Chigi *Katsuogi*

merely decorative ornaments on the shrine roof. The top end (with some exceptions) is usually finished with a vertical edge when the *kami* is male and with a horizontal edge when the *kami* is female. Similar designs can be found on *Haniwa* buildings that date to the fifth century. The design can be traced back to second-century China.

Katsuogi

These are short round pieces of wood that lie along the shrine's roof ridge at regular intervals. They are derived from the timbers used as weights on thatched roofs to prevent movement by strong winds. Again, function has been replaced by a decorative role. These are found particularly on shrine roofs that have no curves or that are influenced by the style of the *Ise Jingū*. The name is said to be derived from the similar-sounding name of small Japanese dried fish whose shape is similar. Both *chigi* and *katsuogi* seem to have been popular toward the end of the Tumulus period of the great sepulchral *Kofun*. The incident in the *Nihongi* in which Emperor Yuryaku[13] forbade the placing of *katsuogi* anywhere but on Imperial palaces (*miya*) indicates that they had come to indicate status. This appears to have been around the fifth century, from which time shrine architecture can be historically documented.

PRINCIPAL TYPES OF SHRINE STYLE

Aidono

The *Aidono* (joint-hall) style is a modification of divine brightness (*shinmei*) whereby two shrines are joined together but each is provided with a separate door to the *haiden*. *Kasuga Taisha* is thought to be the oldest, but *Kashima Jingū* in Ibaraki used this style as early as 649. *Kashima Jingū*, which enshrines Take-mikazuchi-no-mikoto, dates to 1619. Nearby and closely related is *Katori Jingū* which enshrines Futsu-

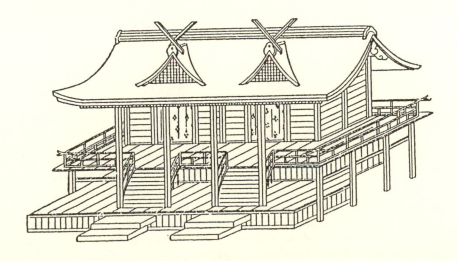

nushi-no-mikoto (known locally as Iwainushi-no-mikoto), who assisted in the work of bringing the land of Japan into being. The *honden* of *Katori Jingū* dates to 1701.

Asama

The name comes from the *Asama Jinja* in Ōmiya near the base of Mt. Fuji. The *Asama* style involves the modification of *gongen* by the addition of an upper story. The lower floor, surrounded by a balustraded veranda, is in *Hoden-zukuri* style. The second floor is in *nagare* style with *chigi* and *katsuogi*. The entire building, apart from the roof, is painted in vermilion

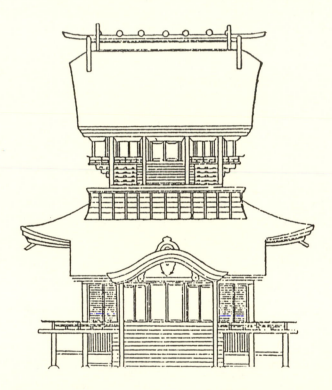

lacquer, with the eaves and rafters in blue and yellow. It is consequently very dynamic in appearance. Also called *Sengen Jinja,* it is sacred to Mt. Fuji and to Konohana-Sakuyahine, the consort of Ninigi-no-mikoto. The incident in which she marries is narrated in both the *Nihon Shoki* and the *Kojiki*. Legend has it that Asama-Okami saved Yamato-Takeru-no-mikoto when he was ambushed on a moor set on fire by assassins. *Asama* first appears in 1223. It was destroyed more than once and rebuilt; the present buildings date to approximately 1604, with modern restoration work having been carried out in 1926. *Asama Jinja* has over 900 branch shrines.

Gion

The most famous shrine in the *Gion* style is *Yasaka Jinja* in Kyoto (formerly known as *Gion Jinja*), last rebuilt by order of the fourth Tokugawa shogun, Ietsuna. It began as a *Tenjin* shrine beside the *Gion-ji*, which was built between 859 and 876. It was first rebuilt after a fire in 1070 in a form similar to its present one, which is famous for the annual spectacular *Gion Matsuri. Gion-zukuri* measures approximately 14 meters on each side and is surrounded by an aisle 2 meters wide that is similar to the classic *shinden* style modeled on the palaces of the ancient nobility. The main

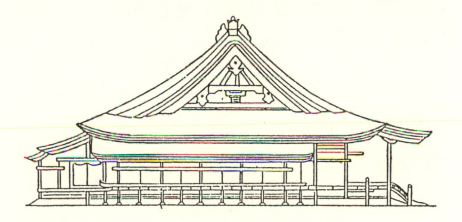

structure and the central part are in *Irimoya-zukuri* style, whereas the right, left, and rear aisles are covered by a feather-edged roof. The steps up to the floor level in front are also covered. The unusual style does not appear to be the result of Buddhist or Chinese influence, but rather of the tastes in house design of the wealthy being applied to shrine building. The interior layout of the rooms is more reminiscent of a temple than a shrine; this underlined its possible origin in house architecture.

Gongen

Gongen means "incarnation." The style became most popular during the early Edo era after it was used in the construction of the *Tosho-gū,* the *Tendai Shinto* shrine in Nikko where Tokugawa Ieyasu was enshrined in 1636. The front roof resembles a Buddhist temple; the main roof joins the

two principal buildings of the complex with a sheltered walkway between. It is heavily lacquered and adorned with carvings. Shrines closely affiliated with esoteric or semi-esoteric Buddhism frequently adopted the *Gongen* style. The *honden* and *norito-den* are usually in *Irimoya-zukuri* style. Three areas make up the complex, the middle one of which is sometimes the same height as, and sometimes lower than, the rest. The center room joined the hitherto unconnected *haiden* with the *honden*. This is probably the origin of the modern form of *Jinja Shaden* in three parts: *haiden*, *heiden* or *noritoden*, and *honden*.

Hachiman

Hachiman, the most widely enshrined of all *kami*, came to be in the popular mind a *kami* of war, particularly after expansion of the cult under Yoritomo

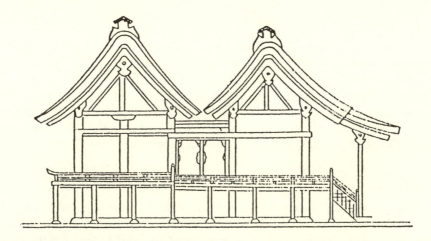

during the Kamakura age. The original shrine at Usa in Kyushu dates to around 765–766. It was replicated in the *Iwashimizu Hachiman-gū* in Kyoto (which enshrines Emperor Ōjin, 270–312) probably around 859, and in the *Tsurugaoka Hachiman-gū* in Kamakura (although the Kamakura shrine incorporates *Gongen* style.) The principal point of development is the addition of a separate hall for worshippers. There is thus a *honden* (main building) as well as a *heiden* (worship hall) connected and covered by sweeping roofs that meet to give the shrine its distinctive form. Under these is a gutter known as the golden gutter. The Hachiman cult also offers protection to localities. In the case of the Kamamura shrine, this includes the entire Kanto plain.

Hie

Hie style is named after the *Hie Jinja* at Sakamoto below Mt. Hie near Kyoto. It enshrines Oyamakui-no-mikoto (also known as Yamasuie-no-onushi-no-kami), the *kami* of Mt. Hie. The *Hie*-style roof has a pent-roof

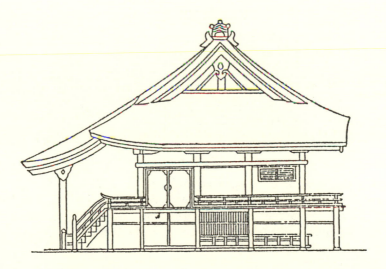

on three sides and a small additional roof in front covering a flight of stairs to the floor level. The style combines Buddhist and Chinese influence with native Japanese styles. During the Edo period, the name *Hie* was seldom used. It was better known as *Sannō* (mountain king) because of its association with the Buddhist *Tendai* sect, whose headquarters is the *Enryaku-*

ji on Mt. Hie. The Chinese characters of the Tokyo *Hie Jinja* differ from the older *Hie,* although it is a branch shrine.

Irimoya

This style grew from a roof form called *Irimoya.* It consists of large gabled roof combined with a smaller sloping roof further down. It has neither *chigi* nor *katsuogi,* suggesting an early palace style. The *Kashihara Jingū,* which enshrines Emperor Jimmu at Unebi near Nara, is the most

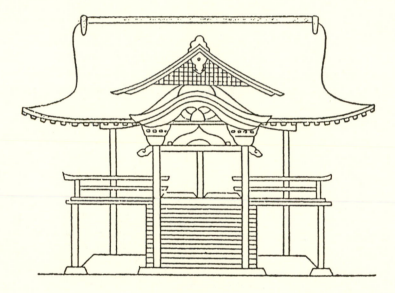

famous of this type. It was approved and built in 1890 after the tomb of Emperor Jimmu had been officially "identified" by the government in 1863. There are very few branch shrines because the cult of Jimmu Tenno was never very popular. Other shrines in *Irimoya-zukuri* style are *Hiraoka Jinja* in Osaka, near which is the *Kofun* style tomb of Emperor Nintoku, and *Mishima Jinja* in Izu.

Kashii

The *Kashii* style of northern Kyushu is retained in the *Kashii-gū* to the north of Fukuoka City, which enshrines Emperor Chuai and Empress Jingu, who moved their palace there because of a rebellion. The shrine claims to date to the eighth century and to have stood facing the Imperial Palace. The curiously complicated style includes a *honden* roof in *Irimoya,* whereas other parts have a *sugaru* gable. A veranda goes around all six sides, and

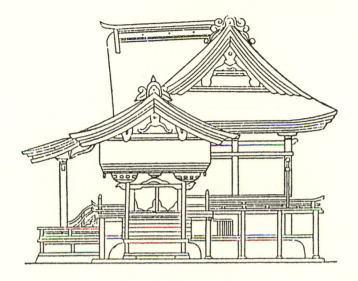

a covered staircase constitutes the entrance to the *haiden* in front. The buildings were last reconstructed in 1801.

Kasuga

The *Kasuga Taisha* in Nara (established by the Fujiwara family around 709) marks a new era in shrine architecture. Straight lines were replaced by sweeping roofs on the Chinese model, with even the *chigi* becoming

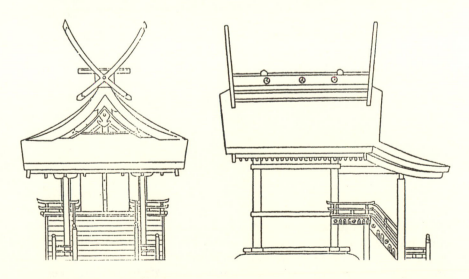

curved. Red, gold, and vermilion were introduced to decorate the wood-work. The name *Kasuga* designates a complex of four small buildings set up in a row. *Kasuga-zukuri* is supported by columns and the roof is thatched with *hiwada* (Japanese cypress bark). The style resembles *Taisha,* with the practical addition of a roof over the staircase to prevent it from becoming wet and slippery. At the time of construction it was surrounded by a *tamagaki,* a sacred fence, which was changed into an encircling veranda (*kairo*) in 1178. The present shrine was last constructed in 1862.

Kibitsu

The *Kibitsu Jinja* in the suburbs of Okayama is a rare style of shrine building with the largest *honden* of any shrine. It stands over 20 meters by 16 meters and was erected in 1390 by the third Ashikaga shogun, Yoshimitsu. The *norito-den* was added in 1402. The previous buildings were destroyed in an early fourteenth-century natural disaster. The *Nagare*-style *honden* has three sections surrounded by an inner aisle, and an outer aisle

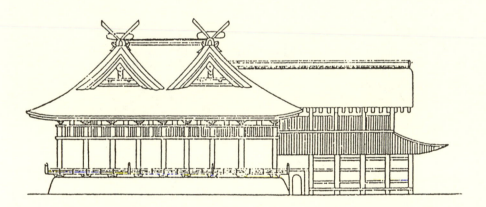

encircled by a balustraded veranda. It sits on a raised base called a *kame-bara* because it resembles the belly of a turtle. Floors and ceiling heights rise progressively inside the complex. The outer walls are of natural wood; the interior is partly painted in vermilion and partly in black lacquer with occasional gold metal fittings. The roof is thatched with *hiwada* and the ends are finished with *chigi*. Two *Irimoya* roofs are added, which gave rise to the name *hiyoku irimoya* (wings-abreast-*irimoya*).

Nagare

After the arrival of Buddhism, when shrine architecture took on Chinese influence, the subsequently popular *Nagare* style gave roof lines a new flowing form. The best known modern example is the *Meiji Jingū* in Tokyo. The classic *Kamigamo* and *Shimogamo Jinja* in Kyoto date to the seventh century. Compared to the other older shrines, they are relatively small. This suggests their origin as portable shrines (*mikoshi*). The roof sweeps over the stairs and the area in front of the building.

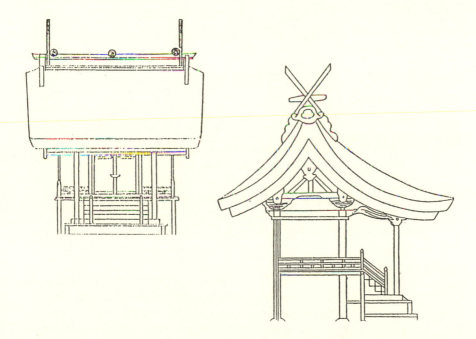

Otori

This is a variation of *Sumiyoshi,* but with three posts on the long side and an inner and outer sanctuary layout. The original *Otori Jinja* in Osaka (which legend dates to the time of Emperor Keiko) was burned down in 1905. The design includes a *honden* and a *norito-den*; but, like *Sumoyoshi,* it has no veranda. There are two doors and a staircase at the front, as in the *Taisha* style. Enshrined is Otori-no-Muraji, who has been identified

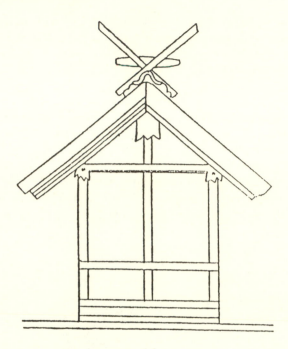

with Yamato-Takeru-no-mikoto (according to shrine publications) and with Ameno-Koyane-no-mikoto.

Shinmei

This is associated particularly with *Ise Jingū*[14] and is marked by the extra-large *chigi* and the ten *katsuogi* that line the roof. The *Naikū* (inner shrine) is consecrated to Amaterasu, the *kami* of the sun (hence the name "divine brightness"), and the *Gekū* (outer shrine) enshrines the *kami* of grain, Toyōke-no-kami. This establishes a direct connection with the *Takaya* style and its function. The buildings at Ise are erected according to design instructions that, until 1945, could not be imitated in order to preserve the sanctity of their character. The Grand Shrines of Ise are the finest and only surviving example of *Yuiitsu Shinmei* (unique *shinmei*), assuming that in ancient times there may have been others like it. Legends have the *Naikū* being moved from Kasanui near Nara in March, 5 B.C., and the *Gekū* from Tamba near Kyoto in 478 B.C. The *shikinen-sengū* (rebuilding) requires 200,000 craftsmen; in 1993 it cost approximately U.S. $30 million to complete, almost all subscribed voluntarily.

The building is surrounded by a veranda on four sides with a wooden staircase up to it. To support the projecting roof, two pillars—sometimes called *mune-mochi-hashira* (ridge-supporting pillar), *osa-hashira* (small lying-between pillar), or *futa-hashira* (two pillars)—right and left, go through the veranda. One explanation of these is the idea of using a tree as it stood. The *shin-no-mihashira* (heart pillar) is a large log standing under the center of the floor. The pedimental roof is thatched with *kaya* and the edge is covered by a *hafuri-ita,* a dust board, to which the *katsuogi* and *chigi* are attached.

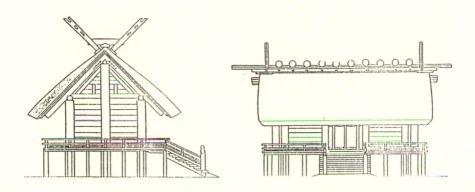

Atsuta Jingū in Nagoya is a distinctive example of *Shinmei* in that it is long in frontage and short in depth. The lower part of its pillars (larger than the upper) is buried deep in the ground. It enshrines Atsuta-no-kami along with Amaterasu, Susano-o-no-mikoto, and Yamato-takeru-no-mikoto, the possessor of the Imperial sword who died in the vicinity. Originally built in the *Taisha* style, the shrine was rebuilt in 1893 and then again in 1935 in *Shinmei* style. It was partially destroyed during World War II but was refurbished in 1955. The land area is 200,000 square meters, including small groves of camphor trees more than 1,000 years old.[15]

Sumiyoshi

One suggested origin of the style is the temporary buildings of that period erected for special festivals. *Taisha zukuri* is quite different but, like *Taisha,* eventually came to be a title of rank rather than design. Not all shrines bearing the title *Taisha,* such as *Kasuga Taisha,* are in *Taisha* style.

Sumiyoshi is similar to, but larger in appearance than, *Otori. Sumiyoshi* is longer in depth, its plane is oblong rather than square, and it has an inner and outer building. It is constructed of straight line timbers and has

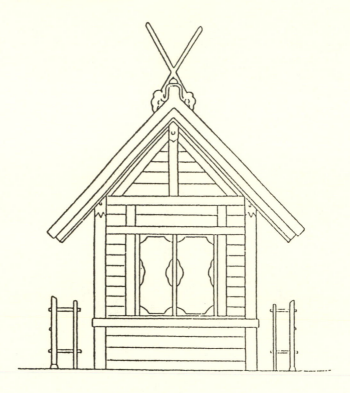

neither veranda nor central pillar but is surrounded by a low wooden fence. The roof is gabled and supported by large round posts and is marked by tall ornamental *chigi* and *katsuogi*. The *honden* doors face and open to the front. The head shrine in Osaka is made up of four buildings and was last rebuilt in 1708. It is a guardian shrine for the ocean and for sea-faring people; it rose to fame because of its association with Empress Jingu.[16]

Taisha

Izumo Taisha was modeled on palaces built by powerful lords and re-ferred to in the mythology of the Kofun period. The present buildings at Izumo date to 1744 and, like *Ise Jingū*, are made of undecorated natural wood.

The *Taisha* style consists of four compartments surrounded by a balus-trated veranda. Its most distinctive feature is the large central pillar, the *shin*, or *kokoro-no-hashira* (heart pillar), and the *daikoku hashira* (throne pillar), over one meter in diameter. To the right, facing the side of the

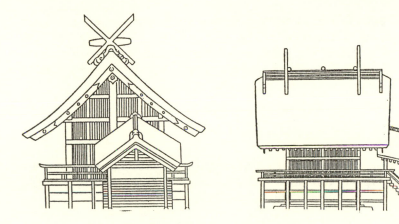

building, is the entrance with a steep wooden staircase. The *kami* nation-wide are thought to go to Izumo in October for matchmaking. The great festivals of *kami-ai-sai* and *kami-ari-sai* are celebrated there.

Yatsu-Mune

Yatsu-mune means "eight-roofed" style. Both sides of the *haiden* have a small "wing" roof attached to the main roof, whose style follows *Gongen*. Most *Yatsu-mune* shrines have either five or seven roofs. The term *eight* follows the Chinese usage (as in "eight-fathomed palace") to mean large. The *Kitano Tenmangū* of Kyoto is perhaps the best example of *Yatsu-mune* architecture. Built in 1607, it enshrines Sugawara Michizane (844–903)[17] as Tenjin, the *kami* of learning. One special feature of the design is a room between the *honden* and the *haiden* known as the *ishi-no-ma* (room of stone). Some scholars think that the two buildings were originally separated by an open space, which later came to be a room (hence the other name,

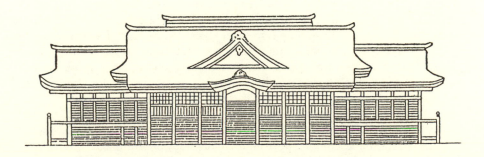

ishi-no-ma-zukuri). The style of the *Kitano Tenmangū* has been replicated in other shrines such as the *Hokoku Jinja* in Kyoto, which enshrines Hideyoshi, and the *Osaki Hachiman* in Sendai. After the construction of the *Tōshō-gū* in Nikko, *Gongen* became a general term for that style along with *Yatsu-mune* and *Ishi-no-ma-zukuri.*

THE TORII

The *torii* marks the entrance to the sacred grounds of a shrine. There are a variety of types of *torii,* each with a unique history. Regardless of origin, the *torii* is inseparably identified with the image of Shinto.

Meaning of Torii

The word *torii* seems to be ancient Japanese, as is the concept itself. However, an accurate account of its etymology is uncertain. Several solutions may be considered,[18] although none seems very credible. The origin of the name and the idea itself is probably best left open to debate.

Development of the Torii

The oldest *torii,* such as at Ise, were made of plain unpainted *hinoki* or other native trees. From the Nara period, in keeping with changes in shrine buildings, red became common and *torii* came to be made of stone. Bronze, iron, and even porcelain came into use during the Tokugawa period (1603–1867), although the latter proved not to be durable. Concrete *torii* have been built, sometimes to minimize cost but often to meet the requirements of fire regulations as well.

The *torii* need not match the architectural style, although they often do. Some styles of architecture have no matching *torii*; some *torii* styles have no matching shrines. Straight-lined buildings are usually accompanied by straight-lined *torii,* but exceptions may be found. Reasons may vary from the wishes of a donor to the feeling of a priest as to the kind of atmosphere, spiritual energy, or aesthetic impact that a *torii* should have.

Some shrines may have only one *torii*; larger shrines may have several at different stages on the *sandō,* the winding road leading to the shrine buildings. *Torii* may also stand at a distance from a shrine, or even mark the extent of the shrine's territory. They may also be used to mark sacred rocks or trees, by being placed in front of them. *Inari Jinja* are famous for the large numbers of red *torii* that line the road to the buildings; the *torii* are usually presented by shrine supporters. The world of the *torii* exhibits all the fascination and complexity found throughout *Shinto* itself.

Elements of the Torii

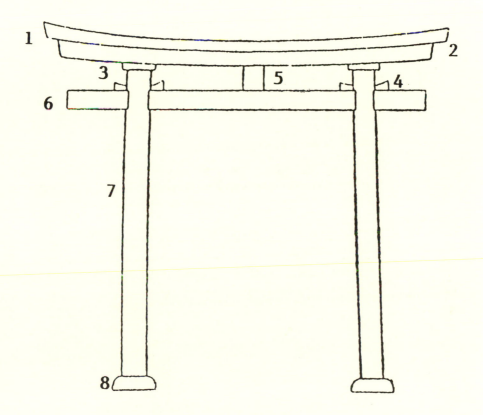

1. *kasagi*—upper cross beam
2. *shimagi*—under upper beam
3. *daiwa*—upper cross beam rest
4. *kusabi*—lower cross beam wedges
5. *gakuzuka*—tablet or inscription holder
6. *nuki*—lower cross beam
7. *hashira*—vertical beams
8. *kamebara*—vertical beam supports

TORII STYLES

Churen

This name also reads *shimenawa torii* and is probably one of the oldest styles, consisting simply of two posts with a rope tied loosely across the top.

Hachiman

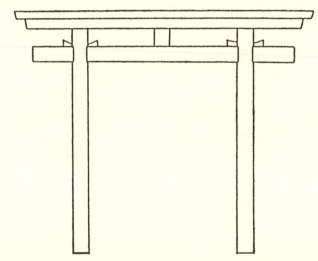

The formal *Hachiman* style originated during the Heian period (794–1185) and is closely modeled on the *Kasuga torii*. The *kasagi* and the *shimagi* are cut slantwise. Not all Hachiman shrines, however, have a *Hachiman torii*. Many have a *Ryōbu torii*.

Inari

This first appeared during the late Heian period. It is also called the *Daiwa torii*, named from the round *daiwa* that support the *Ishimagi* and

the *kasagi*. The *Fushimi Inari Jinja* in Kyoto is famous for the large numbers of *torii* within its grounds, only a few of which are actually *Inari*.

Ise

The *Ise torii* is also called the *Jingū torii* because it is associated only with *Ise Jingū*. It follows the same pattern as *shinmei*, except that the *kasagi*

is pentagonal and there are two *kusabi* holding the *nuki* in place. The *kamebara* is made up of pebbles from the bed of the nearby Isuzu River, which runs beside the *Naigū*. This is found only at the *Naigū*, the inner shrine; the *Gekū*, the outer shrine, has a *torii* with no pebbles around the base.

Karahafu

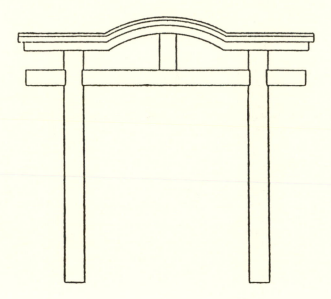

Kara meant "something new" (from China) and could be taken to be an innovative development of the *Kasuga torii*. It stands in front of the *Itsukushima Jinja* in the grounds of the Imperial Palace in Kyoto. Taira-no-Kiyamori (1117–1181) is said to have designed it. Its stone suggests that it predates the sixteenth century. The style is also known as *Tohafu*.

Kashima

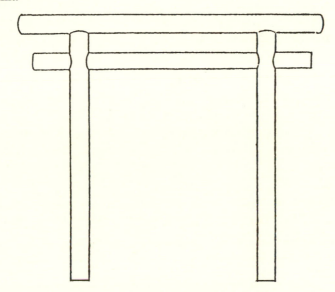

The *Kashima* style is associated with the *Kashima Jingū* in Ibaraki. It is also found frequently in the area surrounding the *Kashima Jingū*.

Kasuga

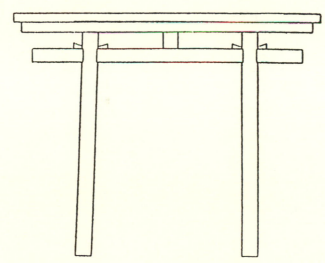

The *Kasuga torii* was the first to be painted red and the first to be seen with the *shimagi,* the under upper cross beam, at *Kasuga Taisha.* The double-wedged *nuki* goes through the *hashira.* The Chinese-influenced decoration of the shrine dates to 768.

Kuroki

The "wild tree" is probably the most primitive and simple entirely wooden form, made of unscraped bark. The *nuki* is attached firmly across and between the *hashira* but does not break into them. *Nonomiya Jinja* to

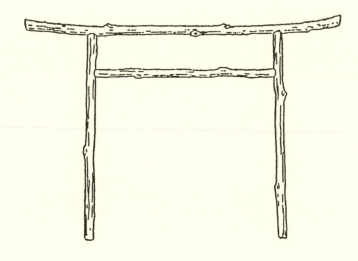

Amaterasu (located in a bamboo grove) has such a *torii.* It was the place designated for the worship of Amaterasu by an Imperial Princess appointed as *saiō* of the *Ise Jingū* after a three-year period of purification.

Mibashira

The design is made up of three *Kasuga torii* joined to produce a three-legged (*sankyaku*) *torii.* The best example, built in granite, is found on a small piece of land in a pond beside the *Kijima Jinja* in northwest Kyoto.

There is another a good example in the Ukyo ward of Kyoto at the *Konoshima Jinja*. The style is sometimes known as *Sanchu*.

Miwa

The triple composition of the *torii* at the *Omiwa Jinja* near Nara suggests its other names: *Sankō* (three lights), *Waki* (side), and *Komochi torii* (parent with child). It dates from the twelfth century and is found both with

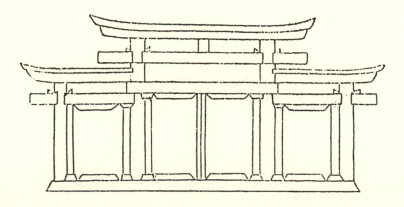

and without doors. The enshrined *kami* of the *Omiwa Jinja* is Omono-nishi-no-mikoto, the guardian *kami* of *sake*-makers.

Munetada

The *Munetada* is the last of the oldest type of *torii* that made use of straight lines, although there is a slight hint of a change of form. The best

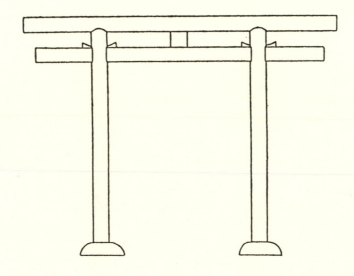

example is the second *torii* on the *Munedata Jinja sandō* on Yoshida Hill in Kyoto. Munetada Kurozumi (1779–1850) founded *Kurozumi-kyō*, an Edo period Shinto sect.

Myōjin

The "gracious *kami*" style is probably one of the most fashionable and commonly found styles in shrines throughout the country. It stands on a

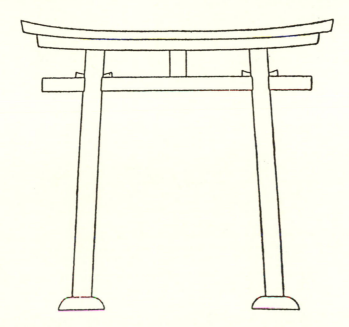

low stone base instead of being buried directly in the ground. The *Kamo Jinja* in Kyoto and the *Meiji Jingū* in Tokyo have excellent *Myōjin torii*.

Naigu-gen

This style resembles the *Ise torii* except that is *hashira* are octagonal. The prime example is the *Daigengū-Jingū* in Kyoto.

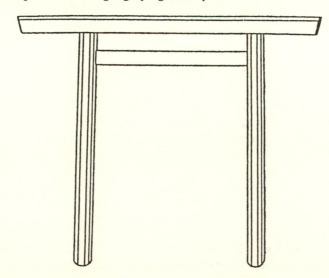

Nakayama

The *Nakayama torii* is not well known. The main *Nakayama Jinja* is in the village of Ichinomiya in Okayama. The *torii* is over 9 meters tall and

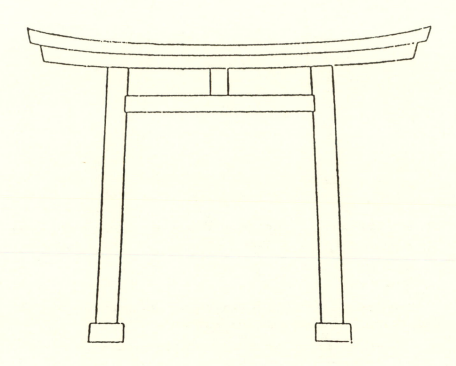

was erected in 1791. The *Kasagi* and *shimagi* are curved, but the *nuki*— which does not penetrate the *hashira*—is straight. The *honden* was completed 1559 and enshrines Kanayama-hiko-no-mikoto.

Nemaki

Nemaki means "wrapping the foot," so named probably because the bottom part of the posts are wrapped in wood or stone to prevent decay. The wrapped part is always painted black; the rest is red or vermilion. There is often an extra covering above the *kasagi,* which is painted black also. The *Fushimi Inari Jinja* of Kyoto has a *Nemaki*-style *torii.*

Nune

No specimens of this exist at present, but it is found frequently in art and is considered quite unusual. It is similar to *Inari* with the addition of two angled posts built in to the *gakuzuka*.

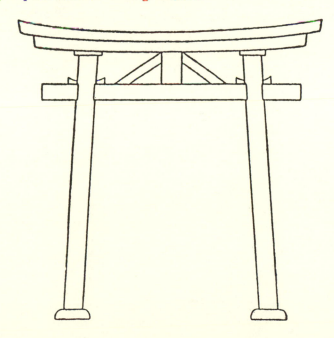

Ryōbu

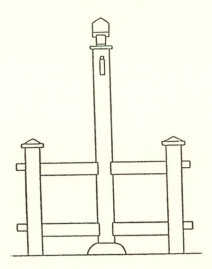

This style is associated with dual Shinto and is distinctive because it has additional support in front of and behind the *hashira*. It is also called the *Shikyaku* (four-legged), the *Gongen,* the *Sode* (sleeve), or the *Waku* (framed) *torii*. The best example, commonly seen in brochures, is the *Itsu-kushima Jinja torii* on the sacred island of Miyajima in the inland sea. Last rebuilt in 1875, it stands in the ocean and towers 18 meters in height.

Sannō

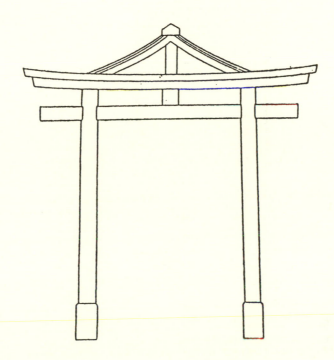

The *Sannō* style is unusual because of its peaked top (*gashho,* "a joining of hands") above the *kasagi.* It has a rain cover called the *urako* with a *tokin* on the top, like the hat worn by *yamabushi.* The best example is at the *Hie Jinja* near Lake Biwa. It is sometimes called the *Sogo* (synthetic), the *Gassho,* or the *Hie torii.*

Shinmei

The style of "divine brightness" clearly reflects the *Kuroki* style. The absence in both *Shinmei* and *Kuroki* of the *gakuzuka* is evidence that they predate Chinese influences.

Shinmon

Some shrines, like the *Nikkō Tōshōgū,* have a *shinmon* (*kami*-gate) rather than a *torii.* This is common in *jingū-ji* (shrine-temples) of *Tendai Shinto* or *Shingon Shinto,* which combine Buddhism and Shinto. In the right and left alcoves of some of these *shinmon* may be seen the *Ya-Daijin,* the arrow ministers of state who guard against misfortune. The figures also represent two *kami,* Toyo-Iwamado-no-kami and Kushi-iwamado-no-kami, who are thought to be the sons of Futodama-no-mikoto. They are also sometimes taken to be Ame-no-oshihi-no-mikoto and Ame-no-tsukume-no-mikoto, who guided the descent of Ninigi-no-mikoto to the Land of Reed Plains. The overlap of Buddhism and Shinto accounts for the multiple identity. There are various styles of gates according to the main architectural style of the buildings themselves. The principal ones are as follows:

Rōmon: This is a general term for gate as well as the term used to identify the special gate used by *chokushi.*

Sōmon: This usually refers to the outer gate or the first gate after the outer one.

Yotsu-ashi-mon: The name designates the style of four round pillars holding the gate.

Yatsu-ashi-mon: This style has eight square pillars to support the four round pillars to which the door is attached.

Kara-mon: *Kara* (Chinese) style has gates at both front and rear, as well as at right and left. It came into use during the Kamakura age.

Zuijin-mon: This is the gate style that enshrines the guardian *kami* of the gate, one on the right side and one on the left. These were originally Buddhist *Ni-O*; but after the separation of Buddhism and Shinto, in many cases they were replaced by *kami* dressed in Heian Court style.

Where there is more than one gate, they are normally identified as follows:

Ita-gaki: outer gate
Soto-tama-gaki: first inner gate
Uchi-tama-gaki: second inner gate
Mizu-gaki: third inner gate[19]

Sumiyoshi

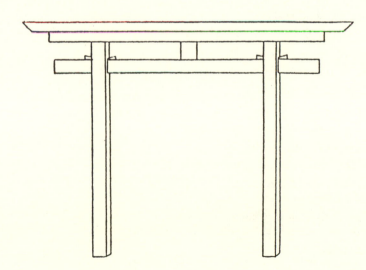

The *Sumiyoshi torii* is distinctive because the *hashira* are square, an unusual feature in a *torii*.

SHRINE GROUNDS

In addition to the *shaden* and *torii,* there are many other features of shrine grounds. None are purely decorative. They all have a symbolic meaning related to the worship of the *kami* and have been added at various stages in the development of Shinto and each individual shrine.

Layout of Ise no Ichinomiya, Tsubaki Dai Jinja—Mie Prefecture

Tsubaki Grand Shrine is one of the oldest sacred places in Japan. It boasts the Iwakura no Mifune, where Ninigi no Mikoto, grandson of the *kami* of the sun, first set foot on earth after his descent from the high plain of heaven. The enshrined *kami*, Sarutahiko Okami is head of the earthly *kami*. His wife, Ame-uzumo-no-mikoto, performed the famous dance that enticed Amaterasu, the *kami* of the sun, out of hiding to restore light to the world. The incumbent priest, Guji Yamamoto Yukitaka, is the ninety-sixth generation of the Yamamoto family to be high priest of the Shrine. While the shrine grounds have features that are unique to its history, it follows the pattern of most shrines.

1. Mt. Nyuodogatake
2. Kunimi Peak
3. Tsubaki (Camellia) Peak
4. Mountain trails used to climb the mountain for purification—a five-hour climb.
5. Onbe River
6. Konryu Myōjin Waterfall (used for purification rituals of *misogi shuhō*)
7. Honden (inner sanctuary)
8. Haiden (worship sanctuary)
9. Heiden or Kaguraden (outer sanctuary)
10. Shamushō (Shrine offices)
11. Side Sanctuary to Ame-uzume-no-mikoto
12. Tea House (presented by the late Matsushita Konosuke of Matsushita Electronics Corporation)
13. Grave of Sarutahiko Okami (Graves are not found in shrines because of the impurity associated with death. This may not apply in the case of a *kami*.)
14. Iwakura no Mifune
15. List of shrine donors
16. Shishi Koma Inu
17. Gyōmandō for performance of Shinto/Buddhist rituals
18. Purification Hall

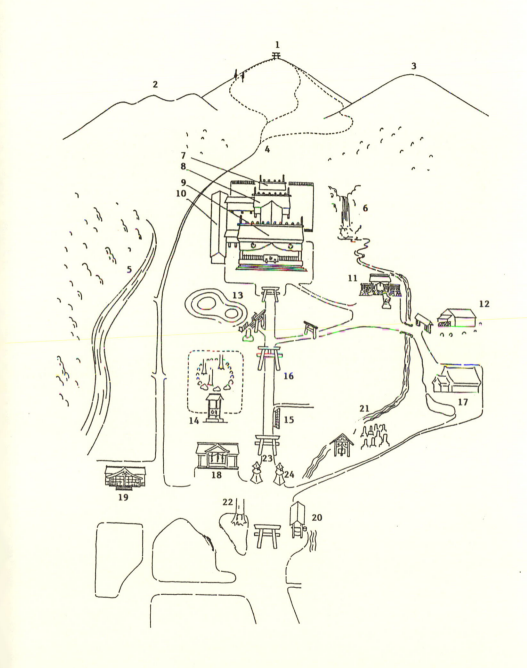

19. Sanshuden
20. Te-mizuya (Ablution Pavilion)
21. Daimyōjin River
22. Shimboku (the sacred tree, a 900-year-old Japanese cypress, or *hinoki*)
23. Omote Sandō (main approach to shrine buildings)
24. Tora (stone lanterns)

Shimenawa

The twisted rope marks out a place, object, or person that is sacred, has been purified and freed of pollution, and thereby is frequently renewed. Its origin is traced to the rope placed in front of the *Ame-no-iwato* in which

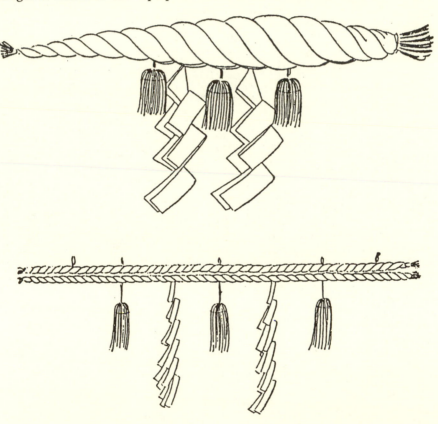

Amaterasu hid herself. The first part of the rope to be woven is placed on the right, because the left side is considered of higher rank than the right. The rope is woven to the left; and from it, seven, five, and three strips of straw may be hung. The seven, five, and three are sometimes taken to mean the three *kami* of creation and the seven heavenly and five earthly *kami*, although this is speculation. Between these, *Yu-shide* or *Gohei,* zig-zag shaped folded paper strips, are hung as symbolic offerings to the *kami.*

Shishi Koma Inu

Shishi means "lion" and *Koma Inu* means "dog from Koma," a district of ancient Korea. They are taken sometimes as lions or dogs, sometimes as both. They stand a short distance inside the *sandō* behind the main *torii.* There are several variations. Sometimes both have horns, sometimes neither has. Sometimes both are open-mouthed or closed-mouthed. Most frequently, one mouth is open and one shut. They are usually made of stone but in some cases of bronze or wood. Their role is perceived to parallel the *Ni-O* at Buddhist temples, namely, to prevent bad spirits from entering the shrine precincts.

One improbable explanation of their origin is that they were introduced after the subjugation of Korea by Empress Jingu as a mark of the willingness of the Korean people to serve Japan as faithfully as a dog. Equally far-fetched is the suggestion that Empress Jingu's expedition was led by a dog, which became the symbol of victory. In the Chinese Court, figures of lions and dogs stood at the right and left of bamboo or silk screens to prevent them from moving in the wind. The Chinese also often placed such creatures at the entrances to important buildings. Either of these latter accounts is more plausible.

Toro

Within the ground of every shrine are numerous large standing lanterns (*toro*) which, like many other items within shrine precincts, are gifts of donors or parishioners who wish to contribute to the support of the shrine.

Ishi-toro   Kane-toro   Kane-toro   Tsuri-toro

There are several types of *toro*. The most common are made of stone, although they can be made of metal, wood, or a combination of materials. There are also hanging types. The wooden ones tend to resemble nine-teenth-century gas streetlights; they have rectangular frames on top of large thin poles and are frequently painted red. They may also bear the names of the corporation or individuals who donated them. Originally designed to bear live flames, most are now lit by electricity. At night they give shrine precincts a distinctive atmosphere and contribute significantly to their aesthetic appearance.

Additional Buildings and Artifacts

Numerous other buildings are found among the *shaden* within shrine grounds. The names of the principal ones may vary from one locality another, but the following are the most commonly used designations:

Kagura-den: The building or raised platform on which *kagura* (sacred dance) is performed.

Gishiki-den: This is where weddings or other such events are celebrated. In some shrines the *haiden* and *heiden* serve the same functions as the *kagura-den* and *gishiki-den*.

Shamushō: Shrine business office.

Harae-dō: Place of purification.

Te-miuzu-ya: Trough for washing the hands and mouth upon entering the precincts of a shrine. Long-handled ladles called *haidatsu* sit on it.

Saikan: Place for the purification of priests prior to the performance of ceremonies.

Shinsen-den: The sacred kitchen in which the food offerings to the *kami* are ceremonially prepared.

Homotsu-den: The repository of all sacred or valuable artifacts belonging to the shrine.

Mikoshi-gura: The building where the portable shrine (*mikoshi*) is housed between festivals.

Kiyome-no-ike: In addition to buildings, many shrines have a small pond, sometimes known as a *kiyome-no-ike* (pond of purification), probably a lingering reminder of the origins of all Shinto rituals in lustration.

Hashi: There may be a bridge across the pond, frequently in the *Taiko* style, rounded like a drum. One of the most famous examples is found inside the grounds of the *Sumiyoshi Taisha* in Osaka. The grounds of most shrines are either designed in garden form or have a garden within them.

Sandō: The approach road to the shrine precincts, which is normally curved at some point so that the retreating worshipper does not turn his or her back on the *kami*. Some *sandō* are old and very long. *Ōmote Sandō* in central Tokyo's

Harajuku district is the main approach road to the *Meiji Jingū*. The *sandō* of the *Hikawa Jinja* in Ōmiya City runs through the center of the town. Shops now rent land for business along it, but the sacred trees cannot be removed. The shops are built around the trees, which protrude through the roofs and make a most unusual sight.

Bunsha and Massha: Branch Shrines and Side Shrines

Most major shrines have branches for the creation of which the spirit, or *mitama,* of the *kami* is divided. Shinto thought sees the spirit of the *kami* on an analogy with fire. Fire is not diminished by being divided. Neither is the *kami*. The four principal designations are as follows:

Bekkū (betsu-gū): "independent shrine"

Bunsha: "separated shrine"

Massha: sometimes understood as *matsu-sha,* "branch shrine"

Sessha: sometimes understood as *setsu-sha,* "embraced-shrine"

The first two are usually independently established shrines in a location separate from the head shrine; the second two are subsidiary shrines within the precincts of a large one.

The term *wakamiya* is used to denote shrines in which the multiplied spirit of a *kami* is enshrined. There are three main varieties, although there are many local variations. There are *wakamiya* in which the *kami* is that of the main shrine. There are those in which the *kami* is or are the offspring of the *kami* of the main shrine; and there are those in which the angry *mitama* of the *kami* is pacified.

Yashikigami and Kamidana

The *yashikigami* and the *kamidana* are found in and around dwelling places. The *yashikigami* (*kami* of the house) is usually found in a miniature shrine standing in a propitious corner of the courtyard or grounds of a large house. Traditionally, these exist for the veneration of household ancestors along with the spirit of the land *kami*. The *kamidana* (*kami* shelf) inside the building is a miniature shrine/altar usually brought from the shrine to which the house is attached as an *ujiko*. These can also be seen inside Japanese-style restaurants (especially *sushi* restaurants), company offices, railway stations, police stations, timber yards, and particularly on the premises of any of the traditional trades or occupations of Japan (e.g., carpentry, entertainment, or *sake*-brewing). Each has its guardian *kami* as well as the district ones; consequently, the *kamidana* may enshrine more than one *kami*. The *yashikigami* and *kamidana* should be treated like normal shrines and should receive fresh *shinsen* every day, particularly rice, water, salt, and *sake*. Various items may be changed at each New Year, such as the *shimenawa*. Normally a priest makes an annual visit to attend to them and to offer a small festival to the *bunrei,* the divided spirit of the *kami.*

NOTES

1. See the discussion of "Kami Associated with Natural Phenomena" in Chapter 4 of this book.

2. Architecture in Christian churches reflects cultural traditions ranging from Byzantine, Baroque, and Gothic to the austerity of the Reformed tradition. Layout may reflect different theologies of the sacraments, but they neither determine nor indicate which divine being is worshipped. It is thus possible to discuss church architecture in a general way. In the case of *jinja shaden,* the format of the buildings is derived from a complex of historical associations, including the *kami* enshrined.

3. Divination of locations (*uranai*) by geomantic methods continues not only in the Imperial Household. In 1986 the residents of Motherwell, an industrial town south of Glasgow in Scotland, were surprised when officials from Kibun, a food company that was planning to open a factory nearby, chose their site after two Shinto priests in full *shozoku* performed *oharai* and released two wild geese to determine the most propitious location.

4. Removal of a shrine can be thought to be disastrous, because the community loses its *kami*. Owing to soaring land prices in central Tokyo, the *Hakkan Jinja* on Ginza's Namiki Dori was forced to rethink its location in the mid-1980s. It was a shrine to which businessmen came by day and entertainers by night, seeking good fortune. A building was erected on top of which the *shaden* were reconstructed, connected to the earth below by a pipe that linked the *shaden* with the soil upon which they formerly stood! The *Jinja Honchō* did not approve of this unusual idea.

5. See the Chart of the Development of Shinto in Chapter 1 of this book.

6. Among the oldest of these is the *Tsubaki Dai Jinja,* which I have already discussed.

7. See the discussion of "Shrine Statistics and Ranks within the Kokka Shinto System" in Chapter 1 of this book.

8. Natural materials (normally *hinoki,* Japanese cypress) are used. I wrote in my previous book that I had seen Buddhist temples in concrete but never a shrine. However, fire regulations in Tokyo required that the *Karasumori Jinja* in Shimbashi be rebuilt in concrete. The name means "forest of crows," which may suggest what Shimbashi looked like a couple of centuries ago. Today, not only are there no crows, but there are no trees and the shrine sits on a much smaller plot of land between numerous large buildings. Considering land values in central Tokyo, is this evidence of the sacredness of shrine lands?

9. In addition to materials published by individual shrines, my sources on *shaden zukuri* and *torii* included Yamauchi Akira, *Jinja Kensetsu* (Jinja Shimpo, Tokyo, 1937), an older text that is interesting because it effectively relates the shape

of shrines to mountains. It was written before World War II, when accounts of Japan's sacred places were not permitted to raise sensitive issues about origins outside of the Japanese archipelago. Useful as a source in English, but equally dated, is Akiyama Aisaburo, *Shinto and Its Architecture* (Kyoto Welcome Society, Kyoto, 1936).

10. In the middle of the parking lot at the Tokyo Airport at Haneda, there is the red *torii* of a shrine. The shrine was removed to make way for the buildings and the runway. Various disasters took place after the airport opened, which were attributed to the distressed *kami*. Although new shrine buildings had been erected nearby, it was decided to pacify the *kami* by replacing the *torii*.

11. See Yamauchi, *Jinja Kensetsu*, pp. 44 ff, on *Tenchi-Gongen* and *Takakuya*. The *Asahi Shimbun* of 22 May 1992 reported the finding of the oldest yet *Takakuya* artifact in Japanese cypress at Shimomagari in Shiga Prefecture, dating to the early third century.

12. Watanabe Yasutada, *Nihon no Bijutsu Series Ise to Izumo* (Shinto Art: Ise and Izumo Shrines), Heibonsha Survey of Japanese Art, Vol. 3 (Weatherhill, Tokyo, 1974), pp. 104 hr ff, discusses the origins of shrine buildings.

13. *Nihongi*, XIV: 6 and 39–41.

14. On *Ise Jingū* see also Vol. 18 of the Shogakkan Series on *Meiho Nihon no Bijutsu* by Soga Tetsuo on *Ise to Nikkō* (Shogakkan, Tokyo, 1982), pp. 1–28. The text also contains an excellent discussion of the origins of the structures of *shaden* and *torii*, along with seventy pages of illustrations. The section on Nikkō should be consulted for details on *Gongen-zukuri*. See also Watanabe Yoshio, *Jingū to Ise-Shi, Nihon no Bijutsu*, Vol. 12 (Sueisha, Tokyo, 1979).

15. On *Atsuta Jingū*, apart from the shrine's own publications (issued around 1940) there is a study by Shinoda Yasuo, *Atsuta Jingū* (Gakuseisha, Tokyo, 1968).

16. See the discussion of "Sumiyoshi Taisha" in Chapter 4 of this book.

17. See the discussion of "Kami Derived from Historical Personalities" in Chapter 4 of this book.

18. Possible explanations are (1) that in ancient times, it may have been the gateway to ordinary dwelling houses using existing trees. It would not, therefore, be stylized as it came to be in later times. It could also have been the gate of the fence that surrounded some ancient houses. (2) It has been linked to the *Ame-no-iwato* in which Amaterasu hid in anger. One version of how she was induced to come out involved the building of a wooden frame where cocks could perch and crow. *Torii* thus become *tori* (bird) and *i* as a shortened version of the term *iru*, meaning "to be." (3) *Torii* as "bird" and *iru* as "enter" suggest the place where people entered and birds perched (birds were used to tell the time). (4) It has been suggested that the term comes from the Chinese character for "heaven" (*Ten* in Japanese and *T'ien* in Chinese). This is unlikely, because *torii* were erected before the arrival of Chinese characters into Japanese culture.

19. These names may vary locally. In the case of *Izumo Taisha*, for example, they are called respectively *ara-gaki*, *mizu-gaki*, *tama-gaki*, and *suki-bei*.

Chapter 6

Rituals, Festivals (Matsuri), Liturgies (Norito), and the Shinto Priesthood

RITUALS AND OHARAI

The main rituals of Shinto center around the concepts of *tsumi* (impurity) and its removal by *oharai* (purification.)[1]

Tsumi (Impurity)

Tsumi has a broad range of meanings including "pollution," "sickness," and "disaster," as well as "error." Certain actions, situations, or uninvited circumstances can cause impurity and must be dealt with by avoidance or by ritual purification. Two broad categories of *tsumi* may be distinguished, although within them can be found many specific kinds.

Ama-tsu-tsumi. Corresponding to the *Ama-tsu-kami,* the heavenly *kami,* there are *Ama-tsu-tsumi,* or heavenly impurities. These are typified by the outrageous behavior of the *kami* of the stars, Susano-o-no-mikoto, which was so offensive to Amaterasu.

Kuni-tsu-tsumi. Corresponding to the *kuni-tsu-kami,* the earthly *kami,* there are *Kuni-tsu-tsumi,* or earthly impurities. These include afflicting injury or death, immodest behavior, the use of magic, certain contagious diseases, damage done by harmful birds, wounds (*kega*),[2] and other things that may be beyond human control. Human beings may be morally responsible for some of these, but for most they are not. Herein lies the important difference between *tsumi* (often incorrectly translated as "sin") and "sin" referring to actions or conditions for which people may be held morally responsible (assuming that the doctrine of original sin is not considered a philosophy of moral determinism). Impurities in Japan include things that happen to people that can damage their lives, whether they will them or not.[3]

Magatsuhi-no-kami. There are also *Magatsuhi-no-kami* of temptation (from the land of *Yomi*) whose influence can only be dispelled by the *kami* of purification, the *naobi-no-kami*.[4]

Harai (Purification)

The only method of removing *sumi* is purification, or *harai*, which takes three basic forms:[5]

1. *Harai* is performed by a priest using a *harai-gushi*, a wand of paper streamers that is symbolically waved over the place or person to be purified.

2. *Misogi* involves lustration with water, either by hand, in small buckets, by crouching in a river or in the sea, or by standing under a flowing waterfall. Participants wear a loincloth or kimono-style robe, or are simply naked.

3. *Imi* involves avoidance of certain words or particular actions. For example, the word *kiru* (cut) must never be used at the time of a wedding. The word *deru* (go out) is taboo also. This presents a challenge for the master of ceremonies, who must announce the ceremony of cutting the cake and the ritual going out and coming in of the bride and groom as they change clothes in the ceremony of *ironaoshi*, in language avoiding these terms. People who have suffered a recent bereavement will not attend an occasion of celebration because death is associated with impurity.

Ceremonies of Purification

Priests perform many kinds of purification rituals throughout the year. The principal ones are described here, although others may be performed at the request of parishioners. They are rituals that the priests will travel to perform.

Jichin-sai (ground-pacify-festival). This is the ceremony of ground-breaking in which a priest will "pacify" the *kami* of the ground where a new building is to be erected. He will first set up a *himorogi* (sacred space) bounded by a *shimenawa* (sacred rope) and then perform *oharai*. Such ceremonies are held daily for new projects, new houses, new road works, or construction of any kind. Their purpose is to pacify the *kami* of the area who may be disturbed, and to guarantee the safety from misfortune of all who will work on the project.

Yaku-barai (misfortune-purify). This is the calming of a troublesome *kami*, or the purification of a person to avoid the years of life when disasters most frequently happen. It is sometimes misleadingly translated as "exorcism," a concept that belongs to the Western dualistic system of thought wherein good and evil, God and the Devil, are viewed as rivals battling for the soul of man. No such dichotomy exists in Japanese thought. Even the Buddhist deities of hell were downgraded in significance and softened in appearance after they arrived in Japan. Japanese thought inclines toward monism because of its doctrine of harmony; by contrast, Western thought inclines toward dualism, making use of the dialectic of confrontation for the development of new ideas and the enactment of social change. The Japanese, however, do believe in the realities of misfortune and calamity and try to ward these off by means of purification ceremonies. The Takashima Daira housing complex in Tokyo experienced a large number of suicides during the early 1970s when people jumped from the roofs to their deaths. Not even barbed wire restrained them. The residents finally arranged for a Shinto priest to perform *yaku-barai* in the center of the area, hoping that the reason for the tragedies would be removed.

The *yaku-doshi* are the years of misfortune in adult life, age thirty-three for women and age forty-two for men. People will go to a shrine for *yaku-barai* to ward off misadventures that may occur during these critical times in life. The sense of auspicious and inauspicious times is deeply ingrained in the Japanese mind, and certain days and dates are avoided (*imi*). Many business corporations follow such practices meticulously even to the present day with regard to the timing of new developments, company events, or overseas trips.

Kotsu Anzen Oharai. Travel safety of all kinds, whether by car, airplane, or bus, may be the subject of purification for the traveler. Cars may be purified at shrines, and bus companies usually have a priest purify new vehicles before they go into service. Northwest Airlines brought its newest and largest 747 jumbo jet to Tokyo in 1988 to exhibit it and have it purified by a priest.

Special Cases of Oharai. Oharai can be performed in different ways and in different seasons. Home-cleaning for New Year is called *susu-harai.* Purification after a death is sometimes called *fujo-harai.* Beginning election campaigns, opening new businesses, inaugurating a new company, cutting the tapes to open a new section of railway—all are occasions when *oharai* is appropriate. The purpose of these exercises is to rid the place, person, or object of impurities that could be causes of misfortune.

Shinzen Kekkon: The Shinto Wedding Ceremony. The central act at a Shinto wedding is the purification of the couple and the families followed by the drinking of *sake* to commune with the *kami* before whom the wedding is contracted. The ritual is still called a wedding; but in its structure it is the same as all Shinto rituals, having purification as its central feature. Otherwise, it follows all the other cultural features of Japanese wedding celebrations. Shinto shrines perform a large percentage of Japan's weddings, in the same way that Buddhism accounts for the bulk of the nation's funerary rites.

Misogi Shuhō: Waterfall Purification. This may also be done in different of ways but is normally performed late at night or at first light of dawn, with the place of purification lit only by a brazier of burning wood. Participants are led by a *michihiko,* who leads the groups through the stages of the ritual. Men normally wear a *fundoshi* (loincloth) and a headband called a *hachimaki.* Women wear the headband and a white *kimono* garment, although the use by women of only the loincloth is not unknown.

After performing various calisthenic exercises to stimulate the soul and prepare it for the ritual, candidates make their way to the fall. The leader performs a number of ritual movements, which include pouring *sake* into the falls and throwing salt into it and upon all those taking part. The leader may also perform several secret hand signs, including one in which the nine squares of existence are cut and rid of impurities. The leader enters the fall first and then, one by one, he directs each person to follow. Each completes the same sequence of actions and steps back into the fall, taking the weight of water on the back of the neck and shoulders. The words "*Harae tamae kiyome tamae rokonshōjo*" are shouted (an invocation to wash away impurities from the soul and from the six elements of the body) until the leader signals the person to come out.

Misogi has been regaining popularity since the end of the Pacific War, when shrines were able once again to perform religious ceremonies. Some shrines have a *misogi-kai,* an association of practitioners who visit the shrine regularly to perform *misogi.* The revival of the religious culture of Shinto and the restoration of its spirituality have been significant features of its development since the postwar Constitution was put in place.

Salt as a Purifying Agent

Salt is also used as an agent of purification. This is because salt water is considered a more powerful agent of purification than ordinary water. Salt is seen in many places and is used on many occasions in Japan. It is used as an offering on Shinto altars along with water and rice. Salt water is consequently also seen as a powerful purifying agent.

Salt is thrown by *Sumo* wrestlers each time they enter the *dohyō,* which is a sacred area. Before each tournament, Shinto priests perform the *Dohyō Matsuri* in which the ring is purified. Offerings from the rituals are buried in the middle between the white lines behind which the wrestlers face each other before each bout begins. One famous *Ōzeki* (junior champion), had a weak knee; and in the preparatory walks to the middle of the ring before the bout began, as well as throwing salt in the air he always threw some on his knee. I have personally seen a baseball team, after a string of defeats, arrange to have salt thrown into the dugout by a priest or even by the manager in the hope of warding off the misfortunes that kept the team from winning.

Everyone who attends a funeral receives, among other items, a small packet of salt for self-purification upon returning home. It is sprinkled over the entrance to the house to prevent the pollution of death from entering the mourners' homes. Restaurants and, not infrequently, bars as well as regular businesses may place two small piles of salt outside their doorway, one on each side, after washing the entranceway and before any customers arrive. It is intended to ensure that good customers will come and that the evening's business will be successful. Doubtless, the ancient property of salt as an astringent is the origin of its use as a purifying agent. Its use as a central item of liturgy is one unique aspect of Shinto and the Japanese tradition that does not find ready parallels in other traditions.

Misogi harai under the waterfall also involves the use of salt. After regular *oharai,* the people taking part move toward the fall and are sprinkled with salt again. They take three mouthfuls of *sake* with salt in it, which are spat out as part of the ceremony to purify the mouth one last time. Japanese *sake* is also a purifying agent used in Shinto rituals and found on the Shinto altar.

Imi

Many ancient customs that continue in contemporary Japanese society lie behind the penchant for choosing good days on the Oriental Zodiac for business trips and important events and for avoiding bad days for weddings or any other significant venture. These are cases of *imi,* the avoidance of high-risk times in favor of times that are conducive to good fortune and prosperity.

ŌHARAE NO KOTOBA AND NORITO

Harai is accompanied by the recitation of a *norito,* or address to the *kami,* consisting of specially chosen words that are designed to have a pleasing sound. This derives from belief in *kotodama,* the mystical and spiritual power residing within words. It is based on the ancient Japanese belief that beautiful words brought about good fortune and words that were the opposite brought about misfortune. Therefore, the choice and the method of reciting words was of the utmost importance. *Imi no kotoba* (words of avoidance) refer to any words or sound that are displeasing to the *kami.*

The model for all *norito* was laid out in the *Engishiki,* a code of regulations and procedures that dates to the tenth century. The first recorded injunction to perform *harai* at a national level is recorded in the *Nihongi* (Book IX), when the widow of Emperor Chuai called for a great purging of offenses at all levels. As a result, on the last days of June and December at shrines throughout the nation and in the Imperial Household the words of the *Ōharae,* or Great Purification, are repeated. The words of the *Ōharae* are a classic of Shinto and have been respected and recited for centuries. Many commentaries have been written on the *Ōharae* from various points of view. It provides information about the background, the culture, and the character of the Japanese of old and indicates where their sensitivities in belief lay. It consists of 900 characters, and performers of Ōharae are required to memorize the entire text.[6]

The goal of oharai in all its forms is the restoration of the state of purity known as seimei-shin (or akaki kiyoki kokoro), the basis of communion with the kami. It is characterized by four conditions of the kokoro (heart): namely, akaki kokoro, a bright heart; kiyoki kokoro, a pure heart; tadashiki kokoro, a correct or just heart; and naoki kokoro, a straight heart. These become the basis of all proper actions and conduct by people duly purified.

SHRINE FESTIVALS

Matsuri

The heart of all Shinto activities and of every shrine is the festival.[7] Thousands are held nationwide every year, ranging in scale and size from the great festivals such as the Chichibu Yo Matsuri in Saitama, which attracts over a quarter of a million people each year, to tiny village festivals that attract only a few hundred local parishioners. Matsuri possesses great breadth of meaning. The word matsurigoto in early times implied government and was the origin of saisei-itchi (unity of worship and government), an idea revived in Kokka Shinto during the nineteenth century and derived from ancient Japan as a sacral society.[8] The Meiji era government was endeavoring to present itself in these terms.

The event at which the community offers its collective worship to the kami is the festival, the organization of which is a major social activity in itself. The council of shrine leaders who take charge of the planning and organization enjoy doing so not just because they are keeping the festival in existence but also because part of the entire festival is intended to perpetuate reverence for the kami and to show the dependence of the community upon its divine protector. Not all shrines organize their own festivals, but large shrines host numerous festivals every year.

The festival is but one part of the annual cycle of events at all shrines throughout the country. Each shrine has its own set of annual events, most of which are related to agriculture, in particular to rice planting, rice protection, and rice gathering. The primary symbolic acts are still performed by the Imperial Family, who plant the first seedlings of the year and harvest the first grains, which are offered to the Imperial divine ancestor, Amaterasu, at the Ise Jingū. Other shrines celebrate in a similar way according to their own local customs, and it is around these that the yearly cycle of events is built.

Structure and Meaning of the Festival

Festivals follow a basic sequence of events to which local communities add particular activities (described subsequently) and a touch of local color depending upon the occasion.[9] No matter the festival and no matter the place, the fundamental sequence of events follows a tripartite structure: the invocation of the *kami,* the offerings to the *kami,* and the final communion with the *kami.*

Invocation of the Kami. This part consists of inviting the *kami* in proper fashion to visit and meet the people. The shrine is specially cleaned and the priests undergo purification before commencing any activities.

Shūbatsu. The priests in full ceremonial dress purify themselves in order to take part in the rituals. The inner building (*honden*) of the shrine complex is opened up and the *goshintai* viewed by the priests. This is performed after purification and is a ritual conducted entirely by the priests themselves, with no lay witnesses present. Sometimes, prior to the purification at the shrine, priests perform *misogi* by throwing buckets of water over themselves, or under a waterfall, in a river, or in the sea, depending upon where the shrine is located. This is called *shubatsu* or *kessai.* Priests are also expected to practice abstinence (*saikai*) before major festivals. Thereafter, the people taking part in the festival are purified so that the *kami* may be ceremonially invoked and invited to come to the shrine.

Opening of the Gate. Along with the participating leading laymen in robes of state, the priests form a procession that moves down the *sandō,* the approach road to the shrine, to meet the *kami* at the appointed place. Here the duly purified laypersons become responsible for transporting the *kami* into the shrine and throughout the community. The *kami* may be borne in a *mikoshi.* The meeting is effected; and the *kami* usually accompanies the procession to the shrine building, where the most sacred place is opened. The community follows the procession to the shrine, each group having assembled in its locality bearing the *kami* to the shrine. When everyone is assembled within the shrine grounds, the next stage of the festival can commence.

Offerings to the Kami. The *kami* is welcomed to the community and by the community, and then offerings are made. The offerings and order of events are as follows:

Shinsen. The offerings usually placed on the altar are rice, salt, water, rice wine (*sake*), rice cakes (*omochi*), fish (usually *tai* sea bream), seaweed (*konbu*), vegetables, grain, and fruit. The *Shinsen* are prepared in a purified and spotlessly clean kitchen called the *Shinsen-den.* There are various kinds, according to the way in which the foods are prepared: *jukusen* is cooked food, *seisen* is raw food, and *sosen* is vegetarian food containing no fish, fowl, or flesh of any kind.

Aisatsu (Greetings). The chief priest (*Gūji*) delivers an address of welcome.

Gifts are presented to the *kami* from the parishioners. These usually include flowers, money in special envelopes, food in rice bags, and *sake* in special drums called *taru*. These are usually on display in the public buildings of the shrine.

Entertainment: Music and Dance, and Martial Arts. Classic forms of entertainment have long been associated with shrine festivals. Although they are often performed in different places, their roots lie in Shinto rituals. There are two main categories: music and dance activities, and sports activities.

Music and dance include several separate forms that are arts in their own right. *Kagura* is a classical Japanese dance performed by shrine maidens (*miko*). Dances have a central place in Japanese religion; it was a dance that enticed Amaterasu out of the cave. The Chinese characters are *kami* plus "happy." Among the other dances seen at festivals is the *shishi-mai,* known also as the lion dance. It is performed as an act of purification and as the central event in the life of some shrines, taking place once only every two or three years. Several men or youths are under a long sheet, which becomes the body. One is inside the large wooden head. To the music of the *fue* and the rhythm of drum beats, the lion performs a sequence of dances. The animal portrayed need not be a lion but is usually described as such. In fact, in various parts of the country it may take a quite different form. The dance itself probably originated in China, where the creature in question was a dragon. Sometimes the lion mask has horns or is identified with the deer (suggesting a Buddhist influence).

During the festivals themselves, when the wagons are being drawn through the streets, various musical activities take place. There may even be a kind of "musicians' loft," a raised platform on which costumed musicians beat the *taiko* drums and blow flutes until they are exhausted by keeping alive the rhythm and atmosphere of the festival.

Bugaku is another genre of classical Japanese dance with special music. The instruments used here and in *gagaku* are described later in this chapter under "Ritual Instruments and Utensils."

The entire cycle of *Noh* drama has its roots in Shinto. *Kami* are portrayed in the introductions to the various epics.

As in other cultures, martial arts provide opportunities to select the fittest and strongest men in each category. They are also staged for the entertainment of the *kami. Yabusame* is costumed mounted archery from horseback at standing targets. The importance of the *hama* (arrow) and its power to break misfortune is underlined in this sport. *Budō* includes martial arts such as *Kendō,* Japanese sword-fencing; or *Sumo,* Japanese wrestling. Although in the later twentieth century it has become a televised sport in its own right, the Shinto associations of *Sumo* remain.

Removal of the Shinsen. The offerings are removed from the altar and taken away for various uses. Sometimes they are used by the priests or given away. Sometimes they are consumed at the *naorai* or given to parishioners to take home.

Closing of the gate. The main events involving the priests conclude with the closing of the gate and the consequent closing of the inner sanctum. The priests have finished their work, and there remains only the sacramental act of drinking *sake* with the *kami* to bring everything to an end.

Communion with the Kami (Naorai). Casks of *sake* are broken open and drunk from a wooden *masu*, a square cup made of Japanese cypress. This gives the *sake* a distinctive taste. The combination of the aroma of the wood and the taste of the *sake* is probably one fragrance uniquely associated with Shinto and Japan. This aspect of the festival is peculiar also to Japan— social drinking as a religious act to commune with the *kami* in addition to the ritual use of *sake*. This happens after any major festival and often turns into a party with the organizers, the High Priest, and other priests present. The *naorai* is held not only after festivals but after *misogi* or other shrine rituals and activities. It is typical of the Shinto approach to life and the *kami*, one of celebration in a festive mood. Communion with the *kami* also enriches the communion of the people among themselves.

Chinkon (Calming of the Soul). This is a form of silent meditation within the shrine precincts at the close of major rituals (sometimes including festivals) when people reflect upon the significance of what they have been doing. They try to both conserve and draw from the experience they have had while performing the rituals. *Chinkon* takes place after the *misogi* rituals but before the *naorai*. Although it is a Shinto concept, it was popularized by Buddhism during the Heian period and was associated specifically with the calming of angry souls held to be responsible for the natural calamities that plagued the city of Kyoto from time to time.[10]

Ceremonial Wagons

The most extravagant and colorful aspects of the *matsuri* are seen when the *kami*, after being welcomed, is carried around the community, village, or town. Sometimes an *omikoshi* (portable shrine) is carried by groups who dance and reel vigorously around the streets. If the town is beside the coast, they might even bounce it into the sea. Sometimes there is more than one *omikoshi* and these might be jostled and charged playfully into each other. In areas where *omikoshi* are not used, great wagons are pulled through the streets instead. These are known as *dashi* or *yatai* and are of various designs. The following models indicate different styles peculiar to certain regions and festivals. Each district within a region may have its own wagon for these events.

Iwate Danjiri Festival Gikuruma (10 meters tall). Drummers and Musicians are located inside the wagon, which is pulled through the streets by members of the *ujikosodai* of each district. This festival is renowned for

Iwate, Takayama, and Kyoto Gion Festival Wagons

the speed and vigour with which the wagon is rushed through the streets, causing frequent damage to houses and sadly, the occasional fatality.

Takayama Festival Yattai (18 meters tall). Like the other wagons, each part of this vehicle has a name and a symbolic meaning. The wagon transports the *kami* of the community through the district it protects. The drummers and players of the *fue* sit inside and play as the wagon is hauled through the streets.

Kyoto Gion Festival Hoko (23 meters tall). These wagons are made of wood, and on account of their size, they weigh several tons. They are decorated elaborately in many colors and ornamented with numerous metallic plates and hanging artifacts.

Nen-chu-gyō-ji: Annual Events and Festivals

There may be local variations, but the following are basic and no shrine would omit any of them.[11]

Oshōgatsu (New Year). This event is the largest celebration of the year. The act of going to a shrine at New Year is called *hatsu mode* (the first shrine visit) and is performed by approximately 90 million people. The *Meiji Jingū* in Tokyo usually has 2.5 to 3 million visitors within the first seventy-two hours of the New Year. Police with microphones appeal to people to make their prayers short and keep moving to let others in.

Setsubun-sai. This festival is Chinese in origin but is performed at most shrines to mark the beginning of spring. The throwing out of ill fortune and the coming of good fortune are symbolized by the throwing of beans. The ritual usually commences with the High Priest of the shrine firing an arrow, the symbol of the power to break bad fortune; it climaxes in the throwing of beans over the worshippers, who gather them and take them home for good luck.

Haru Matsuri (Spring Festival). This festival is held to ensure the safety of the rice planting.

Natsu Matsuri (Summer Festival). This is held to protect the crops from pestilence and blight during the hot seasons.

Aki Matsuri (Autumn Festival). This festival is a ritual of thanksgiving for the gathered harvest.

Organization and Planning

For local shrine festivals it is the shrine elders, the *ujikosodai* or the *ujikokai,* who are responsible for seeing that the entire cycle of annual events takes place. Parishioners are called *ujiko*. In shrines where there are no priests permanently appointed, the lay leaders are sometimes called the *miyaza* or *to-za*; they conduct *naorai* at various times of the year between festivals to seek the protection of the *kami*.

Sampai

This formal act of showing reverence at a shrine can be performed by anyone at any time of the year. It can be associated with special events or activities and can also be an accompaniment to occasions such as purification of one's car or the start of a new business. Individuals or groups undertaking *seishiki sampai* perform the usual actions appropriate to anyone worshipping at a shrine. The layout of the shrine grounds and their artifacts is designed to facilitate the movement from entrance to the completion of the act of reverence.

Temizu-no-gi (washing of hands and mouth). The first ritual is performed at the *te-mizuya*, the ablution pavilion at the entrance to the precincts. A small ladle (*haidatsu*) with a long handle is used. Water is scooped from a trough of running water and, with the ladle held in the right hand, a little is poured over the left. The ladle is then transferred to the left hand and the right hand is similarly washed. Thereafter, returning the ladle to the right hand, more water is poured on the left hand, some of which is taken into the mouth. This is emptied in front of the trough, the ladle is rinsed, and the ritual is completed. The worshipper may now proceed to the shrine precincts proper.

Sūhai (showing reverence). In front of the *heiden* the worshipper stops, probably throws a coin (an offering called a *saisen*), and follows the ritual of *ni-hai-ni-hakusho-ippai* (two bows, two claps, and one bow.)[12] This may vary somewhat within different shrine traditions. Some shrines call for three claps and others four. However, this sequence is probably the most common. To the average worshipper at a shrine, this is standard behavior; after perhaps buying a talisman or an *ema,* he or she returns home. For those performing the full rituals, there are two or three additional stages.

Oharai (purification). In the next important part of the ceremony the worshippers enter the *heiden,* where they kneel facing the altar. A priest then formally enters (*shikiten-kaishi*). After beating the *taiko* drum and perhaps playing the flute, he intones the words of a *norito* and then waves the *harai-gushi* over the worshippers to purify them (*shūbatsu-no-gi*). The priest then recites another *norito* to please the *kami,* and the *kami* alights on the evergreen *sakaki* in the rite known as *koshin-no-gi.* Offerings are dedicated (*kensen-no-gi*) and the *kami* is formally addressed in the *norito-sojo.*

Tamagushi-hoten-no-gi (offering the tamagushi). Worshippers then move from the *heiden* to the *haiden,* where they stand in front of another altar with a sacred table some distance in front. The evergreen *sakaki* tree provides branches and leaves with *gohei* attached. The principal worshipper or group leader receives one of these from the priest. He turns it so that the stem faces the altar and places it in front of the symbols of the *kami.* The sequence of two bows, two claps, and one bow completes the ceremony. *Saimotsu* is offered by the group or the individual, with special offerings of money being given to shrines for such services. The *tessen-no-gi* then takes place: the offerings that have been made are removed. The ritual is completed by the *shoshin-no-gi* in which the *kami* ascends heavenward from the *sakaki.*

Naorai. After completing all the rituals, worshippers file out of the *haiden* to a place where the shrine maidens are waiting to pour a little *sake* onto a flat dish from what looks like a silver teapot. The *sake* is drunk and the worshippers receive various gifts from the shrine (in return for their donations) along with protective talismans, sacred *sake,* and some shrine literature. These are usually presented in an attractively designed paper bag bearing the logo of the shrine. After this the worshippers return home.

Hatsu miya mairi

The birth of a baby is one occasion when a similar sequence is performed. The ritual is then called *hatsu miya mairi* (first shrine visit), when the infant is received as a parishioner of the *kami*. It is performed on the thirty-second day after the birth of a boy and on the thirty-third for a girl.

Ema

One other feature of shrine precincts is the large wooden frames (sometime covered) to which are tied small wooden tablets, on the back of which prayers may be written. These are called *ema*, which means "picture of a horse." Horses were traditional offerings to the *kami*. In place of these, the wooden pictures were created. Nowadays they depict not only horses but features of the particular shrine, the animal symbols of the Oriental Zodiac, and other local features. They are very attractive and are often collected by folk art enthusiasts. They are hung in the *ema-den* and contain prayers that are often touching in their simplicity and honesty.

RITUAL INSTRUMENTS AND UTENSILS

Musical Instruments

In festivals and religious rituals involving *gagaku*, the classical courtly music, a variety of instruments are used.[13] These can be classified into two types.

Uchi-mono (percussion). This category includes the *sanko* (three drums), which are the *taiko*, the large drum that sits on a stand in all shrines and whose deep sound marks the beginning of a ritual; the *kakko*, which in *gagaku* keeps time; and the *shoko*, a smaller accompanying drum. Like the *taiko*, the *kakko* is beaten with two sticks. Groups may also play several *taiko* together. *Sasara* are pieces of wood clapped together. They are also used prior to announcing bouts between higher ranked *Sumo* wrestlers.

Sankan (wind: three reeds). These instruments are classical. They include the *fue*, a short flute-like instrument with six holes; the *sho*, a complicated instrument of seventeen bamboo tubes of different lengths arranged in a circle; and the *hichikiri*, an instrument that is a species of the straight flute or flageolet and that has nine holes.

Shrine maidens may use *suzu* in dances. It is a tambourine-like device with bells that can be made to ring simultaneously by a flick of the wrist. There is a more complicated version (used also by Buddhist priests) shaken during purification. The bell was used for exorcism in India and China and is an implement of purification in Shinto.

Non-Musical Objects

Various other accessories are used or are found in and around buildings where Shinto rites take place.

Goshiki-ban. In shrines where Buddhism and Shinto had close relations in the past, there are numerous shrine items to which colored ribbons are attached. These are in five colors; each color[14] is associated with a direction and has a particular meaning.

Color	Direction	Meaning
kuro black	North	*aramitama*—origin, beginning
murasaki purple	(same as black where found as an alternative)	
ao blue or green	East	*kushi-mitama*—life, creation
aka red	South	*sachi-mitama*—harmony, expansion
shiro white	West	*nigi-mitama*—integration, power
kiro yellow	Middle	*nao-hi*—creativity, unity

Ryōbu Shinto explains these in the following way, along with the *kami* appropriate to each color and direction.[15]

Direction	Kami
North	Ame-no-Hiwashi-ara-hi-no-o-kami
	(*hiwashi* means "eagle of the sun")
East	Kushi-hi-mitama-no-o-kami
South	Sachi-hi-mitama-no-o-kami
West	Nigi-hi-mitama-no-o-kami
Middle	Ame-no-minaka-nushi-no-kami

The *kami* colors and directions are given complicated explanations. However, the colors feature prominently in many shrines, hanging inside the *heiden* in the form of five streamers approximately 2 meters or more long and 10 centimeters wide. They are also seen attached to the *suzu*, which many *miko* hold when they are performing *kagura*, and to the *hama*, the arrow that breaks bad fortune.

Gohei. These zig-zag strips of paper have been mentioned. The other reading of *gohei* (*mitegura*) is of uncertain origin. The use of *gohei* as offerings or as attached to the *amagushi* may have begun with the practice of offering cloth to a *kami*, which is still sometimes done by the Emperor. Paper came to be substituted just as the *ema* was substituted for the real horse—although white horses are still found at some shrines, the most famous being the *Tōshō-gū* in Nikko.

The shape of the folds and the number of folds varies according to the esoteric beliefs and practices of individual shrines and priests. *Gohei* may vary in color. Red is sometimes used along with white.[16] They may be made in metal or, as in the *Kibitsu Jinja*, of a gold-colored material. These surely

Examples of Gohei

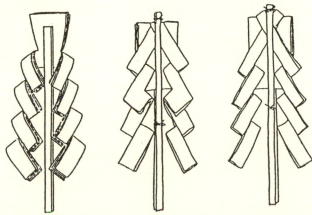

reflect ancient origins and possible relationships with Buddhism. Silver is commonly associated with Korea, as gold is with Buddhism in Japan.

Saikigu. There are numerous important utensils used in all religious ceremonies. Some of these have been mentioned, but a more careful and complete description is necessary in order to see the degree of minute detail that each ritual entails. The principal ones are as follows:

sambō: the tray used to carry offerings

oshiki: a tray with an edge of thick wood around all four sides

hassoku-an: an eight-legged table that is set up to bear the offerings

heihaku: offerings

shinsen: food offerings

tamagushi: a sacred branch offered to the *kami*

takatsuki: a sacred utensil used to bear the offerings. This is now usually made of lacquered wood. Everything else is made of *hinoki*. There are two types of this utensil; the *kaku-takatsuki*, which is square, and the *maru-takatsuki*, which is round.

The utensils are seen at every Shinto altar. When *jichin-sai* is being performed, they are set up inside the *himorogi*. After the ritual is over, the *saikigu* are removed and only the *shimenawa* remains, joining four long branches.

GOSHINTAI AND SHINZŌ

The technical definition of *Goshintai* (honorable-*kami*-body) is the object in which the *mitama* of the *kami* is found within the shrine buildings. It is treated with great respect; but it is not worshipped as a holy relic, as in the case of religions of crass superstition or crude magic.

Goshintai may or may not be found within the *honden* of a shrine. Shinto's lack of statuary and iconography is passed over all too frequently by those who wish to assert the superiority of Buddhism over the more primitive Shinto. Yet Judaism is not attacked as "primitive" on account of its lack of statuary. The *goshintai* is another distinctive idea of Shinto, something associated with the *kami* but not worshipped instead of the *kami*. In that sense, in spite of all its particularity, Shinto can see the power of *kami* in abstract terms.

Because the *goshintai* is rarely seen or talked about, little is known about any of them. Indeed, in some shrines the most sacred place in the *honden* is in fact empty. There is simply nothing there. In others, a mirror inside a bag acts as the *goshintai*. In other instances it is an object associated with the *kami*, a bamboo comb or some unusual item. Swords can be found as *goshintai*, although such cases are rare. Often they are wrapped in sacred cloths or hidden in boxes and never brought out. Prior to the Meiji Restoration some shrines did have statues that dated back to the twelfth or thirteenth century, when Shinto art developed somewhat. Most of these were an admixture of Shinto and Buddhism and, in the majority of cases, were destroyed by government order. Some did survive. In the mountain *Tengu Jinja* near Hakone, the *goshintai* is actually a statue of Buddha. In cases where the shrine may have no *honden,* the implication is that a nearby natural object functions as both, perhaps a mountain or (in the case of small shrines), a tree, a waterfall, a rock formation, or even an abalone shell. These cases are dependent upon the locality. Shinto art in the form of *Shinzō* does exist.[17] However, portrayals of *kami* in that form usually depict them in court dress (from the Heian period, when the practice began under the influence of Buddhism). The painting or sculpture becomes a *yorishiro*, a place where the *kami* resides. It is therefore not merely a work of representational art.

SHRINE SYMBOLS

Shrines have various identifying logos or symbols. In shrines that had a past relation with Esoteric Buddhism in particular, various types may be seen.

The *tomoe* is similar to the Chinese *in-yo* (*ying-yang*) symbol, except that it is divided into three sections. These are explained in various ways, one being Heaven, Earth, and Humanity.

Hoshi-no-tama is most frequently found as an ornament or in a design related to Inari shrines. *Hoshi* means "star," and *tama* means "spirit" or "ball." Again, no convincing explanations appear to exist.

Sanmi-sangen, the three principles according to which life is understood, can be set out in the geometrical form of a superimposed triangle, circle, and square.[18] Although a great deal of supplementary explanation would be necessary to acquire a complete understanding of it, the basic format is easy to grasp if it is diagrammatically presented. It brings together numerous aspects of Shinto in a framework that unites cosmic and earthly existence in meaningful relation.

THE SHINTO PRIESTHOOD

The Shinto priesthood[19] is ancient and honorable and traces its origins to the sacral society that was ancient Japan. The duties of a priest are to serve the *kami,* to engage in religious activities based on *Jinja Shinto,* and to administer shrine business. Many shrines are served by hereditary priests. Some priestly families go far back, although the Meiji government policy about shrines did affect some of these. Many, however, preserved their heritage and remain in their traditional succession. The communities they belong to expect this of them.

Priestly Vestments: Saifukingu

The dress worn by the priests, although possibly older in origin, was stylized during the Heian age and reflects the court dress of the period, suitably modified for liturgical purposes. The principal items are detailed here.

Headgear. Kanmuri is used when priests are in full dress for special ceremonies.

Robes. Ho is the outer garment worn over the other robes. It is also known as *sokutai, ikan,* or *saifuku.* Traditionally, the colors purple, red,

Sanmi-Sangen

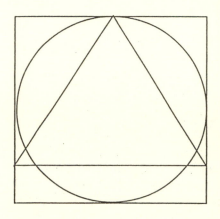

THREE PRINCIPLES 三光の原理		
▲	●	■
GAS 気体	LIQUID 液体	SOLID 固体
☆	☽	○
STAR 星	MOON 月	SUN 太陽
MISSION 使命	LIFE 生命	DESTINY 宿命
SWORD 剣	JEWEL 玉	MIRROR 鏡
FUTURE 未来	PRESENT 現在	PAST 過去
TRUTH 真	VIRTUE 善	BEAUTY 美
WISDOM 知	MAN 人	COURAGE 勇
SALT 塩	WATER 水	RICE 米

green, light blue, and yellow reflected Court rank. In modern times these have been reduced to black, red, and light blue. The *saifuku,* made of white silk, is designed in the same way as the *ikan* and is used for most religious rituals.

In addition to these is the *kariginu,* which also originated during the Heian period. There are many colors, selected according to the age and rank of the wearer as well as according to the seasons of the year.

Accessories. Shaku is a sceptre-like flat piece of wood carried by priests in the same manner as ancient Court officials carried them to indicate authority. In China, a shaku is carried to signify a message of state. *Asa-gutsu* are shoes worn during the Heian period by the nobility. They were made originally of leather, are now made of lacquered wood; the *asa-gutsu* are worn by Shinto priests when they perform rituals.

Priestly Training and Gradations

There are two principal institutions where people can study to become priests. There is a Faculty of Shinto Studies at Kokugakuin University in

Examples of Priestly Robes

Tokyo, which began as a center of the study of *kokugaku* (national learning). There is also Kogakkan University in Ise, which trains priests to recite the liturgies and understand the meaning of the rituals. Candidates may enter a college, qualify, and then attach themselves to shrines; or they may simply join a shrine and receive status at the lowest rank after basic training, supplementing their rank and status with further studies.

There are two ranking systems. One is within the shrines; like promotion in a company, it depends upon seniority and service (among other considerations). It is also in some cases related to who will inherit a shrine. These ranks are determined within individual shrines. Alongside this is a system of ranking priests according to their experience, accomplishments, and tests set out by the Association of Shinto Shrines.

The ranks are denoted by the color of *hakama* a priest may wear. A priest may be highly ranked in his own shrine but still have a lower grade in the national system. The ranking system known as *kai-i* is as follows:

jokai: purity. This is granted to priests who have served for twenty years or more at the rank of *negi* or above and who hold the rank of *meikai* at Grade 2.

meikai: brightness. This rank and the two below it are granted on the basis of education, general learning, training, and experience at a shrine.

seikai: righteousness.

chokkai: uprightness.

Ranks of the Priesthood within Individual Jinja

Gūji: the chief priest of a shrine

Gon-Gūji: the assistant chief priest of a shrine

Negi: senior priest (there may be more than one)

Gon-negi: assistant senior priest (there may be several)

Kannushi: priest (there may be any number)[20]

Miko: shrine maiden (unmarried daughter, often of a parishioner) who assists at rituals and performs sacred dances (*kagura*)

Itsuki-no-miya or *Saishu*: the highest of all ranks, traditionally a female of the Imperial Family, who was known as the princess devoted to the *kami*. The office exists now only at the Grand Shrines of Ise.

Shrine Organization and Life

In large shrines, the routine and rituals of the day are fixed throughout the year; whether or not visitors come to the shrine, these are followed. When there are special rituals or festivals, these are performed in addition to the daily chores. A typical day might be as follows. Around 6:00 or 7:00 A.M., a senior priest in full robes makes his way assisted by several junior priests to open the doors of the *haiden,* where he performs a ritual involving a *norito,* the *taiko,* and the *fue.* Specially prepared offerings (*shinsen*) are brought and placed on the inner altar in the *honden.*

After this has been completed, the younger priests are joined by others who brush the gravel on the *sandō,* the approach road inside the shrine precincts, so that worshippers will walk on freshly cleaned pathways. Stone entranceways are washed with water, and the shrine offices (*shamushō*) are opened by 8:00 A.M. At that time the act of morning worship (*chō-hai*) takes place, involving all the shrine priests and staff. The *norito* is recited, the staff purified for the day, and announcements made about the day's events and duties.

Later in the day, sometimes as early as dusk but sometimes as late as 9:00 P.M., the offerings are removed and the large wooden front doors of the main buildings are closed again until morning. The times may vary in accordance with local customs and traditions. Shrines where *misogi* is practiced may close later, because *misogi* is usually performed late at night or early in the morning.

A shrine is a place of activity every day, all year round. Weekends tend to be busier because people have leisure time to take their cars for road safety purification or to seek *oharai* for personal reasons. People who do so go to the shrine office and register and then wait for their turn to have the rituals performed. They pay for these services, which enables the shrines to receive an income. Parishioners may also make appointments for priests to perform rituals at their new homes or their companies or to mark a special event in the family. Even casual visitors may be eligible for such services if the shrine *kami* is well known for some special capacity, such as assisting at childbirth or in passing examinations. In such ways, shrines offer care for all aspects and stages of life.

NOTES

1. The material for this section is drawn from a variety of sources, including works by Ono Sokyo, Muraoka Tsunetsugu, Katō Genchi, W. G. Aston, various publications of the *Jinja Honchō,* and individual shrines.

2. The term *kegare* is also used to describe specific types of impurity caused by child-bearing, menstruation, disease, and death. These occurrences affect not only the individuals concerned but those around them, including family members. If the presence of *kegare* is ignored, *tatari* (misfortune) may come as a warning. Restrictions on women performing shrine functions at certain times have been gradually

relaxed, although in conservative quarters they may still be strictly enforced. A U.S. boxer's woman manager was not allowed to enter the ring because it had been set up in the *Sumo* hall over the *dohyō*, a place considered sacred to the *kami*. She had to be content with coaching from a distance.

3. See the discussion of Shinto and Ethics in Chapter 10.

4. *Maga* means "confusion."

5. Other types of purification including *goma*, the fire rite, are used in *Shugendō*.

6. See *Sourcebook of Shinto* (Greenwood Press, forthcoming) for text and translations.

7. Materials and resources consulted for this section include the following: *Matsuri no* (*Gurafu-sha, Karagurafic* 8), (Gurafusha, Tokyo, 1980); Naoe Hiroji, *Matsuri to Nen-chū-Gyō-ji* (Festivals and the Cycle of Yearly Events) (Sakura, Tokyo, 1980), p. 289; Makita Shigeru, *Kami to Matsuri to Nihonjin* (Kami, Festivals, and the Japanese People) (Kodansha, Tokyo, 1972), p. 185; Yanagita Kunio, *Nihon no Matsuri* (The Japanese Festival) (Kadokawa Shoten, Tokyo, 1956), p. 232; *Nihon no Matsuri* (Japanese Festivals), 8 vols. (Kodansha, Tokyo, 1982); *Nihon no Jinja to Matsuri* (Japanese Shrines and Festivals) (Jinja Honchō, Tokyo, 1970). The literature on festivals is massive; specialties include types of festivals, regions of Japan, and shrines and cults.

8. Emperor Meiji frequently made reference to *saisei-itchi*. See the discussion of "Kokka Shinto: State Shinto" in Chapter 1 of this book.

9. The Institute of Japanese Culture at Kokugakuin University under Professor Ueda Kenji commenced a series on special festivals and their meaning in the 1980s.

10. See the discussion of *Tenjin* in Chapter 4.

11. See Nishitsunoi Imasayoshi, *Nen-chū-gyō-ji Jiten* (Dictionary of the Cycle of Yearly Events) (Tokyodo, Tokyo, 1958), p. 972.

12. The act of clapping is more formally called *kashiwade*.

13. Volumes abound on Japanese arts, including *Gagaku, Kagura,* and *Noh*. These are produced simply for appreciation of their artistic merits without reference to Shinto.

14. Although explanations vary slightly, the colors are standard and are also found in Buddhist temples.

15. Directions of the compass also are important aspects of the Oriental Zodiac. They relate to the cycle of twelve years believed to have influence upon people depending upon the year in which they were born. Many priests practice fortune-telling according to these principles.

16. Red and white in combination mark a celebration.

17. For a fuller discussion, see Kageyama Haruki, *Shinto Bijutsu, Nihon no Bijutsu*, Vol. 18 (Shibundo, Tokyo, 1967). There is an English version, *Arts of Shinto*, which is Vol. 4 in a series published by Weatherhill, 1973. Statuary and painting are discussed from p. 46 onward.

18. For a modern exposition by an authority on the subject, see Yamamoto Yukitaka, *Shinto to Tomo ni Ikeru* (Tosho Shuppan, Tokyo, 1988), pp. 223 ff.

19. The *Jinja Honchō* is the final source for correct information on the structure and organization of the modern priesthood, although there are many local variations as well as shrines outside the system. This excludes shrines that are designated Kyōha, or Sect, Shinto.

20. The term *kannushi* means "person who belongs to the *kami*." An alternative (Chinese-style) term is *Shinshoku,* which has the nuance of "serving the *kami*." *Tayu* was the fifth rank at Court and was used by priests. It is now obsolete in that usage.

Part III

SHINTO SECTS

Chapter 7

Kyōha (Sect) and Tsūzoku (Folk) Shinto

NON-INSTITUTIONAL RELIGIOUS MOVEMENTS IN JAPAN

Alongside government-recognized and government-supervised shrines, independent and unofficial movements arose and flourished from time to time. This section and the next address these cultic, unorthodox, and often enigmatic movements. They are not part of *Jinja Shinto* as such, but even a cursory examination reveals that they were inspired by the Shinto tradition. Also, when great shrines rose to prominence, they frequently became "cultic" in the popular sense, the cultic nature of Japanese religion being one of its most prominent characteristics. *Izumo Taisha* enshrines the *kami* of the mythology but also has its own Sect Shinto support group, further evidence that abundant distinctions exist and that drawing lines of demarcation in Shinto is never simple. In order of discussion, I first examine the ancient mountain cults; second, the distinctive features of asceticism in Japan; and third, the topic of *Shugendō*. Thereafter I examine the thirteen sects of *Kyōha Shinto*.

SANGAKU SHINKŌ AND ASCETICISM

In researching the appeal and challenge of cults rooted in the folk tradition, it is necessary to understand the importance of mountains and the significance of practicing ascetic rituals in them. Mountains were believed to be the residence of spirits, principally spirits of the dead who watched over and assisted the living. Mountains themselves were often considered to be *kami* and were accorded special reverence. Ancient Japanese religion was largely based on a fascination with mountains, the roots of *Sangaku Shinkō*. Climbing mountains and living in mountains always seems to have been associated with natural spirituality. Many old Shinto shrines and Buddhist temples are located on the peaks of mountains, which in modern times require railways, paved roads, and cable cars for convenient access. How they were built and how people lived there in the past is a matter of speculation. Kūkai chose *Kōyasan* as the site of the *Kongōbu-ji*, and Saichō chose Mt. Hie for the *Enryaku-ji*. Nichiren received his spiritual enlightenment on a mountain. Climbing Mt. Fuji has been a religious act for centuries, usually an act of purification. In some rural areas, boys reaching puberty purify themselves still by climbing a local mountain. The *Kumano Junrei*, the pilgrimage of the Kumano region, is essentially an exercise in mountaineering by people dressed in Heian age costume. The famous blind women shamans practice their art on Mt. Osore in Aomori Prefecture. The list could go on.

The essential role of mountains in Shinto in particular, and in Japanese religion in general, also has lent a distinctive character to the style of Japanese asceticism.[1] If we define an ascetic as someone who lives at the center of his or her spiritual energy, then the manner in which that energy is channeled toward achieving a particular state of mind or body depends upon the ascetic's perception of the self. If the self is viewed as evil, then it may merit punishment, as in medieval Western asceticism. On the other hand, if the self is capable of improvement, the purpose of the discipline correspondingly becomes positively targeted at such improvements, which is the dynamic behind Japanese asceticism. Buddhists speak of the *soku-shin-jō-butsu*—literally, "one who becomes a Buddha in the flesh." Shinto similarly aims at transforming a human being into a living *kami*. In the mountain tradition of the Buddhist/Shinto amalgam the full flowering of these ideals can best be seen.

SHUGENDŌ: BEGINNINGS TO THE HEIAN PERIOD

Shugendō dates to the Nara period, or perhaps even earlier. Most likely much of its early leadership came from the mainland of Asia, although it was not long before the Japanese reverence for mountains began to encourage the development of indigenous forms. Shugendō is often primarily associated with Buddhism rather than Shinto, and it is probable that the earliest developments began within Buddhism. However, as the movement grew, its peculiar character came to express as much the insights of Shinto as those of Buddhism.

The most famous of the early holy men (*ubasoku-zenji*) was the legendary En no Ozunu mentioned in the *Shoku Nihongi*[2] during the reign of Emperor Mommu (r. 687–707). He is described as having been expelled from Mt. Katsuragi to Oshima in Izu after being betrayed in some way by a disciple called Karakuni no Muraji Hiratori.[3] He was credited with powers that included being able to invoke demons to do his bidding and to punish those who disobeyed him. Legend also tells that he compelled a spirit to build a bridge from Mt. Katsuragi to Kimpusen.[4] In later times he came to be regarded as the historical founder of Shugendō, which would date the rise of mountain asceticism to the early Nara period, before the arrival and development of Esoteric Buddhism in Japan. However far back mountain asceticism in Japan actually goes, it seems that the Nara period had its own traditions and that the later influx of Buddhist esotericism led to the growth and amalgamation of these groups into the class of people who came to be known as *shugenja*.

Descriptions of the early ascetics are limited. En no Ozunu's four practices were apparently picking fruits, drawing water, collecting firewood, and preparing vegetarian food. Early ascetics may have set up small Tibetan-style cave altars in the quest for spiritual powers from what they felt were energy spots. They were not well organized or formalized either in dress or manners (as they became in later days), but it was to express the activities of these people that the term *Shugendō* was invented. *Shugendō* uses three characters—*shu* (self-cultivation), *gen* (the beneficial effect of austerities), and *dō* (way), giving the generic meaning of "the way to spiritual power through discipline." Practitioners were called *shugenja*, people seeking to acquire these powers. The other name for *shugenja*, *yamabushi* (people who lie down and sleep in mountains), is better known and more popularly used than *shugenja*, which remains a rather technical expression.

In the early Nara period, three basic elements existed from which later practices developed to become the complex mass of rituals and disciplines recorded during the Kamakura age. Seclusion for long periods in caves close to rivers or waterfalls and devotion to particular *kami* were the first two, which reflect Shinto ideals. In Heian times a variety of esoteric rituals derived from Buddhism were added to them. The goals of Shugendō thus expanded to include the search for supernatural powers through ascetic and esoteric rituals conducted in secluded and holy mountain areas with power places.[5] All these features are still identifiable in modern Shugendō, as studies of groups at the Dewa Sanzan confirm.[6]

Other figures around whom legends grew included Soo (831–918) of Mt. Hiei, who lived near the Kasuragawa Falls in the western foothills of Mt. Hira and who focused on the Buddhist esoteric deity Acala; Enchin (814–891), who founded the *Mii-dera*, the headquarters of the Temple school of Tendai; and Shōbō (834–909), who lived on Mt. Yoshino. Specific mountain regions came to be identified with Shugendō, the most important of which were the Kimpusen range and Mt. Kastusuragi, the three shrines of Kumano, Mount Ishizuki in Shikoku, Daisen in Chugoku, Hakusan and Tateyama, Mt. Nikko, and the famous Dewa Sanzan (three mountains in modern Yamagata Prefecture—Hagurosan, Yudonosan, and Gassan).

In the Omine range linking Kimpusen and Kumano where there was a well-known "ascetic path," several groups were already established by the

Location of Dewa Sanzan

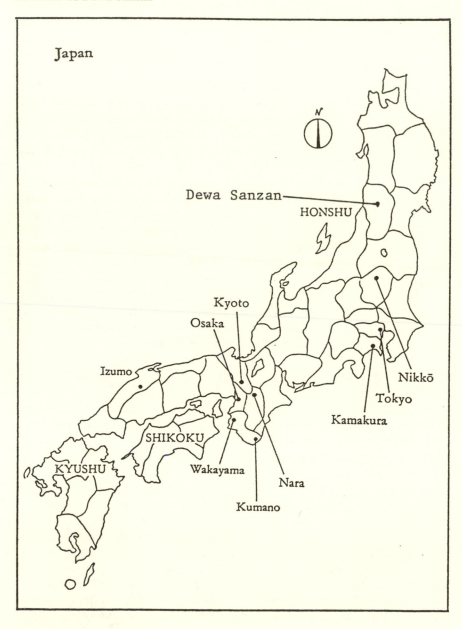

Japan

N

Dewa Sanzan

HONSHU

Kyoto

Osaka

Izumo

Nikkō

Tokyo

Kamakura

SHIKOKU

KYUSHU

Wakayama

Nara

Kumano

Heian period, principally at Ozasa, Shonoiwaya, Zenkidani, and Tamaki-yama. This made it the informal capital of ascetic practice in central Japan by the twelfth century. The *Kumano Sanja* or *Sanzan (Hongū, New,* and *Nachi* shrines) have a long and interesting history. Heian period stories of the origins of the shrines,[7] associate the founding with the Buddhist avatar *Ojishin* of Mt. T'ien-t'ai in China. He is said to have visited Mt. Hiko, Mt. Ishizuki, the Kannokura sanctuary of the New Shrine, and *Asuga Jinja* before finally descending to the *Hongū* in Kumano in the form of the moon. The moon appears, of course, in the Kumano Mandala. Eight years after the legendary date of the descent, a hunter in pursuit of a wild boar saw three forms of the moon among the trees of the mountain. He asked them what they were and they replied that they were the *kami* of Kumano. Thus, Tendai Buddhism and the *kami* of the moon came to be identified in Kumano.

Official records of the shrines[8] relate the foundation of the *Hongū* to a priest called Zendō; the *Nachi* was founded by a monk called Ragyo, who landed in the southern part of Kumano. By the late Heian age, it was claimed that En no Ozunu himself went on a pilgrimage to Kumano, performing purification rites en route.[9] This seems unlikely, but the story illustrates the tendency within Japanese culture in general and Japanese religion in particular to trace origins to a mythological person of great status in order to enhance status. Such must have been the prestige of both Kumano and Kimpusen that after difficult beginnings, they were able by the Heian age to make such claims. It was in the succeeding era, however, that the organizational aspects of Shugendō reached maturity.

SHUGENDŌ IN THE KAMAKURA PERIOD AND AFTER

By the eleventh century, Kumano and Kimpusen had become established as the leading centers of mountain asceticism and had begun to develop both discipline and order. Kumano became the center of the *Honzan* sect (Tendai), and Kimpusen hosted the *Tōzan* sect (Shingon).

The Honzan Sect

Links with Tendai Buddhism began when the Imperial Family and members of the nobility began to make regular pilgrimages to Kumano. Ascetics from all over the country began resorting there to form various *shugen,* orders with different traditions, customs, and practices. Pivotal to this development was Zōyo (1032–1116), a Tendai priest of the *Mii-dera* who guided Emperor Shirakawa on his 1090 Kumano pilgrimage.[10] When he was subsequently appointed governor of Kumano, the Kumano *Sanja* became directly related to the *Mii-dera* and consequently to the Tendai sect. Jokei, the son of Emperor Go-Shirakawa, became a Tendai priest and abbot

Map of *Shugendō* Locations

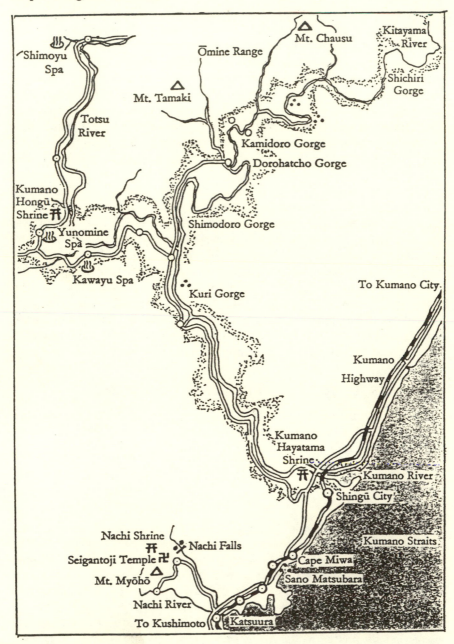

Shimoyu Spa

Mt. Chausu

Kitayama River

Ōmine Range

Shichiri Gorge

Mt. Tamaki

Totsu River

Kamidoro Gorge

Dorohatcho Gorge

Kumano Hongū Shrine

Shimodoro Gorge

Yunomine Spa

Kawayu Spa

Kuri Gorge

To Kumano City

Kumano Highway

Kumano Hayatama Shrine

Kumano River

Shingū City

Nachi Shrine

Nachi Falls

Seigantoji Temple

Kumano Straits

Mt. Myōhō

Cape Miwa

Sano Matsubara

Nachi River

To Kushimoto

Katsuura

of the *Shogo-in*, which in effect related the abbacy to the governorship of Kumano.

Shugenja in Kumano came to be known as *sendatsu* and their followers as *danna*. Highly ranked teachers called *oshi* received stipends for leading people to mountain power places. Many *sendatsu* as well as *oshi* became very wealthy owing to the large numbers of followers who came to their areas for purification and guidance. This added further prestige, as well as power, to the *Shogo-in*, which in turn appointed the *Higashiyama Nyakuoji Jinja* in Kyoto (strongly backed by the Ashikaga shogunate) as the supervising shrine of the *Kumano Sanja* in the fourteenth century. The system was expanded and remained under the administration of the *Shogo-in*, which consequently became the headquarters of what came to be known as the *Honzan* sect. It claimed to be the orthodox tradition of Shugendō, hence the name *Honzan* (original mountain), with En no Ozunu as founder and Zoyo as patron of the sect.

The Tendai monk Enchin (founder of the *Mii-dera*) was said to have been engaged in ascetic practices at Omine and Kumano in the hope that the temple would support it. Organizational structures began to firm up by the mid-fourteenth century. Abbott Ryoyu of the *Shogo-in* established places for ordination at Jinzen on Mount Omine and Nakatsugawa on Mt. Matsuragi. The *kasumi* system also was introduced around the same time, whereby influential *shugenja* established an independent area of authority called a *kasumi*. Lower-ranked *shugenja* were appointed with designated districts inside each *kasumi*. By the fifteenth century, *Shogo-in* abbots began making nationwide tours to all outlying centers to inspect *shugenja*. Abbot Doko (1430–1510) was particularly active. The Honzan sect claimed in its biography of En no Ozunu that he had visited all these places, a propaganda claim to legitimize the efforts of the abbots of the *Shogo-in* and to enhance the status of the sect. The headquarters remains the *Shogo-in* in Kyoto.

The Tōzan Sect

The other great sect of the era was associated with Kimpusen in Yoshino, which had become a center for *shugenja* from shrines and temples around Nara. The group was made up of thirty-six centers,[11] mostly temples that had strong links with the *Kofuku-ji* in Nara. The *Tōzan* sect grew out of this assorted group of shrines, temples, and their respective *shugenja*. Its name literally means "this mountain," implying equal status with Honzan. Headquarters were established at Ozasa on Mt. Omine, which received cooperation from both Eastern and Western Halls of the *Kofuku-ji*.

The Tōzan traced its roots to Shōbō, who founded both the *Daigo-ji* and the *Ono-ha* of Shingon Buddhism (thus its link with Shingon). A Muromachi era legend claimed that Shōbō had received the spiritual seal of En no Ozunu and the Imperial Seal of Emperor Jomei (r. 629–641), which had subsequently been entrusted to two *shugenja*—Uchiyama, an *Oshuku* (leading master guide), and Sakuramoto, *Ninoshoku* (assistant master guide) of the order—another counterclaim to orthodoxy. Shōbō was also said to have led a pilgrimage of the greatest thirty-six *shugenja* into the Omine range of mountains from Yoshino, which was supposed to account for the thirty-six centers noted. Novices first had to join one of the thirty-six identified leaders, who would present their names to the entire group assembled at Ozasa. The image of Shōbō as founder was strengthened by the late Muromachi era, when the group slowly began to separate from the *Kofuku-ji* and move closer to the *Sambo-in* of the *Daigo-ji*, confirming the link with Shingon. Its headquarters remains the *Sambo-in* of the *Daigo-ji*.

Other centers of Shugendō grew up in different parts of the country, but their attachment to one or another sect or group demonstrates the pre-eminence of the Honzan and Tōzan sects. The structure of Shugendō and the development of the two sects and their various branches as well as their lingering influences is an aspect of Japanese religion that merits more attention than it has received.

Regional Shugendō

Some provincial practitioners of Shugendō attached themselves to either Honzan or Tōzan, whereas others tried to become independent. Four groups were particularly prominent.

Haguro-san. This group in Yamagata Prefecture still retains a distinct identity within the tradition. *Haguro yamabushi* are recorded as having visited Kyoto as early as the late tenth century, although the first historical references and the oldest records date to the thirteenth century.[12] Although it claimed many grounds for an independent existence, most likely *Haguro shugendō* originated from the *Honzan-ha*. The *yatagarasu* is the messenger of *Haguro-gongen*, which further strengthens the possibility of links with Kumano. The additional fact that three mountains are revered may further parallel Kumano. The area functioned as headquarters for all Shugendō in the Tohoku area. By the late Edo period, over 4,000 *yamabushi* practiced on Haguro. Both Shingon and Tendai priests performed ascetic rituals on *Haguro-san*, with married Tendai-affiliated ascetics and *hijiri* practicing the *nembutsu*. Shugendō was proscribed by the Mejii government, so *Haguro* suffered like all other centers. *Dewa-Jinja* became the most important center of the revived *Dewa-Sanzan* after the Pacific War, when Shugendō re-established itself.

Nikko-san. This group claimed to be founded by Shōbō and developed by Benkaku, who became abbot in 1210 and who was renowned for his ascetic practices at Kumano (indicating links with Tendai Buddhism). He founded the *Komyo-in* on *Nikko-san*; this became headquarters for all the *shugenja* in the region. The demise of the center at *Nikko-san* was the result of poor political judgment. *Nikko-san*, it appears, was on the side of the Hojo family during the campaigns of Hideyoshi, with the result that its lands were confiscated by Hideyoshi after the Odawara campaign. By the late sixteenth century it had been replaced by the *Zazen-in*, another sub-temple of the same area. The *Nikko-Tōshōgū* is a Tendai Shinto shrine, which indicates the earlier links; the mountain area, like the *Dewa-Sanzan*, still breathes its ascetic past.

Hiko-san. This is the name of a Kyushu mountain. *Hiko-san* priests were first identified as demanding the removal of the governor at Dazaifu and the banishment of vice-governor Fujiwara no Nagafusa in 1094.[13] It is also recorded that in 1181 Emperor Goshirakawa added *Hiko-san* to the areas under the control of the New Kumano Shrine in Kyoto, which explains the relationship between *Hiko-san* and Kumano. *Hiko-san* included several holy places; the southern Peak of the World Body (the historical Boddha, Shaka), the northern Peak of the Dharma's Body (Amida), and the central Peak of the Female Body (the one thousand–armed Cannon). Over one hundred priests and two hundred *shugenja* were recorded as having lived there at one time, making it one of the largest centers of Tendai Shugendō. *Hiko-san*, like *Haguro*, was strategically located in a military sense and was protected by Prince Yasuhito, the son of Emperor Gofushimi (r. 1298–1301). The niece of the military governor of Buzen province married the prince, who received in return a residence and the abbacy of the *Nyoho-ji*. This gave *Hiko-san* peace and prosperity to develop not only its own style of rituals but a theology and a metaphysic of Shugendō as early as the sixteenth century.

Katsuragi-san. In contrast to the esoteric, *Katsuragi-san* was associated with the more esoteric cult of the Lotus Sūtra. Twenty-eight pilgrimage stations, representing the twenty-eight chapters of the Lotus Sūtra, ran from the Tomogashima Islands (near modern-day Wakayama City) to Nijo-san in Yamato. The guardian of all *shugenja* was considered to be Kongō Zāo Gongen, whom it was believed had appeared to En no Ozunu in a vision during the seventh century. According to one account, En no Ozunu (again invoked in the interests of credibility) was in a cave meditating upon a protector for those entering the mountains. Maitreya appeared to him along with Cannon and the Buddha. Nevertheless, he continued meditating until Zāo Gongen appeared, whom he felt was the best guardian for himself and Kimpusen. From the Kamakura era legends of this kind became wide-spread, which does suggest that Zāo Gongen had become an important *kami* of shugendō.

Each center of Shugendō had its own traditions, customs, and beliefs. One example of the diversity of the various regional groups was the existence in Omine of mythical child attendants of the *kami* known as *dōji*.[14]

Their unique role indicates how the Shinto tendency toward particularism interacted with the cosmology and metaphysics of Buddhism.

The Yamabushi-chō

One of the main sources of information about the *yamabushi* is the thirteenth-century register called the *Yamabushi-chō*, which lists many practices of the Kumano region. *Shugenja* dressed in orange tunics, wore *hakama* trousers and special headgear, and carried wooden boxes on their backs. Three accessories considered necessary for entry to the mountains were a wooden case (carried on the back); a conical-shaped, broad-brimmed hat; and a Shinto *harai-gushi*. This may have originally been made of paper, but weather considerations may have been the reason that in later ages *shugenja* came to carry a *suzu*. Although this is associated more with exorcism in India than Shinto, it came into widespread use and is still used in some shrines.

It was widely thought by older scholars that *yamabushi* merely hiked in the mountain ranges from Yoshino to Kumano (or from Kumano to Yoshino) through what is now the Kumano-Yoshino national park, although more recent research suggests that they formed temporary settlements at specific locations. However, entry into or exit from the mountains was ritualized. Buddhist and other sacred objects or artifacts were given to the *shugenja*. Rituals and practices began to become standardized during the Kamakura age, and much of modern Shugendō was developed during that period. Formal entry into the mountains commenced with the ritual beating of a novice with a staff to awaken him into awareness of the Tathagata or the Buddha whose power was being sought. This was followed by the confession of sins (which in the case of Kumano was performed by hanging over a cliff by a rope that is briefly released)[15] and purification in a waterfall. Consumption of food and water was minimal.

Sacred fires using small piles of wood set up in pillars (*hashiramoto goma*) were prepared and lit as a form of *oharai*. Initiation into esoteric mysteries followed these rituals performed on a regular basis along with instructions on how to draw energy from power places in the mountains. When the designated period was completed, there was a formal departure from the mountains. The concepts underlying disciplines such as *Sen-nichi-kai-hō-gyō*[16] and be traced to these early practices.

Two sets of practices are distinguished in the *Yamabushi-chō*. One was concerned with the life-support activities of the ascetic; the other pursued the quest for spiritual power. From about the fifteenth century, ten disciplines were made obligatory for anyone wishing to enter the mountains formally for ascetic practice. These included the beating to awaken the senses, the confession of impurities, the weighing of *karmic* bonds to determine how much guilt was being borne, the abstaining from drinking water and from eating cereals, the pouring of water on the body for purification, ritual wrestling, dancing, and *hashiramoto goma* with esoteric rites. Each act was considered to correspond to one of the ten worlds of Shingon Buddhism through which people passed on their way to enlightenment. The ten worlds listed by Kukai were the worlds of hell, hungry spirits, animals, demons, human beings, heavenly beings, *shravakas, pratyekabuddhas, bodhisattvas*, and finally the world of the buddhas.[17] A *shugenja* who correctly performed the rituals could progress through the ten worlds and attain Buddhahood in the flesh, according to the separate philosophies of Shingon and Tendai. Also from the fifteenth century, symbolic explanations of both rituals and locations were invented to intensify the meaning of the rites; this displays yet another interesting feature of Japanese religion. The Omine mountains, for example, were interpreted in terms of *Ryōbu Shinto*, the Kumano end being the Womb Mandala and the Yoshino end being the Diamond Mandala. The pilgrimage route thus carried the *shugenja* in a symbolic way either upward to enlightenment or downward to hell, depending upon where he began.

An additional feature of the activities of *shugenja* explains how so many grew rich and powerful; they acted as guides for the nobility who made pilgrimages from the Heian period onward. They led courtiers and *samurai* as well as ordinary people in performing rituals, offering prayers, and guiding the pilgrims through the requirements of the pilgrimage. *Shugenja* were attached to teachers who owned hostels, which in turn were used to collect revenue.

The Kumano guides, for example, traveled all over the country to spread the teachings of the cult, acquiring believers and helping to establish branches of the Kumano tradition. A sutra mound excavation at Nachi records that a *shugenja* called Gyoyo toured the country in 1176 and enlisted 69,000 followers. This was probably the peak of that sect, although Shugendō continued to exist until the Meiji government banned it. The *Kumano Junrei*, like the *Dewa-Sanzan*, was revived after the Pacific War.

Shugenja Dress

There are various styles of *Shugenja*, which is one reason for the controversy about whether Shugendō is Buddhist or Shinto. The *Tōzan-ha* members shaved their heads like Buddhist priests, whereas the *Honzan-ha* kept their hair and grew it long. The dress as well as the doctrines reflect Buddhist, Shinto, and perhaps even popular Taoistic ideas, thereby defying simple categorization. This very syncretism may justify calling it Japanese.

The dress of the *shugenja* remains essentially as it was, reflecting the cosmological philosophy of the Ten Worlds of Esoteric Buddhism. There are many forms of dress according to sect and rank. White, indicating purity, is the Shinto contribution to outward appearance. *Shugenja* wear a white tunic and a special tassled stole, symbolizing the Diamond realm and the Womb realm. A small pillbox-like hat symbolizes Mahavairocana. Leggings and straw sandals are worn with a fur apron over the seat, a *juzu* is wound around the arm, and a ceremonial staff or wand and a large conch shell that represents the path of the *shugenja* toward Buddhahood are carried. Two ropes hang from the waist, wooden cases for religious articles and necessities are carried on the back, and a conical broad-brimmed straw hat is carried to symbolize ultimate rebirth as a Buddha. The uniform transformed the *shugenja* himself into a walking mandala, which united in his person the human and physical with the potential power of the Buddha and the supernatural. The costume was a constant reminder of the meaning of the pilgrimage and the goals of Shugendō.[18] The following diagram and list illustrate some of the basic elements carried by all mountain ascetics.

1. *Tokin* is the skull cap. This is an adaptation of a hood, made now of twelve folds which represent the twelve worlds in esoteric Buddhism. It is also thought to have the power to protect its wearer against evils and dangers in the mountains and is used as a drinking cup.

2. *Suzukake* is the distinctive colored robe which evolved into four main styles.

3. *Nenju* or *juzu* is the Buddhist rosary, which is made of rough stone beads.

4. *Hora* is the conch shell blown to proclaim the Buddhist law. It is also used for group communication in the mountains.

5. *Oi* is a portable altar carried as a backpack containing the Buddhist writings

and necessary work tools. It is covered by a *katabako*, a small box. The *oi* is considered female and the *katabako* is considered male.

6. *Kongozue* is the "diamond cane," used for climbing; in esoteric Buddhism it represents the hardness of true wisdom.

7. *Hiogi*, a cypress fan, is carried by *shugenja* of rank to symbolize the fanning of the flame induced in the ritual of *goma*.

8. *Hashira-nawa* is the rope used in climbing mountains.

9. *Waraji* are the straw sandals which are the only correct footwear of the mountain ascetic.

TSŪZOKU: POPULAR SHINTO

Local cults and rituals, along with popular but uninstitutionalized *kami*, are usually designated as folk Shinto. Cults grew around figures such as *Tengu*, a mythical object of devotion in many parts of Japan. Shrines can be found in various isolated locations that are strange admixtures of Shinto and folk culture. Some of that folk culture contains strands of Taoism, which entered Japan but was effectively contained and transformed by the mid-Nara period. Traces remain, for example, in the tales of the *Hagoromo*, young women in swan-like feather robes who descend to earth to bathe. The *Nagu Jinja* in Takeno enshrines Toyokanome-no-mikoto. Legend has it that an aging couple, finding a *Hagoromo* bathing, took the feather robe without which she could not return to her supernatural world. She agreed to become their adopted daughter and brewed a delicious *sake* that made them very wealthy. They then turned her out and she wandered until she came to the village of Nagu, where she settled and became Toyokanome-no-mikoto, transforming herself into a *kami* of cereals. In ways like this the idea of the world beyond, the *Toyoko-no-kuni* of the *Nihongi*, the mysterious sacred realm of *kami* became intertwined with folk ideas. Developments such as this, dating to the Nara period and before, produced many sites for shrines that literally grew out of the popular religious mind.

Such religious mentality never disappeared and re-emerged in various forms of popular syncretism. It reflects the Japanese dislike for drawing hard and fast distinctions. By government order, institutions based on syncretism had to decide whether they were shrines or temples after the Meiji Restoration, but many did not totally comply with government requirements. The ones that did were able to return to their former ways after 1946. Such phenomena illustrate the syncretistic tendencies in Japanese religion that traditionally revered the *kami* and the Buddha and followed the teachings of Confucius. The constitutions of the early Japanese merchant houses, such as the House of Mitsui, included exactly these injunctions in their practices. They counseled against excessive fervor about religion but required the basic observances of religion by all House members. This syncretism produced new movements from time to time, and it is from the mass of such movements that the various sects of Kyōha Shinto emerged during the later Edo and early Meiji periods.

Two movements that characteristically combined reverence for the three great strands of Japanese religion were *Shingaku* and *Hōtoku*. Both arose and flourished during the Edo period and were, in many ways, among the most typical products of the popular syncretistic ethico-religious mentality encouraged by the government.

Shingaku

Ishida Baigan (1685–1746)[19] founded a movement that is usually classified as popular Shinto. The central ideas were both religious and ethical; the strong moral teaching included elements of Buddhism and Confucian virtues. It had a strong foundation in Shinto, particularly stressing the worship of Amaterasu and of one's own *uji-gami*. It also included elements of Zen thought and some aspects of neo-Confucian cosmology, which it combined into simple precepts for the daily life of ordinary people.

The movement began in Kyoto and spread nationwide. It primarily stressed the improvement of the heart (*kokoro*, a concept that remains very important in the teachings of the New Religions), hence the name *Shingaku*, "heart-learning." The idea of "heart" in Ishida's thought encompasses the seat of the emotions and the source of actions, although normally in Japanese the *hara* (stomach) is viewed in this way. Ishida thought that the heart can be cultivated as a source of good actions. His use of *kokoro* is remarkably similar to the use of *lev* (heart) in the Hebrew tradition. Ishida's movement widely influenced ordinary people and was easily combined with whatever local institutions they belonged to or shrines or temples with which they were affiliated. It still survives in indirect forms and continues to be in the background of many new religious movements, just as it lay in the background of Sect Shinto.

Hōtoku

Ninomiya Sontoku (1787–1856),[20] a peasant farmer sage, was the founder of this movement, which has a remarkable history and whose followers in modern times include some distinguished Japanese intellectuals. The term means "repayment of indebtedness" and was the basis of a movement that later became popular with the Japanese government at the time of the creation of State Shinto. The debt was the debt of people to ancestors, parents, and to Heaven and Earth for all they have given to mankind.

Originally, Ninomiya's purpose was to devise schemes for economic development in rural areas, and he considered that certain moral and mental attitudes were essential to the development of any successful economic theory. He believed that if people do not have a reason to work or do not see it as an integral part of the meaning of life, they will not be motivated. Consequently, he created a religious ideology around the concept of *Hō-toku*; and the idea of repayment of indebtedness dovetailed with reverence for Buddha, *kami* worship, and the practice of Confucian values. His teaching had four basic elements. He stressed sincerity of mind (*shisei*), the virtue of industrious labor (*kinrō*), the ideal of a planned economy (*bundo*), and the virtue of yielding to others (*suijō*).

On the fiftieth anniversary of Ninomiya's death the Ministry of Home Affairs decided to promote the idea in the interest of national development, so it formed *Hōtoku* societies all around the country, stressing loyalty to the house (*ie*) and to the family of the nation. Repayment of indebtedness was now subtly redirected toward the Emperor, the *kami*, and the State as well as toward parents and ancestors. According to records of the times, the Ministry of Home Affairs became sarcastically renamed the *Hōtoku Naimushō*. It serves as another illustration of the way in which the government manipulated people's natural sensitivities and feelings for reverence toward sacred objects to strengthen the Imperial image and the centrality of the *kokutai*. The Ministry of Education had a statue of *Ninomiya Kinjirō*, the symbol of the cult, placed in every school playground established during the Meiji period. Depicted as a barefoot boy in Japanese dress carrying a bundle of sticks, he was used as a model for moral education. He was presented as a boy who endured misfortune and hardship to exemplify all the Japanese virtues.[21] Young people were encouraged to follow his courageous and determined example, to study diligently, work hard, and live in a sacrificial manner.

Although they are not purely Shinto, both *Shingaku* and *Hōtoku* are important simply because they employed a view of human nature that is associated with Shinto. Grasping the significance of these two movements aids in understanding the new religions.

Local Cults and Kami

Under this category may be listed some of the *uji-gami* that small and sometimes large shrines set up for the protection of local areas, old family residences and other special places, events, people, or natural phenomena. There were approximately 70,000 of these listed after the Meiji Restoration, so a detailed discussion of them is not possible. However, alongside these were numerous *kami* to whom people resorted but who are not always formally enshrined. These include the *shichi-fuku-jin*, the seven *kami* of good fortune. Traditionally, Japanese communities were organized around two shrines and two *kami* or sets of *kami*. First was the ancestral *kami* of the community, a historical founding figure or a great benefactor. The other was the *kami* of the land itself, the creative *kami*. Herein probably lie the origins of the *uji-gami* concept, the *kami* of the family. In some regions, after individuals passed away there was a custom by which that person was recognized as a *ji-kami*, a land *kami*, thirty years after death. The *ji-kami* in time shaded into *kami* such as the *ta-no-kami*, the *kami* of the field. *Dozoku-shin* (kinship-related *kami*), although somewhat vague, have as their main function to strengthen the relationship of the individual to the locality and to seal that relationship with reverence for the area *kami*. The existence of countless numbers of local *kami* left plenty of room for the emergence and development of regional cults. It is from these roots and the complex of phenomena discussed earlier in this section that the popular movements of the Edo period grew along with the movements later known as *Kyōha Shinto*.

KYŌHA SHINTO

Kyōha Shinto refers to various independent sects that grew up especially during the late Edo period and that received special status from the Meiji government. The basic difference between Shrine Shinto and Kyōha Shinto is that although both have deep roots in folk religion, Kyōha sects, because they were historically later in developing and grew self-consciously, could identify a founder, and a formal set of teachings and may even have produced some sacred writings. Most tended to come from simple background. Their teachings were correspondingly simple and had a great appeal to ordinary people. This new development within the world of Shinto allowed for the growth of new cults and new ideas in a way that had not been seen since the Kamakura period.

The distinction between Shrine Shinto and Sect or "Religious" Shinto had one unfortunate repercussion. It made possible the later claim that Shinto was not in fact a religion, because "religious" types of Shinto could be distinguished from Shrine Shinto. It was a policy of the Meiji government to use reverence for the Emperor as the basis of State Shinto. State recognition of Sect Shinto commenced in 1876 and was completed by 1904. Part of the reason for this recognition was to make the distinction between folk Shinto and government-approved rituals clear and unambiguous. Scholars such as Yanagita Kunio and the professors of the University of Tokyo, as civil servants, were required to offer arguments that the government-required observances of State Shinto did not violate the freedom of religion that was technically permitted by the Constitution, because Shinto was a folk way and not a religion.

Kyōha Shinto sects are usually classified under five headings. There are the Pure Shinto Sects: *Shinto Tai-kyō, Shinri-kyō,* and *Izumo Ōyashiro-kyō*. The Confucian Sects are *Shinto Shusei-ha* and *Taisei-kyō*. The Mountain Sects are *Jikkō-kyō, Fusō-kyō,* and *Mitake-kyō*. The Purification Sects are *Shinshu-kyō* and *Misogi-kyō*. The three Faith Healing Sects are *Kuro-*

zumi-kyō, Konkō-kyō, and Tenri-kyō. Historically, these may be divided into the religious groups that developed before the Meiji Restoration; those that reflect the strict religious policy of the government; and those that had a pre-Meiji beginning but came into line with the Meiji government policy. On etymology, kyō means "teaching" and ha means "sect." Kyō-ha refers to Shinto sects with explicit teachings that were transmitted to believers, as distinct from shrines that had less articulate cultic beliefs surrounding an enshrined kami.

In contemporary terms, it appears to be a declining movement. Statistics suggest that the entire Kyōha Shinto group is losing support, having lost nearly one million members between 1975 and 1985. It registered a total membership of 6,093,557 in 1975. The comparative figure in 1987 was 5,182,085 (which represents roughly a 16 percent decrease). Reasons for the decline may be explained in various ways. Undoubtedly, the further Japan moves from the Meiji period, the less likely these movements are liable to be perceived as relevant, unless they introduce major changes in their teachings. The changed social climate between 1950 and 1990 must also be a factor leading to reduced recruitment; and many new religions came into being during that time that are probably much more attractive to younger people.

Pure *Shinto* Sects

Shinto Taikyō. The movement for independent recognition of the thirteen Kyōha sects by the government, spearheaded by *Shinto Taikyō*, began in 1882 and lasted through 1908 (from Meiji 15 to Meiji 41). By looking at the development of Shinto Taikyō it is possible to understand not only the various steps in the recognition of the Kyōha movement but also how Kyōha Shinto in general and Shinto Taikyō in particular played a significant a role in the rise of Japanese nationalism alongside *Kokka Shinto*.

The Meiji government did not initially pursue a consistent policy toward Shinto. Shinto Taikyō,[22] a product of the Meiji period mentality, began in 1873 with the founding of the *Taikyō-in*. This was intended to be the central organization of the domestic missionary activity of Shinto, following the injunction of Emperor Meiji: *"Taikyō sempu no mikonotori"* (to revive the great way, Shinto, in his era). The *Taikyō-in* was dissolved after factional struggles and, instead, the *Shinto Jimukyoku*, the Office of Shinto, was established. After the separation of religion from politics (*seikyō-bunri*) had been declared in 1882, the *Shinto Jimukyoku* was renamed *Shinto Honkyoku* and Viscount Masakuni Inaba was elected as the first president (*kanchō*). He defined the basic doctrines of Shinto Taikyō in response to which the Ministry of Home Affairs recognized it as a sect, distinguishing for the first time between Sect and State Shinto. Inaba can be given credit for both forming Shinto Taikyō as it is now known and for making space within the government system for other forms of Sect Shinto.

His successor was Inaba Masayoshi (appointed in 1898, or Meiji 31), whose main work was the organization of both teaching and teachers. Sect Shinto began to rise in popularity because it was seen to be in harmony with Japan as a land of the *kami* (*shinkoku shiso*), an idea that had been revived for ideological and propaganda purposes during the Sino-Japanese War at the turn of the century. The next president, Honda Kojo, took up office just before the Russo-Japanese War. He meticulously observed government injunctions to stimulate nationalism. *Shinto Honkyoku* along with Buddhism and Christianity encouraged the nation to confront Russia, merely acting in common with all other religious movements of the time. The sixth *Kanchō*, Hayashi Gosuke, decided to replace the name *Shinto Honkyoku* with *Shinto Taikyō* in an effort to establish a measure of independence from government pressure. Thus, it continued to promote the great teaching (*Taikyō*) until the end of the Pacific War, when its status came up for review. In 1951 it was recognized by the Ministry of Education as a religious corporate person (*shūkyo hōjin*) and received the formal identity of Shinto Taikyō by which it is still known.

Like other movements in the group, Shinto Taikyō underwent a transformation after the Pacific War; as a result, the emphasis of its teaching ceased to be upon *kannagara* as a way to unite the nation and focused instead upon *kannagara* as a way of peace and harmony. The transformation is indeed remarkable. The new ideals were to be achieved by the composition of *waka* poems, the practice of calligraphy, the way of tea, and the practice of martial arts such as *Aikidō*. By means of these, people would become closer to the *kami*, a doctrine that became the focus of Shinto Taikyō. The name still retains nationalist overtones, but the content has been thoroughly revised.

Although it is no longer overtly missionary, Shinto Taikyō drew up plans for expansion in 1965. An enlarged headquarters was to be a base for energizing of the spirit of the Japanese people and for functioning as the central office buildings of all religious movements in the group. The plan was not carried out through lack of resources.

Beliefs and Teachings. The influence of the president seems profound in the formation of an outlook on life by believers, but Four Great Beliefs (*Shinto Taikyō Yon-dai Shinjō*) that are defined as the basis of the movement are more orthodox in their content.

1. *Tentoku* (heaven-virtue) refers to Ame-no-minakushi-no-kami, who is considered to be the cosmic law of time and space and to be the source of goodness, love, morality, and inspiration from whom human beings receive wisdom and virtue.

2. *Chi-on* (earth-benefit) is the worldview aspect of the teaching that centers on the visible form of Ame-no-minakushi-no-kami as *inyo-nishin*.

The positive and negative *kami* are Taka-musubi-no-kami and Kami-musubi-no-kami. These three form the *zoka-sanshin* (the three *kami* of creation) in an orthodox interpretation of the mythology.

3. *Shōjō* (purity) refers to the phenomenal world of human life that is relative and limited by time and space. Although they are born from the *kami*, human beings become egocentric in order to survive, because of their environment. The struggles that result from this destroy harmony, so humanity becomes estranged from the spiritual world. Believers are expected to express and achieve truth (*shin*), goodness (*zen*), and beauty (*bi*). These have a purifying effect. By removing impurities through ritual purification (*harai*) and calming the soul (*chinkon*), they may return to the level of the *kami*.

4. *Kōmyō* (light-bright) deals with how to live life. When people follow the will of the *kami* by realizing their own dignity and that of others, and when they live close to the *kami* in the spirit of *shōjō*, an ideal society will come about. Hatred and conflict will be replaced by peace and love.

For other ideas, it is necessary to turn to the sect's main publication, *Shintoshinshi*, a quarterly magazine written by and for believers. Half of its forty pages from a typical 1988 edition were devoted to the activities of the eighth *kanchō*, Shinada Shohei, his own *waka*, or *waka* written in praise of him. In his position close to the *kami*, he is able to give advice to others on how to achieve that ideal state. Articles explained how he had met and knew the world's principal leaders. Believers reported supernatural experiences, such as hearing the voice of the *kami* or being assisted to perform impossible tasks because of inspiration from the teachings of *Taikyō*. The cultic side of the movement remains strong, although Shinada's teachings still resemble more traditional values. Indeed, a strong vein of nationalism can still be detected.

This is most evident in the content of some of the *waka* composed by the president:

> *Kore wa mi wa chichi-haha no mono-kami no mono-umiko no mono-ada ni sumajiki.*
> "My body belongs to my parents and ancestors, the *kami* and my descendants—so I must not waste it in selfish pursuits."

This is his understanding of *kannagara-no-michi* based upon the concept of *Nihonjin to shite no dogi*, the natural spirituality of the Japanese people derived from *ko-shin-dō* or *ko-dō* (the ancient way).

Through ideas like these Shinto Taikyō sees itself as a traditional form of religion that needs to be spread in Japan to confront the problems of modern society. The Japanese will receive wisdom only when they return to the ancestral faith. Present-day Japan is represented as being overlaid by "colonial" culture, and therefore the traditional Japanese spirit has been set aside. This position is ethnocentric and mildly extremist, but at the same time it is claimed that the *Taikyō* has elements and a spirit that can be beneficial to people all around the world. It has points in common with other religions that, it is argued, show no grounds for conflict.

Shinada expresses great respect for Emperor Meiji, the *tennōsei* (emperor system), and the Imperial Rescript on Education (*Kyōiku-chokugo*), which was condemned after the war as being one source of Japanese militarism. Shinada claims that the essence of its teaching was simply the ideal of the upright heart (*naoki kokoro*). These ideas are also expounded in *waka*:

> *Nippon mo zokkokuka shite rōmaji wa sengo chimata ni hanran sen to su*
> "Japan after the war is in a colonial state with romanization flourishing everywhere."
> *Nihongo no shinka shirashime nihongo o sekaigo ni made hiromen to omō*
> "Let the world know the value of Japanese language and make it a world language."
> *Kokubō no kyōka nakushite Nihon no heiwa to anzen nashi toshi omō*
> "There will be no peace and security in Japan without strengthening defense."
> *Shin taiko shūkyō kyōryoku nakariseba sekai heiwa wa eikyu ni kuru nashi*
> "World peace will never come unless we practice the will of the *kami* and all religions cooperate in this."

Organization and Believers. Since 1951, Shinto Taikyō has remained important and influential for its size because it technically remains the official representative of all Kyōha Shinto groups, although most of these have outgrown it in size. At a religious summit held on Mt. Hie in August 1987, the president of Shinto Taikyō intoned the *norito* for peace on behalf of all thirteen Kyōha sects. Shinto Taikyō originally embraced shrines and groups that had neither the size, economic power, nor originality of belief to be independent. Fully 194 shrines came under its jurisdiction in this way. Regardless of the differences of specific beliefs, all follow common roots in Shinto.

Group education is under the control of teachers (*kyōshi*) who may have any one of fourteen ranks (*kyōshi shokkai jūyon dankai*), including titles such as *Dai-kyōjo* (at the top) or *Gon-dai-kyōjo* and *Chū-kyōjo* (further down).

The headquarters of Shinto Taikyō is the *Shinto Taikyōin* in Azabu, Tokyo. There is a meeting on the twenty-first day of each month, open to anyone, at which teachers and believers interact. The monthly meeting and the ranking system are relics of the Shinto missionary movement ideal of the early Meiji period. There is still a director of missions (*senkyō buchō*). The position of *kanchō* is filled by direct election. Unlike religious groups in Japan that depend heavily upon the charismatic power of one leader, Shinto Taikyō seems to be like an institution in the Western sense with a system of order that carries it from year to year.

Enshrined in the *shinden* of the headquarters in Azabu shrine are the heavenly *kami*, the earthly *kami*, and the *yao yorozu no kami*. There seems also to have been a dispute around 1882 as to whether or not Okuni-nushi-no-mikoto was enshrined early on. A calligraphy by Prince Arisugawa speaks of the *Tenshin-chinshin* (the *kami* of Heaven and Earth), the *Kashikodokoro* (the shrine in the Imperial Family Ancestors). Shinto Taikyō is totally dependent upon *gojozai* (dedicated offerings) and *osaisen* (offerings made when approaching the *kami*). Each April a budget is submitted to the Shinto Taikyō committee, which governs all future courses of action. Its faithful number approximately 45,000.[23]

Shinri-kyō. The sect was founded by Kannagibe (later Sano) Tsunehiko (1837–1910), who claimed to be the seventy-seventh descendant of a *kami* called Nigi-hayahi-no-mikoto, one of the *kami* attending Amaterasu Ōmikami. The Kannagibe family were originally practitioners of medicine; but because of the influences of foreign learning upon medicine, their activities became confused with Christianity. Sano himself wished to go into medicine, but for fear of being mistaken for a Christian believer he decided to propagate the family teaching instead. Between 1882 and 1886 he claimed to have received divine revelations in his dreams, which gave him confidence in both his divine mission and his divine ancestry. The sect was given government recognition in 1894; it became a part of *Ontake-kyō* initially but separated in 1908 and became an independent sect. Sano's brother, Takane, and his son Izuhuiko became the principal exponents after Sano died in Kyushu in 1910. Groups gradually began to emerge, initially in northern Kyushu and expanding from there. The tradition is maintained by direct descendants who use either Sano or Kannagibe as a family name.

The name *Shin-ri-kyō* includes the basic character *kyō* (teaching). *Shin* is the same character as *kami*. *Ri* (principle or reason) is a Confucian concept. *Ron-ri-gaku* (argument-principle-science) became the Japanese philosophical term for Aristotlean logic. *Ri* in Confucian thought referred to the principles of order within the universe. Thus, *Shin-ri-kyō* means "Teaching of the Divine Order."[24]

The sect sought to promote the national language and, like Shinto Taikyō, the writing of poetry, *kagura* (sacred dance), and flower arrangement. *Kami* revered include the three central *kami* of creation (the *zoka-sanshin*) and the principal *kami* of the *kami-yo*. The basic doctrines make use of the idea of the spirit of words (*kotodama*), indicating that the concepts are grounded in the classic ideas of Shinto. This becomes much clearer with a grasp of the basic doctrines.

Beliefs and Teaching. The fundamental ideas[25] do not depart far from traditional Shrine Shinto in that the *kami* are revered and proximity to the *kami* remains the condition for human happiness. To achieve this, believers must purify their own hearts and then their surroundings. With blessings from one's ancestors, happiness will come about through these improvements. Shinri-kyō claims that people are reincarnations of their ancestors and that if there is unhappiness or misery, the essential cause lies with the ancestors. The root of unhappiness is due either to the fact that some ancestors did not rise to divinity or to the negligence of individuals in paying adequate respect to their ancestors. Ancestors must be properly served in order to bring about the best possible conditions in the present. This becomes the power to protect one's own offspring and to guarantee survival to posterity. The duties are listed in the articles of Shinri-kyō.

Article I: Follow the teachings of the High Ancestor (the divine ancestor of the Kannagibe family), Nigi-hayahi-no-mikoto, to make clear the meaning of *kotodama* and to understand the doctrines of *Shin-ri*.

Article II: Believe in the limitless, miraculous power of all heavenly *kami* and in the indivisibility of the physical and spiritual worlds. When the heart is made pure and conduct rectified, hardships and illnesses are healed. If we act, we will attain; if we pray, the divine power will operate. But believers must neither say nor do that which is opposed to the truth. (Truth means beliefs of the sect, not forensic or scientific truth in the Western sense.)

Article III: Repudiate heresies and delusions as contempt for rulers and father and weaken the evil cause of severing ancestral relations. Keep deep gratitude toward one's origins. Everything in the world is the creation of the divine will, might, and purpose. Acceptance of the way of the *kami* and submission to it is the essence of Reason, the true Way. (Confucian influences show here as well as Shinto, particularly in the idea of rectifying conduct.)

The principal teachings are summarized in the Ten Negative Precepts. Correctly observed, not only do these precepts guarantee making the best of one's existence, but when the human will conforms to the divine will, people of later generations are guaranteed to succeed them. Material prosperity in this world and bliss in the world to come is the goal. (Shinto emphasis upon happiness in the present is echoed here.) The Ten Negative Precepts of Shinri-kyō contain the principal teachings to be observed:

1. Do not transgress the will of the *kami*.

2. Do not forget your obligations to your ancestors; especially do not forget the kindness of the founder.

3. Do not transgress the decrees of the State.

4. Do not forget the profound goodness of the *kami* whereby misfortune is averted and sickness is healed.

5. Do not forget that the world is one great family.

6. Do not forget the limitations of your own person.

7. Even though others become angry, do not become angry yourself.

8. Do not be slothful in your business.

9. Do not be a person who brings blame to the teaching.

10. Do not be carried away by foreign teaching.

The teaching referred to in the ninth precept means the claim that the "*kami* is good, principle, and nature." Through ancestors, people receive part of the "good"; and it becomes each person's mission in life to carry on the work of the ancestral wills. The *Shin-ri*, the divine principle, is active in all the universe and becomes incarnate in people. Consequently, when individuals duly revere their ancestors and follow the Way, the divine principle becomes realized in the world. The way of Heaven and Earth coincide and there is harmony and peace as well as the prospect of true happiness.

The Ten Negative Prohibitions are supplemented by a set of principles called *Oboe* (Things to be Learned and Remembered) or *Kyōkun* (Lessons for Today):

1. In one day, today, do not have a spirit of laziness.

2. Today, do not say or do falsehoods.

3. Today, do not be poverty-stricken unless because of a shortage of divine will.

4. Today, no matter what happens, do not lose your temper.

5. Today, do not harbor a spirit of vanity.

6. Today, no matter what worries befall you, do not despair.

7. Today, do not feel bitter toward people or work.

8. This honorable day is all for the sake of the compassionate *kami* of Heaven and Earth. If it is at all possible for us to repay this honorable debt, we should seek to spend the day in happiness and enjoyment.

Omamori are available for protection; rituals and ceremonies of divination and reverence for the dead are considered necessary expressions of belief and are basic forms of Shinri-kyō practice.

Sensitivity to the spirit of words (*kotodama*) is evidenced by the preservation of distinctive terms and expressions that are embodied in rituals and addresses to the *kami*. Shinri-kyō also has special seventeen-syllable formulas called *Kai-kai* and words that express the spirit of *Shin-ri*. It also has numerous expressions for some of its central ideas, such as *Mitama-mono-orisuga-kami-wa-yosete* (to bring the spirit close to the *kami* in search of the human-*kami* boundary), *Waga-kokoro suga-suga shi* (to purify one's heart through divinity), or *Kannagi-kan-uranai* (to tell the future and one's fortune by means of divine rituals and practices). *Chinkon* is defined as balancing and harmonizing the soul to rectify its workings through introducing the divine into it.

Organization and Believers. The headquarters of the sect is in Kokura, in Kita-Kyushu. The fourth-generation head of the organization (in 1991) was Kannagibe Takehiko (born in 1948). The largest concentration (250,000) of the 1,500,000 members of the movement is in Kita-Kyushu, but groups of believers are found in areas such as Eastern Chūgoku, Kinki, and other parts of the south. Followers are referred to by the name *Kyōshin-to* (learner-believers of the faith) and are divided into *kyō-to, shin-to,* and *shin-ja.* The most pious are sometimes elevated to the title of *yokusan-in,* which is subdivided into fifteen ranks. Teachers of Shinri-kyō themselves are graded into fifteen ranks. Groups of believers meet in "churches" (*kyo-kai*), a common expression used in Sect Shinto.

Izumo Ōyashiro-kyō. The sect dates to 1874, when the 80th governor of Kuninomiyatsuko (Izumo Province), Senge Takatomi, was also the *Guji* of *Izumo Taisha.* He left the *ujiko* of *Izumo-ōyashiro,* the shrine supporters' organization, to form the *Izumo Taisha Kei Shinko,* which recognized Izumo no Kuni nomi yatsuko and had Ame-ho-hi-no-mikoto as its head. Meiji government policy to use Shinto for national goals centered on the worship of Amaterasu and the *zoka-sanshin* but did not encourage the worship of Okuni-nushi-no-mikoto. It also placed restrictions upon the activities of all religious groups.

In 1882, *Taisha-kyō* was authorized as an independent sect under the leadership of Senge Takatomi. Although its main purpose was to popularize the worship of Okuni-nushi-no-mikoto, it also sought to promote the Great Way of the *kami* for the purpose of cultivating national character. This brought it into line with the ideals of the *kokutai* taught by the Meiji government and made it more acceptable.

After the end of the Pacific War, the organization was freed from state control; by 1951 *Izumo Taisha* had repossessed *Izumo Ōyashiro-kyō.* It has a separate existence although it is under full control of the shrine authorities. It functions nationwide as a base for the support of the shrine. The Senge family, hereditary priests of the shrine, now head the sect.

Beliefs and Teachings.[26] Members of the sect strive to follow three fundamental ideas:

1. To make our hearts upright and to govern our bodies.

2. To have compassion on those who are less fortunate than ourselves; and by giving instruction to those who defy the divine will, to lead them to enter our upright fellowship.

3. To devise ways of realizing genuine happiness and of attaining that spiritual power which pierces through all things both revealed and unrevealed and which exists both now and hereafter.

The sect has a complete statement of goals and expectations of itself and its members:

Those who have entered into this church, while reverently thanking and worshipping the divine goodness, should first and foremost accept and embody the divine purpose of loving their fellow men, should keep in mind the duty of improvement and achievement, and should give expression to moral sincerity. If one is merely greedy of divine blessings and is regardless of human duties, if one is selfishly lacking in concern for others, such a person desecrates the divine goodness and defies the divine purpose of love for others. He does not understand human duty and betrays the principles of the church. One should abandon the distinction of "other" and "self" and should consummate a heart of compassion for his fellow men, ever mindful of the fact that acts of knowing the truth and doing it are not performed merely for the sake of one's own interests, ever knowing that suffering and blessing, advantage and disadvantage, are to be shared widely with others and not in violation of the divine purpose of compassion and equality and not in injury of the good faith of one's fellow men. We believe that these are the main principles of human morals and the gist of one's duty in giving thanks for divine blessings. Therefore the believers of our church, by adding to and extending the benevolence of spirit which we have received as a natural endowment and by showing gratitude for divine goodness, should perform in the world with common duties of humanity. In the world to come such people will shine with the glory of those who have become *kami*.

Organization and Believers. The relationship between the *Izumo Taisha* and the sect illustrates the manner in which some traditional and acknowledged shrines relate to independent groups. Among the most important festivals at *Izumo* are the *Kami-ai-sai* and the *Kami-nari-sai*; these are celebrated in October, when it is believed that the *kami* of Japan all assemble at *Izumo*. Bonfires are lit on the beach to welcome and send off the *kami*. Supporters of *Izumo* come from all over Japan for that event.

The number of registered followers was 1,116,577 as of 1989. The sect's headquarters is within the shrine offices of *Izumo Taisha*.

Confucian Sects

Shinto Shūsei-ha. This sect was organized by Nitta Kunimitsu, who claimed descent from Nitta Yoshisada, an early fourteenth-century warrior renowned for his belief in the virtue of loyalty. Nitta was born in Awa (Tokushima Prefecture) on 5 December 1829, and he died in November 1902. His Confucian and warrior backgrounds inspired him to try to master the arts of both pen and sword. Although the *samurai* class was in decline by the early nineteenth century, in the classic tradition he studied the Chinese classics and the way of the *bushi* in an attempt to discover the proper bearing for a warrior and a gentleman scholar.

At the age of twenty he began to promote the teachings of Shinto as he understood them for the enlightenment of his fellow countrymen. Members of the Oshi clan opposed his activities and began successful slander campaigns, after which he was imprisoned. However, as often happens, his imprisonment had the effect of inducing "enlightenment." His writings before and after the imprisonment period indicate the nature and depth of his conversion experience. After his release, he became more determined than ever to work for the improvement of public morality (in the Confucian sense). With a show of public spirit, he and his companions tried to bring Shinto to greater prominence, stressing moral obligations, patriotism, and its own status as a Great Way. He wished to teach people to become good citizens, to serve in the military if required, and above all to make Japan's economy prosperous by whatever sacrifice was required. These themes found favor with the Meiji government, and he finally was vindicated when the sect was formally recognized in 1876. So successful did he become that he received ten citations and honors from the Imperial Court for his good influence on society.

His teachings, although Confucian in character, claimed to be drawn from the classic texts: the *Kojiki*, the *Nihongi*, the *Kogo Shūi* (Mythological Annals of Japan), and the *Shi Sho Go Kyō*. Reflecting the influence of the *Chu Kun Ai Koku*, in his thought the Imperial tradition was supremely to be revered. He belonged to the *So nō Jōi* faction, which tried to exclude all foreign influences from the developing nation. He definitely reflected the ideology of the period, which called for people to act morally, be loyal to the Meiji government, work and support their families, serve the country, and make Japan great.

Shūsei-ha typifies the blending of Confucian influences with Shinto to generate social ethics that promoted ideals such as loyalty, filial piety, and respect for government authority. It makes use of fundamental Shinto concepts such as *kami* but combines them with elements of the cosmology of neo-Confucian thought and other syncretistic beliefs.

The name *Shūsei* consists of *shūri* (to repair) and *kōsei* (to consolidate). Both terms come from the *Kojiki* in relation to the work of Izanagi and Izanami; in combination they imply a conservative philosophy.

Beliefs and Teachings. The teachings[27] as set out in the publications of the sect illustrate the syncretism of Nitta's original ideas:

1. The myriad forms and manifold network of the universe, including man and the moral world and all things whatsoever, have come into being through the spiritual activity of the true deity of creation, and the soul of man is of one substance with this heavenly deity. The principles of this sect consist of the protecting and careful fostering of this superlatively good soul.

2. Izanagi and Izanami, at the command of the *kami* of Heaven, improved and consolidated this country, including peoples, creatures, grasses, trees, and all

things whatsoever. Accordingly, in *shuri kōsei* (strengthening, making secure) lies the fundamental law of the evolution of the universe; and in truth, the progress of mankind and the advancement of society are due to the operation of this one principle.

3. *Shūri kōsei* is also the process of observing faithfully the moral law and the means by which the affairs of family and society are administered. The purpose is brought to realization through the glorious and radiant virtue of Amaterasu-Omikami.

4. *Kogamesai* means the character of Amaterasu to be radiant and virtuous, which lays demands upon individuals to approximate their lives and conduct to this ideal.

The sect reveres the three central *kami* of creation (*zoka-sanshin*). Together with Izanagi-no-mikoto and Amaterasu they are known as the *Go Chu no Amastsu Kami*. In combination with the myriad of *kami* (*yao yorozu no kami*), they are revered under the general name of *Shu Sei Tai Shin*, the Great Kami of *Shu Sei*. *Tai Shin* is the Chinese (and therefore Confucian) style of reading of *Okami*.

Nitta's Ten Commandments for daily life are model Confucian values:

1. Practice and acquire the way of *shuri kōsei*.
2. Worship the *kami* and repay their virtue.
3. Be always conscious of the grace of one's ancestors and thank and worship them.
4. Stir up *Yamato-damashii* (the warrior spirit of Japan) and thank the Emperor for his grace and serve him.
5. Act in a moral way and strengthen your will.
6. Attend to your business and work for the success of your family.
7. Maintain temperance and frugality and always live within your means.
8. Use Japanese-made products. Don't be attracted by foreign countries.
9. Do what you have said and say what you have done. Live honestly.
10. Bear trials, patiently. Have faith in *Shūsei dō* and perform *kōsei* to complete and fulfill your mind.

Commandments 4 and 8 were eliminated after 1945 as being too nationalistic, although the Japanese preference for domestic products seems to remain a national trait.[28]

Organization and Believers. The leadership consists of designated teachers who have received a five-day training course during which the doctrines are taught formally by the older teachers. The nuance of "teachers" approximates to "missionaries" because they are seeking to spread their teachings nationwide. Once teaching status has been given, teachers engage in ascetic practices such as *misogi*, or in acts of self-denial.

Currently, the center of the sect's religious activities is in Shizuoka Prefecture on a mountain where the worshippers revere *Shinto Shūsei Ha Tai Gen Shi*. Principal ceremonies occur on April 4 and 5 and November 24 and 25. The original head office was in Saitama Prefecture but was moved to Suginami Ward in Tokyo. There are a total of 152 branches and 929 official teachers, 671 male and 258 female. Recorded membership in 1989 was 40,610, compared to 408,000 before the war. Leadership in 1989 was in the hands of fourth-generation Nitta Kunio (born in 1972).

Branch activities center on a monthly ceremony called *Tsukinami Sai*, the main festival. Counseling services are also offered. Members may consult with their teachers on personal matters and may receive advice followed by *oharai*, which shows the combined Shinto and cultic elements of the movement.

Taisei-kyō. This sect was founded by Hirayama Shosai (1815–1890), born as Kuroda Katsuensai and adopted as a Hirayama, who in time became a foreign affairs official of the Edo government. He was a loyal follower of the Tokugawa regime and served it as a *samurai* in several capacities, including as a member of the Council of the Shogun. Like *Shūsei*, he was concerned to use Shinto forms to promote neo-Confucian values. Because of his loyalty to the Edo shogunate, he was confined in 1870 by the Meiji government to Shizuoka. There he studied *Taidokokugaku Shinto* under Munihide Honso, after which he became a priest of the *Hikawa Nichie Jinja*. The new sect was approved on 19 September 1879 under the name *Taisei-Kyōkai*. In 1882 it became *Shinto Taisei-Kyō*. Like other Kyōha sects, it professes to worship Amaterasu and the three central *kami* of creation. The sect reveres seven other *kami*: Amano-onchu-no-kami, Koho-Sanrei-no-kami, Shinko-Sanrei-no-kami, Tensho-kodai-o-kami, Izanagi-no-Mikoto, Susano-o-no-Mikoto, and Okuni-Nushi-no-Mikoto.

Beliefs and Teaching. By observing the Three Teachings and the Five Statements contained in the sect's sacred texts, an individual can eliminate his or her tendencies to excessive preoccupation with self and can commence becoming a *kami*.[29] The three teachings are designed as gates, which is a Buddhist style of expounding a teaching as a way to a place or to a path that leads to enlightenment:

1. *Hoken-Kyō-mon*: having the courage to resist the evil spirits that possess people.
2. *Gyōho-Kyō-Mon*: knowing the holiness of the way, to construct relationships that properly express filial piety.
3. *Shinkyō-Kyō-Mon*: believing that people have good spirits and can always be reformed if they make the effort.

The name combines *Tai* (great), *Sei* (achievement), and *Kyō* (Teaching). The root term *taisei* carries the nuance of successfully completing a task.

The Five Statements are descriptions of or propositions about the world as the sect sees it. These are combined with recommendations about how people should live to benefit from it by achieving the goals of the sect:

1. *Kenyū Mujini*: this world and the world after death are one and the same.
2. *Shisei kan*: a nation is not divided.
3. *Jōju Anraku*: always live peacefully and try to enjoy life.
4. *Shinjin Dōki*: *kami* and human beings will return to the same origin.
5. *Fukumei Tenshin*: report to the *kami* and open the door to understand the teachings.

The Precepts of Taisei-kyō are stated as follows:

1. To observe the ownership of the *kami* of Heaven and Earth and the distant worship of the spirits of successive generations of Emperors and of the deities of the Imperial sanctuaries.
2. To observe the divine commandments that are imperishable as Heaven and Earth and to strengthen the national organization.
3. To make clear the way of human conduct as revealed by Heaven.
4. To train ourselves in devotion to the true law and to strengthen the foundations of inner tranquility.
5. To unite the temporal and spiritual worlds with a clear understanding of the meaning of life and death.
6. To study science and technique and to encourage business enterprise.
7. To carry on religious rites and ceremonies after the manner of successive generations of Imperial Courts.

The sect also teaches the doctrine of improving human instincts by means of the twelve Oriental Zodiac signs. Fortune-telling based on these birth signs can be used to select propitious days or compass directions to promote the success of events and projects. Although in fact these ideas originally came from popular Chinese Taoism, they have become a large part of Japanese culture and are extensively used in shrines and in Buddhist temples as well as by non-religious professional fortune-tellers. Annual sales of fortune-telling publications are in the millions of copies.

Organization and Believers. The original headquarters was at Haramachi in Koshikawa. Air raids on Tokyo during 1945 destroyed the main shrine, which was moved to Kurumsaka in Ueno and then to Kojimachi. The current head shrine is *Tensho-San-Jinja* in Shibuya-ku near Harajuku Station in Tokyo. The movement is organized into churches with central places of worship at seven designated shrines. In 1938 the membership was listed as 727,974 believers with 2,689 teachers, 209 churches, and two shrines. In 1973 it was listed as having one shrine, 51 churches, 10 propagation centers, 471 teachers, and 178,649 adherents. In 1988 these figures had dropped to 237 teachers and only 60,342 adherents belonging to 19 churches. The number of propagation centers was down to 6, although the group claimed 7 shrines. This suggests that the movement is in decline, a phenomenon noted in connection with other Kyōha sects.

The present leader is fifteenth-generation superintendent Iida Kingo, who trained as both Shinto priest and *yamabushi*. His personal philosophy centers on the ideas of *kami*, great nature (*daishizen*) and thanksgiving (*kansha*), which he sees as a virtue on a par with love in the Judaeo-Christian tradition.

Mountain Sects

Jikkō-kyō. The sect was begun by Hasegawa Kakugyō (born in 1541) in order to worship the three *kami* of creation, to worship "from afar" the *Kashikodokoro* in the Imperial Palace, to revere Mt. Fuji, and to pray for the body politic. Its goals are still to expunge human vanity, to eliminate academic controversies from religion, and to ensure or enforce these precepts, hence the name *Jikkō* (enforcement). The name *Kakugyō* means "block-discipline" and is derived from Hasegawa's alleged practice of standing on a block of wood for long periods to commune with the *kami*, hence the rather severe image of the sect.

Reverence for Mt. Fuji can be traced to before the Heian period. Literature of that period and earlier contains many mythological and legendary tales about Mt. Fuji and the *kami* of the mountain. One narrative explains that Fuji was visited by a *kami* called Miogi-no-mikoto, who requested lodging for the night. Fuji refused and the visiting *kami* went instead to Mt. Tsukuba. In retaliation for the inhospitality, he decreed that Mt. Fuji would always be covered with snow so that it would become isolated. The early collection of Japanese poetry called the *Manyōshū* depicts Mt. Fuji with awe and splendor as a *kami*:

> Lo, there towers the lofty peak of Fuji
> The clouds of heaven dare not cross it.
> Nor the birds of the air soar above it.
> It is a kami, mysterious . . .
> It is our treasure, our tutelary *kami*.
>
> The snow that crowns the peak of Fuji melts on the mid day of June
> And that night it snows again.[30]

Fuji was still an active volcano until 1707, so the image of awe and unapproachability is quite appropriate. To calm the volcano, shrines were built to revere Sengen Taijin Ō Kami, Fuji being an object of prayer and reverence rather than the place of asceticism it later came to be.

By the twelfth century, shrines and temples began to appear on and around Mr. Fuji. Matsudai Shonin, also known as Fuji-Shonin, built the first known temple, *Dainichi-ji* (Great Sun Temple). He was an associate and friend of the cloistered Emperor Go-Toba, who retired to become a Buddhist priest. The Buddhist symbol for Mt. Fuji was male (a bodhisattva); the Shinto *kami*, Sengen, was considered female. Reflecting on this problem, Matsudai concluded that the world of the *kami* transcends male and female dichotomy. This helped to afford Mt. Fuji an ever more special status and placed the realm of the *kami* beyond physical or metaphysical dualism.

The various mountain cults already in existence throughout Japan provided a natural background for the development of the reverence of Mt. Fuji, and different groups grew up around the Fuji cult. Hasegawa Kakugyō's movement combined awareness of the Fuji cult with a significant message appropriate to the age, which became the basis of its popular appeal. From the end of the Muromachi period until the more stable Edo period, social turmoil encouraged the emergence of spiritual leaders who offered peace. Hasegawa's father appears to have instilled in his son's mind the idea that he was born to be such a leader. He made many visits to Shinto and Buddhist sacred places and finally arrived at Mt. Fuji, where he was struck by the natural beauty of the mountain. At another mountain, Oshudakkakotsu, Hasegawa met an ascetic from whom he learned the practice of standing on a block of wood to meditate. He was told to go to Mt. Fuji to practice meditation in this way. Here the legend arose of his having stood on a block of wood for 2,000 consecutive days seeking to attain the ability to release the spirit from the body (*ominuki*) so that the spirit could become united with, and receive the words of, the *kami*.

Hasegawa returned home. Following the deaths of his parents he set off once again, but this time he offered himself as a teacher. He went to live inside the crater of Mt. Fuji, where, legend has it, he sheltered Tokugawa Ieyasu when he was seeking refuge. When an epidemic broke out in Edo, Hasegawa went to the city and prayed for the sick. His efforts resulted in many miraculous cures, so he gained a favorable reputation as a healer. However, the government became suspicious of him, as it was of any potential religious leaders. But his help to Tokugawa Ieyasu guaranteed his safety. He returned to Mt. Fuji and lived there for thirty years, teaching that all the *kami* lived there. The principal *kami* in residence was Sengen-dainichi (a name that combines the *kami* with the *bosatsu*); there were others, although not always those named in the Japanese mythology. After Hasegawa's death his disciple, Kuruno Nichigyō, tried to systematize his teaching and successfully integrated many groups and individuals who practiced mountain folk religion.

Hasegawa's teachings came to be interpreted in numerous ways, and two main schools emerged. The *Kōsei* school emphasized ascetic practices and rituals on the mountain. The eventually more powerful *Miroku* school of *Fuji Ko* was founded by Ito Jikigyō; *Jikkō-kyō* emerged from this school. Ito thought that too much emphasis was being placed upon ascetic rituals performed on the mountain itself, and he came to believe that there should be a physically less demanding but equally spiritual path that people could follow. Consequently, many priests of the *Miroku Ha* (school) were part-time, pursuing a secular occupation while serving as priests of the group.

The early eighteenth century was a time of plagues and famines. Merchants began stockpiling crops to force high prices, which caused farmers to revolt against merchants and bureaucrats. Distressed by such social chaos, Ito Jikigyō added Miroku to his name and tried to teach values and ethics. He believed himself to be the incarnation of the bodhisattva Miroku, and he preached accordingly. When Ito appeared to end a cholera outbreak, he was accused of being a hidden Christian (*kakuri kirishitan*), but after investigation he was proved not to be. His daughter, Ito Hanako, served as the next High Priest of the group. She was followed by Ito Sangyo, who tried to further separate the group and its activities from ascetic practices.

The next notable leader of the *Miroku Ha* was Kotani Sanshi Rokugyō, who claimed that the *kami* of the nation's shrines were incapable of solving the problems of the *Sengoku Jidai* and therefore could not be believed. He declared that the world was under the care of Moto-no-chichi-haha, the Father and Mother of everything. This *kami* resides on Mt. Fuji but is unrelated to Takami-musubi-no-kami. Kotani spent much time in Kyoto lobbying (with no success) to gain Imperial recognition. He even suggested that Tokugawa Ieyasu should be worshipped as the bringer of peace to the nation. Kotani changed the Chinese characters for *Fuji* from those of the mountain to those representing the idea that the sole belief was filial piety, in fact a Confucian ideal.

After reaching the age of sixty-six Kotani began to expound his own teachings, using traditional ideas to which he gave his own peculiar interpretation. He tried to simplify religious belief for the benefit of ordinary people. His basic principle was that each individual possessed the potential to become a *kami*, an idea found in various forms in almost all popular movements from the Heian period onward. He interpreted Ito Jikigyo's concept of *Tenchi-Furikawari* (the opposition of Heaven and Earth) so literally that he wore his kimono outside in and wrote the strokes of Chinese characters in reverse. He also began proclaiming that women should dominate men, that the farmers should dominate the *samurai*, and that the Tokugawa government should dominate the Emperor. After visiting Nagasaki, he also argued that Japan should end its closed country policy. This lost him the support of some of the younger *Kokugaku* scholars who were interested in promoting national learning based upon Shinto. Kotani died in 1841, and his followers began reflecting upon how to seek official recognition in such a way that the teachings would not be banned.

The *Kosei-Ha* branch was headed at that time by a Buddhist priest, Tokudaiji Sangyō. Kotani and Tokudaiji met during one of Kotani's visits to Kyoto. Tokudaiji was impressed by Kotani and actually joined *Fuji-ko*, although he did not renounce his Buddhist priesthood. *Fuji-ko* was renamed *Fuji-dō*, after which Tokudaiji assumed the leadership. To achieve recognition for Kotani's work, Tokudaiji felt that an appeal to the government was preferable to an appeal to the Emperor. The government rejected the appeal on the grounds that any associations of common people were potentially subversive, so no groups were permitted to practice religious rituals on mountains. Nevertheless, Kotani's son continued a group that tried to put the *Fuji-dō* teachings into practice by being involved in various public-spirited activities.

Tokudaiji, on the other hand, began changing the teachings of Kotani by first eliminating all references to Buddhism. The *kami* of the mountain was changed to Tengochushu, the central *kami* of the universe, probably to accommodate the *Kokugaku* scholars. Kotani's son refused to acknowledge the proposed changes; and Tokudaiji went back to the ideas of Moto-no-chichi-haha, although his proposals foreshadowed the forced separation of Shinto and Buddhism by the Meiji government. After the Meiji Restoration, Tokudaiji retired from the Buddhist priesthood and sent a messenger, Shibata Hanomori (who became the effectual founder of the sect), to Tokyo to start *Jikkōsha*, which was to prepare *Fuji-dō* to become a pure Shinto sect. Kotani's son again rejected the "Shintoization" but was ejected by Tokudaiji. Kotani's group became *Fuji Dō Koshin Ko*. It continued to exist as a social welfare group working in the Kanto region until its support finally dissolved after World War II. It had its final meeting in 1955 and dissolved itself with a membership of 95.

Tokudaiji's mainline group began to work in harmony with the nationalist and Emperor-centered ideology of the Meiji government, which stressed the virtues of loyalty and patriotism. In 1872 the *Kyōbu-Shō* began its program of indoctrination, and it was then that Tokudaiji and Shibata successfully sought recognition by the government for their teachings. *Jikkō Sha* was formally acknowledged in 1873 as a religious sect that could be supervised by the *Shinto Jimukyoku*. A headquarters was built in Tokyo in 1878, Tokudaiji died in 1879, and in 1882 the group became independent from the *Jimukyoku* and was permitted to call itself *Shinto Jikkō Kyō*. Shibata then became the first High Priest. Although he claimed descent from Hasegawa and others, he did not make use of their teachings except for some of Kotani's ideas, which he incorporated selectively. Although Kotani had been opposed to "Shintoization," Shibata structured *Fuji-dō* in such a way that conformed to the ideology of the Meiji government.

Beliefs and Teaching. These[31] are summarized in the Three Tenets of Jikkō-kyō. Shibata proposed three basic ideas that the government found acceptable (particularly Tenets 2 and 3):

1. To believe that Mt. Fuji is the spirit of truth and therefore the soul of the Earth.
2. To pray for the unbroken Imperial Line and the lasting dignity of the *kokutai*.
3. To work so that the high and the low are friendly and diligent in their occupations.

In order to become closer to the common people, Shibata simplified the teachings of the sect and introduced basic practices that people could follow. The *kami* that were worshipped included the three central *kami* of creation, the *Kashiko-dokoro-Jinja* within the Imperial Palace, and, of course, Mt. Fuji.

The next leader was Chuyo Udonmo, Shibata's first son, who was a world traveler and lecturer. In an address at the first Parliament of World Religions in Chicago in 1893 he tried to speak of universal elements in religion, although he maintained the particularism that is characteristic of Shinto thought. He chaired a conference of Shinto, Buddhist, and Christian leaders in Japan and led them to agree that even though they would continue to promote their own interests, they would also promote the interests of Japan and its national development.

Organization and Believers. The leader in 1988 was the great-grandson of Shibata, operating from a headquarters in Omiya City in Saitami Prefecture. The sect does not proselytize but survives simply by being handed on within families. This has resulted in a decline in membership. The postwar liberation of religion also contributed to the decline by permitting group splintering, a tendency in Japanese religion from early times. *Jikkō-kyō* has 57 churches throughout Japan, although only about 20 are of any size. It has 1,033 teachers; all have been trained at the headquarters, which mainly issues sect publications. The membership was estimated at 400,000 before World War II but in 1988 was posted at approximately 106,620. On August 3 of every year, thousands of believers dress in white and climb Mt. Fuji, shouting "*Rokkonshōjo*," or "purify the six organs of sense" (the eyes, ears, nose, tongue, body, and mind). However, the group does not have a shrine on or near Mt. Fuji. It is a form of reverence from a distance. The sect also practices divination, spells, and invocations according to believers' requests, a clear reminder of its roots in the folk tradition. No traces whatsoever of its Buddhist heritage are present in either its beliefs or its rituals.

Fusō-kyō. This sect also claims Hasegawa Kakugyō as its founder. It did not become an independent sect until 1882, by which time it was under the leadership of Shishino Nakaba. Shishino was born in Satsuma-gun, in what is now Kagoshima Prefecture, and he died in 1884. The original name was *Fuji-Ichizan Kyōkai* (The One Mt. Fuji Association); it enshrined Sengen Okami but was changed to *Fusō-Kyōkai* as the result of a complex play on words. The change of title of the sect, *Fusō*, came from an old and poetic name for Japan, *fu* (meaning "to save") and *sō* (referring to a Chinese legend of a mulberry tree that stood in the sea to the east of China). The meaning gradually changed to refer to the land of the sunrise, and the sect as the teaching of the sect whose teaching protects the country. In 1878 it became *Fusō Kyōha*; in 1883, it became *Fusō-kyō*. It aimed at revering the divine virtue of creation, reverentially holding festivals for the *kami* of Heaven and Earth, and furthering the way of the *kami*. The sect taught and believed in the mystical spirit and unique power of Mt. Fuji. Its teachings were explained and practiced by divination and incantation; it demonstrated this by performing rituals that include removing the heat from fire and other ascetic rites. These rituals are still performed at various shrines and festivals throughout the country.

Beliefs and Teaching. Because *Jikkō-kyō* and *Fusō-kyō* claim the same founder, this suggests that there might be an overlap in their teachings, which to a certain extent is true.[32] However, there are also marked differences that led them to become independent movements. *Jikkō-kyō* is active and ascetic. Fusō-kyō is passive and contemplative. *Fusō-kyō* reveres the *zoka-sanshin*, Amaterasu-Ōkami, and Ubusuna-no-kami in addition to the *kami* of Mt. Fuji (Kono-hana-saku-ya-hime-no-kami), which did not change after the war. This is somewhat different from *Jikkō-kyō*. Fusō-kyō's objective is the happiness and prosperity of the nation rather than that of the sect's members.

The principles of the sect are stated as follows:

1. To worship the immeasurable and limitless goodness of the *zoka-sanshin* and to revere the *Amatsu-kami* and the *Kunitsu-kami*.

2. To cultivate the great truth of Shinto (*Kannagara*) and to understand the significance of life and death.

3. To cultivate the forms and ceremonies of the Imperial Country and make the sacred ceremonies conform to the standards of the royal court of the past.

The beliefs in this regard are close to those of *Jikkō-kyō* but were modified after the war to remove the ultra-nationalistic elements in favor of strengthening the more folk Shinto teachings. As with the other movements, there was a tendency toward a more humanistic view of *kami* within the general reinterpretation of the older doctrines. This occurred along with loss of members as new cults began to offer similar ideas, but in a more up-to-date form. Fusō-kyō was so strongly committed to the unity of worship and government (*saisei-itchi*) that the disappearance of that principle almost denuded its teaching not only of context but also of a great deal of meaning.

Organization and Believers. The organization in its prewar strength numbered over half a million. The chief priest of the sect as of 1989 was Sugiyama Ichitaro (born in 1937), and its headquarters was in Matsubara-cho, Setagaya-ku, Tokyo. Statistics of the same year reported 82,000 believers served by 978 teachers and priests in 81 churches.

Ontake-kyō (Mitake-kyō). Of the three sects concerned with mountains, the largest and most active is *Ontake-kyō*. It was founded by Shimoyama Osuke, an oil merchant in the city of Edo who became a mountain ascetic (*gyōja*) of Mt. Mitake in the Japan Alps between Nagano and Gifu Prefectures. The mountain itself had been revered from time immemorial by peasants of the area, who still refer to it as *Ontakesan* (Honorable Great Mountain). Hence the sect is known as Ontake-kyō. Its roots are, like the other mountain sects, deeply embedded in the folk tradition and beliefs of *sangaku shinko*. Shimoyama became interested and set about trying to identify the *kami* revered there. Mt. Mitake (Mitake Ōkami) was the only known name until Shimoyama claimed that it was a collective name for Kunitokotachi-no-kami, Onamuchi no-kami, and Sakuna-Hikona-no-kami. To these he added Tenshin-chigi, Rekidai-korei, and Ubusuna-no-kami. At first the sect was closely related to *Tosei Kyōkai*, but it was given government recognition as an independent sect in 1882.

Beliefs and Teaching. The beliefs[33] of the sect are set out in five clauses that express the essence of the founder's ideas. To meet the demands of the Meiji government, they included strong sentiments of patriotism:

1. To follow the instructions of the teachers of the church, to exemplify divine reason and human benevolence in conduct, and not to violate the sacred will of the great *kami* of Mitake.

2. Especially to preserve in their hearts reverence for the *kami* and love of country, to honor and obey the Emperor, to conform to the decrees of the State, and by constant diligence in business to lay the foundation of a prosperous land and a strong military (*fukoku kyōhei*).

3. To follow the teachings of the great *kami* and to keep the peace in patience, never to slander others, and to reveal modesty and reverence in conduct.

4. Always in uprightness and integrity to value the truth and never to speak words of deception.

5. To practice fraternity and be as brothers together, and as evidence of the possession of such a spirit to labor to assist travelers of whatever country they may be in their troubles and sickness.

The ideals of the sect reflect the values of the Meiji era, particularly in clause 2, which speaks of the ideal of a prosperous country and a strong military. Like other groups of the Kyōha tradition, these ideas have undergone modification in the postwar era.

The sect is also famed for some of its more than fifty special ceremonies and rites. The principal act of reverence involves climbing Mt. Mitake while chanting "*Rokkonshōjo*" for the purification of the body and senses. This takes place on August 8 of every year and is similar to activities of other mountain groups. There are three shrines on the mountain: The *Omiya*, or Great Shrine; the *Wakamiya* (young shrine); and the *Yamamiya* (mountain shrine), which is located on the summit.

In addition, the sect practices *chinka shiki* (a fire-calming ceremony performed by walking barefoot over a red-hot charcoal fire) and *kugatachi shiki* (a ritual in which boiling water is sprinkled on the body after the heat has been subdued). The purpose of these rituals is the purification of the believer after a hot element has been subdued. Among other places, these rituals are performed at Hanno City in Saitama Prefecture (firewalking) on April 15, and at Otake Town—also in Saitama Prefecture—(boiling water rituals) on May 3 of each year. They attract large crowds because of their spectacular and dramatic nature. Besides these spectacular rites, there is *meigen shiki* (ritual use of a bow string), *shimbu shiki* (sacred dance), *ibuki ho* (deep breathing), and *kame ura* (divination using a tortoise shell).

The rituals reflect two strong folk aspects of *Ontake-kyō*. First, is its interest in healing and medicine, which developed as a basis for belief in other Kyoha sects that focus on healing. The secrets of the quasi-magical rites are also transmitted by the *kami* of Mt. Mitake to believers. Shamanistic group leaders can become *kami*-possessed and can teach special revelations to believers, who may find themselves in a charismatic state. Such groups assemble and roam the mountain from time to time seeking to induce ecstatic states.

The ceremonies are designed not only to heighten spirituality but also to secure the power and blessing of the *kami*, prosperity, longevity, guidance for the future through special revelations and disclosures, and happiness after death. These elements of universal appeal have enabled *Ontake-kyō* to retain its attraction in the midst of all the new religious groups that Japanese society has produced, particularly since the end of the Pacific War. **Organization and Believers.** The headquarters of the sect was formerly located in Osaki in Tokyo but moved to Futana-cho in the city of Nara. Omomo Yoshio took over leadership in 1989. The membership in 1990 was 622,280, compared to 2,051,000 in 1930 (which displays the same trend as noted in the other groups—although less dramatic, probably because of continuing reverence for Mt. Mitake). Members belong to 310 churches, which have an additional 153 branches served by 2,912 licensed teachers.

Purification Sects

Shinshū-kyō. A separate group of sects makes the idea of purification itself the sole concern of their activities and beliefs. The *Shinshū* sect was founded by Yoshimura Masamochi (1839–1916), a member of the great Shinto family of Ōnakatomi. After the Meiji Restoration and the *Shim-butsu-bunri* declaration by the government, he was able to advance his ideas; they emphasized a Shinto purged of all Buddhist elements whatsoever going back to the era before the Nara age. The sect received formal recognition from the government in 1880. Yoshimura himself became the first Head Priest of the movement. He declared the following as its goal: to learn the way of the *kami* in silence; to master the national rites; and to pray for the eternity of the Imperial Family, the health of the Emperor, the prosperity of the country, and the peace of the world along with an abundant harvest of grains and cereals. In fact, much folk religion remains within *Shinshū-kyō* despite all declarations of purity.

Beliefs and Teaching. Basic to *Shinshū-kyō (kami*-learn-become sect) are the ideas of harmony of *yu* (the world of the *kami* that is unseen) and *gen* (the world that human beings inhabit and that is seen).[34] The teaching of the sect emphasizes that it is by actions that people become kami. This is the basis for the ascetic rituals practiced by the group. In April and September, believers practice the two ascetic semi-magical rituals already discussed under Ontake-kyō, namely, the fire-calming ceremony (*chinka shiki*) and the sprinkling of boiling water on the body (*kugatachi shiki*). These are considered to be forms of purification; according to the traditions of the sect, no one has ever been injured or harmed by performing them.

Four other rituals are also performed, often in conjunction with the first two. In *misogi ho*, cold water is poured over the believers for purification. *Batsujo ho* is a form of meditation that claims to rid the personality of bad attitudes such as anger and selfishness. There is also *mono-imi ho*, abstinence from certain foods and drinks; and *shinji ho*, a procedure designed to lead to "divine possession" of the believers, which testifies to the shamanistic aspect of the sect.

According to the formal teachings of the sect, observance of the Three Elements of Shinto will enable the believer to take part in such rituals and achieve the perspective that comes from the union of *yu* and *gen*:

1. A believer should seek to achieve the spirit of a *kami* by practicing *oharai* purification (which may include the rituals described previously).
2. A believer should be well trained when he reaches the level of teaching required for practicing *oharai*. Those who have performed these rituals may become teachers of the sect.
3. A believer should reach harmony with the *kami* and pray for the repose of others' souls.

The kami revered by the sect include the three *kami* of creation, Amaterasu, and the successive Imperial spirits. However, three special *kami* are revered: Sokotsutsu-no-mikoto, Nakatsutsu-o-no-mikoto, and Uwatsutsuo-no-mikoto. These *kami* have a role in purification and are typical of the purification sects. The revered *kami* of the sect did not change after the war. The sect also has Ten Precepts to guide the believers' way of life. The Ten Precepts (*Kyōken Jikkajō*) of *Shinshū-kyō* are very much in line with the teaching of Shinto Taikyō in its Meiji period form:

1. Worship the great *kami* of the sect.
2. Pacify the spirit, for it is part of the spirit of the *kami*.
3. Practice the way of the *kami*.
4. Revere the divine origin of the State.
5. Be loyal to the ruler.
6. Be zealous in filial piety toward your parents.
7. Be kind to others.
8. Be diligent in business.
9. Preserve steadfastness within your heart.
10. Cleanse away the impurities of the body.

Precepts 4 and 5 explicitly demonstrate Meiji period ideology, but *Shinshū-kyō* also displays roots that combine traditional Jinja Shinto with the purification aspects of mountain and folk religion. These elements have survived alongside certain ambiguous feelings about the ideological elements.

One feature of the sect that is most explicitly Shinto is the idea that primarily in ritual and ceremonies is religious truth not only set forth but also grasped and experienced. By purifying the spirit and then coming to know it, it is possible to come to know the *kami* and consequently to heighten human spirituality. Thus, the sect is also known as *Mugon no Oshie* (teaching without words), because it believes that human beings can become *kami* by actions and rites.

Organization and Believers. In 1930 the sect had 770,000 members with a headquarters in Komazawa, Tokyo. It was there that the rites of *chinka shiki* and *kugatachi shiki* were performed traditionally twice a year, on April 9 and September 17. In 1989 the membership stood at 289,203 belonging to 166 churches led by 665 clergy. The headquarters is now located in Setagaya Ward in Tokyo, and the leader is still a member of the Yoshimura family.

Misogi-kyō. The sect was founded by Inoue Masakane (1790–1849), whose real name was Ando Kisaburo. From his distinguished *samurai* father he inherited a morbid concern for the world and its sufferings, as a result of which he became preoccupied with the problems of how to help the sick, the poor, and the aged and how both health and home could be optimally preserved. He traveled, studied, and became a disciple of *Shira-*

kawa Hakoke, a Shinto sect that taught *misogi* and breathing. From this sect he received a teaching license. He then went to Edo as head of the *Shinmeigu*.

Inoue expressed dissatisfaction with the religious policy of the Edo government, for which he was arrested and imprisoned several times. Finally the government exiled him to Miyakejima in 1843, where he died. He was succeeded by a group called *Tokami-ko* (distant *kami* group), which emerged in 1872 but split into two. One part merged with Taisei-kyō. The other, formed by Sakata Tetsuyasu as *Misogi Kosha* in 1883, was given government recognition in 1894 and became Misogi-kyō. Its principal object was to enhance the divine teachings of *misogi*, purification in a river based on the belief that cleansing of mind and body in flowing water was the most effective way to remove *tsumi*. The term *misogi* is said to be derived from the verb *misogu*, which means "to cleanse with water."

Inoue himself was a product of the Shinto/Buddhist/Confucian value system of the Edo period, practicing medicine along with his studies of Shinto ideas. His legacy of writings formed the basis of the history and doctrines of the sect after his death.

Beliefs and Teaching. Inoue taught three methods of improving life: *misogi harae*, proper breathing, and the practice of thrift in matters of daily life.[35] *Misogi* purifies people, and breathing brings them close to the *kami*. The core of Shinto he expressed in these terms: "Shinto is in the house of plain wood, under the thatched roof, with the mirror on the shelf."

The Five Precepts of Misogi-kyō are as follows:

1. Revere the *kami* and respect the Emperor.
2. Worship the *kami* every morning and evening.
3. Do not be deceived by any foreign religion.
4. Be industrious and show gratitude toward the country.
5. Do not disobey the teachings of the founder of the sect.

Inoue believed that the three most efficacious agents of purification in Japan were the *Sanshu Jingi*, the Three Sacred Treasures of the Imperial Regalia. By their amazing power, all forms of impurity, could be removed. He taught that if believers repeated the *norito* of the sect's main ritual, committing all of life to the will and purposes of the *kami*, purification would be effected. The central ritual of *misogi* is performed in Misogi-kyō by repeating the formula *Tōkami emitame, harai tamai, kiyome tamo* ("distant kami, purify and cleanse us we pray").

Breathing as a discipline Inoue based on the idea that the origin of this world is the breath of the *kami*. Consequently, through controlled breathing it is possible to be in communion with the divine. Controlled breathing for religious purposes (*ibuki*) is practiced by other sects also.

By *thrift* Inoue meant not to eat much or live richly: "People who eat much and richly get ill, make their hearts dark and their lives cheap, and they often become idle. Gluttons are people who do not think about the hunger of others or of assisting them in their sufferings. They think only and exclusively of themselves." These words are taken from Inoue's *Shinto Yuiitsu Mondō Shō*, in which he wrote in some detail about his life and teachings.

There is also the doctrine of *Anshin Ritsumei*, the belief that people should not worry about day-to-day concerns but should focus on long-term development goals. *Kami* reverenced by the sect include the three *kami* of creation, Amaterasu, and other select *kami* including Misogi-oshie-no-Ōkami.

Organization and Believers. The sect headquarters was located in Daito Ward in Tokyo opposite *Inoue Jinja* (established in 1880), where the founder is enshrined. The *Inoue Jinja* was renamed *Misogi Jinja* when the headquarters was moved from Uneo to near Yatsugatake after a brief relocation in the Setagaya Ward of Tokyo. The transportation of the *Jinja* from Uneo itself is an interesting story. It seems that a temporary shrine was erected in Setagaya until the rural shrine buildings had been completed. During the removal of the *kami* from Uneo, photographs were taken. Every photograph showed a mysterious ball of light flowing over the procession, although none was seen by anyone at the time. Believers claim that it was the self-disclosure of the *kami* to the people.

Besides the *Misogi Jinja* there are approximately 50 branches (*bunin*) throughout Japan to which the sect's current 98,560 members belong. Its highest prewar membership was 343,000 in 1938.

Under the rules laid down for succession, the organization is headed by the *Kyōshu*, who is appointed after examination by a committee of high officials. By coincidence the *Kyōshu* in 1990 was Sakada Yasugi, a son of the previous *Kyōshu*, but the position is not hereditary. There is an elaborate hierarchy of priests and management levels to which members may aspire after recommendation by the branch head (*bunin-chō*) and appropriate examination by the board of officials.

Priests train by attending three-day sessions four times a year at the *Misogi Jinja*, where they practice the rituals, study the doctrines, and undergo strict self-disciplinary training. Followers attempt to visit the shrine itself once a year to witness the priests performing the shrine rituals. The headquarters is now located in the Setagaya Ward of Tokyo.

The movement underwent upheaval with the separate establishment in Tochigi City in Tochigi Prefecture of the *Misogi-kyō Shin-ba*, which was legally constituted as a religious corporate person (*shūkyō hōjin*) in 1989. It lists 18,935 members in 5 main churches under the guidance of 238 spiritual advisers.

Faith-Healing Sects

Kurozumi-kyō. We now examine the first of the sects that centers on healing. The founder was Kurozumi Munetada (1780–1850), who was enshrined as Munetada Daimyōjin in 1872. The sect was recognized by the government in 1882. Its history and development are related to the key dates in the life of Kurozumi himself. Born as the third son of a low-ranking priest of the *Imamura Jinja*, Kurozumi was a Shinto believer but was deeply influenced by the values of neo-Confucianism. He regarded filial piety as the highest good and resolved at the age of nineteen to honor his parents by becoming a *kami* during his lifetime. When his parents died in 1912 he was devastated, because his purpose in life had been to please them. He contracted tuberculosis and abandoned his mission. As death came near, he was moved to the veranda (*engawa*) of the house to revere the sun again and was completely healed. It was also in performing an act of reverence toward the sun, in November 1814, that he received a divine revelation. When he faced the east, he inhaled the sun's rays and felt transformed. This experience of unity with the divine came to be known as the *Tenmei Jikiju*, the Direct Receipt of the Heavenly Mission. At this point his new life as a religious teacher began.

From 1815 to 1843 he began to collect a group of disciples through his faith-healing as a Shinto priest. He was subject to various criticisms; and in 1816 a document from the Chief Priest ordered him to refrain from healing by charisma, which was considered to be beyond the tasks of a shrine priest. This led to serious conflict. From 1825 to 1843 Kurozumi became involved in alternate periods of seclusion within the shrine and active periods of proselytization outside.

From September 1825 to May 1828 he confined himself to the shrine for 1,000 days, a traditional discipline called *sanrō* or *okomori*. When he was outside preaching, village headmen welcomed him because he taught traditional values, which they felt would be helpful in discouraging peasant rebellion. He was gladly heard and supported by the local rural leadership. It was during this time that he formulated the Seven Household Principles of the sect.

Ultimately, the incompatibility between the particularism of the shrine of which he was priest and the more general nature of his message became critical, so he resigned his office of Senior Priest (*negi*) at the shrine in 1843 and passed it on to his son Munenobu. The followers he had gathered then became followers of Munetada himself, but they consisted mostly of peasants. The *samurai* felt that his teachings were not suitable to their needs.

From 1843 until his death in 1850 Munetada developed his teachings and continued to gather followers. After his death the task of recognition was achieved in 1856. But in 1863 the Okayama region condemned it as counter to the *samurai* spirit. After the Meiji Restoration the group cooperated with the idea of creating a state religion, but it still had difficulty because of the general ban on faith-healing. The Bureau of Shinto Affairs made it into *Shinto Kurozumi Ha*, a sect recognized in 1876 that was permitted both to proselytize and to conduct daily rituals and activities.

Beliefs and Teachings. The sect expresses its beliefs in its Five Teachings, its Seven Articles, and its proverbial sayings.[36] The Five Teachings are as follows:

1. Be always truthful.
2. Leave your fate to Heaven.
3. Do not be selfish.
4. Always be cheerful.
5. Use life productively.

The Seven Articles are as follows:

1. Don't be impious because you were born in the *kami no kuni*.
2. Don't be angry and don't worry.
3. Don't look down on others with arrogance.
4. Don't make your mind worse by dwelling on the wickedness of others.
5. Don't neglect your occupation as long as you are healthy.
6. Don't be faithless once you have entered the path of faithfulness.
7. Don't neglect to express *kansha* (thankfulness) every day.

Worshippers should pledge reverence to Amaterasu every morning and inhale fresh air. In the evening they should lie on their backs and apply strength to the stomach to ensure a sound mind and body. *Kami* reverenced include Amaterasu, Munetada Daimyōjin, and the *kami* of Heaven and Earth. These did not change after the war.

The Proverbs of Kurozumi-kyō elaborate upon these ideas. "When the heart of Amaterasu-Ōmikami and the heart of man are one, this is eternal life." "When the heart of Amaterasu-Ōmikami and our hearts are undivided, then there is no such thing as death." "When we realize that all things are the activity of Heaven, then we know neither pain nor care." "Forsake flesh and self-will and cling to the One Truth of Heaven and Earth." "Happy is the man who cultivates the things that are hidden and lets the things that are apparent take care of themselves." "Of a truth, there is no such thing as sickness." "If you foster a spirit that regards both good and evil as blessings, then the body spontaneously becomes healthy." "In truth, the Way is easy." "He who abandons self-knowledge and spends his days in thankfulness grows neither old nor weary. He knows only joy and happiness." "Both heaven and hell come from one's own heart." "Oh, the sadness of wandering in the devil's prayers." "If in one's heart one is a *kami*, then one becomes a *kami*; if in one's heart one is a Buddha, then one becomes a Buddha; if in one's heart one is a serpent, then one becomes a serpent." "Nothing in all the world calls forth such gratitude as sincerity." "Through oneness in sincerity the men of the four seas are brothers." "All men are brothers. All receive the blessings of the same heaven." "The suffering of others is my suffering; the good of others is my good."

Sermons, Counseling, and Healing. A basic part of the activities of Kurozumi-kyō includes sermons and preaching, which are not normally part of Jinja Shinto activities. Sermons stress that problems arise from lack of harmony with the divine and teach that the solution to all problems lies in restoring the harmony between man and the *kami*. Sermons make use of loud claps (*kashiwade*), and believers also clap twice (in the manner of saluting a *kami* at a shrine) whenever the words of the founder are quoted.

Counseling and healing are practiced, but these are considered subordinate to the source of all problems, namely, the heart (*kokoro*) that is out of harmony with the divine. Once that harmony is restored, all will be well. Medicine is not ignored, but it is regarded as useless because problems of a medical nature are merely symptoms of deeper problems, and removing the symptoms is only half a cure. *Majinai* is used as a form of healing in which a minister transfers from his or her own *nippai* the energy of the sun to the diseased person. In *nippai*, a believer sits facing the sun and inhales the *yōki*, the essence of the deity; this can be transferred from the minister to the sick. Like other groups, Kurozumi-kyō offers a full range of services and rituals. However, these are recognizable both as folk Shinto and as common to many other traditional religious movements.

Organization and Believers. The churches are divided into wards (*kyōku*). Each ward has a director who facilitates communication between them. The largest numerical support is in Okayama, which has three wards and a large concentration of churches. The next in number are Hiroshima, Tottori and Shimanne Prefectures, followed by Shikoku, Hyogo, Nara, and Tokyo. The majority of followers live in Western Japan, but precise statistics are not kept. The operation of the group derives from Shrine Shinto, although it differs in numerous ways. Local relations with shrines vary, so there is a divergence of styles within the sect. Most churches have a layman's meeting called a *Tenshinko*. This involves rotating assemblies convened from time to time for the reading of the liturgy of the Great Purification and also for sermons, healing, and a common meal. Large rural churches may have up to fifty such meetings; urban churches may not have any.

Kurozumi-kyō belongs to the *Kyōha Shinto Rengōkai* (Association of Kyōha Shinto Groups). It also belongs to the World Congress for Religion and Peace (WCRP), thus it is a liberal group that does not attack other movements but is always willing to cooperate with other religions. One unique aspect of Kurozumi-kyō is its claim to be a religion that helps the weak. It has an excellent record in welfare work for the severely handicapped. This was begun when the Japanese government was not as positive as it might have been in providing special facilities for the disabled. The organization now trains personnel for this kind of work from various parts of Southeast Asia. Although churches do exist in the United States, Brazil, and Peru, there is no propagation activity because it is against the policy of the group.

The membership was listed in 1989 at 295,225. These members belonged to a total of 340 churches led by 2,906 clergy and teachers. Eighty percent of the membership lives in rural areas. There are three categories of membership: *Shinja* (believer), which can refer to anyone who maintains a relationship with a church; *Michizure* (follower), which can be interchanged with "believer" but is more limited in its connotation because it refers to a dues-paying member; and *Kyoto*, which indicates households or individuals who traditionally have ancestral and funeral rites performed by the ministers of Kurozumi-kyō.

Churches (*kyōkai*) and shrines (*jinja*) are combined in Kurozumi-kyō. The church is for the pastoral activities of ministers, which is distinguished from the liturgical functions of shrine priests. Normally the *kyōkai* is adjacent to the *jinja* and is entirely supported by the group concerned. The exterior, however, resembles a shrine. The minister usually attends the shrines and their duties. The head shrine is the *Munetada Jinja* in Okayama City. The Head Priest of the shrine, the *Gūji*, is usually a younger brother of the Patriarch. Although in style the churches resemble shrines, instead of a *torii* outside there are two posts joined at the top by a straw rope (*shimenawa*) on which is hung paper strips (*gohei*). The inside of the altar area has two sections. One is for the ancestors of the church; the other represents the place for reverencing Amaterasu, the *kami* of the sun.

The daily worship of the sun is the central act of worship in Kurozumi-kyō. It is called *nippai*, and the best time for *nippai* is sunrise. Recitation of the Great Purification Prayer is called *nissan*. Those who cannot offer daily prayers themselves but wish to have them offered on their behalf may have this done. It is called *nikku*. In addition to the usual rituals such as *hatsumode* (first shrine visit of the New Year), there are two other important annual observances: the *Tōji Taisai* (Winter Solstice Festival) and the *Ōbarae Taisai* (Great Purification Festival), which is performed every six months. The winter solstice commemorates the experience of the founder when he received his mission and the summer festival coincides with the summer solstice, thus making use of the longest and shortest days of the year. The movement of the sun is acknowledged; this remains a basic tenet of the sect.

The ministers of the churches perform the normal range of purification rituals to cover events such as groundbreaking, the birth of a child, success in examinations, and safe travel for success at work. Special requests for liturgical purification are called *kinen* and are usually paid for in cash or kind.

Konkō-kyō. *Konkō-kyō* means literally "teaching of the golden light." It was founded by Kawate Bunjiro (1814–1883), who was born a peasant in Okayama Prefecture and brought up with a religious faith from childhood. Physically, he was not very strong. The dramatic turning point in his life occurred when he was forty-two years of age. His stepmother, younger brother, stepfather, two sons, his daughter, and his two cows died one after the other, precipitating for him a life-and-death sense of crisis. He retained his faith in *Konjin, Tenchi kane no kami* and decided to devote his life to helping people in their difficulties by acting as an intermediary between God and man. He devoted himself to *Toritsugi* mediation. He did not intend to create a movement, but such was his success and popularity that people gathered around him and a movement came into being. Later he received the name Ikigami, Konkō-daimyōjin, the gracious living *kami* of the golden light; from this, the name of Konkō-kyō was born.

As we have seen, the Tokugawa government regarded all popular religious movements with suspicion. Consequently, Konkō-kyō was suppressed in its early years. The founder eventually visited the powerful and influential Shirakawa family in Kyoto, which gave him permission to preach the *Konkō* teachings. After the Meiji Restoration, his status of priest was withdrawn and he was forced to stop mediating and preaching. The pressure was so great that many people deserted the movement. However, the Governor of Okayama responded to a petition that requested permission for religious activities on condition that nothing would be said against the government. Only Kawate was permitted to engage in religious activities, which enabled Konkō-kyō to revive. It soon began spreading; and by 1880, especially because of an outbreak of cholera, its numbers increased dramatically. When Kawate died in 1883 the need for a formal organization became clear. The followers felt that it was best classified as a Shinto group, so the *Konkō-kyōdan* was established as an official religion in 1885 and as an independent religion in 1900. During the Taishō period, when nationalism was being fostered, Konkō-kyō members had to do their duty to the State. They agreed to be patriotic but not cruel. Followers offered condolences to bereaved families in Japan and sent missions to build free medical centers in China. They also created language schools and junior and senior high schools.

After World War II, with freedom of religion established, the followers tried to reform Konkō-kyō, especially where it had been either compromised or reformed by the government. The Scriptures were rewritten to express more closely what the founder felt, and a festival for the founder began to be held annually. In 1964 South America (and later, North America) became new centers of the mission. In 1983 the first centenary festival was held and a new canon, *Gorikai*, was published.

Beliefs and Teachings. These are found in various publications and writings of the founder as well as in many proverbial sayings.[37] Kawate believed that people should enjoy happiness and prosperity and that man can glorify God through happiness and prosperity. The highest human ideal of participating in the glory of God can be realized by living one's everyday life to the fullest. The mediator helps to solve the problems of everyday life so that people can live more effectively and freely. Reward after death is not as important as effort within life. In this way Konkō-kyō mirrors the outlook of Shinto, although other elements are clearly present. "Pray earnestly this very day: God's blessing descends on your own heart. Pour out your heart to God with absolute trust in Him, at any time and at any place. Neither time nor space matters to him."[38]

Like Kurozumi-kyō, Konkō-kyō has a set of proverbs. "God is the Great Parent of your real self. Faith is just like filial obedience to your parents." "Free yourself from doubt. Open and behold the broad way of truth. You will find your life quickened in the midst of the goodness of God." "With God there is neither day nor night, neither far nor near. Pray to him straightforwardly and with a heart of faith." "With sincerity there is no such thing as failure. When failure to accomplish your purpose in prayer arises, then know that something is lacking in sincerity." "Bring not suffering upon yourself by indulgence in selfishness." "One who would walk in the Way of Truth must close the eyes of the flesh and open the eyes of the spirit." "In all the world, there is no such thing as a stranger." "Your body is not for your own freedom." "Do not bring bitterness to your own heart by anger at the things that are past." "Do not profess love with your lips while you harbor hatred in your heart." "One should not be mindful of suffering in his own life and unmindful of suffering in the lives of others."

The concept of God in Konkō-kyō resembles that of Christianity. Human beings are the children of God. However, Konkō-kyō does not believe in creation, but in *aiyokakeyo* (coexistence). God and men cannot exist without each other. If all human beings were to disappear, God would also cease to exist. The world is as it is now. The idea of *ikigami* is equally important to see how the concept of God is understood in practice. In Konkō-kyō teaching, a human being can have God within himself or herself whenever one's thoughts are directed toward the right beliefs. Good will equals God's will. When one possesses such a will, one becomes an *ikigami*. It is not necessary to consider life as a preparation for death and afterlife in which a person can be one with God. This is related to the fact that there is no formal act of confession in Konkō-kyō teaching. There is instead the concept of *okizuke*, making one realize the virtue of something through the problem of wrongful deeds rather than by punishment. In keeping with the spirit of Japanese asceticism, the emphasis is positive. The mediator tells someone who is sick to appreciate the importance and value of being and staying healthy, which implies the philosophy of positive thinking. Believers are encouraged to thank the natural order for its benefits (this shows how closely Konkō-kyō retains the Shinto spirit that lays stress on the world as it is now).

Human nature is respected, and believers are not expected to fight human nature in the interests of reason. Prohibitions exist only in a very basic sense. Members can eat and drink what they will, providing they recognize these as gifts of God. Some prohibitions are moral admonitions:

To know the true way but not to walk in it.

To speak sincerely but to have no sincerity in the heart.

To see another's fault but to commit one's own.

Konkō-kyō is a very liberal religion that sometimes prefers to regard itself as a way of life. Believers may carry out wedding and funeral ceremonies at different religious organizations with no impediment. Indeed, there is no one doctrine that everybody should follow regardless of circumstances. Although the mediator bases his advice on the life of the founder and his teachings, he addresses problems in a person-to-person way so that flexibility is possible and the doctrine can be chosen according to each problem.

Konkō-kyō Scriptures are passages that describe the interaction of various farmers of the time with Konkō-daijin. In these accounts, his teachings are implied. They being with an explanation of how the founder was encouraged by God to devote himself to mediation. The divine call, which took place in November 1859, is called the *Rikkyo Shinden*. Thus began Kawate's service to Tenchi kane no kami. His wife became a "widow" by divine command to permit her husband to concentrate on his mediation work. The Scriptures list the *Tenchi Kakitsuke* (Heaven and Earth's Reminder); this hangs on the wall of every Konkō-kyō church. It is inscribed with these words: "Through Ikigami Konkō-daijin to Tenchi kane no kami with heart and soul pray. The Divine favor depends on your own heart. On this very day, pray." When they are praying, believers say the *kakitsuke* out loud. The Scriptures do not have "Biblical authority," partly because of the lateness of their composition and revision.

The eclecticism of belief makes it easy for Konkō-kyō followers to adapt their beliefs to different situations and to the problems of daily life. In this way it attracts and holds followers. Values include the principle that human nature is something to be treasured and disciplined. People are taught to realize their enormous potential and to express it honestly and sincerely. Prayer should occur often and be a basic part of the follower's daily life. It should be natural and spontaneous, not over-ritualized. In the *Kyoten*

Gorikai, Konkō-daijin exhorts believers to "practice faith like going up the rungs of a ladder. Work at it rung by rung, then your gratitude will increase day by day."

Konkō-daijin also stressed the importance of toleration, not only of other human beings and animals but even of insects. Followers should endure misfortunes and hardships and learn from them. There are not prohibitions with regard to drinking alcohol, smoking, and eating, which underlines the Shinto characteristic of striving to satisfy human nature and not to contest its character.

Organization and Believers. Organization is very democratic. Individual churches are set up, financed, and organized locally. In Hongo-sanchome in Tokyo, for example, the church was founded by a lady who had trouble at home that led to a divorce. Alone and unhappy, she turned to the teachings of Konkō-daijin and was able to rebuild her life. A new church came into being through her experience. She was the grandmother of the minister serving there in the 1980s.

There is no central authority. The headquarters receive only 3,000 yen per member per year. The ministers call the organization "circular," meaning that the churches encircle the headquarters. It is not a hierarchically structured organization, which is in keeping with its liberal style. There are 1,517 churches (60 of which are in Tokyo), with 4,362 ministers and 447,759 listed members as of 1989. Individual churches vary in size, but the interiors of the churches have certain features in common. On the left is a Shinto-style altar for worship of the ancestors of the followers of that church; on the right is an altar honoring Konkō-daijin.

The lives of believers are affected in many ways. Educational and research activities are carried out by twelve kindergartens, two junior high schools, and two senior high schools; a seminary for ministers; and an institute for advanced studies. A hospital, public library, and two scholarship foundations have been set up to express the Konkō-kyō ideal in action. There are also two associations for ministers, one for young people, a women's association, a society of believers, an association for girls and boys, and a group of missionaries who do prison work.

Followers of Konkō-kyō tend to be individuals rather than families. This is explained by the headquarters body as a result of Konkō-kyō being relatively young and not yet established as a family tradition. Within churches there are two groups: believers (*Shin-to*) and members (*Kyō-to*). The former attend church fairly regularly and adhere to the teachings of Konkō-daijin. But they need not devote themselves entirely to the *Konkō* way of life. They may practice Shinto or Buddhism at the same time. If they choose to become members, then they must become totally committed. This is done in an act called *Kashiki* or *Kikyoshiki*. Thereafter all family ceremonies are performed in the Konkō-kyō church.

Rituals performed in Konkō-kyō churches center on the founder's practice of mediation. The task of the mediator is to stand between the members of the community and God and to express the hopes and desires of the people as holy and pure desires presented to God. The mediator may also offer advice to members based on his knowledge of the life of the founder. Mediators are available during specified hours in the church each day. A believer may visit the church to seek mediation or advice. Prayer is the main activity, and people are reminded that they must pray for others as often as they pray for themselves. The basic form of prayer is to clap four times, bow, clasp the hands, pray, and conclude with four claps. There are set prayers that are intoned, but no hymns. Ceremonies are held in honor of God, the founder, and the church's ancestors on three Sundays of the month. There is a special festival in the fall (corresponding to the *aki matsuri*) to commemorate the founder. The spring festival (*haru matsuri*) honors God. Festivals use rice, water, and *sake* as in normal Shinto festivals. Believers hear the teachings of the founder and are invited to reflect on their own lives. After the ceremony, people talk and drink *sake* in the style of a communion with the *kami* and with each other (*naorai*). Unnecessary ritual is minimized in line with the founder's injunction: "when practicing faith do not abandon everything else and immerse yourself in faith obsessively. Practice faith effortlessly, as when you eat a bowl of barley gruel."

Because human nature is considered to be basically good (in line with the general Shinto outlook), ascetic practices or ecclesiastical rituals are not considered to be replacements for benevolent and unselfish acts in daily life. Following the natural order (as a farmer would see life) is taught and encouraged in Konkō-kyō. Like Kurozumi-kyō and Tenri-kyō, Konkō-kyō is a fully developed religion with a range of activities and beliefs that give it wide appeal to different age groups and sectors of society.

Tenri-kyō. Tenri-kyō means "Teaching of Heavenly Reason." The sect was founded by a female shaman called Nakayama Miki (1798–1887). Using a very simple doctrine, she encouraged people to seek *kanrodai sekai* (perfect divine kingdom). The movement was first considered to be a branch of Yoshida Shinto, but in 1880 it changed its affiliation and since then has been recognized as one of the official thirteen sects of Kyōha Shinto. The founding date is usually given as 12 December 1838.

Its distinctive feature is that it is considered to be genuinely monotheistic in the Western sense. Nakayama Miki received a revelation from Tenri-o-no-mikoto, the heavenly divinity known as Oyagami, "Parent God." After the revelation she became *Kami no Yashiro*, the living shrine of the *kami*. "God revealed himself through Nakayama in order to deliver people from individual sufferings and social evils, and to prepare for the coming of *kanrodai sekai*." This was taken to be union with God the Parent.

Nakayama Miki, or Maekawa Miki (her real name), was the eldest daughter of Maekawa Masanobu, who lived in the province of Yamato at

Sanmaiden (Nara Prefecture). She showed early signs of being charismatic and began as a devout member of Pure Land Buddhism. Although she wanted to become a nun, she was married in 1810 to Nakayama Zembei. In 1838 she had a vision that transformed her life and to which she devoted herself wholly and totally, neglecting her family, which eventually fell into poverty. She began performing healing miracles and teaching that divine protection was attainable through a life of sincere piety. She developed a form of worship characterized by ecstatic dancing and shamanistic practices. Her concept of *kanrodai sekai* was interpreted by the government in political terms, which led to extensive persecution for many years.

In 1853 Zembei died and Kokan, Nakayama's youngest daughter, went to Osaka to extend the new cult. During the time she was in Osaka a fire destroyed the Nakayama house, and over the next ten years the family had extreme financial problems. During this time, Nakayama Miki wrote *Mikagurauta* and *Ofudesaki*, which became the basic manuals of Tenri-kyō. In December 1864 the *tsutome-basho* (place for service) was built, and this became the first Tenri-kyō church.

After the Meiji Restoration the Japanese government classified Tenri-kyō as a Kyōha sect, and in this way it slowly began to gain formal recognition. However, it also had to make some changes in its form and order so that it conformed to government regulations. In 1872 a Department of the Imperial Government was established to examine the main doctrines of all the religious bodies in Japan. In July 1874 a formal notice was sent to Prefectural Governors and Head Priests concerning a prohibition on selling protective charms and offering prayers. This was the beginning of a period of intense police interference, which resulted in the seizure of some of Tenri-kyō's religious artifacts in October 1874. In September 1875 Nakayama was forced to report to the prefectural government and was arrested for disobeying religious ordinances. Followers were forced to give up their faith, and police had orders to stop people from assembling near her home. She was eventually released from prison but was arrested again in 1882 and charged with confusing Shinto and Buddhism, which had become a crime during the Meiji period.

It was not until 1885 that official authorization of Tenri-kyō was given by the Central Office of Shinto. After formal recognition, the head church of Tenri-kyō was moved from Tokyo to Jiba. On 26 January 1887 Nakayama began advocating the *Kagura Zutone* (salvation dance), which was also banned by the police. On the premise that the laws of God were more important than the laws of man, the dance was performed at Jiba, during which Nakayama passed away. She was considered to have reached a spiritual state; that, along with her *hinagata* (model life), became the two basic concepts of Tenri-kyō.

Iburi Izo (1833–1907) succeeded Nakayama as the leader through whom God spoke. He was Nakayama's most trusted disciple, and he made a collection of his revelations in a work called the *Osahizu*, which was responsible for the emergence of the structured Tenri-kyō system.

Beliefs and Teachings. Tenri-o-no-mikoto (God the Parent) revealed himself through Nakayama Miki as the creator of the world.[39] He announced his will to save all mankind by emphasizing charity and the healing of disease through acts of mental discipline and faith. The purpose of life is *yokigurashi*, to be happy and free from suffering. (It is interesting to note the Buddhist concern with suffering and the use of Shinto shaman ideas to remove it.) To achieve the pathway to a happy life, several stages of development and faith are required.

First is the need to comprehend God the Parent. Tenri-o-no-mikoto revealed himself in three ways: as "the original and true *kami*," then as *sukihi* (the moon and sun), finally as *Oya* (parent). It has been suggested that there may have been some influence from the *kakuri kirishitan* (hidden Christian) beliefs. As the creator *kami*, God the Parent shows himself to be the true God who made Heaven and Earth and by whom life and the world are sustained. The moon and sun are manifestations of the God parent and remind us of his creative power. Finally, as *Oya*, the parent God teaches not only that he must be revered but also that there is a parent in Heaven whom people can trust and in whom they can confide. "My daily concern is solely how best I may help my children."

God the Parent taught that *tsutome* and *osazuku* constitute the way of saving mankind known as the *tasuke-ichijo*, through which the world will find prosperity and universal peace. The *tsutome* service is performed by seekers of *yokigurashi* with their hearts united, through which they can receive salvation and grace from the parent God. *Osazuke* is the gift of God to special aspirants who are accepted as missionaries after a careful test of character. They become free from pain and disease because suffering, sickness, and unhappiness are the result of the misuse of the mind, which makes an individual unable to receive divine protection from the parent God. Sympathetic toward mankind, the parent God urges people to seek the right path and to reform themselves accordingly.

Prayers in Tenri-kyō are intense and devotional. They are offered at 7:00 A.M. and 7:00 P.M. There are three simple steps in offering prayers. First, believers reflect on the events of the day, past or coming. Second, they recite the words: "*Ashiki o harote taskue, Tenri-o-no-mikoto*" (Please remove the evil and help, Divine Heavenly Wisdom). Then they listen for the voice of the parent God: "*Chotto hanashi kami no iu koto kikande na, Ashikina koto o iwande na*" (Listen to what the parent God says and do not speak of evil things). There is a final word of exhortation: "*Ashiki o harote tasuke sekikomu ichiretsu sumasu kanrodai*" (Wipe away all evil and let the world live in the Kingdom of Perfect Wisdom). Third, the *ostutome* is concluded by the repetition of these words three times. Believers bow three times toward their *Oyasama* shrine.

Three actions are considered necessary to achieve salvation. First, there is *osazuke*, the divine grant to be received that enables an individual to become an agent of God and to perform works for others. Second, there is *hinokishin*, the daily service to be performed. Third, numerous pilgrimages to *Jiba* are encouraged for the continued renewal of faith. If these three things are undertaken with careful devotion, a happy life free of sickness and pain will result.

Another important theme is that of *kashimono-karimono* (things borrowed, things lent). Because God is the creator, human beings cannot claim anything as their own. The body is something received from God on loan; therefore, people cannot do with it just as they please. Sickness is a warning that our bodies are not being used properly. To please God, we should make full use of our bodies as long as possible, being careful not to abuse them. When we die, we can return our body to God with gratitude for having had it to serve us. According to the *Osahizu* of 14 February 1889, "You have borrowed your body from Me. Only your mind is your own property and the workings of your mind shall influence your body." Thus, God is declared to have spoken through Nakayama.

Reincarnation (*innen*) is a belief of Tenri-kyō that is very similar to the Buddhist belief. The *Osahizu* of 3 October 1900 states it thus: "Do not think that a man lives only one life. He will be reborn over and over again. Hark and listen carefully: Your offspring will inherit the consequences of your previous lives." The soul is considered immortal; by *denaoshi*, temporary absence from the world, individuals are prepared for rebirth.

Ethics in Tenri-kyō consist of teaching about the *yatsu no hokori*, the eight kinds of dust: greed, stinginess, partiality, hatred, animosity, anger, covetousness, and arrogance. These are said to be the sources of all human unhappiness. Tenri-kyō does not view man as evil but sees his soul as covered by these different kinds of dust, which prevent him from shining. Once these are removed, the spirit can shine again and salvation will come. The pursuit of *makoto shinjitsu*, or sincere piety, is the goal of the faith and can be achieved through the three actions that lead to salvation.

Organization and Believers. Between 1889 and 1894, divisions of churches were established all over Japan. In 1892 the head church was promoted from the sixth to the first rank in Shinto. In August 1899 the Head Priest applied for independent status from Shinto, but this was denied. In 1901 the school of Tenri-kyō was established and a second application for independence was made. This was refused again on the grounds that the church doctrines were not clear. Three applications and seven years later, the Home Ministry licensed Tenri-kyō on 27 November 1908. Regardless of government interferences, Nakayama's teachings remained intact and Tenri-kyō began to spread outside of Japan in the United States, Taiwan, Korea, and China.

In 1920 the sect was reorganized and the country was divided into ten diocese. After 1945 the *Fukugen* movement undertook the purification of Tenri-kyō teaching because it had been influenced by State Shinto and nationalism. This movement redefined Tenri-kyō and separated it from Kyōha Shinto. On 30 April 1970, Tenri-kyō withdrew from the *Kyōha-Shinto Rengokai* (Alliance of Kyōha-Shinto Sects). By around 1980 it claimed nearly three million believers. In 1989 it reported 1,754,570 members in 15,417 churches led by 185,088 clergy, as well as 20,039 missions throughout the world. It can be considered the most successful and the largest of the modern developments in Sect Shinto, although it now disclaims that identity.

Why has Tenri-kyō been so successful? One reason may be its simplicity. The *Ofudesaki* is written in *waka* style in 5-7-5-7-7 syllables, which was a popular literary form in the late 1800s and early 1900s. The doctrines are simple and the removal of the eight forms of dust by the Shinto ritual of *oharai* is cultural common sense. The idea of Oyagami, the parent God, is psychologically reassuring; because the parent God is everywhere, it accords naturally with Japanese spirituality, its reverence for nature, and its pursuit of harmony and peace.

Social service is prominent. It includes children's homes, homes for the mentally retarded, day care centers, crisis centers, homes for the aged, and kindergartens. Believers express their gratitude to the parent God by showing kindness to others.

PARALLEL DEVELOPMENTS

Crosscultural parallels have been noted with regard to these groups. In view of the fact that the similarities with Christianity in some cases are striking, some comments seem appropriate. The Kurozumi-kyō teaching, for example, is similar to that of Jesus of Nazareth, whose metaphors were drawn from the fishing and farming world and who was concerned to deliver men from the present evil age into the Kingdom of God. The founder of Christian Science in the United States[40] had a career very similar to that of Nakayama Miki, and she taught doctrines of healing that are remarkably close to those of Tenri-kyō. Similarities exist at other levels. Parallel ideas in the crosscultural setting are always interesting to note, although they may give rise to spurious speculation, especially if the search centers on causal links.

We should not make too much of such "coincidences." The influence of latent Christian ideas cannot be ruled out—especially from *Kakuri Kirishitan*, whose ideas eventually became an admixture of Christianity, Shinto, and Buddhism. This alone would explain a great deal. The influences have been identified in many and even conflicting forms. However, two observations can help to establish a more objective context. First, there are universal religious elements of appeal (as in mysticism and meditation) that transcend traditions and can be found everywhere. These can exist independently of each other in forms that resemble one another despite contrasting cultural backgrounds. Sociological, economic, or other reasons may account for their appeal at one time rather than another, but they remain as constants wherever they exist. Second, there are "mechanisms of belief" that seem effective for certain types of believing people (as in divination and healing). A sect may have success simply by addressing its appeal to the right type of person. Both healing and divination are widespread in religious cultures. Universality of presence or appeal seem to me more preferable as explanations of parallels than tenuous causal links that seek to connect A and B across cultural boundaries in ways that invariably require manipulation of facts. Seeming parallels are probably best left as such, being viewed as no more and no less than interesting cases of coincidence. Whether or not such parallels constitute evidence of truth is a separate metaphysical issue that is best left aside here.

CHANGE AND CONTINUITY IN KYŌHA SHINTO

Without anticipating the discussions in the next chapter, it becomes obvious that there is considerable overlap between Sect Shinto and the New Religions. Murakami Shigeyoshi, a Tokyo University authority on Japanese religion, has commented that Kurozumi-kyō is not the first among the New Religions but is the last among the religions of feudal Japan.[41] Indeed, in the views of some scholars Kyōha Shinto should be classified as an early manifestation of the New Religions (a position with which I would not take issue, except to say that I think it is helpful to distinguish them in order to understand the nature of continuity that has survived throughout the different eras of change).

One line of argument has suggested that there are three phases of New Religions: the nineteenth century, the 1920s, and the postwar era. That is a convenient device for describing them in historical sequence. However, viewed from another standpoint—namely, the content of beliefs—they can indicate a continuum of thought and tradition rather than a series of new developments. The ultra-nationalistic tendencies of the Meiji period and the early years of Shōwa were toned down after the Pacific War, but other essential elements remained, including everything from enshrined *kami* (with some exceptions) to rituals and practices.

The central doctrine of meliorism that is common to all the sects as well as to the New Religions, the belief that human effort alone can save the world, remains as one basic element of continuity. The problems of the world lie within individuals, therefore the salvation of the world must begin there. Counseling of individuals always takes the form of pointing to defects in their attitudes or disposition that lead to the miseries they are experiencing. This confers on these movements their timeless qualities in spite of the fact that they present themselves as speaking for a new age. It is interesting to compare the teachings of the Kyōha groups with each other and then with some literature from the New Religions. The relationship of change and continuity thereby becomes much more apparent.

GENEALOGY OF NEW MOVEMENTS FROM KYŌHA SHINTO SECTS

The clearest evidence of continuity is set out in the following listing of all the new movements that have grown out of the Kyōha Shinto sects, according to the latest research on the subject.[42]

Shinto Taikyō
Inari-kyō
Okami-kyō
Omiwa-kyō
Katori-kon Kon-kyō
Kannagara-kyō
Maruyama-kyō
Shizen-sha
Shinto-kan Shin-kyō
Shinto-shin Shin-kyō
Shinto Kami-no-Michibiki-kyō
Shinto-Tenkyo-kyō (Nojō)
Shisei Mahashira-kyō
Tengen-kyō
Tenzen-kyō
Mizuho-kyō
Yayama-kyō

Ontake-kyō
Ontakesan Soma-hon-kyō
Ontake-kyō-shusei-ha
Shinsen-kyō
Shinto-kokusei-kyō
Shintoku-kyōdan
Chikakuzan-Minshukyo-kyōdan
Tenji-kyō
Chokurei-kyō
Nichigetsu-kyu (Tokyo)

Fusō-kyō
Ishizu-chi-kyō
Isuzu-kyō
Daihinomoto-kyō
Omisora-kyō
Konpira-kyō
Shinso-kyō
Sei-ei-kyō
Daidō-kyō (Fukushima)
Tenshu-kyō
Tenchi-kyō (Kyoto)
Fuji-kyō
Fuji-mi-ho
Fuji-hon-kyō
Shinno-domyo
Kobo-shu-Kobo-en
Minetaka Inari Daisha-kyō

Jikkō-kyō
Shinto Konpira-kyō
Meiji-kyō

Shinri-kyō
Seishin-kyō
Chosei-kyō
Chintaku-reifu-shin-kyō
Hinomoto-kyō

Hino Oshie
Hinomoto-kyō
Mitama-kyō

Shinshū-kyō
Kamino-Michibiki-kyō
Tensho-kyō (Kyoto)
Meisei-kyō

Tenri-kyō
Seikai-shindō-kyō
Daidō-kyō
Hikawa-kami-Ichi-jō
Hinomoto-shinsei-kyō

Taisei-kyō
Shugen Dō-kyō
Tenchi-kyō (Hyogo)

Shrine-derived
Ishizuchi-Hon-kyō
Izumo-kyō
Nihon Jingu-Hon-chō
Yamato-kyō

GENERAL SOURCES

For Chapters 7 and 8, general sources include the following: *Shukyonenkan* (Yearbook of Japanese Religions) (Government's Agency for Cultural Affairs, Tokyo); the extremely valuable *Shin Shūkyō Jiten* (Encyclopedia of New Religions) (Kobundo, Tokyo, 1989). The *Shinshū-kyō Gaido* (Guide to the New Religions) (Best Books, Tokyo, 1989) produced for the *Shin Shukyo Kenkyukai*, or New Religions Research Association, offers a profile of the largest eighty groups as of 1 January 1988. D. C. Holtom, *The National Faith of Japan* (Kegan Paul, London, 1938), pp. 189–286, offers a prewar account in English of the Kyōha sects. Sect publications are listed where they exist. English translations are borrowed from these where they exist.

NOTES

1. William James, *Varieties of Religious Experience* (Gifford Lectures at Edinburgh University, 1901–1902) offers a vivid account of the *via negativa* of medieval European asceticism that punished the body to save the soul. This contrasts with the *via positiva* of the Japanese *gyōja*, whose search for spiritual enlightenment implied an ascent from *homo sapiens* to *homo excellens*.

2. Kitagawa, *Religion in Japanese History* (Columbia University Press, 1966), pp. 38–45. He was also known by other names, including En no Gyōja.

3. *Karakuni* (referring to China or Korea) adds further weight to the thesis that many early ascetics associated with Buddhism came from the Asian mainland. Because Japan was still learning the secrets, the existence of a Japanese leader such as En no Ozunu becomes significant.

4. Recorded in the *Nihon Ryōiki* (which dates to around 822) is an anthology of Buddhist moral educational stories centered on the consequences of good and

bad behavior in life in terms of the Buddhist law. See Nakamura Kyoko, *Miraculous Stories from the Buddhist Tradition* (Cambridge University Press, 1973).

5. See Keith Dowman, *The Power-Places of Central Tibet* (Routledge and Kegan Paul, London, 1988), which is based on the work of a famous Tibetan Khampa lama, Jamyang Kyentse Wangpo (1820–1892).

6. H. Byron Earhart, *A Religious Study of the Mount Haguro Sect of Shugendō* (Sophia, Tokyo, 1970).

7. The story is recorded in the *Kumano Gengen Gosuijaku Engi* (Record of Divine Incarnations at Kumano), compiled during the tenth century.

8. *Kumano Hongū Betto Shidai* (Details of the Superintendent of Kumano Hongu).

9. This is found in the *Shozan Engi* (Narratives of the Origins of Several Mountains). The story has been taken as suggesting that the ascetics on Mt. Katsuragi and in Kumano had some degree of communication.

10. Emperor Go-shirakawa made twenty-three pilgrimages to Kumano.

11. The centers and provinces were as follows: Abe, Kongosan, Miwa, Kamamnokuchi, Bodaisan, Narukawa, Momohara, Shigisan, Koten-ji, Kayahara, Matsuo, Yata, Ryozen-ji, Horyu-ji, Nakanogawa, Nishi Odawara, Chosho-ji, Tonomine, Yoshino Sakuramoto, Uchiyama Eikyu-ji, and Hatsuse (in Yamato); Koyasan, Negoro Teranishi, Negoro Terahigashi, and Konakawa-dera (in Ki); Makio, Kamio, Takakura, Wada, and Nakagawa Ushinotaki (in Izumi); Fushimi and Kaijusen-ji (in Yamashiro); Iwamoto-in and Umemoto-in of Hando-ji (in Omi); Tanjo-ji (in Setsu); Segi-ji (in Ise).

12. The reference is in a text entitled *Azuma Kagami* (Mirror of Eastern Japan), an account of the Kamakura shogunate written between 1266 and 1301.

13. The reference is found in the *Honcho-Seiki* (Chronicles of the Reigns of the Imperial Court) by Fujiwara Michiari (ordered by Emperor Toba).

14. The eight main *dōji* of Omine were the *Kenzo Dōji* (protector and patron of the *Zenji no shuku* center); *Gose Dōji* (protector of the devotees of various teachings and patron of the *Tawa no shuku*); *Koku Dōji* (who reflected universal unchanging love and was the patron of the *Sho no Iwaya*); *Kenko Dōji* (protector of those keeping the precepts and patron of the *Ozasa no shuku*); *Aujo Dōji* (who clamed disturbances, subdued evil, and was patron of the *Tamaki no shuku*); *Kosho Dōji* (who illumined the universe and was patron of the *Jinzen no shuku*); *Jihi Dōji* (who preserved the Mahayana teachings and was patron of the *Suiin no shuku*); *Jona Dōji* (who overcame and removed karmic obstacles and was patron of the *Fukikoshi no shuku*).

15. Paul L. Swanson, "Shugendō and the Yoshino-Kumano Pilgrimage," *Monumenta Nipponica* 36, no. 1 (Spring 1981): 55–84.

16. John Stevens, *Marathon Monks of Mt. Hie* (Shambhala Press, Boston, 1988).

17. These are part of Shingon cosmology. See Kukai, *Shoji Jisso Gi* (The Meaning of Sound, Word, and Reality), tr. in Yoshito S. Hakeda, *Kūkai: Major Works* (Columbia University Press, 1972), pp. 240–241.

18. For reference to the costume of the *Yamabushi*, see Earhart, *Religious Study*, pp. 25–32; and Ishihara Akitaro, *Nihon no Bukkyō Shuha no Subete* (Daihoronkaku, Tokyo, 1981), pp. 232–234. This book gives drawings and explanations of all *Yamabushi* and *Shugendō* costumes.

19. Regarding Ishida Baigan, see Robert N. Bellah, *Tokugawa Religion* (Free Press, Glencoe, 1957).

20. Regarding Ninomiya Sontoku, see T.R.H. Havens, *Farm and Nation in Modern Japan: Agrarian Nationalism* (Princeton University Press, 1974); see also studies by Ohe Seizo.

21. The Ministry of Education raised a proposal in 1988 to restore these statues, which had been removed after World War II as symbols of the old value system. Some may still be seen in isolated rural areas where the work of demolition was never completed.

22. In addition to published documents, much of this material was taken from records of a research group visit to the headquarters of Shinto Taikyō in Azabu in central Tokyo in 1988. In included an interview with Kanchō Shimada Shohei, whose gracious cooperation and illuminating explanations are most gratefully acknowledged. *Meiji Hyakunen to Shinto Taikyō* is the main publication (*Tokyo Life*, 1965).

23. Shinto Taikyō has given rise to sixteen independent sects. (See the list at the end of Chapter 7.)

24. Although there may be similarities in the form of analogous Confucian origins, the use of the concept of Divine Principle in the Unification Church (which originated in South Korea) should not be confused with that in *Shinri-kyō*. Beyond the incidental resemblance of name, the two have no relationship whatsoever. There is no relationship either with the new cult *Om-shinri-kyō* or its political affiliate, *Shinri-tō*.

25. Sano Itohiko in *Uchū* (January 1930). See also Murakami Shigeyoshi, *Kokka Shintō to Minshū Shūkyō* (Yoshikawa Kobunkan, Tokyo, 1982); Furuno Masato, *Gendai Shinto Gaisetsu* (Sankibo Shuppanbu, Tokyo, 1931); *Nippon Shūkyō Jiten* (Kobundo, Tokyo, 1985); and Kono Shozo, *Shinto Taiko* (The Gist of Shinto) (Japan Culture Association, Tokyo, 1936).

26. The principal texts of *Izumo Taisha-kyō* are *Gokyogo*, *Shinri-Nyumon*, and *Shinri-no-Koe*. See the volume on *Izumo Taisha* (*Nippon no Jinja*, series 3) by Senge Takamune (Gakuseisha, Tokyo, 1968), pp. 249–261. *Izumo-kyō* was separately incorporated in 1951, as are several other *Izumo* groups.

27. *Shinto Shuseiha Kyōri* (Doctrines of Shinto) (Shusei-ha, Tokyo, 1928).

28. Meiji era Kyōha groups and prewar New Religions found it necessary to incorporate these themes in order to receive government recognition. These—along with the *kami* revered—in some cases underwent changes after 1946, as the discussion on New Religions demonstrates.

29. Information in this section was obtained from Shiraishi Umekichi, *Shinto Taisei-kyō Shudo Shimpo Ryakkai* (issued by headquarters, no date); Ogasawara Haruo, *Shinto Shinkō no Keifu* (Pelicansha, Tokyo, 1980).

30. *Manyōshū* poems nos. 319 and 320 attributed to Takahashino Mushimaro. Many of these ancient verses display powerful emotions that were heavily suppressed in later ages. The contrast between the mood of the *Manyōshū* and that of the teachings of the New Religions, for example, shows how heavily still the legacies of Edo and Meiji hang upon modern Japan. (For a modern rendering, see *The Manyōshū*, tr. by H. H. Honda, Hokuseido Press, Tokyo, 1967, p. 31).

31. Shibata Magotaro, *Fujidō Toden Kyogi Enkaku* (Fujido Headquarters, Tokyo, 1917); *Jikkō Kyō no Raireki* (Jikko-kyo, Omiya) and *Jikkō-Kyō Shinpai Go-Onreisho* (Jikko-kyo, Omiya) (The Prayer Book of the Sect); Okada Hiroshi, *Jikkō Kyō to Fuji Do Koshin Ko* (Jikko-kyo, Omiya) (issued by headquarters). The climb-

ing season of Mt. Fuji begins with the *Fujimode*, the first climb, on July 10. It is a festival of ancient origin that begins at the main shrine in Fujiyoshida city. The climb by Shinto priests and believers reaches the peak before sunrise, and a booming *taiko* drum greets the sunrise of the first climb. See *Nen-chū-gyō-ji Jiten*, ed. Nishitsunoi Masayoshi (Tokyodo, Tokyo, 1958), p. 703.

32. Sources were obtained from headquarters.

33. Sources were obtained from headquarters.

34. Information in this section was obtained from the following: *Shinshū-Kyō* (Shinshū-Kyō Dai-Kyo-Cho, Tokyo, 1982); Sugano Masateru, *Kyōgi no shori* (A Guide to Teaching) (Shinshu Headquarters, Tokyo, 1928).

35. Sources include the following: Inoue Masakane, *Shinto Yuiitsu Mondo Shō* and *Ikun Shu* and *Kono Yo no Kamisama-Inoue Masakane no Shogai*; and an interview very kindly given by Mr. Kuroiwa Akihiko, manager of the Tokyo Headquarters.

36. Sources include the following: *Kurozumi Kyōshō* (Texts of Kurozumi-kyō) (Kurozumi-kyo Nisshinsha, Okayama, 1974); Hara Keigo, *Kurozumi Munetada* (Yoshikawa Kobunkan, Tokyo, 1964); Ebina Danmasa, *Kirisutokyō no Mitaru Kurozumi Kyō no Shinri* (Kurozumikyō Kenkyū Siryo Okayama); Helen Hardacre, *Kurozumikyō and the New Religions of Japan* (Princeton University Press, 1986); Kurozumi Muneharu (Chief Patriarch of *Kurozumi-kyō*), *The Teachings of Munetada Kurozumi* (private paper); and Willis Stoesz, *Kurozumi Shinto: An American Dialogue* (Anima, Chambersburg, Pa., 1989).

37. Sources include the following: Fujii Kineo, *Hito wa Minna Kaminoko* (General Headquarters of Konkōkyō, Okayama, 1984); *Konkōkyō: A New Religion of Japan* (General Headquarters of Konkōkyō, Okayama, 1958); Matsui Fumio, *Konkō Daijin: A Biography* (Konkō Churches of America, San Francisco, 1972); Delwin B. Schneider, *Konkōkyō: A Japanese Religion* (ISR Press, Tokyo, 1963); Yasuda Kozo, *Konkōkyō Scriptures* (General Headquarters of Konkōkyō, Okayama, 1983); *Konkō-kyō Kyōten* (The Sacred Texts of Konkō-kyō) (Konko Headquarters, Okayama City, 1920); Miyake Toshio, *Heiwa o Ikiru* (Kodansha, Tokyo, 1989); head of the *Konkō-kyō* of Izuo.

38. *Kurozumi-kyō: A New Religion of Japan* (General Headquarters, Okayama, 1958).

39. Sources include the following: *Tenrikyō Kyōka Honbu* (A Short History of Tenrikyō) (Tenrikyō, Tenri City, 1960); Masuno Michioki, *Tenrikyō* (Tenrikyō Head Church, Tenri, 1928); Henry Van Straelen, *Religion of Divine Wisdom* (Salesim Trade School, Tokyo, 1957); *Tenri Yearbook* (Headquarters, Tenri City, 1992).

40. Parallel developments with Christian Science are extremely interesting, empirically in terms of making crosscultural comparisons and philosophically in terms of grasping common roots and elements of religion and religious development in cosmic as well as historical and sociological settings. For historical data, see A. C. Bouquest, *Comparative Religion* (Penguin, London, 1958), p. 198. See also Nakamura Hajime, *A Comparative History of Ideas* (Routledge and Kegan Paul, New York, 1986).

41. Murakami Shigeyoshi, *Japanese Religion in the Modern Century* tr. by H. Byron Earhart (University of Tokyo, 1980).

42. *Shin Shūkyō Jiten*, p. 66.

Chapter 8

Shinto and the New Religions

THE NEW RELIGIONS

The New Religions of Japan, the *Shin Shūkyō* or *Shinkō-Shūkyō* (in contrast to the older established religions known as *Kisei Shūkyō*), are well-known features of Japan's postwar religious and cultural landscape. The Ministry of Education, which keeps statistics on religious groups, identified over two thousand in 1987. These range from small groups with as few as a hundred followers and one spiritual leader to vast denominations like the Nichiren Buddhist movement *Soka Gakkai,* which claimed at its peak to have had 16 million followers. With the exception of the Unification Church (which originated in Korea) and one or two foreign Christian groups, all the movements have developed indigenously. They present a strong argument for the fact that religion continues to play a role in Japanese society; furthermore, they represent certain traits of character within Japanese religious life that seem to be typical of all periods of Japanese history and that reflect and support patterns of continuity in Japanese society and values.

In discussing these newer religions "related to" Shinto, it should be explained that they may not necessarily (or in some cases not even consciously) be derived from Shinto or shrines, although many are. In contrast to the groups that have Buddhist leanings, those listed here are based upon and influenced by ideas that can be derived from the Shinto tradition in one form or another. There may not be overt Shinto connections, but the central ideas and practices are closer to Shinto than to any other tradition in Japan.

A prima facie survey of the New Religions may suggest groups of ideas that seem to conflict with each other and that have in some cases only tenuous links with Shinto. More careful investigation will show that in spite of apparent contradictions, which are often aggravated in translation, they nevertheless have common themes. Much of the research for this book was supported by visits to either the headquarters or meetings to which non-members were admitted. Through interviews with group leaders and the metaphors they used, my initial confusion began to fade in the face of recurrent patterns. Although I recognize that these groups are distinct, it could also be argued that there is much in common among them—and that the matters in common are more significant than the differences. Readers may judge for themselves.

It is difficult not to be struck by the parallels with Kyōha Shinto discussed in the previous section. In some respects only time separates these movements. The *Kyōha Shinto Rengōkai* (Association of Sect Shinto) originally included only the thirteen official sects. After 1949 many new groups entered, increasing its member groups to seventy-five. At that point some of the New Religions joined the great stream of the evolution of Japanese religion. Although they have different origins, different leaders, and belong to different eras, they all seem similar and very Japanese. Herein also is a sound reason for rejecting the crisis theories of the New Religions. The religious liberation of 1946 allowed suppressed movements to flourish and encouraged them to be less nationalistic, to think in terms of the wider world. This was a welcome development; many of the groups are now involved in movements such as the World Conference for Religion and Peace (WCRP) and the International Association for Religious Freedom (IARF), and others perform good works in numerous areas of society. If these tendencies continue as Japanese religions enter their "international age," it bodes well for the future.[1] Before examining the common features of the sects, I offer a few critical observations on some of the general theories about the New Religions.

THEORIES ABOUT THE NEW RELIGIONS

The earliest theories concerning the New Religions argued that they were religions of apocalyptic crisis, the immediate crisis being the World War II defeat, the subsequent pains of Occupation, and the rebuilding of both society and economy. The use of the term *crisis* was extended by some observers to encompass social crisis in a broad sense, similar to the changes overtaking Western society at that time. Macfarland Neill's *Rush Hour of the Gods* was one early example that attracted great attention when it was published. Harry Thomsen's *The New Religions of Japan* was the other best-known work along these lines, a discussion slightly more insightful in its conclusions than some. For example, Thomsen noted the role of charismatic figures in the formation of new religious movements, but he did not appear to see its broader historical perspective. Other major works on the New Religions tended initially to follow the same arguments and even included some Japanese writers,[2] although it is interesting to note that none of Japan's major writers on religion (e.g., Nakamujra Hajime) gave serious credence to these theories.

The theories of crisis are unsatisfactory, first, because they lack historical perspective. The role of shamanism goes deep into Japanese history. It is a simple fact that the type of religious movements of the postwar period have been seen emerging at all stages of Japanese history, in times of relative quiet as well as in times of crisis. The growth of the various sects of Kyōha Shinto is a long tale of "new religions" emerging during the Edo period, when they were defined and then approved by the State as recognized sects. They were probably as novel to the people of their day as the New Religions are to the present. In other words, creating new movements has always been a feature of Japanese religious life.

A second unsatisfactory feature of the crisis approach to the New Religions is that they fail to take account of the changed nature of the Japanese Constitution after 1946. The abolition of State Shinto and the freedom of religious belief under the Constitution permitted the revival of shrines that had been suppressed during the *Jinja Gappei* period, when the government put all shrines under State direction. This fact of liberation meant that pent-up energies could be released, which was probably as important a factor in the sudden explosion of cults as was the critical situation that the nation was facing. Spiritual rootlessness, as Kitagawa has remarked,[3] remains a condition of the postwar society that many of these groups seek to cure. However, it is a condition of malaise, not of crisis.

Third, discussions have tended to focus on Buddhist groups as a consequence of the mistaken but commonly held view that Japan is essentially a Buddhist nation upon which Shinto was imposed by the government. Nothing could be further from the truth. Nakamura Hajime had made the point that the Japanese government came to Buddhism not in the interests of the salvation of the people's souls but in the interests of strengthening Japanese tribalism.[4] Buddhism was absorbed into Japanese culture, but the price was total accommodation to Shinto. Western observers in general have been excessively captivated by Buddhism in Japan, particularly Zen, and have consequently failed to see that Buddhism in Japan is Japanese first and Buddhist second.[5] Consequently, the religious movements that have their base in Shinto have been researched and documented less than their Buddhist counterparts. Many of the New Religions are in fact Buddhist, but what has been said about continuity with the past is also true of them. The largest and most influential of the new movements within Buddhism share three common factors: (1) they were started before the war under different names; (2) it was the constitutional separation of State and Religion that permitted them to flourish; (3) they are based on the Lotus Sūtra and they look to the Kamakura age priest Nichiren as their spiritual ancestor. Furthermore, in spite of declared statements on the subject, they all practice ancestral reverence in some form. In other words, they are new in one sense but extremely traditional in another, which is precisely what makes them so enigmatic.

Finally, by not looking thoroughly at the nature of Japanese folk religion, theories that emphasize the crisis aspect of the New Religions fail to grasp the essentials of Japanese religiosity and the Japanese perception of spirituality. These are equally important elements of the tradition. The fundamental place of Shinto attitudes and what they impart to any perception of religion is a vital ingredient of a full understanding of the background to the growth of new religious phenomena in Japan. The elements of shamanism, divination, counseling, and healing are at the roots of spirituality in Japan in every age. If the *Kyōha Shinto* and the *Shinkō Shūkyō* groups are a response to any kind of crisis, perhaps it is to the general problem created by the impact of modernization[6] on traditional Japanese society, a process that has been going on since Commodore Perry first challenged the closed society of the Edo period. The Japanese of the late twentieth century are still coming to terms with that process—within which World War II was but a part, as have been the subsequent phases of economic growth. Perhaps it is a parable on the consequences of so much happening in such a short space of time. Japan moved further and faster than any other nation in the world within the same time span and may still be paying the price of the pressures generated.

CHARACTERISTIC FEATURES OF THE NEW RELIGIONS

Charismatic and shamanistic leadership can be traced as far back as the Yamato clan, which showed its leadership through women shamans who were married to the earliest clan leaders. The sacral nature of kingship, a principle that has never been absent in Japanese social development, can be seen there; the pattern is replicated in the new religious groups that emerged within the changing circumstances of Japanese history. The influence of fortune-tellers in contemporary industrial Japanese society is testimony to the fact that when Japanese religious life lacks vigor, all that seems necessary is the emergence of a powerful shaman for a new movement to be born.

Most of the New Religions (like the Kyōha Shinto groups) have a designated leader or founder who is reverenced in a special way and whose life story represents the values that have become a basic part of the organization. This is also true of corporations, which often display cultic features. The Matsushita *Kaikan*, a museum containing the story of Matsushita's founder, is presently celebrated in a reverential way that gives the sense of a place of worship as well as a museum. The cultic and the corporate have much in common.[7]

The importance and frequency of spiritual healing are significant features. Many of the leaders were interested in healing for one reason or another, and several made astonishing claims about the powers they could summon to produce miraculous cures. Some claim that these are not miracles; others believe they are. Nonetheless, the supernatural is being tapped and spiritual energies appear to be released that bring cures to some individuals and that enhance the spiritual status of the leader and the group. In this regard, *Kurozumi-kyō* spans both older and newer religions.

Covert nationalism is a feature of the postwar New Religions that echoes history. Prewar groups were explicitly tied to the values of ultra-nationalism as a condition of government recognition. Some underwent changes after the war, introducing themes such as world peace or well-being. However, amid the talk of world peace and the development of humankind, we often find assertions that Japan is somehow spearheading a new emerging civilization or playing a messianic role. Similar narcissistic thinking can be found in Japanese Christianity, which is further proof of how deep the inclination is to think in these terms.

I use the word *covert* because some of these religions have imposing titles suggestive of a world vision, yet the tendency remains to see the world saved by the insights of a Japanese leader. Here, the messianic and the nationalistic converge in the pattern set by Nichiren, who declared of Japanese Buddhism in the Kamakura age that once purified by his teaching. Buddhism as a whole would be purified. Japanese Buddhism would then save Asia, and Asia would save the world. The nineteenth-century Christian thinker Uchuimura Kanzo (1861–1930) wrote in the flyleaf of his Bible a vow that shaped his life when he was working in a hospital for retarded children in America in the 1880s: "I for Japan, Japan for the world, the world for Christ and all for God." Unless I misread him, Christ is mediated to the world by Japan! But here the charisma and vision of a leader combine in a deep-seated respect for national identity. Most of the new religious groups existed before the war under different names and had to survive the pressures of militarism and constant government scrutiny and suspicion. Names were changed and new beginnings made, but aspects of the continuity remain and the teachings of the founders are still the norms of doctrines.

Ancestral reverence is central to the recognition and resolution of all human problems. Each of the groups discussed here lays great store on revering ancestors properly and on seeing oneself as a link between past and future, being responsible toward both. This metaphysical view of history seems crucial to Japanese self-understanding. It embodies the nation's deepest spirituality and is used by the new as well as the older religious traditions to show people where they stand in time and how they should view themselves and their duties in terms of past and future.

Stress on purification as a means to deeper spirituality is as old as Shinto itself. It is frequently expressed within these groups in their concerns for the individual to maximize development in all respects. Underlying the power of purification is the belief in the fundamental goodness of human nature, a doctrine that seems basic to Shinto in whatever form it takes. The problem of evil is seldom discussed in ways that the Western mind would find satisfactory. This relates to the metaphysical issue of dualism versus monism in Japanese thought and the cultural influences that a predominantly monistic way of thinking may exert.

Stress on happiness is frequently combined with the demand that believers accept the world as it is now as being the best possible of all situations. The doctrine of *imanaka*, a very old Shinto term, can be heard in the background of many of these ideas and should be considered one of the key concepts of the Shinto tradition as well as an outlook on life that is common to all religious strands of Japanese culture. Even the Buddhist groups in the New Religions are concerned with happiness. The well-known research institute established by Matsushita Konoskue is called PHP (Peace, Happiness, and Prosperity), terms that belong to the tradition whereby the *kami* wish for people to be successful in business and to prosper. The objective of spiritual healing is to promote happiness, and happiness is often associated with the concept of harmony. This brings us to another common feature: the older Confucian ethics.

Confucian ethics in different forms have been taught in Japan ever since Prince Shōtoku (574–622) formulated his famous Seventeen Clause Constitution (in reality a set of moral guidelines), stressing harmony as the first principle for the order of society. The same may be said of the Kyōha sects, in which Confucian values are as strongly in evidence as they are throughout Japanese history.

Even the purists of the *Kokugaku* school were not averse to falling back on Confucian ideals, even indirectly. Although Confucianism is never mentioned as such, the values are identifiable. The inheritance is from the Meiji period, when the values were made the moral foundation of the Constitution in such a way that they linger to the present in forms of feudal thought and practice, some more obvious than others. Ancestral reverence, parental respect, and values related to husband and wife reflect the Confucian relationships; without these, the moral matrix of Japanese society would be extremely weak. Although they can be labeled Confucian, they have been adapted and changed in a Japanese way so that they are now truly Japanese values. Therefore, they inevitably feature in every new group that seeks to restore or rebuild the moral fabric of Japanese society.

Other characteristics could be adduced, but the foregoing seem to me to be sufficient evidence of common ideas and common traditions. Not all the New Religions that are Shinto-inspired are discussed here. The number is too great even to list. What follows is an account of a number of the most prominent groups that display aspects of Shinto in their activities. I also note that healing plays an important part and that they are trying to address ageless concerns rather than offer panaceas for the problems of the present. However, human and existential problems linger that none of the New Religions seem to be able to address in a meaningful way. The nature of evil is one. A sensitive Japanese student of mine made the following critical point in a seminar: "Faithful people are betrayed, honest people become sick, and people who work hard remain poor. These religions do not address questions like this at all."

The Western mind would expect a rational approach to these realities. But perhaps it is the more "intuitive" Japanese approach that distresses the Western mind. The New Religions probably satisfy the Japanese mind with their soothing aesthetic approach to problems to the same extent that they perplex the Western observer. If they did not, they would not have such large followings. Likewise, the failure of Christianity in Japan[8] may well be partly the result of the application of rational methods to problems that Japanese culture considers to be fundamentally emotional perceptions of the world. It is as though the New Religions are concerned not to understand the questions but simply to offer acceptable answers.

CONTRASTS WITH ESTABLISHED RELIGIONS IN JAPAN

The distinction can be overstressed because the cultic and the institutional can fade into each other, as developments within Kyōha Shinto demonstrated. However, certain points of difference can make the distinction clearer to the outside observer.[9]

First, nearly all the New Religions look to a historical founder (*kyōsomsama*), the person upon whose inspiration the movement is based and from whose experiences it is derived. That person is revered and in some cases considered to be a *kami*, as in Kyōha Shinto. In contrast, Jinja Shinto and its shrines can point only to the mists of time and declare that their origins lie in the beginnings of Japanese civilization, with the *kami* of the mythology rather than with subsequent historical personalities. Even where historical personalities are enshrined, such figures are in no way considered founders of the shrine, as the case of Sugawara Michizane proves.

Second, their New Religions' teachings are more clearly set out than the vague and less defined beliefs of the shrines themselves. In the case of Jinja Shinto shrines, the object of offering prayers may be for some general good like a good marriage, childbirth, passing examinations, or success in business. Intellectual content is minimal although rituals can be complex. New Religions have articulated sets of beliefs and rules to guide the behavior of believers.

Third, in the new movements the distinction between clergy and laity in terms of both status and function is vague. Indeed, some movements (particularly the Buddhist ones) style themselves movements for "laymen." The Shinto priest, by his training in rituals and by his skills in reciting *norito* as well as by his dress and demeanor, is better qualified to approach the *kami* than the average believer. Furthermore, shrines are frequently in the hereditary possession of priestly families. This tendency can be found in New Religions that have reached the second generation and desire to establish a pedigree of tradition.

WORLDVIEW OF THE NEW RELIGIONS

In spite of all their apparent differences, the New Religions share an almost identical worldview. By *worldview* I do not exactly mean the German concept of *Weltanschauung*—which is heavily metaphysical (and which Japanese religions are not)—but rather a sense of the position of the individual, his or her religious beliefs, and the meaning of these against a loosely conceived cosmic background within which that meaning can be experienced and understood. It is not explicitly defined in any objective sense and therefore cannot be the object of systematic philosophical exposition. It is defined rather in terms of points of reference that serve more like guides through the sequences in a mandala than a charted map of cosmic geography. It is not a worldview that answers questions and gives a sense of meaning to human history and human development. It is thoroughly integrated into Japanese culture as its background and therefore shares all the presuppositions that lie within it. Consequently, its exposition is extremely difficult without a good grasp of the fundamentals of the culture itself.

It is best described as a set of concentric circles in which the individual *kokoro* (heart) or *tamashi* (soul) is at the center. Surrounding the soul is the body, which is part of the next circle, Japanese society. Beyond this is everything between the oceans around Japan and outer space! That may be called *Kannagara* (The Way of the Kami), *Daishizen* (Great Nature), or some other name with a cosmic connotation. The message of religion is designed to keep the harmonious balance of these circles. If the energizing principle of the system is grasped and followed, then all will be well. If not, then sickness, misery, and unhappiness will prevail. The individual has to learn how to integrate properly with society and beyond in order to avoid suffering. The cultivation of the *kokoro* in moral terms and the elimination of all tendencies to egoism in thought and behavior will result in the fulfillment of material and spiritual longings.

The serious problems of life are addressed in this way. They are seen not to be deficiencies within the structure of creation. Rather, they are traced to the individual, whose defective attitudes are the source of the problem. There is nothing wrong in the cosmos that the adequate moral cultivation of the individual will not set to rights. Consequently, Western solutions to social problems, political action, or public protest are dismissed as ineffective. Only collective moral cultivation can improve society. The healing of society cannot be performed by drastic means. The same holds true of the human body, whose illnesses are the result of an uncultivated *kokoro*. A Japanese proverb says this most succinctly: "*Kurushimu mo tanoshimu mo kokoro no mochiyo*" ("Our suffering as well as our happiness is governed by how we bear our *kokoro*").

Because all problems are located within the individual and not in the social environment, healing begins when moral values are realigned to harmonize with the system in which people live. Only in this way can the individual reach the fulfillment of his or her highest potential. The individual life comes to have meaning only from being part of the religious group, which in turn permeates the entire Japanese cultural and social system. In this, people can enhance the power to find happiness (i.e., by subordinating the self to its immediate social environment). Here the Confucian elements in the worldview emerge. The delicate issues of authority and obedience become important. The self becomes cultivated by becoming selfless and by training in the various cultural and martial arts that enhance the self (e.g., calligraphy, flower arrangement, or *aikidō*), a principle already observed in Kyōha Shinto. The individual thus grows into the system and becomes a part of it.

Other aspects of the worldview[10] could be discussed, but the ones just mentioned should suffice to indicate not merely features of the general worldview but also some similarities between worldviews found in Kyōha Shinto and those found in the New Religions. This is a clear case of continuity being more noticeable than change.

PRINCIPAL NEW RELIGIONS RELATED TO SHINTO

Ōmoto-kyō

Origins and Development. The name of the movement means "The Teaching of the Great Origin"—an expression, according to sect records, invented by the foundress, Deguchi Nao, in 1892 when she planted a flower, the *Rhodea Japonica* (Ōmoto in Japanese), and in a *kami*-possessed state uttered the words "This is the Ōmoto, the Great Foundation of the World: the teachings of the Great Beginning, the First Cause, shall be preached." To this incident Ōmoto-kyō traces its origins. Thereafter the circumstances of the life of Deguchi (1837–1918) became the basis of the development of the movement.

She came from a poor background and was married to Deguchi Masagoro, whose circumstances were little better than those of her own family. However, she was by nature pious, hard-working, and sincere; and after being widowed, she began to have visions and experiences of being the medium of a *kami*. The critical event took place in the New Year of 1892, when she had a vision of herself in a great hall meeting with a pious-looking man in the presence of her late husband. The vision occurred repeatedly, and finally she was able to ask the name of the spirit that was seeking to make contact with her. The spirit identified itself as Ushitora-no-Konjin. Thereafter she began preaching and making strange utterances for which the suspicious authorities imprisoned her. She scratched her ideas on the walls of the prison cell with a nail, and these became the beginnings of the sacred book of Ōmoto, the *Ofudesaki*.

She also predicted the coming of a fellow-believer whom she called the Master. In 1898 a young man named Ueda Kisaburo visited her, claiming that he too was a believer in Konjin, and he married into the Deguchi family. He than became Deguchi Onisaburo (1871–1948), and from his efforts the development of Ōmoto-kyō as an organized sect began. He too had come from a poor family and had experienced a severe depression when his father died. To find relief, he began practicing ascetic exercises in the mountains of Takuma. He also had revelations of Heaven and Hell and was taught the truth of the universe and the destiny of the world—in a way, it has been said, reminiscent of Dostoevsky's *The Dream of a Ridiculous Man*. He believed simply that his mission was to save the world by improving human society. His own revelations thus matched those of Deguchi Nao, and the combination formed the basis of the expansion of the Ōmoto-kyō teaching.

Government recognition of the movement was withheld for a number of reasons, partly because the teaching was heavily monotheistic and partly because of its innate suspicion of new movements that implicitly criticized then-contemporary society by proposing programs of "reform." Worst of all, Deguchi was publicly preaching that human salvation began with the salvation of ordinary people, the masses. Such tendencies were viewed as revolutionary and consequently as menacing to government authority and Imperial prerogative. Police action against Ōmoto-kyō was brutal and repressive. On charges of lèse-majesté, the headquarters was destroyed and many members arrested, charged with violations of the Maintenance of the Public Order Act, and imprisoned. This happened twice, during 1921 and 1935. In 1942 Deguchi was released after six years and eight months in prison.

Deguchi Onisaburo's own life was filled with dramatic incidents, including his return in chains from an aborted mission to China in the company of *Aikidō* master Ueshiba Morihei, with whom he maintained a close relationship. His remaining years were spent teaching quietly. After the war, the movement gained fresh momentum and became active in defending the postwar peace Constitution. It also developed a strong inter-faith approach to religious dialogue, particularly with Christianity in the United States.

Beliefs and Teachings. The main teachings[11] are contained in the founder's *Ofudesaki* and in a book entitled *Reikai Monogatari* (Tales of the World of the Spirit) written by Onisaburo. The powerful apocalyptic mood of the message may have been one reason for its appeal. The following lines are from the foundress when she was imprisoned: "The Greater World shall burst into full blossom as plum blossoms in early Spring. The time for me, Ushitora-no-Konjin, the Primal *Kami*, to reign has finally come. This is a dark age! If things are left as they are, order will never prevail in the world. Therefore, the world shall be reconstructed under the protection of the One Ruling *Kami* where peace will prevail for all ages to come." This was powerful imagery for an illiterate peasant woman and, not surprisingly, words to make the government uneasy. Although she had never knowingly come into contact with Biblical writings, her prophecies and warnings resemble them, as do her concerns for social reforms.

Onisaburo supplemented her ideas by his writings, which he composed after his first release from prison in 1921. As well as documenting his own spiritual pilgrimage, he stated the fundamental Doctrine of Ōmoto-kyō and the three great Rules of Learning. "Konjin Kami is the all-pervading Spirit in the universe. Man is the minister governing all Heaven and Earth. When unity of man and *kami* is attained, he commands unlimited power and authority." The Rules are as follows:

1. Observe the true phenomena of nature and you will think of the body of the one true *kami*.
2. Observe the unerring function of the universe and you will think of the energy of the one true *kami*.
3. Penetrate the mentality of living creatures and you will conceive of the soul of the one true *kami*.

The divine is believed present in the human heart because they are interdependent. The divine becomes omnipotent only when man cooperates in the salvation of the world. This means the reconstruction of the world by the reorientation of the social value system. "Man must live in religion. Not one thing that man does is outside the sphere of true religion."

The themes of universal brotherhood and justice also lie at the heart of the teachings of the foundress. This stems from the belief that Konjin is the universal *kami* concerned about all mankind. Ōmoto-kyō sees itself as without prejudice or discrimination. There is a belief in life after death, which can be either direct transport to Heaven or a journey through a series of stages until pure spirituality has been achieved.

Purification from evil follows the traditional Shinto style. In 1901 the foundress, in obedience to Konjin, sent to the *Ame-no-Iwato* from which water was drawn that was then mixed with the wells of *Omoto*. This was taken to the island of Meshima, where Konjin was believed to be enshrined. She poured the water into the sea with the words, "Unshitora-Konjin, we humbly pray you with your power . . . to make this pure water from Moto-Ise circle the seas of the world, turning to clouds . . . to rain, snow, and hail, watering the five continents, cleansing corrupt spirits, washing away impurities, and building a paradise on earth." This first act of universal purification became a model for future Ōmoto-kyō rituals. At the time of *Setsubun*, priests perform a ritual for purification of the universe in the *Miroku-Den* of the headquarters from 7:00 P.M. until the first light of dawn. The normal Shinto practice of *oharai* is followed throughout the year at all other festivals.

Although it has universal elements, Ōmoto-Kyō remains close to the spirituality of Shinto from which it drew inspiration, particularly the Shinto sense of the idea that man is a child descended from the *kami*. In that belief it is quite orthodox, although the application of the idea has unique aspects.

Organization and Believers. The movement is administered from a headquarters in Kameoka City in Kyoto-fu. Its holy place is the *Miroku-Den* and the *Kinryū-Den* (Pavilion of the Golden Dragon) in Ayabe, which is near Moto-Ise. The island of Meshima in the Sea of Japan is sacred because the foundress went there in 1905 to pray and receive revelations, as is Kamishima in the Sea of Japan, where Hitsujisaru no Konjin is enshrined. The head in 1989 was Deguchi Kyotaro, a great-grandson of the foundress.

Ōmoto-kyō developed during the crucial inter-war era but lost momentum and appeal during the postwar liberal years. It peaked during the inter-war era, when it claimed two million followers. It claimed only 200,000 registered believers in 1989. Why did such a dynamic movement decline so dramatically? Perhaps the eschatological message had been partly realized by the postwar changes in Japanese society. Perhaps its reported prewar political activities confused people as much as did its postwar concentration on art, education, Esperanto, and social welfare, which was probably too sophisticated for that moment of history. It had been dealt severe blows by the police and the press but did not explode with a postwar revival; it remains relatively small, although it is still one of the larger Shinto-based New Religions.

Shinrei-kyō

Origins and Development. Shinrei-kyō came into being after World War II. It is described by its followers as a "super religion" that in some way transcends both religion and science as hitherto known. The name combines *kami* (spirit) and "teaching" and is declared to mean "Teaching of the Divine Spirit." The miracles that divine power made possible to its founder are what believers claim differentiate it from other faiths. It claims that miracles do take place and that these are without parallel in any other religion. Consequently, it explains itself through case studies that demonstrate how its principles work. Miracles are the authenticating proof of Shinrei-kyō beliefs.

Otsuka Kan'ichi (1891–1972), the founder, was born the son of a wealthy merchant in Tokushima. From childhood he showed prodigious capacities in the area of fortune-telling, predicting the future, and being an inventor. At age sixteen he went to various famous centers of mountain religion in Japan, not to learn Buddhism but to confirm his own spiritual powers. He then came to believe that Japan had a role to play in the process of world transformation. By making the nation's spiritual heritage known and available, Japan will contribute to the peace of the world. When the divine power of Shinrei-kyō is released, a new world order comes into being. Shinrei-kyō itself is thus the herald of the coming age. The movement is described by its followers as "the dawning world movement, the ultimate principle that makes the planets move, the true Shintoism and the spiritual sun rising in Japan."

Otsuka himself first put pen to paper in 1911 after extensive travels in Korea, Manchuria, and Mongolia. In a pamphlet entitled *Dainippon-seishin* (The Spirit of Great Japan) he warned that Japan's involvement in war against Germany would lead to catastrophe. Holding firmly to the ideals of salvation for the people and the realization of world peace, he founded Shinrei-kyō. After his death he was enshrined in Akigawa City in a place sacred to believers and known as the *Korin-kaku*.

Beliefs and Teachings. The basic teaching[12] centers on the idea of miraculous healing. Through a process of skull expansion (which happens to every follower), brain cells are activated and the mind is calmed; through being able to make sound judgments, believers are enabled to develop themselves to the fullest. The founder himself is declared by believers to be a *Shinrei-no-okami* (a *kami* spirit, great *kami*) who is one with the *kami* of the universe and one with the generative power that brings the universe into being, a doctrine derived from Shinto. *In-en-ga* is the principle of explanation used. *In* is "cause" and *ga* is "effect." *En* refers to invisible and external forces that shape human destiny by affecting the cause-effect relationship. One's present sufferings are the result of one's own and one's ancestors' wicked deeds. (This idea is partly Buddhist, but the importance of ancestors may once again be observed.) Shinrei-kyō believers claim to die a natural death in such a way that their bodies will not experience rigor mortis, death spots, or putrid odors. This enables the sublime transmigration to take place from death to a new life thereafter.

The Dawning World Movement idea was initiated by the founder in the early 1970s to stress Japan's role in international relations as a creator of world peace. He argued that the focus of international religions was shifting from West to East and that the core of human existence was rejecting materialism for what he called *seishinteki bunmei*, or spiritual civilization. The idea of *seishinteki bunmei* is not clearly defined but suggests a type of society different from that of modern Japan, wherein, according to Otsuka's views, material things had come to be dominant. At best, his views can be considered as containing authentic visionary elements. At worst, they can be interpreted as calling for a return to a more traditional type of society.

Distinctive Features. The annual cycle of events is reminiscent of the *gyōji* of a normal shrine—a pattern common to most religious groups in Japan, especially those based on Shinto. Monthly gatherings and special ceremonies lead to the purification of the spirit, the key to health and healing. The practice of *sai*, or *matsuri* (festival), is explicitly Shinto. There is, for example, the *Tsuninamisai* (Lunar Festival) held on the third of each month except in January, May, and November; the *Shinnensai* (New Year) celebrated on January 3; the *Kaikyo-kinensai* (commemoration of the founding of Shinrei-kyō) held from February 11 to 12; the *Kyōso Seitan-sai* or *Shunki-taisai* (Kyōso-sama's birthday) held on May 3; the *Mitama-sai* (Calming the Souls of Ancestors) on August 15; the *Shuuki-taisai*, a counterpart of *Shunki-taisai*, held on November 3; and the *Misogi-sai* (Purification Festival) held on December 31.

At these and other festivals, *go shinsui* and *okumotsu* (water and food charged with divine power) are taken home to be consumed as sources of receiving the miraculous power of the founder. At the various ceremonies and Sunday gatherings, claps and bows toward the altar confirm the degree to which Shinto practices are being followed. Unique to Shinrei-kyō is the act of offering special thanks to the *Kyoso-sama*, who is considered to have been the human manifestation of a divine providence, the classic concept of a *daimyōjin* or an *ikigami*. One of its points of appeal for modern Japanese may be that it does not put any demands upon people to improve their lives actively, but rather encourages them to depend upon a figure like the *Kyoso-sama* to achieve it on their behalf. It may thus be viewed as a religion of dependence. It seems to suggest that human effort is not required; but to achieve the goals of the religion, considerable effort is in fact required.

Organization and Believers. The founder's widow (known as *Kyōbo-sama*) took over leadership after her husband's death. She came to be an intermediary between the founder and the members, because it was she who first recognized the divine power in him. The organization claimed 171,484 members in 1989, as well as 300 associate members who subscribe to Shinrei-kyō publications. Also listed were 165 instructors. There are seven churches located in Akasaka, Aobadai (in Tokyo's *Meguro-ku*), Sapporo (in Hokkaido), Kitami, Nagoya, Nishinomiya, and Ashikawa. There is no priesthood, but there is a division called the *Jimkyoku* charged with the responsibilities of organizing events, ceremonies, and religious services for members. But the office staff and the members are not distinctively divided.

There are two subordinate organizations within Shinrei-kyō. One is *Shinrei-jihō-sha*, which publishes a bimonthly newspaper, *Shinrei-jihō*, intended primarily for non-members. It also publishes books that are records of miracles experienced by followers. There are seven volumes of *Kiseki no Izumi* (The Fountainhead of Miracles) that detail the cure of diseases considered fatal by the Ministry of Health and Welfare. They include miracles to people, animals, plants, and inanimate objects; painless childbirth; "sublime transmigration"; business prosperity; skull expansion; and skeletal reformation.

A separate movement was *Nippon Seishin Fukko Sokushin-Kai* (Society to Promote the Restoration of the Soul of Japan). Its aim is to restore the true Japanese spirit, which has been lost in the midst of the great economic changes of the postwar world. A monthly newspaper entitled *Keimei Shimbun* (The Cock-Crowing Newspaper) seeks to promote "enlightened activities." During the 1970s much effort was expended on propagation, particularly on university campuses. This aspect of mission work is still pursued vigorously. Open training sessions and *happyō-kai* are held at which individuals report on the miracles they have experienced.

Mahikari

Origins and Development. The *Sukyō Mahikari* was founded by Okada Kotama (1901–1974), as he later named himself. Formerly a soldier and a businessman, his body was occupied by Su-no-Kamisama in 1959 when he received a revelation to become *Sukuinushi-sama* (Master of Salvation). As a young man he injured his back in a horse-riding accident, which resulted in a disease of the thoracic vertebrae. His condition was pronounced incurable by medical specialists. Given only three years to live, he decided to devote himself to religion. After the three years had elapsed he was still alive and, mysteriously, his disease had disappeared. He went on to found several military aircraft–manufacturing companies, becoming wealthy in the process. The U.S. bombing raids at the end of World War II put an end to his business, and he became bankrupt and joined *Seikai Kyūsei-Shūyo* (a religion of world messianity).

Working hard to pay off his debts, on 27 February 1959 at 5:00 A.M. he received his first revelation. He was informed that religions up to that time had not exposed the truth fully, but that to him the fullness of Divine Truth would be revealed as to no other. He was told that his mission was to "purify" the world through the power of the True Light, which radiated through his hands. He also had the task of unifying world religions and building the World Shrine in order to enshrine the Almighty Creator God and to awaken people to the reality of the spiritual world.

During the 1960s and 1970s, *Sukuin-sama* traveled internationally and met various world religious leaders, including Pope Paul VI. On 13 June 1974, ten days before his death, he officially handed over his divinely commissioned mission to his daughter Sachiko. She is now known as *Oshien-ushi-sama* (Master of Teaching).

Beliefs and Teachings. The connection that human beings can have with God is established during a three-day seminar (*kenshu*).[13] A divine pendant is worn around the neck; called an *omitama*, this assists in the channeling of the True Light through the individual. By raising one's hand, any individual can become a channel that focuses the True Light. The Mahikari definition of True Light is "Divine Light" or the "Light of Almighty God," which not only heals people physically but also imparts "wisdom, will, and emotion that gives progressive understanding to souls and removes spiritual impurities that may have accumulated over hundreds of thousands of years."

The sacred text from which the teachings are drawn is the *Goseigen*, interpreted by Okada's idea of *genreigaku* (the science of interpreting words by spirit). The practice of radiating light from the hands is called *Makihari no Waza*. No special human qualities are needed to acquire this power. The ability to perform this act after only three days of training is explained by the belief that the world in which we live is a place where rapid spiritual, mental, and physical purification is needed to prepare mankind for the holy civilization that will come about after the cataclysm of the near future. A new world will emerge in which people will live in harmony with God and with each other. Before achieving worldwide harmony, however, human problems must be solved at the domestic level. Individuals must find health, happiness, peace, and material welfare through the understanding of the spiritual dimension and the practice of *Mahikari*. People experiencing domestic strife, for example, are represented as victims of the vengeful spirit of a previous life. Escape from the problem through divorce or a new lover not only builds bad *karma* for the future but ensures that the problem will recur. Only through the True Light can one's ancestors as well as one's self be progressively purified. The same principles can be applied to politics and other areas of human activity. Improvement of one's spiritual makeup is the key to improved performance in many areas of life, from education to economic success. Mahikari publications are designed to give evidence of the success of the movement in achieving these spiritual results.

Distinctive Features. Strong influences of Shinto can be seen in the concepts of purification and *goshintai* (a scroll with power to purify and protect). Mahikari recognizes the entire Shinto pantheon but places the bodhisattva Kannon on top. Although Mahikari meeting places seem to be churches, by installing a *goshintai* the church building in fact becomes a shrine. So Mahikari can enshrine *kami* as in normal Shinto practices. Buddhist elements are present, particularly the sense of transmitted bad *karma*. However, the importance of ancestral reverence points to its traditional Japanese character. It also makes use of other Shinto practices, including the *Ōharae no Kotoba* and *kotodama*. Before radiating the True Light, believers must chant the prayer *Amatsu Norigoto* in a bold and clear voice because the combination of words and syllables has spiritual power. This is clearly derived from the Shinto concept of *kotodama*, the soul power of words. When Mahikari is being explained to the non-believer, the Buddhist elements are underlined along with other ideas technically supported by Christian writings. The point is to indicate the movement's syncretistic and eclectic style, which of course is another characteristic feature of Japanese religion in any era.

The chief deity of Mahikari is Su-no-kami or Mi-oyamoto-su-Mahikari-o-mikami, the creator of the entire world who sends out a supernatural light, *Mahikari*, which is the secret of the power of the religion. This *kami* is the source of all the gods of other faiths, Amaterasu in Shinto, Jehovah in Judaism and Christianity, Allah in Islam. These are all forms that are appropriate to their own historic situation. Mahikari claims that there is only one origin of religions and one origin of all human races. The theme may have a universal sound, but there is implicit ethnocentrism in the claim that the origin of all races and religions is to be found in Japan.

Mahikari has an explicit eschatological doctrine of an apocalypse in which man's fallen condition will be punished by a dreadful calamity (*hi-no-senrei*, baptism of fire), after which only 20 percent of the world's population will survive. This eschatology is quite detailed and teaches that the world exists in two forms, material and spiritual. There is *Reikai*, where only noble spirits can live, and there is *Yukai*, where most spirits live in two hundred levels, the lowest of which is Hell. The individual likewise has two parts, material and spiritual, which are divided into *Reitai* and *Yutai*. This resembles a combination of Chrisian Gnosticism of the first century A.D. and Buddhist cosmology and eschatology.

Organization and Believers. The total number of followers in Japan was listed as 419,482 in 1989. The headquarters is located in Takayama City in Gifu Prefecture. Among its unusual members is Antonio Inoki, a retired professional wrestler who turned politician and was elected to the House of Councillors in 1986. He is also famous for his wrestler/boxer fight in Tokyo with then boxing Heavyweight Champion of the World, Mohammed Ali. The movement has branches in North America and considers itself capable of becoming a world religion.

The sect under Okada Keishu (the founder's adopted daughter) was forced to separate in 1978 from the original *Seikai Mahikari Bunmei Kyōdan*. It was led thereafter by Sekiguchi Sakae following a court battle for leadership occasioned by Okada's death in 1974. The court awarded the succession to Sekiguchi, whose group numbers just over 80,000. There is also the breakaway *Shinyūgen Kyūsei Mahikari Kyōdan* founded in Yoda Kuniyoshi, and the *Subikari Kōha Seikai Shindan* founded by Kuroda Minoru in 1980. The latter has 4,500 members and 75 lecturers. All practice Okada's *Mahikari no Waza*. The two major groups have active overseas branches. The *Sukyo Mahikari* has 150 branches in Europe and Africa, 30 in North America, 70 in South America, and 50 in the Pacific region. *Sekai Mahikari Bunmei Kyōdan* has only about 18 overseas stations.

PL Kyōdan

Origins and Development. The sect can be traced to *Hitonomichi Kyōdan*, a 1931 prewar movement, and even further back as the successor to *Tokumitsu-kyō*, founded in 1912 by Kanada Tokumitusu (1863–1919). The terms in the title of *PL Kyōdan* were inserted for a specific reason, namely, the unhappy experiences of *Hitono-michi Kyōdan* in prewar days.

Although in principle religious toleration appeared in Japan with the revoking of the ban on Christianity and was included in Article 28 of the Meiji Constitution, in fact freedom of religious practice did not occur in every sense. Tokumitsu founded the new group during the business boom of World War I and it found great acceptance, especially among the merchants of Osaka. It died, however, with its founder; Miki Tokuchika then founded a successor movement in the mid-1920s. The name *Hitonomichi* was adopted in 1931.

The Kagoshima branch changed its name but failed to get permission from the prefectural government for the changes. When the police were informed of this, they prosecuted the leader; in 1931 he was convicted and sentenced to ten days in detention. A lawyer by the name of Matsumoto Shigetoshi believed this violated the constitutionally established freedom of religion, so he challenged the law under which the police exercised such surveillance. He demanded that the Supreme Court review the laws concerned. The Court ruled that the police were entitled to do whatever was necessary to maintain peace and order and to ensure the implementation of the duties of subjects. The judicial system was in effect unable to resist the authority of the government administration and consequently lost its independence. It accepted the principle that the government had the right to control thought, religion, and education. It is also interesting to note that seemingly out of fear for their own situation, other leaders of new religious movements accepted the Court ruling without demur. They in effect undermined their own freedom by doing so. This paved the way for frequent arrests of various religious leaders on the charge of lèse-majesté. Although the group did nothing wrong, the hysterical Japan of the 1930s was no place for such a movement. Hitonomichi changed some of its doctrines to match the needs of the time, but still with no success. For example, although Amaterasu was revered, the movement was told that it did so in a vulgar and disrespectful manner.

It was in fact the structure of Hitonomichi that alarmed the police. A unit consisted of five people plus a leader. Five units made a group (of thirty people). In Hyogo alone there were 200 groups in close network. There were nine districts with a district chief. Thus, a leader could give a message to the nine leaders and they in turn to the groups, and finally to all units. This was too dangerous in the view of the suspicious police, who did not like any kind of group activity they could not control. In the eyes of the government, any group was capable of subversion and of threatening the government's power. Hitonomichi was considered a threat and therefore dissolved.

The founder of PL Kyōdan was the son of the founder of Hitonomichi Kyōdan. He described the persecution his father had faced as the "egoism of state power." Even when Hitonomichi tried to accommodate itself to State Shinto, it was still treated as subversive and attacked. Consequently, the basis for the name *Perfect Liberty* appears to be a statement of a point of view in relation to the absence of freedom that was characteristic of prewar pressures within Japanese society.

Kanada, the founder of *Tokumitsu-kyō*, was born in 1863. He had a childhood interest in religion, particularly Shingon Buddhism, and was a devotee of its founder, Kōbō Daishi. Like his ideal, he jumped off a cliff and injured himself but found illumination in the prowess of his act. When he married into the Kanada family, he changed his name to Tokumitsu and then established a successful cutlery business. Although he was not able to devote himself fully to religion, he became a teacher of the Kyōha-Shinto sect of *Mitake-kyō*. His *Tokumitsu-kyō* was originally a group within *Mitake-kyō*. When news of his miraculous powers began to spread, followers began to increase—not least of all among the business community, especially in Osaka. In 1912 Kanada met a Buddhist priest named Miki who had been born in 1871. At age ten Miki began various disciplines at the *Manpukuji*, head temple of the Obaku Zen sect. He met Kanada at a time when he (Miki) was having great doubts about Zen teaching, and he decided to become a follower of the *Tokumitsu* teachings. In 1916 Miki abandoned his Buddhist status and became a follower of Tokumitsu-kyō. He received the name *Tokuchika* from Kanada. Kanada died in 1919 and was given the title *Kakurioya* (Hidden Founder/Parent) of the PL Kyōdan.

Tokuchika followed Kanada's dying request to plant a *sakaki* tree at the place of his death. He worshipped there daily, having been told by Kanada that a "good man" would appear one day and that another three revelations would come. After five years of waiting, Miki had the three revelations himself—so he became the awaited "good man.' In 1924 he founded the successor to Tokumitsu-kyō, called *Jindō Tokumitsu-kyō* (The Human Way Tokumitsu Teaching). This distinguished it from *Shinto Tokumitsu-kyō*, which still exists as an independent sect (registered as *Fusō-kyō*). The main emphasis of the new group was humanistic, with stress on husband-wife and parent-child relations. After gradually spreading, it became popular and its name was changed in 1931 to *Hito no Michi*.

In 1936 the leadership passed from father to son, and thereafter persecution began. Tokuhara was detained for investigation and died under arrest at the age of sixty-nine. The movement was forcibly disbanded. However, Hito no Michi believers continued their faith in secret through Tokuchika, who was also imprisoned and remained so until the end of the war. When religious freedom was proclaimed after the war, believers wished for the religion to be restarted. With some hesitation Tokuchika organized the *Perfect Liberty Club*; but after the constitutional guarantee of religious freedom from 29 September 1946, he established the PL Kyōdan in Tosu in Saga Prefecture. Tokuchika is referred to as *Oshieoya* (Teaching-Parent) and Tokuhara became known as the official founder of PL Kyōdan.

Beliefs and Teachings. PL Kyōdan is also known as the "religion of art."[14] It seeks to elucidate the way to the eternal peace and welfare of mankind by promoting the realization that all men are children of God, and by making people attain a state of mind whereby both they and others become blessed and happy through freely and powerfully expressing their individuality in the interest of fellow men and society under the motto "Life is Art." Its teachings distinguish between the Divine Law of Great Nature (*Daishizen*), which was revealed by the Divine to Miki, and Human Law, which is the ethics created by human art. The concepts of "Life is Art" and man's life as a continuous succession of "self-expressions" mean to engage in the creation of art by expressing the self in conformity with the Divine Law while also acknowledging human laws.

The Divine Law is stated in the form of Twenty-One Precepts for Life, known as the *Shosei-kun*. It was revealed to Tokuharu Miki, the father of Tokuchika, five years after the death of Kanada. Later, Tokuchika received it at Hiroshima in 1947. The official PL Kyōdan translation follows (which accounts for eccentric English usages):

1. Life is Art.
2. The whole life of the individual is a continuous succession of self-expressions.
3. The individual is a manifestation of God.
4. We suffer if we do not manifest ourselves.
5. We lose ourselves if we are swayed by our feelings.
6. Our true self is revealed when our ego is effaced.
7. All things exist in mutual relation to one another.
8. Live radiantly as the sun.
9. All men are equal.
10. Bring mutual happiness through our expressions.
11. Depend on God at all times.
12. There is always a way for each person.
13. There is one way for men and there is another for women.
14. All things exist for world peace.

15. Our whole environment is the mirror of our mind.

16. All things make progress and develop.

17. Grasp the heart of everything.

18. At every moment man stands at the crossroad of good and evil.

19. Practice at once whatever our first inspiration dictates.

20. Attain the perfect harmonious state of mind and matter.

21. Live in Perfect Liberty.

Of the twenty-one, only seven are actually precepts (numbers 8, 10, 11, 17, 19, 20, 21). The remaining fourteen may be divided into doctrines or assumptions about people, about the world, and about God. Numbers 2 through 6 are a set of propositions that expound the nature of the individual. Numbers 1, 7, 14, 16, and 18 are in reality metaphysical propositions, and number 9 seems to be borrowed from the U.S. Declaration of Independence. Numbers 12 and 13 do not appear to sit well together, and number 13 seems to reflect strong Confucian influences.

PL Kyōdan is monotheistic and believes in a parent God called Mioya-Ōkami. It is claimed that by himself man can do nothing, and that the power of nature controls everything man does. *Daishizen* also controls the progress of all creation. There is a great power in the universe, which human beings can receive if they live in accordance with the power and flow of Great Nature. This is God, the great power, the spiritual power that controls life and every human activity. God manifests himself in man, and man therefore makes self-expressions with the knowledge that God is his sustenance to lead to a perfect artistic life. God is also working for the betterment and improvement of man. However, there is also a sense in which man and God are different: "Man is God manifested as a human being, but Man is not God Himself and remains man, but possesses the essential qualities of God."

At the moment of birth, the individual receives the spirit of the parent God Mioya-Ōkami and thus life is sustained. When he or she dies, the spirit returns to God while the body remains on earth. It is the possession of a body, intellect, individuality, and the desire for expression and life that makes human beings surpass all other beings. But they can become their best only when they are in close relation with God. Salvation is achieved through spiritual and material efforts. Members must listen to the teachings, attend morning services, and show through their financial contributions how serious they are about attaining salvation. Members should visit the Holy Land (the headquarters in Osaka) at least once. Salvation comes by means of these relationships as well as the "divine function" of the founder, who mediates salvation from God to man.

PL Kyōdan stresses art and the artistic as a model for life. "Life is pleasant and interesting because man has this desire for self-expression, and because man is made to feel joy and satisfaction by endeavoring to manifest this desire. The progress and development of human society can be said to be based on this boundless desire for expression. The result of the self-expression must be the creation of art."

According to the book *Perfect Liberty: How to Lead a Happy Life*, an artist is someone who devotes himself completely to his work without thinking of anything else. In this way an object of art is created. The reward of such creativity is spiritual pleasure or religious exaltation. The artistic life brings about happiness, the joy of the artist. Thus, if the purpose in life is to create art (i.e., to express oneself), there can be nothing but happiness in life and unhappiness cannot exist. However, if people forget God, life ceases to be artistic and such individuals will meet difficulties and misfortunes. The environment does not develop favorably, nothing happens as desired, and illness may occur. Sufferings and misfortunes are *gasho*, warnings from God. If the events are recognized as a warning, then there is hope. The believer goes to the Master (Miki) or a consultant to ask for a *kokoroe* (prescription). The problem is diagnosed and a treatment for the misfortune is proposed. If time is too short, the Master saves the believer by vicariously accepting his sufferings.

According to PL Kyōdan teaching, everything in the world can be used for the creation of art. Human beings are social beings, surrounded by many others who can share their joys. Self-expression must never be a hindrance to others or bring misfortune on society. It must be a blessing to the individual and to society. "A joy shared with others becomes a joy twice blessed."

There must also be harmony in the home of the artists. Every member of the family should strive to fulfill his or her respective task in a peaceful, joyous, and pleasant mood without any restraint or hindrance. The ultimate goal of PL Kyōdan is world peace. As more people embrace it and live artistic lives, the more evils will vanish and the world will become a lovelier place—indeed, a world of perfect liberty.

Organization and Believers. The membership was listed as 2,200,424 in 1990 under the direction of 28,937 teachers. The headquarters is in Osaka-fu. Expansion of the movement occurred principally after the war; it began in December 1948 when the headquarters was moved to Shimizu in Shizuoka Prefecture. In March 1952 a ground-breaking ceremony was held near Osaka, where the Eternal Headquarters were to be set up. In December 1953 the Head Offices were moved to Osaka. By 1955 the Eternal Headquarters in Tondabayashi were ready for occupancy, and the Holy Land of PL Kyōdan was completed with the erection of the Divine Hall. In addition to these projects, an eighteen-hole golf course was built overlooking the Divine Hall along with a Youth Hall; a hospital; a high school, *PL Gakuen* (famous for its baseball team); and a finishing school.

In January 1960 the nephew of Tokuchika, Miki Takahito, was designated *tsugioya* (next leader). In 1961 Tokuchika's wife was given the title of *kagemioya* and empowered to dispense Divine Teaching (*mioshie*). Her daughter Shirahi was also considered able to dispense spiritual wisdom. The leader in 1989 was Miki Takahito, who succeeded on the death of Tokuchika in 1983.

Seicho-no-Ie

Origins and Development. The name *Seicho-no-Ie* was the name given by the founder, Taniguchi Masaharu, to a cultural magazine he first published in March 1940. In commenting upon the state of affairs of human life in a semi-philosophical way, Taniguchi began the process that led to the formation of the new movement. He was born the son of a Karasukara-mura farmer in Hyogo Prefecture on 22 November 1893. His parents were poor and he was given up for adoption at the age of four. He spent his childhood in Osaka and graduated there with top honors. He states in his autobiography that he considered himself in some way different from his brothers, desiring that he be set aside by the *kami* for a special purpose. He was very able, but his teachers regarded him as too self-possessed. He entered Waseda High School and finally Waseda University, but according to some accounts, due to a failed romance he dropped out in his third year.

He went to work in a factory of a company called Settsu Boseki in Akashi; but after an argument with the managers, he quit. While trying to find a place for himself in society, he happened to read an edition of a magazine called *Suisei* that contained an article about spiritual healing. This led to an interest in Ōmoto-kyō, at that time a new and controversial religion combining several ideas that attracted Taniguchi. He was fascinated by the Ōmoto-kyō claim that the world would soon be rid of all evil and that the present age would be followed by a new age of purity. Although he was critical of some aspects of the movement, he joined it and became editor of two publications of the sect, *Ayabe Shimbun* and *Shinreikai*. He then began to develop his own disciplines, including wearing an inexpensive robe tied with a rope, by reason of which he called himself the "St. Francis of the Ōmoto-kyō." He also fasted for days at a time and performed ritual *misogi* in rivers in order to purify himself. Around that time the Ōmoto-kyō belief in the end of the world was generating social hysteria, which drew it to the attention of the police and the government. Charges were pressed on the grounds of its disturbance of the peace and incitement to revolution. The leaders were arrested, and Taniguchi's house was searched. The group met again and became more dogmatic about the benefits of belonging to it after the last judgment had taken place. Some thought they would become rulers of other states, including Britain, the United States, and China.

In the midst of all this chaos Taniguchi fell in love with, and married, a member of the sect in spite of his anxieties about the end of the world. He finally found that the teachings of the group did not satisfy him, and he stopped lecturing and meeting group members. He met Nishida Tenko of

Itto-en but did not find what could satisfy him. He decided to leave Ōmoto-kyō and wrote a collection of essays entitled *Shodo-e*. This widely read and very successful book soon found him many followers. A man named Asano, who had also left Ōmoto-kyō, contacted Taniguchi to work on his new magazine, *Shinrei-kenkyū*. Taniguchi worked for this group as a translator and received a salary. He lived very poorly, dogged by crises. When his pregnant wife was found to be suffering from a disorder akin to heart disease, his thoughts turned to life, values, and suffering. He developed these in writing and sent them to *Itto-en*. He even began a long novel entitled *Kami o Sabaku* (Judging God), which he completed despite weakened health. Before he could collect any royalties, the Kanto earthquake struck on 1 September 1923. He and his wife escaped to Kobe with their lives and nothing else, where their parents helped them. He thereafter worked for various organizations. Finally, through publishing a magazine entitled *Seicho-no-Ie* in March 1940, which expounded his views of the world, his own movement came into being.

Beliefs and Teachings. The name *ie* refers not to a house but to the Great Universe.[15] The term *seicho* means "to grow," that is, to create as the universe is creating and growing infinitely. The great universe is the House of Growth, and members study the rules of life to teach people the rules that make it work. Taniguchi calls the true state of life (*Jisso-no-Sekai*) the *Seicho-no-Ie*. The Buddhist notion of Nirvana (particularly in Mahayana Buddhism) may be similar to this, but Taniguchi thought it was too negative. He thought that paradise should have a more joyful and lively image, so to him *Seicho-no-Ie* means "always growing and infinitely young." It is also regarded as a paradise on earth. He formulated a set of ideas known as the Seven Teachings of Taniguchi:

1. The purpose of the group is different from the other cults in that we worship life and teach people to live in accordance with the natural rules of life.

2. The rule in life is the way to infinite growth of oneself and also a life for each individual that is eternal.

3. We think and we testify to the true evolution of mankind.

4. Materialistic desire (for things such as money) and individual desire are not important. What is important is love. Through the different expressions of love such as prayer, worship, and cherishing, we realize love.

5. We are God's children and we inherit his perfection and have great potential. We are now standing in the era of evolution and we should make the best use of the creation of language and take the whole of mankind into the next great era.

6. We should make use of the best of language in order to reach our goal—that is, to change the present world order to something better. In order to spread our teachings to the world we must do whatever we can, such as publish periodicals, use the radio, hold seminars, and so forth.

7. Our goal is to give people a good education, a correct view of life, and to teach
   them the right way to live. We wish to be rid of all disaster, disease, and any
   form of evil on earth and actually build a paradise on earth.

This is achieved by worshipping life and by harmonizing the individual
with life's rules. Rule 3 and its teaching about "true evolution" is difficult
to understand if it is interpreted in material terms of development. Apparently it is meant to convey the idea of evolution moving toward a world
in which there is no suffering or injustice, no unhappiness, a true paradise
on earth.

Is Seicho-no-Ie a religion? The movement claims not to be a religion, but
a way that transcends religion. Yet the question of whether its content is
religious or not remains a problem. It opposes no religion and claims that
through understanding Seicho-no-Ie people may better understand their
own religions. Taniguchi, in a pamphlet distributed by the Headquarters,
made his point in the following terms:

Seicho-no-Ie (House of Growth) is a house. All other cults are gates (*shumon*) to
the doctrines. The members of a religion are at the gates of the world. To achieve
real awakening one must not wait at the gate, but go deep inside. *Seicho-no-Ie* is
the way into deeper understanding. The opening of truth comes with the philosophy
of the real state of life (*Seimei-no-Jisshō*) which is taught by *Seicho-no-Ie*, and is
also called *Yuishinjitsu Soron*. The philosophy declares that whatever exists is all
expressed by God and God is good, which means that naturally eveything is good.
Nothing is evil, and if it seems to be it is illusory.

In dramatic contrast to Western ideas wherein man must approach God
through pain and suffering, in Seicho-no-Ie thought God does not wish to
see human suffering. Indeed, true religion does not teach people to suffer
for their sins. It teaches them to become happy and free from all kinds of
sufferings. Seicho-no-Ie does not belong with Buddhism, because it does
not teach a renunciation of desire. It more clearly belongs with Shinto,
because it stresses happiness and freedom and doing ordinary things in a
natural way.

Seicho-no-Ie claims to be able to help people understand their own religions better. Therefore, members of any religion can also be members of
Seicho-no-Ie. It could be called a house of refuge for those who are confused by religion. Certainly, people can belong exclusively, but this is not
required because Seicho-no-Ie shows no resistance or opposition to any
other religious groups. The only clear stance is taken in the affirmation that
religions should not call on people to suffer, but to escape suffering in order
to find happiness. (Paradoxically, this may mean the duty to endure to find
peace as opposed to escape from the world.) In this regard it is typical of

the New Religions in its essential point of view, one that is found in many new Buddhist groups as well.

Rituals and Practices. Although members may attend the rituals of other faiths they believe in, the rituals of Seicho-no-Ie are fundamentally Shinto because Taniguchi felt that Japanese would be most at home with these. There are three main rituals of the movement.

First, there is a memorial service for the dead. This is performed three times a year, in spring, summer, and autumn. At the headquarters in Harajuku in Tokyo is an altar over which a sūtra is read (herein is a Buddhist element). The group believes that the dead live on and can be helped with spiritual enlightenment. Seicho-no-Ie takes this ceremony very seriously. In this connection, it supports the idea of the government becoming responsible for the Yasukuni Shrine.

Second, there is a ceremony for the living. People for whom prayers are requested are named and the names are put into a box. The sūtra is read ten times a day for these people, to assist them with spiritual enlightenment.

Third, there is a ceremony of purification. This is performed only for those attending training sessions. Members write on sheets of paper things that are troubling them, and the sheets are burned while the sūtra is being chanted. (This resembles *goma*, the fire ceremony for purity performed in Esoteric Buddhism and in some Shinto shrines.) Seicho-no-Ie teaches firmly that negative feelings cause misfortune and unhappiness. Members avoid using negative words (a Shinto idea, *imi no kotoba*, "words to be avoided") and curses of any kind because they will increase the quotient of misery in the world.

Shinsōkan is a type of meditation performed by members and is the most important ritual. *Seiza* (sitting with legs bent) and *gassho* (hands together in front of the face) are involved. Members recite the *kami-yobi-uta* (the song to invoke the *kami*). Each participant must concentrate on the idea that the knowledge, love, life, happiness, and harmony of the *kami* is flowing through the body, which enables the person to leave the world of senses to enter the world of "truth." The period is concluded by a prayer for peace on earth. This is recommended as a discipline once a day for thirty to forty minutes. It can be done alone, but doing it in a group is considered to afford more energy.

Training sessions are offered for ten-day periods on a regular basis every few months. The day commences at 5:30 A.M., when the first sūtra is read and cleaning begins. At 6:00 A.M. it is time for *Shinsōkan*, and at 6:30 A.M. *Shihōhai* (a Shinto ritual showing reverence to north, south, east, and west as an act of respect to nature) is performed. Breakfast is at 8:00 A.M. and *Shinsōkan* at 8:30 A.M. At 9:00 A.M. the lecture period begins. Lunch is at 12 noon, and lectures commence again from 1:00 until 4:00 P.M. Baths are followed by dinner and from 6:00 to 6:30 P.M. small group discussions take place. From 6:30 to 8:30 P.M. there may be another lecture or a purification ceremony. The day closes at 9:00 P.M. People are encouraged to believe themselves to be part of God and to be capable of experiencing divine power. Illness and misfortune can be cured, and health and good fortune restored.

Organization and Believers. The organization claimed to have 810,644 members in 1989. They are served by 15,991 teachers and lecturers. The present leader is Taniguchi Seicho (born in 1919), who succeeded to the leadership after the death of the founder in 1985. Its headquarters is located in Jingu-mae, Shibuya Ward, in Tokyo near the Meiji Shrine. A house in Nagasaki Prefecture is used for various training purposes.

Sekai-Kyūsei-kyō

Origins and Development. The Church of World Messianity was founded in 1935 by Okada Mokichi. Like Taniguchi of Seicho-no-Ie, he had belonged to Ōmoto-kyō. The movement's first name was *Dainihon-kannonkai* (Great Japan Association for the Worship of Kannon). Okada was instructed by God to build a heaven on earth and to prophesy concerning the last judgment to the Japan of the 1920s and 1930s, which was then in the grip of an apocalyptic mood. The movement began as a Japanese movement but tried to take on the image of a world religion. It followed the recurring pattern of being created in Japan for the Japanese, who then felt the need to spread it for the salvation of the world. This can be seen in the development of new religious movements in different eras, particularly since the Meiji period and after World War II.

Okada himself was born in Tokyo on 23 December 1882. He dreamed of being an artist, but his general physical weaknesses forced him to abandon most of his ideas. His family became impoverished by the earthquake of September 1923 when their business was destroyed. Around that time, he was exposed to Ōmoto-kyō and was attracted by ideas of spiritual healing.

It was in 1926 that he heard a message telling him to prepare for "Heaven on earth" to be manifested as *miroku-okami* and that he was appointed to lead others in the process toward the ideal world. This endowed him with special powers to save others. In 1931 he received another message, which informed him that the spiritual world had been transformed from being dark and painful to being bright and pleasurable. He believed that he was to perform the mission of saving the world. "Heaven on earth," he declared, was a world without illness, poverty, and conflict—a utopian society of health, wealth, and happiness as well as truth, justice, and beauty, all in perfect harmony.

Okada's involvement in Ōmoto-kyō led to his founding the *Dainihon-Kannonkai* in February 1928 with two objectives. First was the goal of communion with the divine; second was the ideal of healing disease through the laying on of hands. The government ordered him to limit himself to one purpose, and healing was chosen. In 1934 he changed the name to *Nihon-Jyoka-Ryoho* (Japan Association for Therapy through Purification). During World War II the movement was suppressed, but it was revived in 1947 as the *Nihon-Kannon-Kyōdan* (Japan Society for the Worship of Kannon). In 1950 the movement split and Okada formed the *Sekai-Meshiya-kyō*, the World Messianic Movement. The final name of *Sekai-Kyūsei-kyō* was determined just after that.

In June 1980 the Mokichi Okada Association (MOA) was formed to engage in activities that would not be affected by Okada's teachings. A great deal of doctrine had been acquired from Ōmoto-kyō. Okada believed that the *kami* of creation, Sozo-shushin, wished to establish paradise on earth, so the organization laid stress on two themes, faith-healing and utopianism. Okada was referred to as *Meishusama* (Enlightened Master) and is believed to have ascended to heaven, where he is still directing the affairs of this world. Just before his death he was arrested but cleared of charges of tax evasion. After his death his widow, Yoshiko, assumed the leadership role as *Nidaisama* (Second Master) until she died in 1962. Their daughter, Fujita Itsuki, became *Sandaisama* after her mother.

The MOA aims at overcoming racial, religious, and cultural barriers by means of art, education, agriculture, and environmental sciences. It seeks to deepen people's awareness of their cultural heritage and its beauty and thereby increase international understanding. The worldwide campaign began in July 1980 following Okada's ideas that the religion could save even America. In one of his speeches he declared that "no other nation besides America is today equal to the task of maintaining peace in the world. It is one of the most urgent tasks of the day to help America to improve the health conditions of her people. I therefore want to stop the spread of disease there and eradicate all existing disease."

The MOA has used International Exchange Programs on Contemporary Art to enable one culture to see others, a window to spiritual heritage. Since 1973 a Japan-Brazil Art Exhibition has been an annual event, and others have been held in the United States. Scientific research is being conducted on natural agricultural techniques promoting proper and healthy growth of vegetables without chemicals that damage the soil and threaten human life. In 1982 a Natural Agriculture International Research and Development Center was established on a fifty-hectare farm in Izu. Farms now exist in Hokkaido, Okinawa, and Nagano as well as in Hawaii, Brazil, and Thailand. The movement is also politically active, supporting the Liberal Democratic Party through its own *Jiyū-minshu-tō-Kyūsei Rengōkai* to actualize their ideals.

Beliefs and Teachings. To create a world of happiness, it is necessary to eliminate the three causes of unhappiness: sickness, poverty, and conflict.[16] Therefore, people must be physically, spiritually, and materially fulfilled.

"Sickness" is perceived not as a deteriorating process but as a form of cleansing. Too much of a good thing can have negative consequences. The body emits waste products daily to purify itself. Sometimes the amount of waste ejected is not enough and "sickness" results. Sickness is like a massive cleaning time, but it can also be painful. The world is understood according to the following diagram:

Reikai (Spiritual World)		*Genkai* (Material World)
Unseen world		The world of the five senses
events we can't see	become	events that can be seen
man is born		dies and re-enters
the *Reikai*		man's life is in the *Genkai*

The *Genkai* is the world we live in; the *Reikai* exists as a world that we cannot see, but where events take place before they happen in the *Genkai*. People come from the *Reikai*, die, and return. This is the meaning of *ojo*. People with special spiritual powers (*reikan*) in all religions and who have glimpses of heaven follow a similar model, according to official teachings. There are 180 levels in which individual existence is located; every existence is located in one of these. There are 60 levels each of heaven, hell, and purgatory. Everyone has *kumori*, the roots of unhappiness. It may take one of the four forms of (1) bad thoughts, words, and deeds; (2) bad deeds performed by ancestors; (3) bad deeds performed in one's previous existences; or (4) external bodies not good for them such as medicine, insecticides, and food additives. These are comparable to *karma* in Hindu thought and must be excised from human life. By lessening *kumori* in one's lifetime, the possibility of good reincarnation is enhanced. The belief structure of the church seems to reflect elements of Shinto along with Christianity, Buddhism, and even Hinduism. Basic is ancestral reverence, which relates to the amount of *kumori* the individual may have to bear. Christianity is presented in the form of the ideal of a Messiah who has come to save people from the Last Judgment.

Among the sect's rituals and practices, purification plays an important role. Two types are practiced. The natural cleansing of the body is called *jotai*. To alleviate pain and facilitate the removal of waste, *jōrei* is practiced. This relates to the purification of other forms of *kumori* such as natural disasters, thefts, or other events that may have an adverse effect on the individual. Sometimes it becomes necessary to take responsibility for deeds that one has not performed, including bad deeds performed by one's ancestors. Teaching number 4 is a practical form of avoidance of bad external influences by eating carefully. Okada conducted a scientific study on "heavenly agriculture," a form of environmental awareness. Research on the farm in Izu has shown the effects of insecticides on human cells, so the natural organic farm has begun to gain recognition. The World Messianity Company distributes safe and wholesome foods.

Okada realized that single-handed accomplishment of his mission was not possible, so he circulated pendants with the Chinese character *hikari* (light) on them. Anyone possessing one of these can perform *jōrei*. Simply by raising the palm toward another person, the power of *Meishusama* flows from that person to the person to be purified. Belief by the second party is not necessary, because lack of faith does not affect the power of the pendant. (This is similar to the practice of Mahikari.)

Aesthetics also feature in the thinking of Sekai-Kyūsei-kyō. It owns the Mokichi Okada Association Art Gallery in Atami, along with another museum. Beauty is important in life and can also be a source of purification. Calligraphy is important as a reflection of the soul. The *Sangetsuryu* school of *Ikebana* (Flower Arrangement) was set up to purify human society and the human heart.

The religion also calls itself *Chōshūkyō*, meaning a religion above religions. The sense of "above" means that it is more comprehensive, being concerned not only with spiritual but also with aesthetic and material aspects of human life. It does not reject other religions but believes it is possible to belong to both Christianity and Buddhism as well. Its name includes *Sekai*, or world, which implies this breadth. It has branches in Brazil and Hawaii and it claims several hundred thousand followers throughout the world. Through them it seeks to purify all peoples of their spiritual and physical *kumori* so that when the Last Judgment takes place, it will not be so severe for those purified. It also seeks through its members to build an ideal human society throughout the world, one that appears to be a balanced combination of both Japanese and Western cultures. To join the movement it is necessary to attend three meetings. At the third one, the *hikari* pendant is given. Members are encouraged to join, not for personal reasons but in order to create a new heaven on earth. However, many people become members to cure bad health or bad fortune, and some have risen to prominence within the movement.

Organization and Believers. The headquarters is located at Gora near Hakone. There is a model displayed of the *miroku-ōmikami* (heaven on earth) called *Saichi*. It is said to be reflected in the *Reikai*, which in turn will be reflected in all the corners of the earth—thus making the *miroku-ōmikami* a reality. The church has three gardens in Japan that depict the three elements of the universe. There is an oriental-style garden in Hakone that symbolizes fire and a Western garden in Atami that symbolizes water. There is also a flat garden in Kyoto symbolizing the earth. These gardens are meant to represent the links between nature and humanity.

The MOA Trading Company was established (originally as Atami Shōjin in 1948) in 1983 to provide natural foods for a healthy and peaceful society and to operate hotels and restaurants for the welfare of followers. The company also provides travel services and produces art goods, books, newspapers, and magazines.

An Economic and Industrial Research Association founded by Kamei Kanichiro in 1947 became a member of the MOA in 1973. It provides the economic input to the concepts of progress necessary to construct the "ideal" society. There are officially 54 churches and 453 mission stations. There were 4,211 teachers (2,181 male and 2,030 female) and 835,756 believers registered in 1990.

Jissen-Rinri-Kōseikai

Origin and Development. The president of the organization in 1990 was Uehiro Eiji, whose father, Uehiro Tetsuhiko, a *hibakusha* (survivor of the atomic bombing of Hiroshima), miraculously recovered after having been about to die. To show his gratitude, he resolved to spend his remaining years working for the benefit of others; to this the beginnings of the movement can be traced. It is therefore an entirely postwar movement. Nevertheless, it does present themes that are familiar in Japanese religious history. "The way of the Japanese people must be thought out again. There is no ideology upon which the Japanese people can build their way of life." The organization is dedicated to rethinking and guiding that way.

Beliefs and Teachings. The organization encourages people to live by the Five Principles:[17]

1. Today, let us not forget our three *on* (obligations of gratitude for parental love, the guidance of our mentors, and duties toward society) and work willingly with pleasure.
2. Today, let us not speak badly of others or speak well of ourselves.
3. Today, let us respond to the wishes of others instantaneously.
4. Today, let us not get angry or feel insufficient or discontented.
5. Today, let us try not to waste *kokoro*, things, and time, but live anew on earth.

The acceptance of inherited problems and the sense of responsibility toward the future is implied in Principle 1. The founder wrote of the idea being like passing the baton in a relay race. Then it is put into your hand, you must take it and go. "Parents" clearly implies "ancestors," as each generation of parents succeeds the next. "Mentors" can be anyone who conveys a better understanding to others.

Principle 2 implies a position of extreme passiveness toward any kind of wrongs. The passivity of Buddhism fits in here, but the stance of *Jissen-Rinri-Kōseikai* is more extreme. Social criticism is to be ignored. The problems of society are due to wrong shadows of the soul; and by cultivating large-heartedness, people will realize that they themselves are always wrong. This seems to bypass the problem of evil in a way that even other Japanese religious traditions would find difficult to accept.

Principle 3 implies performing tasks that one notices need doing, which the founder declares is natural for people to do. Following the way of nature brings the movement close to Shinto, and the stress on keeping harmony with the natural can be traced to the same source. To be able to "notice" what should be done requires a certain spiritual telepathy, which in turn calls for a pure mind—another ideal found among Shinto thinkers.

Principle 4 underlines the idea of *honzen*, or humility. If people accept things as they are, then people may become human beings who live in accordance with nature or the natural. Acceptance of things as they are eliminates the need for a sense of anger or insufficiency.

Principle 5 deals with "unnatural movements of the soul," which lead to its waste. Sickness or unfortunate happenings are warnings that the soul is out of harmony with nature. This would be recognized by Shinto thinkers as similar to *tsumi* or *tatari*. Acceptance of material prosperity and its encouragement, as well as its use to benefit society, accords with the general attitude of Shinto thought toward the physical world.

The emphasis throughout on "now," seen in the repetition of "today" at the beginning of each principle, suggests another root of Shinto, which is stated more explicitly in the present president's principle of "*Kyo ich-inichi shugi*" ("one day at a time, today, principle"). The idea that this world is the best and only place, and that emphasis must be strong upon living and living now, echoes the concept of *imanaka*.

The ultimate goal of human society is harmony. Human beings have a life given to them by "Mother Nature," which they must fulfill as dutiful human beings. This means following the ethics of Jissen-Rinri-Kōseikai. The rules in the system are considered to be not manmade but part of the natural law of the universe, which ensures that everything achieves its best fulfillment and ultimate condition. Harmony is stressed, but discipline is regarded as a basic part of the ideal of harmony. The student must be grateful to the teachers for their strictness as well as for the teacher needing to be strict. The same is true for parents. Contemporary society is plagued by massive information flow, but only that which is edifying should be selected for transmission to others. Members are taught to be sensitive and to respond to others' needs, to prevent them from feeling excluded; in this way, harmony in the true sense is preserved.

The ethics of the movement are natural ones to produce an ideal life. These are applied and very practical, directed to concrete situations and relationships with positive guidance on how to live. The movement's appeal lies in the way in which life can be directed and members need only follow by practicing the rules. Members believe they have an obligation to spread their teaching as a means to making a better world.

One of the basic principles taught in the founder's book, *Anata no Jissen-Rinri*, is that life must be accepted as it is because it has come about naturally in that form. To deny the ego and be led by nature sounds easy, but actually it is very difficult. Unhappiness is a warning that life is not being lived properly. Changes must be made before it is too late.

What a person is may also be the result of what his ancestors did, and in this regard he also must accept the situation. This cannot be evaded or avoided. People are born with every good possibility and a gentle mind; but once they forget about the good of society and the good of others, they quickly come to grief. The teaching of Jissen-Rinri-Kōseikai declares that the worth of a person is measured by the degree to which that person can disregard his or her desires to expend energy in working for others. An open and generous mind is essential. Human beings are not made to live alone. They are born into a society and therefore must learn to fit together to form a valuable whole: this is the meaning of harmony. Respect for others is the basis of the generation of harmony and the energy for the advancement of society.

At the basis of all other forms of harmony is the harmony of the family. The basis of the individual life has to be located within the family, because any potential achievements in human society are possibly only through the family's existence as a foundation of the social order. Husband and wife should stand together on an even basis while following their individual roles as man and woman. The two rules are complementary, and this is what makes harmony possible.

Rituals and Ceremonies. Haya Okiai takes place every day of the year from 5:00 to 6:00 A.M. because the early morning is when people are most refreshed. This is when the five principles are chanted. The *Haya Okiai* is conducted in a room containing a desk above which are the Japanese flag and a photograph of the President. The Five Principles are written on the wall. Meetings involve reciting the Five Principles and then reading a chapter of a book written by the founder. The leader insists on the importance of practical ethics, and then members make short speeches testifying to their successful practice of the ideals.

In view of the teachings, one might expect there to be a ceremony of purification. However, there is not; individuals must see to this at their local shrines or in other groups to which they belong.

Organization and Believers. Jissen-Rinri-Kōsekai is recognized by the Ministry of Education as a socio-educational organization. It is an incorporated body that is non-profit making and dependent upon donations (*shadan hōjin*). It claimed 3.5 million members in 1989, who pay approximately 220 yen per month to be members. The admission fee is approximately U.S. $30.

OTHER SHINTO-BASED NEW RELIGIONS

The list of these religions is far from exhausted by this sampling of the most typical ones. Others have become well known and might have been discussed had space permitted. That list could have included the following: *Nenbyō-Shinkyō, Oyama-nezu-no-Mikoto-Shinji-Kyōkai, Shizen-no-Izumi, Byakko-Shinkōkai, Tenshō-Kotai-Jingū-kyō, Kedatsu-kai, Kyō-sei-shu-kyō, Annanai-kyō, Sekai-Mahikari-Bunmei-Kyōdan, Shinsei-kai, Daiwa-Kyōkai, Shōroku-Shinto-Yamatoyama, Nippon-Sei-dō-Kyōkai, Shin-mei-ai-Shinkai, Shizen-kai, Shizen-sha, Shizen-Shin-Dō, Makoto-no-Ie, Sumera-kyō, Maruyama-kyō, Ko-myo-kai, Heiwa-Kyōkai, Ichi-gen-no-Miya, Kami-Ichi-Jyō-kyō, Dai-Shin-Kyō-kai* and *Tenrei-Shinrei-Kenkyū-Jyō*. All these groups have less than 100,000 members.[18]

One feature of the postwar religious landscape is that many movements come into being and pass out of existence, fragment or amalgamate, in an almost molecular-like manner. There are also literally hundreds of small movements with tiny handfuls of members that cease to exist when the founder dies or disappears.[19] Such movements may not even be registered with the government, but they exist in an ad hoc fashion. Information about them comes to be known only if their doings reach the attention of the press or other media.

COMPARATIVE REFLECTIONS

Cults in America[20] is an interesting text that makes a useful accompaniment to this study, even though Japanese religions do not feature within it. It primarily addresses cults that have roots in American culture, although some Oriental cults are listed. It points in a useful way to common features of the cultic that help to make sense of their appeal in a crosscultural setting. It enables the reader to distinguish between what is universal in the matter of cults and what about these religions in Japan is peculiarly Japanese and distinctively Shinto.

Most cults in the United States have roots in the Judaeo-Christian tradition and emphases that either come directly from Christianity or are in dire opposition to it. Many of America's older cults grew up as new communities became isolated from mainline religious groups. Untutored reading of the Bible produced many of these, such as the Mormon movement. Others grew up as the nation expanded. These would be analogous to the Kyōha Shinto groups. The equivalent to the New Religions might include Scientology; certain television evangelists who place emphasis on healing and other charismatic evidences of power; and new religions of Asian origin. The self-help type of religion preached by Robert Schuller is also reminiscent of the New Religions in Japan, something that people can recognize in its externals as being somewhat traditional but whose content is eclectic.

The sharpest contrasts can be seen here, between the implied worldview and the place of the individual in relation to how problems are defined and "solved." The Japanese cults stress group harmony, whereas the Western ones stress individual dependent faith (implicitly in the cult leader). In that sense, traditional cultural configurations seem to dominate, which may be one reason for their appeal. However, both sets seem to share the common goals of relieving people of the need for thought or decision. Perhaps this is the common root of the appeal of the cultic: release of the individual from the responsibility of thinking or deciding in a free and existential manner.

GENERAL SOURCES

In addition to the specific titles listed in the Notes, books consulted include the following: *Shin Shūkyō Dai-Jiten*; Shinshūkyō Gaido; Murakami Shigeyoshi, *Japanese Religion in the Modern Century* (University of Tokyo, 1980); and various works by H. Byron Earhart, including *The New Religions of Japan: A Bibliography of Western Language Materials* (University of Michigan Press, Ann Arbor, 1983).

NOTES

1. See Stuart Picken, "Japanese Religions and Internationalization: Problems and Prospects," *Japan Foundation Orientation Series*, No. 24 (Tokyo, 1987).

2. Raymond Hammer, *Japan's Religious Ferment* (SCM Press, London, 1961); H. Neil MacFarland, *The Rush Hour of the Gods* (New York, Macmillan, 1967); Harry Thomsen, *The New Religions of Japan* (Tuttle, Tokyo, 1963); Takagi Hiro, *Nihon no Shinkyō Shūkyō* (The New Religions of Japan) (Iwanami Shoten, Tokyo, 1959). Helen Hardacre, *Lay Buddhism in Contemporary Japan: Reiyukai Kyodan* (Princeton University Press, 1984) offers an excellent critique of the crisis theories.

3. Joseph Kitagawa, *Religion in Japanese History* (Columbia University Press, 1966), p. 331.

4. Nakamura Hajime, *Ways of Thinking of Eastern Peoples* (East-West Center Press, Honolulu, 1973), p. 457.

5. Frederick Franck, *The Buddha Eye* (Nanzan Studies in Religion and Culture, New York, 1982) is typical of that approach.

6. Modernization theory sources include the following: S. N. Eisenstadt, *Essays on Sociological Aspects of Political and Economic Development* (Prentice Hall, New York, 1966), and *The Political Systems of Empires* (Free Press, Glencoe, 1963); C. E. Black, *The Dynamics of Modernization: A Study in Comparative History* (Harper Torchbooks, New York, 1966); Jansen et al., *The Modernization of Japan and Russia* (Free Press, New York, 1975).

7. Cultic and corporate in Japan overlap: the corporations' songs and creeds appear very cultic, and the shrines function as guardians of the corporations. Most major corporations in Japan have a shrine affiliation of some kind. See *Kigyo to*

Jinja (Jinja Shinpo Books, Tokyo, 1986), p. 168. This useful study of well-known corporations and organizations explains their shrine affiliations.

8. See Stuart Picken, *Christianity and Japan: Meeting—Conflict—Hope* (Kodansha International, Tokyo, 1982).

9. For a general discussion, see Edward Norbeck, *Religion and Society in Modern Japan*, Rice University Studies, Vol. 56, No. 1 (Rice University, Houston, 1970); Saki Akio, *Shinkō Shukyō* (The New Religions) (Aoki Shoten, Tokyo, 1960).

10. The first chapter of Helen Hardacre's book *Kurozumikyō and the New Religions of Japan* (Princeton University Press, 1986) contains a superb account of the worldview of the New Religions.

11. Sources for this section include the following: Frederick Franck, *An Encounter with Oomoto* (Cross Currents, New York, 1975); *Nao Deguchi: A Biography of the Foundress of Oomoto* (Oomoto Foundation, Kameoka, 1982); Oishi Sakae, *Kaiso-Den* (Teenseisha, Tokyo, 1949); *Outline of Oomoto* (Oomoto Foundation, Kameoka, 1974); Deguchi Kyotaro, *The Great Onisaburo* (Oomoto Foundation, Tokyo, 1973). Deguchi's text, *Ofudesaki*, and the *Reikai no Monogatari* provide basic source material along with the magazine *Oomoto International*.

12. Sources include the following: Matsuno Junko, *"Shinreikyō" Shin Shūkyō Jiten* (Tokyodo Shuppan, Tokyo, 1984); Shinrei-kyō publications in Japanese and English including *Light from the East* (1986), *Towards the Dawning World* (1981), and the *Keimei-Shimbun* newspaper (Shinreikyō, Tokyo).

13. Sources include the following: *Kiseki no Hikari* (*Sekai Mahikari Bunmei Kyōdan*) (Yokasha, Shizuoka, 1990); *Response to Heaven: Additional Wisdom of Mahikari* (Yokosha, Shizuoka, 1990); A. K. Tebecis, *Mahikari* (LH Yoko Shuppan, Tokyo, 1982). The *Goseigen* remains the basic text of the sect.

14. Sources include the following: *PL Kyōdan: Shin no Jiyu* (Believer's Handbook) (Headquarters, Tondabayashi); *Perfect Liberty: How to Lead a Happy Life* (Headquarters, Tondabayashi, 1950); *Essay on the Way of Life* (Headquarters, Tondabayashi, 1950).

15. Sources include the following: Taniguchi Masakaru, *Seicho no Ie to wa Nanika?* (Nihon Kyobunsha, Tokyo, 1987); Editorial Head Office, *Seicho no Ie* (Nihon Kyobunsha, Tokyo, 1984); Hase Akihasa, *Japan's Modern Culture and Its Roots* (International Society for Educational Information, Tokyo, 1982). Because Taniguchi began publishing magazines, Seicho-no-Ie communicates principally through them: *Seicho-no-Ie* for general interest; *Shirohato* for women; *Hikari no Izumi* for new believers; *Risosekai* for young believers; *Risosekai Junior* for junior and senior high school students; *Seishinkagaku* for the general audience with a scientific perspective. Membership for a few thousand yen each year enables believers to have a reduction on magazine costs, which averaged U.S. $1 per copy in 1989.

16. Sekai Kyūsei-kyō texts include *Teachings of Meishu-sama, Prayers and Gosanka, Light from the East, World Messianity: What It Means*. All are issued in English and Japanese from either the headquarters in Atami or the U.S. offices in Los Angeles.

17. Sources include the following: Uehiro Eiji, *Anata no Jissen Rinri* (Practical Ethics for You) (Rinyu Shuppan, Tokyo, 1974); *Ikiru Seikatsu* (The Power to Live) (Dai Shindo, Tokyo, 1955); *Akarui Seikatsu* (Ways to Brighten Your Life) (Rinyu Shuppan, Tokyo, 1954); Sugihara Eiichiro, ed., *Rinrikōsei-Kaiho* (Jissenrinrikōsei-

kai, Tokyo, 1988). Magazines of the movement are *Rinri Kōsei Kaiho* (Ethics Bulletin) and *Seinen to Rinri* (Youth and Ethics).

18. See *Shin Shūkyō Jiten* for further information.

19. One such group, called *Michi no Tomo Kyōkai*, dissolved in crisis on 2 November 1986 when the founder died. This led to the deaths of six women members including the founder's wife, who immolated themselves on a nearby beach.

20. Wills Appel, *Cults in America: Programmed in Paradise* (Holt, Rinehart and Winston, New York, 1983).

Part IV

SHINTO THOUGHT

Chapter 9

Academic Shinto

SHINTO AND JAPANESE THOUGHT

Academic Shinto is a general term used to identify various movements within and among shrines that were overtly more philosophical and theological in their import than ritualistic. However, I do not wish to raise expectations about there being doctrinal positions worked out in a manner similar to Western theological and philosophical debate of the past. Rather, there are expressions of ideas based upon insights and intuitions that ignore many Western-style distinctions such as the one between natural and revealed religion. The doctrine of *kami*, for example, is not standardized in any form; therefore, each movement of thought must be described in terms of its own concepts. In this sense Shinto ideas run like strands of varying-colored threads throughout the entire tapestry of Japanese thought. Shinto and Japanese thought are at times inseparable, although Buddhist and Confucian ideas have been incorporated over the years. These have been woven together in a manner that is characteristically Japanese, selectively, and then adapted to meet the perceived needs of the age. The resultant system of thought and values deserves to be described as Japanese, although foreign elements are present. Their slow induction and steady ingestion into the system has changed their distinctively foreign character and made them very much "Japanese." Nakamura Hajime, the most renowned of Japan's twentieth-century intellectual historians, has described Japanese thought as eclectic (meaning not interested in formal consistency) and (because of the narrow social nexus that it supports) tending toward narrow and often ethnocentric points of view.[1] The particularism noted earlier is also very much in evidence throughout the history of Japanese thought; this should help to explain why, for example, Japanese politicians frequently fail to grasp the significance of the outside world and its potential impact until it has become too late to alter course.

The various currents of thought within the Shinto tradition can be roughly divided into overtly syncretistic and ostensibly purist trends. The syncretistic movements grew up from the early interaction with Buddhism based on the *honji-suijaku* principle in one of its various forms. Three movements emerged related to the main Buddhist movements, Tendai and Shingon in the Heian period, and Lotus or Nichiren Buddhism in the Kamakura period. These were *Tendai Shinto*, *Shingon Shinto*, and *Hokke Shinto*. As a reaction to these, the purist strand emerged in an attempt to identify the unique elements of Shinto apart from the Buddhism. The great thinker Yoshida Kanetomo drew attention to the fact that Shinto had its own tradition prior to the arrival of Buddhism and that Buddhist Shinto was simply a phase. He tried to define the fundamentals of Shinto according to the traditions of his own family and wanted to return Shinto to a purer form, although he acknowledged the distinction between exoteric and esoteric rituals. The growth of neo-Confucian influences resulted in the introduction of Confucian elements into Shinto thought, which were seen both in mainstream Shinto and in the various old and new sects. Finally, during the Edo period the great task of redefining Shinto and Japanese culture along with their relationship was undertaken by the scholars of the *Kokugaku* movement, foremost of whom was Motoori Norinaga.

The discussion here is an outline of the principle ideas of each important thinker and his place within the development of a particular strand of tradition, although the connections do not necessarily flow in any logical sequence. Great dialectical swings of the kind found in European thought are not typical of Japan, where gentle movement to and from older positions is typical. The *Kokugaku* movement lies in the background of the Meiji Restoration. This brings us into the modern period when government interference stunted the growth of new religious ideas in Shinto, a condition that the postwar Constitution brought to an end.

TENDAI SHINTO OR SANNŌ-ICHIJITSU SHINTO

This is the form of Shinto associated with the work of the famous Buddhist priest Saichō (767–822), who was posthumously called *Dengyō Daishi* and who introduced the Tendai sect of Buddhism to Japan from Mt. T'ien Tai in China. The Tendai sect is headquartered at Mt. Hie to the northeast of Kyoto. The sect was presented as a guardian of the country. The northeast was considered most vulnerable to the visitation of disaster, and Mt. Hie was located in that direction. The image grew of Tendai and its temples as guardians of Kyoto. *Sannō* means "mountain divinity"; it was the former name of the guardian *kami* on Mt. Hie. *Ichijitsu* means "truth is absolute;" it is an expression found in the *Hokke-kyō*, the Lotus Sūtra, which is the principal text of Tendai Buddhism.

The sect reached the peak of its development during the Edo period with the work of another distinguished priest, Tenkai (1536–1643), posthumously named *Jigen Daishi*.[2] The *Sannō* cult was the core movement within the tradition, but it is known more for its works of art than for its religious and philosophical ideas.[3] Indeed, in these Shinto Buddhist movements, ideas were more readily expressed in art, ritual, and symbol than in words, a natural tendency of the Japanese way of thinking. Twenty-one Sannō shrines trace their origin to the act in which *Dengyō Daishi* prayed to Sannō to ensure that the *kami* of the mountain would approve of and duly afford protection to the Tendai temple that he proposed to erect. The principal shrine, the *Hie Jinja*, is located to the east at the base of the mountain overlooking Lake Biwa. It is divided into an eastern section that enshrines Oyamakui-no-mikoto, the *kami* of the mountain; and a western section that enshrines Inamuchi-no-mikoto, the *kami* of Mt. Miwa in the modern Nara Prefecture. These two, plus five others, are known collectively as the Seven Upper Shrines and are the heart of the cult. There are also Seven Middle Shrines and Seven Lower Shrines, which makes the total number twenty-one. The number seven in Tendai thought related to the Seven Worlds of Tendai cosmology.

RYŌBU SHINTO OR SHINGON SHINTO

The origin of this form of Shinto, referred to also as "Dual Shinto" or "Shinto of the Two Parts," is associated with Kūkai (773–835), who visited China at the same time as Saichō (during the Tang Dynasty) to study Buddhism and who subsequently founded the totally estoeric (*mikkyō*) Shingon sect. Yoshida Kanetomo (1434–1511) is also thought to have been an important early figure in the movement, because the term *Ryōbu Shinto* most likely did not come into use until after Kūkai's death.

The name *Ryōbu* arose from the combination of two important teachings, namely, the *Taizōkai* (womb, representing the world of embryonic truth) and the *Kongōkai* (diamond, representing the world of unshakable truth). These were also the names of two famous mandalas that symbolized, respectively, passive reasons and positive wisdom. Ryōbu was based on the concept of *honji-suijaku*, the "original incarnation." Each *kami* was thought to represent a *bosatsu* or bodhisattva. Titles such as *gongen* (avatar) or *bosatsu* were given to *kami* to heighten their significance. Kūkai worked extremely hard during his lifetime, visiting mountain shrines in particular; there, many traces of esoteric rituals can still be seen.

Development of Ryōbu Shinto

The Watarai school introduced many new elements into its eclectic theory of Shinto, matching what seems to have been a steady influence and input from Esoteric Buddhism into the Shinto of that period. This is illus-

trated by the creation of texts—such as *Yamatohime no Mikoto Seiki*—
stressing worship of the *kami* with a pure heart.[4] Although they contain
elements of tradition preserved from very early times at Ise, ideas parallel
to the basic Shinto ideas were produced with Shinto concepts (e.g., the
Ōbarae of the Nakatomi clan being given a Buddhist interpretation). The
texts were called the *Ōnakatomi Sūtras* because their recitation was considered favored by Buddha.

Around this time there also grew up a tendency to interpret the principal
kami along the lines of Esoteric Buddhism. This first appeared at Ōmiwa
Jinja in Yamato. A distinguished priest named Bizon was also a devotee of
the *kami* of Miwa. His disciple Shonin propounded as new theory in 1318
according to which Amaterasu descended to earth and appeared as the
kami of Ōmiwa on Mt. Miwa and as the great imperial *kami* at Mt. Kamiji
in Ise. According to Shonin, these three *kami* were in fact one and could
be regarded as a threefold manifestation of the *Dainichi Nyorai*, the Great
Buddha of the Light of the Universe (Sun). They became known as the
"three-in-one." This gave rise to what was later called Miwa Shinto.

The Ise group also developed ties with the ascetic center, Mt. Katsuragi
in Yamato. The group compiled a text entitled *Katsuragi Hozan-ki*,[5] according to which Ame-no-minakushi-no-mikoto transformed himself into
a sacred mirror of the three-in-one and was enshrined in the *Toyōke Jingū*
at Ise. The *Katsuragi Hozan-ki* is one of the most secret and sacred texts
associated with Ise, according to the *Koro Kujitsu-den*[6] of Watarai Yukitada. The *Tenchi Reiki-ki*[7] was actually fourth in a series of the eighteen
volumes that began with the *Nisho Daijingū Reiki-ki*,[8] but it was considered the most important and in this way came to give its name to the entire
series. The texts share common features in the way they offer esoteric explanations of the different elements of the shrine, the location of its buildings, and other aspects of the site. They make use of the diamond mandala
and the womb mandala of Ryōbu Shinto. The existence of the inner and
outer shrines at Ise was explained in these terms. Buddhist arguments appeared that attributed them to that source. The tendency to explain Shinto
(particularly Ise Shinto) in terms of Esoteric Buddhism became widespread.
It was a priest of the Shomyo-ji in Musashi, Ken'a (1262–1338), who was
most active in promoting these ideas. During the Kemmu Restoration (c.
1334), Kitabatake Chikafusa (1293–1354) and Jihen (the older brother of
Urabe Kaneyoshi) composed works on Shinto thought and doctrine. Jihen's
major works include *Kyuji Hongi Gengi*, *Tenchi Jingi Shinchin Yoki*, and
Toyoashihara Jimpu Waki.[9] Chikafusa's representative work is *Gengen-
shū*.[10] In 1419, High Priest Ryohen of Mt. Hiei gave a formal exposition
of his own interpretation of *Tenchi Reiki-ki* and of the section on "the age
of the *kami*" in the *Nihongi* to his disciples. It later became customary to
perform a *reiki-ki* initiation rite modeled on some of the more esoteric
practices of Buddhism. The syncretism was completed, because (according

to Ryohen) even though we may speak of initiation by one term in Shingon esotericism and by another in Shinto, they are in fact the same thing. Another term for *reiki* was *kanjō*.[11]

During the Muromachi period (1336–1573), *Goryu Shinto* appeared. A type of Shingon Shinto, it was heavily influenced by Esoteric Buddhism and was practiced even on Mt. Kōya. It was known originally as *Kōbō Daishi Shinto* but later was officially named *Goryu Shinto*. In parallel to this, an Esoteric Buddhist version of Shinto was created without reference to the Grand Shrines of Ise.

HOKKE SHINTO

The Shinto[12] of the Lotus Sūtra refers to several types of Buddhist thought in which the Lotus Sūtra is taken into Shinto activities. A brief understanding of the relevant aspects of Buddhism is required for background. There are two main traditions of the Lotus Sutra in Japanese religion. The main and orthodox one is its transmission in the history and rituals of the Tendai school as it was introduced from China by Saicho. The other tradition is the more controversial line created by the Kamakura period priest Nichiren (1222–1282). Of all Japanese religious figures he is the most unusual, resembling, in the views of many scholars, a Hebrew reform prophet of the eighth century B.C. rather than a Japanese Buddhist priest. His aggressive criticisms of government and other Buddhists was out of character in Japan. He was exiled and sentenced to death but was miraculously saved.

Nichiren left the legacy of the *Nichiren-shū*, a sect of Buddhism bearing his intellectual imprint and based on the Lotus Sūtra. Three large new religions of Buddhist origin trace their roots to Nichiren, and each reflects a different face of the founder. There is the somewhat conservative *Reiyūkai* (Society of Friends of Spirits), which has its headquarters in Azabudai in central Tokyo. There is the radical *Soka Gakkai* (Association of Value Creation) headquartered at the *Taiseki-ji*, an old temple near Mt. Fuji; and there is the liberal *Risshō Kōsei-kai*, which has its headquarters in Suginami Ward in Tokyo. Its name is explained as *risshō* (righteousness and security for the nation), *kō* (harmony of believers), and *sei* (the ideal of attaining Buddhahood).

Nichiren's name affords a clue to one other aspect of his thought. At the age of twenty-one he returned to his native Boso Peninsula (in modern Chibu Prefecture); and in a mood of dissatisfaction with Tendai rituals, he found his religious inspiration on Mt. Kiyosumi during a sunrise exercise in 1253. It was then that he formulated his famous proclamation, the *daimoku*: "*Namu myōkō Renge-kyō*" ("hail to the Lotus Sūtra"). Nichiren's name reflects this duality. *Nichi* speaks of the sun, and *Ren* of the lotus.

The Tendai tradition had hitherto been known as Hokke (Lotus) Buddhism. Thereafter, the name became attached to Nichiren Buddhism.

Hokke Shinto therefore can refer to two slightly different versions of the same content. Tendai Shinto was a form of Hokke Shinto arising from a union of Tendai Shinto and Yoshida Shinto. There is also a form of Hokke Shinto that has been traced to Nichiren but concerning which almost nothing is extant. Unlike Shingon and Tendai Shinto, in which shrines can still be identified, Nichiren is now known only and completely as a Buddhist figure. It is quite likely that his name was attached to a set of ideas for propaganda purposes at a later date, as was the case with Kūkai. The content of Hokke Shinto, like Nichiren himself, is controversial; therefore little can be said with certainty. Its last known form, which died out because of the Meiji separation of Shinto and Buddhism, was *Remmon-kyō*, founded in 1868 by Shimmura Mitsu (1831–1914).

YOSHIDA SHINTO

During the latter part of the rule of the Ashikaga shogunate (1335–1575) Yoshida Shinto emerged, claiming to be the hereditary principles transmitted to the Yoshida family from its divine ancestor, Ame-no-koyane-no-mikoto, the *kami* whom they claimed supervised the festivities of the *kami* during the *kami-yo*.

The basic teaching of Yoshida Shinto was that the *kami* are the heart and the heart is the *kami*. All things in the universe were created by the actions of the *kami*. Heaven and Earth are books that are lit for understanding by the sun and moon. That truth resides in Shinto, which is the foundation of everything else; the others receive their significance and authenticity from the foundation of Shinto. This perspective led it to be called *Genpon-sōgen-Shinto* (Original Source Shinto). It is also called *Yuiitsu Shinto* (Unique Shinto) or Urabe Shinto, because Urabe was the former name of the Yoshida family.

The background to the development of these ideas is unintelligible without some clarification of the complex relationship of the names of Hirano, Yoshida, and Urabe. The name *Urabe* dates to the era when the roles of the clans were first defined. First and foremost, they were officials in the *Jingikan* (Office of Shinto Worship). From this base they expanded their influence by becoming historians of Shinto and authorities on the classics. To heighten his status, the head of the clan made a point of observing all Shinto taboos—for example, by avoiding any contact with death or the dead whatsoever because of physical pollution, or by abstaining from certain foods, drinks, or activities because of the need for ritual purity.

Around the time of the development of new ideas by the *gekū* of the Grand Shrines of Ise, Urabe Kanekata composed the *Shaku Nihongi* as a compendium of all previous commentaries on the classic text of the Nara age. He was a member of the Hirano branch of the ancient Urabe clan who had originally been in charge of divination by means of tortoise shells in the *Jingikan* of the Nara government. His father, Kanebumi, was an authority on the *Isonokami Jinja*, and his grandfather, Kaneyori, had been an expert in the *Nihon Shoki* as well as in the history of the Hachiman tradition. Their combined efforts and efficiency enabled them to rise steadily to the point at which they controlled several major posts in the *Jingikan*.

They also served as hereditary priests of such important shrines in Kyoto as the Hirano and Yoshida shrines. By the end of the Heian period two families, the Umenomiya and the Awatanomiya, had emerged from the Urabe clan as new families of Shinto priests. The latter were responsible for the worship of the spirits of Emperor Sutoku (r. 1123–1141) and of Fujiwara no Yoriie.

The Urabe clan subsequently developed two main lines of succession, the Hirano and the Yoshida. Kaneyori, Kanebumi, and Kanekata belonged to the Hirano branch. They were more active during the early period. However, by the middle to the latter part of the fourteenth century, the Yoshida line came to pre-eminence beginning with Yoshida Kanetoyo, who composed the *Miyaji Hiji Kuden*.[13] His son was Kanehiro (who was patronized by Ashikaga Shogun Yoshimitsu), his grandson was Kaneatsu, and his great-grandson was the famous Yoshida Kanetomo.

In spite of the academic lineage and the deep and serious scholarship, the shamanistic face of Shinto remained. An incident is recorded from the fifteenth century about the wife of a Yoshida priest becoming possessed by a spirit in the early afternoon. She suddenly began uttering an oracle. The priest quickly purified himself by *misogi harai* and gave her some *sake*. After swallowing a little she completed the oracle, whose contents the priest, for some reason, elected not to record.

The Yoshida family also began to create its own interpretation of the age of the *kami*. The Imperial Prince Sondo, also a Buddhist monk, was instructed in the origins of Japan and Shinto by the Yoshida family, whose teaching in that way gradually attained the status of orthodoxy.

Yoshida Kanetomo (1435–1511)

He was the dominant and pivotal figure of the tradition. His successes relate to both his family background and the age in which he lived. He was the twenty-first generation of the Yoshida Shinto family; he was intelligent, thoughtful, and a well-learned Shinto scholar who brought the system to completion. He reached his mature years amid the horrendous destruction of the Onin War, witnessing the dreadful destruction of ancient and valued artifacts. From the age of thirty-nine he launched himself into academic and religious activities, which occupied the rest of his life.

The construction of the *Saijoshō* was his first major project. It was a hall intended for abstinence and ritual purification, but in fact it was a version of the Hall of the Eight Kami in the ancient *Jingikan*. For this Kanetomo received Imperial authority, calling it the most sacred of shrines. He also received a large donation from Hino Tomiko, the wife of Shogun Ashikaga Yoshimasa. His popular lectures on the *Kamiyo* sections of the *Nihongi* drew large audiences and spread the influence of his teachings. He supplied the ideas of the sect with apt comments and established his own thought almost as the orthodoxy of the age. He claimed in the *Shinto Taii*[14] and in the *Yuiitsu Shinto Myōbō Yōshū* to have derived his ideas from earlier thinkers such as Kanenao and Kanenobu. He argued powerfully for the uniqueness and independence of his thought from any form of Buddhist influence. He declared that the Shinto of his tradition was universal: winds and waves, clouds and mist; movement and stillness, advances and retreats; day and night, the hidden and the manifest; warmth and chill, heat and cold; recompense for good and ill, distinction of right and wrong. He claimed further that there was nothing whatsoever that was not the work of the divine principle taught by the Yoshida school. In speaking of Shinto "of one stream, not two," he was referring to an unrecorded memo of Shotoku Tasishi to the Emperor that Buddhism was the flower and fruit of the true doctrine, Confucianism was the branch and leaf, but Shinto was the root. The eastward movement of Buddhism showed that Japan was the prime nation of the Three Countries (India, China, and Japan). He devised rituals that were adapted from Shingon Esoteric Buddhism with the obvious intent of displacing Buddhism from its prominence by enriching the Shinto liturgy at the expense of Buddhism.

Of interest also is the attempt made by Kanetomo to conceptualize the idea of *kami*. He declared that *kami* was a form of absolute existence that was prior to the formation of heaven and earth. It transcends the principles of *in* (*ying*) and *yo* (*yang*) but can act with them. This power as manifest in heaven and earth is called *kami*. It is called spirit (*rei*) in objects and things, and in human beings it is known as heart (*kokoro*). *Kami*, *rei*, and *kokoro* are words that refer to the same reality. Thus, Shinto protects the human heart, a concept that features in all aspects of traditional and new religions. Kanetomo stressed the importance of purification as one method of preserving and protecting the heart. Regardless of the limitations of his system of ideas, he bequeathed both an intellectual inheritance and a political status to Yoshida Shinto. This was taken up by his principal successor, Kanemigi, under whose influence Yoshida Shinto grew to even greater importance.

Yoshida Kanemigi (1516–1573)

Kanemigi was actually a son of the influential Confucian scholar Kiyo-hara Nobutaka (1475–1550), who was adopted by the Yoshida family and thereby became a grandson of Kanetomo. One important aspect of the period was the spread of shrines across the country in the provinces. This was done not simply by teaching but also by bestowing status upon local *kami* and folk deities. Various privileges include the right to use the title *daimyojin* (gracious *kami*) instead of *gongen*, the term used for *avatar* in Buddhism. This was evidence of the degree to which the power and influence of the Yoshida family over shrines had become established.

In 1485 Kanetomo was requested by Shogun Yoshimasa (1435–1490) to undertake a study of certain shrines around Kyoto, the enshrined *kami*, the corresponding Buddhist deities according to the old *honji-suijaku* theory, their subsidiary shrines, the associated Buddhist temples, their rites, clergy, and history. This added not only to the family's prestige but also to its general expertise in Shinto and its cultic relation to Buddhism.

Kanemigi was well acquainted with the antiquarian aspects of Shinto and followed the study with a commentary on the *Nijūnisha Chushiki*.[15] From 1542 to 1572 he traveled widely in Iga, Ise, Nagato, and other areas, researching records, shrines, and shrine families. One direct result was that the number of families of Shinto priests who came to Kyoto to seek formal affiliation with Yoshida Shinto grew steadily; people came initially from the central region in West Japan but later from the northeast and the northwest. From a list of 120 provincial shrines that received an imprimatur of Yoshida Shinto between 1482 and 1569, the following regions were represented: Kyoto area—79 shrines including 28 in Omi, 1 in Yamba, and 39 others; Chubu—16 including 5 in Echizen, 4 in Mikawa, 3 in Wakasa; Chugoku—12 with 6 in Suo; in addition, there were 10 in Shikoku, and 2 in Kanto.

During this period Shinto community relations went through an important stage of development. Many lay people were given permission to manage and maintain shrines. For example, the *Hirano Myojin Jinja* in Settsu was put into the hands of the village elders, the headman being released from clothing taboos. The *Koita Jinja* in Tamba was given a tablet to be placed on the part of the *torii* intended for the identity markers, indicating that the enshrined being had been given full *kami* status, as was the locally revered being (the Nara monk Dōkyō) in the *Saeki Jinja* in Tamba. Other examples included granting permission to build a *torii* or to have permanent lay people act as shrine caretakers. As small villages moved toward independence, local *samurai* and the village elders became the core of the Shinto priesthood. This was probably the origin of the local *ujikosodai* and the *miyaza*, groups of lay people who maintained the shrines and served the *kami* (the latter groups occurring where no fully authorized priest was serving).

Yoshida Shinto also relaxed certain rigid taboos, permitting the eating of meat for health or allowing some rituals to be performed with warmed water rather than cold. It was even able to release villagers from contractual bonds to other clan members or clan masters. Amulets and talismen were circulated for various purposes (e.g., to pacify the vengeful dead or to protect the home against fire and theft). These reflect the kinds of concerns that may be seen at shrines to the present day, allowing for more contemporary concerns such as road safety or air travel at home and abroad. The growth of village life during the sixteenth century established many of the patterns of life that are still observed. Much of this was due to the influence of Yoshida Shinto, which remained a powerful force until it was severely criticized by the *Kokugaku* scholar Hirata Atsutane (1774–1842). This brought its influence to an end during the latter third of the Edo age.

WATARAI SHINTO AND THE ORIGINS OF ISE SHINTO

During the reigns of Emperors Yomei and Kotoku (recorded in the *Nihongi*) the term *Shinto* was ordinarily used to refer to attitudes of reverence toward the traditional *kami* of the country and people, leaning heavily on the folk way idea. The *honji-suijaku* theory of the Heian period brought it into relation with Buddhism. By the Kamakura period, it had come to be defined as a system of ideas, a "philosophy" that coexisted with Buddhism as a religious and philosophical tradition in its own right. The *Kogi Zui-ketsu-shu*,[16] written in 1256 as a compilation of responses by a Jōdo monk, Shinzui, to questions from Uehara Atsuhiro, defends this position. The fact that alms were offered by believers in Buddhism and Shinto was taken as evidence that the religions were equal and identical.

In the *Tsukai Sankeiki*, Amaterasu Omikami was declared to be the Lord of Shinto, whereas Dainichi Nyorai was the Lord of Buddhism. Shinto, however, could still be found referring to folk religion. It was not until the fourteenth century that the "philosophical" usage became the rule rather than the exception. Expressions then came into use that spoke of the profound meaning of Shinto, of the transformation of Shinto, or of the beautiful spirit of Shinto and Buddhism.[17] Many other texts make similar claims. The *Toyoashihara Jimpuwa-ki* contains a reference to the imperial virtue that extends over heaven, earth, and man that is called the Way of the Emperor. In Japan it is also called the way of the Kami.[18]

As at present, the influence of the major shrines seems to have been decisive. They were largely responsible for the development of both the philosophical and the ritual aspects of Shinto. At Ise, Sannō, and Miwa Shrines, such developments were most apparent. In prohibiting private visits to Ise, the *Engishiki* stated clearly that servants of the Emperor may not visit and make offerings at Ise Grand Shrine at will.[19] However, lack of funds prevented the government from enforcing this order. Income had to be permitted from less official sources, principally from the lands held throughout the country known as *mikuriya*. Central and East Japan were targeted particularly for the development of these land tracts. Buddhist culture was less rooted there than in the rest of the country. Propagandist stress on the mythical origins of Japan and the Japanese race appealed to the emerging warrior class, who derived a sense of identity and purpose from it. Minamoto no Yoshimune made a donation to the Soima *mikuriya* in 1161 with a declaration that the entire land of Dai-Nippon belonged to the Toyoke Shrine and the Imperial Grand Shrines of Ise. Japan, he claimed, echoing the classics, was the Central Land of Reed Plains.

Origins of Ise Shinto

Following these changes in the intellectual climate, the priests of Ise worked hard to achieve hegemony over the eastern part of the country and clearly had much success.[20] Minamoto Yoritomo encouraged the *gon-negi* at Ise most committed to the extension of the cult, presented *mikuriya* and horses to both the inner and outer shrines, and suppressed all resistance to them in the Ise area. His influence was decisive for the growing *samurai* class and had a great deal to do with the establishment of the prestige of the Grand Shrines. By a coincidence of history, it was at this time that the *Tōdai-ji* in Nara fell into ruins after a disastrous fire and was in need of rebuilding. In 1186 a Pure Land monk called Shunjobo Chogen (1121–1206) presented a petition in the form of 600 scrolls of the Great Perfection of Wisdom Sutra to the Grand Shrines of Ise in the company of 60 other monks to seek the cooperation of the Grand Shrines in the rebuilding of the *Tōdai-ji*. The High Priest, Ōnakatomi Tadataka; the chief *negi* of the Inner Shrine, Arakida Narinaga; and the chief *negi* of the Outer Shrine, Watarai Mitsutada, warmly welcomed the delegation and the scrolls, which were to increase the joy of Amaterasu Omikami and Toyōke Omikami in the law and in their own holy radiance.

According to the *Daijingū Shozoji-ki*[21] a courtier known as Tachibana no Moroe (684–757) had been sent by Emperor Shomu during the Nara period to the Grand Shrines of Ise to receive an oracle, which declared that the sun was identical with Dainichi Nyorai. The "sun" was, of course, Amaterasu. This marked the beginning of a new stage in the relationship, which was to develop to the benefit of Shinto over the ensuing eras and gradually reverse the earlier position whereby Shinto was forced to yield to Buddhism and Chinese culture.[22]

Expansion of Ise Shinto

The Ise shrines began to draw large numbers of pilgrims from the thirteenth century onward. The great ceremonies of 1266, and later of 1287, are recorded as having drawn millions of pilgrims. Under the influence of Chogen, many Buddhist priests made the pilgrimage. The *Tsukai Sankei-ki* was used as a guidebook and introduction to the great themes of the *kami* of the Grand Shrines. Tsukai himself was a typical product of the age in which he lived. He was originally a member of the Ōnakatomi clan but had joined the *Shingon-shū* as a priest of the *Daigo-ji*, becoming proficient in the teachings of the *Sambo-in* school. He became Head Priest of the *Daigo-ji* and succeeded to the *Renge-ji*, a temple of the Ōnakatomi clan located on the Tanahashi *mikuriya* not far from the Ise Grand Shrine. He built an institution called the *Dai Jingū Horaku-ji* (literally, "Grand Shrine Temple of Pleasure in the Buddhist Law"), which he used as a base to explain how the native *kami* of Japan appreciated the teachings of Buddhism. He interpreted the nature of the *Geku* and the *Naiku* in quasi-Buddhist terms; this was a difficult position to maintain owing to the rules at Ise forbidding Buddhist priests from entering the shrine precincts because Buddhism was considered unclean.

Various popular explanations were invented to make it possible for Buddhism and Shinto to coexist. One common line of argument was that anti-Buddhist sentiment was actually pretense, and that in fact even though the Ise *kami* outwardly keep themselves apart from Buddhism, they inwardly guard and defend it. Consequently Buddhism, it was claimed, has always depended upon the protection of the Grand Shrines.[23]

These explanations gradually became official doctrines taught by the Outer Shrine (rather than the Inner Shrine) from the early Kamakura period. The *Engishiki* referred to the Inner Shrine as the Grand Shrine. The Outer Shrine was known as the Watarai shrine, indicating the influence of the Watarai family and their role in expanding the cult. By the late Heian period, the Inner Shrine was called the Imperial Grand Shrine and the Outer Shrine was called the Toyōke Grand Shrine. The Outer was slowly beginning to achieve parity with the Inner. In Tsukai's writings, the record of the pilgrimage noted that the *negi* of the Outer Shrine served at both Inner and Outer rituals.

The manner in which the Outer Shrine was presenting its claims aroused the displeasure of the Inner Shrine. In 1282 the Outer Shrine *negi*, Yukitada (1236–1305), who had been relieved of his duties, went to Kyoto to engage in research. He wrote a treatise on the divine names of the *kami* of the two Grand Shrines entitled *Ise Nisho Daijingū Shinmei Hisho*, which he presented to the retired Emperor Kameyama. He was restored to office in 1287. In 1296 there was a controversy with the Inner Shrine concerning the appropriateness of the name *Toyōke Imperial Shrine* in a document referring to the Outer Shrine. Yoshitada made the Inner priests very angry by referring in his defense to the *Zō Ise Nisho Daijingū Hōkihon-gi*,[24] which had been written by a priest of the Outer Shrine. It contained many of the ideas of Ise Shinto as it was being developed by the Outer Shrine. It declared, for example, that *kami* and mind are the fundamental essences of Heaven and Earth and that the body is nothing less than the growth of the five elements. They return to the origin of all things in accordance with the universal mind. *Kami* is revealed through the performance of prayers, and they help the honest and upright. The *Zō Ise Nisho Daijingū Hōkihon-gi* also offered an interesting exposition of the idea of man as a divine being under Heaven who should live in a peaceful world. It is the mind, or heart, that gives residence to the divine, so it should be kept pure. The descent of the *kami* is through prayers and the divine protection is rooted in honesty. Individuals should entrust themselves to the original vow. Once everyone accepts the Great Way, the world revolves peacefully and the sun and moon are bright; wind and rain enrich the country in due season; and the people are at peace. The taint of Buddhism is thus avoided.

These ideas and many like them are found in works written by the generations of Watarai priests of the Outer Shrine, which came to be known as the *Shinto Gobushō* (The Five-fold Shinto Canon). The texts were the *Amaterashimasu Ise ni-sho Kōtai Jingū Go-chinza shidai-ki, Ise Nisho Kōtai Jingū Go-Chinza Denki, Toyōke Kōtai Jingū Go-Chinza, Zo-Ise Nisho Daijingū Hōkihongi,* and *Yamatohime no Mikoto seiki.*[25] These were the definitive works on Ise Shinto (meaning Watarai Shinto).

The essence of the cult was very simple. It stressed four principles: (1) the authority of the Grand Shrine, (2) the sanctity of the Imperial Regalia, (3) the self-awareness of Japan as the *kami no kuni* (land of the *kami*) and (4) the expression of reverence by prayer, purity, and honesty. These principles implied a rejection of the earlier principle of *Shimbutsu Shugo*, the harmony of Buddhism and Shinto. The cult recognized Buddhism as such, but it claimed that Shinto was a religion in its own right, received from one's ancestors to be passed on to one's descendants. This set of ideas was the work of Watarai Yukitada, Watarai Tsuneyoshi, and Watarai Ieyuki.

The *kami* of the Outer Shrine known as Miketsu no Kami is the same *kami* identified in the *Kojiki* and the *Nihon Shoki* as Ame-no-minakushi-no-kami and Kuni-no-tokotachi-no-mikoto. This *kami* is said to have made an agreement with Amaterasu at the time of creation that permitted her to rule the Empire forever. This clearly gave status to the Amaterasu cult. The *kami* of the Outer Shrine was understood to be in charge of water, whereas the *kami* of the Inner Shrine ruled over fire. However, Outer Shrine supporters argued that water was especially important for nourishing everything that exists. This assisted in the *kami*'s development from a *kami* of foodstuffs to one of general fertility and productivity.

To prove the arguments various sources of ideas were used, including the Chinese *Yin-Yang* theory and the Five Elements Theory, as well as Esoteric Buddhist ideas and some Taoist thought. Watarai Ieyuki, the successor to Yukitada, wrote a book entitled *Ruiji Jingi Hongen*[26] in which he attempted to systematize the new Shinto ideas, drawing upon Sung Dynasty records to prove his case.

It is difficult to assess how influential these ideas were on ordinary people, but a nationwide network of believers (similar to the system of Kumano) came into being. This added to the prestige of the Outer Shrine as it gradually carved out its own place in Japanese religious history.

Many of the ideas of Watarai Ieyuki and Tsuneyoshi were used and developed by Kitabatake Chikafusa (1293–1354) into spiritual ideals and practical principles (Kitabatake was a statesman at the southern court in Yoshino at the time). This added to the prestige and power of the Ise cult. Also at this time, the *Nakatomi Ōbarae* was coming to be treated with great respect, growing in prestige as the major *norito* of all Shinto rituals. Strict rules were devised and enforced with regard to the writings of Ise Shinto, the "writings prohibited beyond the river (Miyakawa)." They were forbidden to be read by anyone younger than sixty years of age who was not a member of a small elite, priestly class. This restriction on access further added to their prestige.

Later Developments under Watarai Nobuyoshi (1615–1691)

Properly speaking, this discussion belongs to the Edo period but is part of the history of the Ise tradition. The Watarai family were the hereditary priests of the *geku* of the Grand Shrines of Ise. Nobuyoshi totally rejected Ryōbu Shinto and insisted upon reverence for only the *kami* of Heaven and Earth. He made a clear and distinct separation of Shinto ideas from Buddhism. He affirmed the principles of honesty, mystery, and purity as being based upon the dignity of the Grand Shrines of Ise and the sacred nature of the Imperial Household. He encouraged the development of provincial shrines and tried to heighten ordinary people's awareness of the importance of Shinto. But the ultimate objective was to elevate the place of the Outer Shrine above that of the Inner.

Watarai Shinto might be justifiably called Philosophical or Academic Shinto in that it tried to identify and define a pure form of Shinto, which it then presented as the basis of government and morality. It also showed how Shinto permeated daily life by pointing out systematically that not one normal human activity is unaffected by Shinto. In reality, there were elements of Confucianism, although in its doctrinal aspects there is also an underlying monotheistic universalism. The origins and contents of Watarai Shinto merit much more research and attention than they have received.

SUIGA SHINTO

The thought of Chu Hsi (1130–1200) was used by the Tokugawa government to introduce into Japan the kind of Confucianism it wished to promulgate. The system of thought of Chu Hsi Confucianism was first studied and developed by Fujiwara Seika (1561–1619)[27] and Hayashi Razan (1583–1657),[28] who were both former Buddhist priests and commoners (perhaps a reaction to the previous age as well as release from it). Hayashi was the principal scholar of the Tokugawa shogunate; his contribution was the assertion that the basic relationship of the system was that of Ruler-Subject, which was to take precedence over the traditional Confucian priority of Father-Son. In doing so Hayashi was Japanizing Confucian ideas, but at the same time he was re-framing Japanese thought within Chinese values.

Yamasaki Ansai (1616–1682) was an eminent Confucian scholar whose thought represented the culmination of this approach. He emphasized the Great Way established by Amaterasu and by Sarutahiko-o-kami. He stressed veneration of the *kami* and explained that man and the universe are one, signaling the return to a more clearly monistic pattern of thought. In effect he developed a new branch of the Chu Hsi school, becoming in the process the most notable exponent of Confucian Shinto.[29] His concept of reverence for the Emperor (*sonnō shugi*) tied up with the notion of Japan as the land of the *kami* (*kami no kuni*). The development of these two ideas gave a framework of reference for the definition of the *kokutai* (body politic), a concept that became basic to Tokugawa ideals of education. His school became known as *Suiga*, the "Shinto of Divine Revelation and Blessing." The Great Way, the true way, was that of Ohirumemuchi (another name for Amaterasu). Sarutahiko-o-kami Shinto was part of the sun virtue (*nittoku*) of Amaterasu.

Although Suiga Shinto effectively diminished the influence of Ryōbu Shinto, it incorporated many ideas that were unacceptable to Shinto orthodoxy because of its close relationship with Sung Dynasty Confucian ideas. It was on these grounds, for example, that Motoori Norinaga (1729–1801) rejected it as having preached Confucianism under the guise of Shinto. However, Ansai did in fact encourage reverence for the Imperial House and helped cultivate personal piety within Shinto.

Yamago Sokō (1622–1685) of the Ancient Learning School[30] within Confucianism showed an even greater tendency to be nationalistic or "Japanist" in this way, designating Shinto as the *Seikyō*, the teaching of the sages. Both thinkers contributed to the expanded influence of Confucian ethics as the moral dimension of Shinto, ensuring its place as a fundamental element in the Japanese social value system through modern times.

KOKUGAKU SHINTO

The term *Kokugaku* (national learning) refers to the work of a number of thinkers whose ideas developed around the mid-Tokugawa period, during which they gained slow but steady recognition. Kokugaku thought became more widely discussed, however, after the Meiji Restoration, when it was used to point the Japanese people toward the roots of their nationhood. The search for identity was a necessary and inevitable part of the modernization process for the Japanese, as it is for any nation struggling with the conflict between tradition and modernity. The ideas themselves grew out of various aspects of cultural development during the *sakoku jidai*, the era of the closed country. The name *Fukko Shinto* (Restoration Shinto) was also used to stress the idea of returning to older ways, when in fact the nation was undertaking the structural reforms necessary to equip it for survival in the changing modern world.

Intellectual History in the Tokugawa Period

Concepts that had become familiar to the popular mind included *hohon hanshi* (indebtedness to ancestors and return to beginnings), *gyōki* (the age of attenuation), and *mappō* (the apocalyptic age). These ideas were current during the *sengoku jidai* (the era of civil wars that started around 1470). Lack of central authority produced, among other things, social reforms, a breakdown of the class structure, and the liberation of the individual. After the final victory of Tokugawa Ieyasu in 1615 following the earlier efforts at centralization by Oda Nobunaga (1534–1582) and Toyotomi Hideyoshi (1536–1598), the Tokugawa period came into being. The new shogunate devoted great attention to cultural and educational matters. The new culture was firmly in the hands of the government and did not depend upon priests and nobles, as in the Heian period. It was also totally secular, having been purged of all influences of Buddhism, a religion not well regarded by the Tokugawa House. The forced division of the *Jōdo-Shin* sect into *Higashi* and *Nishi-Honganji* to make two smaller groups indicates the degree of concern it exercised. Rule through culture and learning (*bunkyō seiji*) was the principal policy of the government.

As a reaction to the formal Confucian-Shinto alliance, various alternative schools emerged. One was the *yomei-gaku*[31] which asserted that moral truths were discovered by introspection rather than study, as the Chu Hsi school argued. Nakae Tōju (1608–1648)[32] and Kumazawa Banzan (1619–1691)[33] were the two principal figures of this tradition. The name *Kogaku* (Ancient Learning) began to appear as a reaction to all of these, introducing a new stress upon return to original texts in search for the spiritual roots and true cultural identity of Japan.

Ito Jinsai (1627–1705)

The originator of the Ancient Learning School was Ito Jinsai,[34] who came from a merchant family in Kyoto. He developed a special interest in Confucianism, initially being influenced by Chu Hsi but later developing his own school and becoming famous on that account. His critical study of Chu Hsi led him to doubt whether or not it was actually Confucian. He began to move away from it, trying to bring out the original meaning of the Chinese classics, especially the *Analects* of Confucius and the *Book of Mencius*. He pointed out that Chu Hsi distinguished between primary nature (*honzen no sei*) and physical nature (*kishitsu no sei*) derived from the cosmology centered on the Absolute (*taikyoku*), principle (*li*) and spirit (*ki*). Its methods of self-cultivation were based on the maintenance of respect, *kei* (respectful behavior), and an exhaustive study of *li*. It saw morality expressed in the return to *honzen no sei* through a process of self-realization similar to Western philosophical idealist systems of thought such as that of F. H. Bradley.[35] Morality in this system became the realization of a principle that was achieved through self-reflection and emphasis upon speculative discipline. Ito's conclusion was that the Chu Hsi school was not really Confucian in the pure sense. The tenuous analogies with Buddhism and Taoism simply obscured the original ideas of Confucius and Mencius, which Ito proceeded to define in different terms. Confucian morality was based upon *in* (benevolence) in the sense of an active love toward other people. Love (*ai*) was the Way of Heaven (*Tendō*), the natural way. Human beings expressed this cosmic movement when they showed humanity (*jin*). Morality was thus achieved by practice and cultivation of *jin*, but not though speculation.

Ito's stress on the original meaning of Confucianism and the true meaning of morality represented a way of thinking that was to have profound influence on those coming later in the search for the origins and meaning of morality and moral order. Thus, a new style of Japanese scholarship came into being based on the principle that searching for antiquarian roots was a legitimate activity. It continued in Confucian studies for a time before the spirit transferred itself to the examination of the origins of *Nippon-shugi*, Japanism. Ito's work was continued by his son Togai (1670–1736). Their joint work, a dominant influence in Kyoto scholarship, came to be known as the Horikawa school. Among their followers were many former scholars of the Chu Hsi and Yang Ming schools.

Ogyū Sorai (1666–1728)

The Ancient Rhetoric school of Sorai developed a generation after Ito.[36] It was a dedicated Sinophilism that disdained things Japanese. In contrast to Ito Jinsai's scholarly life in Kyoto, Ogyū worked for the government of

Edo and found patronage in the shoguns Tsunayoshi (1646–1709) and Yoshimune (1684–1751).

Ogyū began his career by studying Chu Hsi and in time founded his own school, which included a special interest in Chinese rhetoric. His teachings were close to those of Ito, although he felt that Ito's views still contained some elements of Buddhist and Taoist doctrines. He sought to further purify Confucian thought and argued that the sage kings Yao and Shun and those of the dynasties of Hsia, Yin, and Chou of the age of Confucius were successfully able to pacify China because they had received the Mandate of Heaven (*tenmei*). This was not Ito's understanding of the natural way, nor was it the same as benevolence (*jin*) and duty (*gi*). It was, rather, a utilitarian ethic based upon the traditional culture of rituals (*rei*), music (*gaku*), punishment (*kei*), and law (*sei*). Ogyū contended that the ideas of way and virtue (*toku*) never existed outside of these four elements of culture and civilization.

Because words (meaning poetry and history) and actions (music) were the central values of that classic age, there was need to clarify both the meaning of words and the character of actions. The study of the Six Classics could thus be the basis for the administration of the entire world, because they cover all aspects of ancient culture. Ogyū contended that Japanese poetry of the past was inferior to Chinese poetry, so he proposed a restoration of literary style based on Chinese writing. His school came to be known as the Ken'en school, which reached its peak between 1720 and 1740.

Two main branches grew up, the first of which centered on the classics and was typified by Dazai Jun (1680–1747).[37] During his first thirty years as a scholar, Dazai moved from Chu Hsi to Ito's school and then to that of Ogyū. He developed an extreme form of utilitarian ethics, being extremely critical of the study of *li* as a way of interpreting the classics. He was a competent literary critic; in his *Dokugo*, a collection of poems, he offers a Chinese perspective on Japanese poetry. He claimed to identify Chinese traits of style in old Japanese work but also insisted that people should study Japanese poetry of the past, which expressed feelings naturally without any artificiality. In this regard, to some extent he anticipated the *Kokugaku* school.

Hattori Nankaku (1683–1749)[38] was the model of the second group, which focused on the study of literature, particularly the prose and poetry of China. Dazai noted that after Hattori had begun to understand Japanese poetry he turned to Chinese poetry, and that after grasping its style he came to excel in it. The efforts of these scholars promoted a deep feeling for Chinese culture and style and a neglect of interest in the Japanese tradition. On the other hand, continued study of the ancient Chinese styles by Ogyū made possible the later critical work of National Learning as a philological movement, because the Chinese styles could not be identified. In all of these scholars, no matter how pro-Chinese, there was a slightly ambiguous attitude toward the object of their respect. They studied things Chinese but somehow wanted to improve things Japanese to the point at which they equaled the Chinese in quality but could be called Japanese. This concern also lies in the background of the *Kokugaku* school.

Kokugaku: National Learning

Confucianism was the great force used by the government during the Edo period to control learning and culture. National Learning grew out of an antagonism to this and to Confucianism, which it saw as an imported ideology. Buddhist and Confucian ideas had dominated Japanese values since the Nara period, which meant Chinese influence. Tokugawa policy was to encourage the syncretistic mixture of Buddhism and Shinto, of temples and shrines, to permit Confucian learning to become the true mark of sophistication and the proper norm for social mores. Confucianism was thus able to disregard Buddhism, and under the patronage of the Tokugawa family it became the official ideology of the state, used to inculcate desirable manners and attitudes. From among the many Confucian schools, a school of Ancient Learning emerged that in part was responsible for the rise of the National Learning movement.

National Learning from its inception showed three very clear anti-Confucian tendencies. First, it appreciated things Japanese and deprecated things foreign as a reaction to the view that revered things Chinese and disregarded things Japanese. This is seen especially in the scholarly goals of identifying what was purely and originally Japanese and in the conception of a Japanese-style moral sense.

Second, it showed a preference for naturalism and simplicity of artistic style in contrast to the formalism, complexity, and artificiality that it saw as hallmarks of the Confucian tradition. The National Learning movement affirmed the emotions and refined and defended this idea through the philological study of the Japanese classics, particularly of the prose and poetic styles of the Heian period. Comments made by Motoori Norinaga must have been revolutionary in that age of gaudiness and formalism. The charges of the "unnaturalness" of Confucian morality and of the "naturalness" of a human moral sense represented a serious challenge to the basis of the Tokugawa social system and its insistence upon a divinely sanctioned order. Ultimately, it was little more than a matter of replacing one ideal of a divine order (invented in China) with another (developed in Japan), but the movement itself enabled people to clarify the central issues involved and to decide which they preferred.

Third, it claimed to be seeking to throw light on the meanings of Japanese words and concepts that were created and written before the introduction of Buddhism and Confucianism. This refers to the *Yamato Kotoba,* the ancient form of the Japanese language that was claimed to have existed before Chinese culture came to dominate Japanese life. The goal of National Learning was thus to define, defend, and propagate in their purest form the moral, spiritual, and artistic values of the ancient Japanese. It began by rejecting Confucian and Buddhist ideas in the Japanese classics and by trying to expose the original and unique spirit of the ancient Japanese people. This was the principal goal of the National Learning movement. From the work of Keichū and its attitude of "seeking the truth," through Kada Azumamaro and Kamono Mabuchi to Motoori Norinaga, we see the emergence of a genuine philosophical spirit and of a critical inquiry, something that never appeared to have existed in Japanese history until them.

Origins in Keichū and Kada Azumamaro

Both the Ancient Meaning school (*Kogigaku*) of Ito Jinsai and the Ancient Rhetoric school (*Kokunjigaku*) of Ogyū Sorai were schools of Chinese philology. *Kokugaku* grew out of the Ancient Learning movement. With the work of Keichū, the National Learning movement developed independently of the Chinese school and came to take on a uniquely Japanese profile.

Keichū (1640–1701)[39] began his career as a Shingon Buddhist priest and scholar who gradually became committed to seeking truth in an uncompromising way. His principal fields of study, the *Manyōshū* and the historical *kana*, aimed at restoring ancient Japanese language. This approach led him to make use of inductive reasoning in trying to infer original meanings and intents. He eventually went far beyond the *Manyōshū* and developed methods to gain insight into the proper way to read the *Tale of Genji* and the *Tale of Ise* as literary works. The moralistic character of Confucian studies had hitherto inhibited this kind of critical and analytical approach, but Keichū's entirely scholarly and objectively critical method gave great impetus to the study of Japanese learning (*Wagaku*).

Kada Azumamaro (1669–1736),[40] the son of the *Gūji* (High Priest) of the Inari *Jinja* in Kyoto, came a generation after Keichū. He first set the goals of National Learning in his search to identify and define the religious, moral, literary, and legal culture of the ancient Japanese through the study of the classics. Kada prepared and presented to the government in 1728 a petition to establish a school (*so gakko rei*). Although he may not have used the term *National Learning* as such, he did speak of state learning. Several aspects of his application are interesting for the future development of the movement. He subdivided National Learning into *kami* way (Shinto), law, history, and literature. The objective was to clarify the true meaning of the classics by removing Buddhist and Confucian distortions. He explained various methods of arriving at an understanding of the ancient mind through the clarification of ancient words and books, and he spoke of the absurdity of interpreting them through the mysterious and the secretive.

The scholarly purpose of National Learning had been definitively set down. However, Kada's work in the study of *kami* way was not as deep as that of the *Manyōshū*, on which he did a great deal of work. In this way he was still within the tradition of Keichū. However, his tendency to express a normative view, as well as his own sense of what was ethical, entitles him to a place in the development of National Learning. He helped to give vent to the suppressed feelings of national consciousness that had been growing steadily within Shinto since the beginning of the Tokugawa period.

Kamo no Mabuchi (1697–1769)

Mabuchi[41] was a direct disciple of Kada. Like those before him, the motivating force behind his work was a reaction to overstylized, overformalized culture and the desire to return to the simplicity of what was purely Japanese. He was born in Hammamatsu, now a modern super express (*Shinkansen*) train stop between Tokyo and Kyoto. The family had a military tradition; one earlier figure, Masada, gained fame at the battle of Mikatagahara in 1572 while serving under Tokugawa Ieyasu. His father was a priest of the New Okabe Shrine in Iba Village, as a consequence of which he took Okabe as a family name. Kamo Mabuchi himself was adopted by the husband of an elder sister and later by another relative named Masanaga, whose daughter he married. Widowed at age twenty-eight, he left that family intending to become a Shingon priest. Unable to do so because his parents did not approve of his plan, he married the daughter of an innkeeper named Umeya in Hammamatsu. There he remained for ten years.

Of his academic training, little is known except what he tells us. He was taught by his mother to value serenity (*yasurakeku*) and refined elegance (*miyabika*), as in the poems of the *Manyōshū*. He was also apparently attracted at a young age to Chinese studies. Most important, he met Kada Azumamaro several times in Hammamatsu on his journeys between Kyoto and Edo and finally went to study with him for the last four years of the old scholar's life. He thus became deeply involved in the learning of the day. In 1737, the year following Azumamaro's death, he returned to Hammamatsu. In 1738 he abandoned the name Umeya, took back the name Okabe, and opened a private school in Edo. He taught Japanese poetry and prose and developed his new ideas until he retired in 1760 at age sixty-four. He died at age seventy-three. Like Confucius, he marked the stages of his life in decades.

He noted of himself that when he was over fifty years old, he came to think that he had some understanding of both ancient things and the classics. At age sixty, the meaning of the *Manyōshū* came to life in his mind and he realized that the thinking of the ancients was accessible through the study of their poetry. This enabled him to finish his work on it. After these efforts, at the age of seventy he declared that he had a sense of accomplishment. During the first period, Ogyū Sorai's thought was still exerting cultural power. During the second period, the work of Hattori Nankaku was growing in importance. The final period occurred when the work of Mabuchi and his new concept of ancient learning came to replace both of the previously dominant schools. His home in Edo in the Hama Ward was in the house called *Agatai* (House in the Fields), where he lived from 1764. Agatai gave its name to his school, which came into being as a new intellectual force in Edo. Mabuchi was a poet and a philosopher, but he was also a very careful scholar. In addition to studying the *Manyōshū*, he worked on the Shinto liturgies and early Imperial Edicts as well as Heian period literature, *Genji Monogatari, Ise Monogatari, Kokinshu,* and the *Hyakunin Isshu.*

To study these texts, particularly the *Manyōshū*, Mabuchi recommended reading a poem five times from an annotated edition (probably the Muromachi Sengaku edition) marked with the *tempon* (Japanese readings) and without trying to grasp the meaning. This philological exercise would enable the reader to observe different word usages. The poem should be read a sixth time or more, but with an attempt at writing other readings into the text. This might generate some confusion but probably would bring previous readings unconsciously to mind. Reading these various versions in a comparative way would probably suggest some readings as preferable and correct. After doing this several times, he recommended a speed reading of other ancient works from the *Kojiki* to the *Wamyo ruiju sho*, the Shinto liturgies in the *Engishiki*, and the texts of the Imperial Edicts of various eras. Contrasts and generic meanings would naturally emerge. Problematic readings, interpolations, and mistakes could then be identified in a way that made the sentiments of antiquity (in the *Manyōshū*) transparent.

Mabuchi's work on the *Manyōshū* carried all earlier work to a great degree of refinement. Uniquely and successfully, he captured the spirit of antiquity in his philology and experienced it himself by becoming able to write poems in the style and mood of that age, which he called the "true mind of the high and upright." He demonstrated the importance of the spirit of simplicity that was at work in the creation of the *Manyōshū* before the advent of either Buddhism or Confucianism.

The essence of the *Manyōshū* as he saw and grasped it was contained in the core concepts of Shinto. In his *Niimanabi* (basic learning), he noted that through all its poems can be found a spirit that is lofty (*takaki*) and direct (*naoki*). There is elegance (*miyabi*) and manliness (*o-shiki*). These terms explain the meaning of the sincere heart (*magokoro*), which he took to be the central theme of the *Manyōshū*. His efforts at imitating the style of the *Manyōshū* demonstrated his mastery of the spirit of the text as well as his acquaintance with the values of the age that had produced it. The Ancient Way gave to National Learning its finest tool of normative analysis, which enabled it to see beyond the outer layers of the past to the pristine spirit at the heart of Japanese culture.

Mabuchi's political philosophy starts from the idea of the body politic (*kokutai*) ruled over eternally by an unbroken line of Emperors. In his *Engishiki norito kai jo* (Introduction to Understanding Liturgies of the *Engishiki*), he brought the poetic and the political into touch by stating that literature is a "medication" for political order, especially in the days of Fuijiwara. The culture of ancient Japan was for that reason indeed excellent. The manly spirit seen in the *Manyōshū* emanated from the Emperor, and it characterized his rule. The ancient and great civilization of Japan was damaged by the intrusion of Confucian and Buddhist ideas. The Imperial Court (along with the national spirit) went into decline in proportion to its interest in academic trivia and complexity of style. Poetry also consequently suffered the effeminateness of the Heian Court. Mabuchi defended the link between poetry and the social order by declaring that poetry was the Great Way, whereas the teachings of Confucius were a lesser way. Poetry, not being based on logic, expressed spontaneous human feeling and consequently could harmonize with the spirit of good government. Poetry could have a soothing effect on the mind and consequently upon government. Logic simply killed what it touched.

Kamo Mabuchi was in effect generating an idealism (or, some might argue, a romanticism) that sought to recreate the life and spirit of the past within the present. Anyone concerned about social order would, in his view, think of the rule of past great Emperors. This would lead to an interest in the literature and culture of those eras. From these the spirit of the age could be learned, especially through poetry, principal of which must be the poems of the *Manyōshū*.

The concept of *zeitgeist* is assumed and used effectively in all of Mabuchi's arguments that idealize the past and make it a model for the present and future. The glories of that past age are a theme to which he returns time and again. From an enhanced aestheticism based on that understanding of the past, he believed that society could move to an enhanced morality. He always referred back to the age of Fujiwara, the Plain of Wisteria of the seventh century, as his datum point, describing those Emperors as people who venerated the *kami* and exercised power with awe and majesty for all to see. The nobility and magnificence of their style pacified the people and made sound government possible.

In the years immediately preceding his death and as recorded in writings such as *Agatai shugen roku* or the *Koku-i ko*, Mabuchi developed ideas that were influential on his successors and that left a foundation for the emerging movement. He continued to stress the ideal of a return to the golden age of Japanese culture, which he dated from the era of Empress Ingu (fourth century C.E.) to that of Emperor Tenji (r. 668–671).

He metaphorically contrasted Japan, the land of the rising sun, with China, where the sun was at its zenith, and India, where the sun had set. The national character of Japan was that of spring, in contrast to China's summer and India's autumn; Japan was a youth compared to the maturity of China and the age of India. In contrast to the elaborate artificiality of these civilizations, Japan was simple and natural. The Japanese had no pompous philosophy, no places, no writing. Roofs were wooden, walls earthen, and clothes of hemp. For almost a millennium the Imperial Family reigned and peace and stability existed. But the Chinese, with their complex doctrines of Confucianism, had lost their Imperial continuity to barbarians. Japan alone followed the Way of Heaven and Earth. Shinto features strongly in Mabuchi's claim that the Shinto *norito* were pure models of ancient style and therefore untouched by Confucianism. Thus, the words of the *Ōbarae* were the basis for understanding the way of the *kami*.

Mabuchi continued to work on the philosophical basis for his position with the outlook of a mature, secular humanist. The *kami* way follows the natural rhythm of Heaven and Earth, which are transformed according to the changing seasons. Belief that *kami* answer prayers or save people from hell he regarded as fanciful superstition. Shinto meant simply revering the *kami*, which led Muraoka Tsunetsugu to label him as holding an atheistic natural philosophy. The atheism is debatable, but his idea of *kami* is not one that is heavily endowed with the supernatural.

He continued also to maintain a lively interest in political questions, praising the military government of Tokugawa Ieyasu and calling it an age that had returned to antiquity. He argued for the necessity to move the capital from time to time to invigorate the national spirit. He also advocated the restoration of the Imperial Court. In a manner that is almost prophetic of events just over a century later, in his *Koku-i Ko* he declared that he was hoping a ruler would appear who embodied his ideals. Such a person, he asserted, could set the world to rights in ten or twenty years. This outlook may have been optimistic, but the ideas he forged during his life became tremendous conceptual weapons in the hands of those who followed him.

Motoori Norinaga (1730–1801)

The greatest exponent of national learning, Motoori Norinaga, gave *Kokugaku* broad perspectives and precise scholarship.[42] Working from Heian Studies (*chukogaku*) and Nara Studies (*jokogaku*), he provided *Kokugaku* with a sound foundation. Although he was regarded as the most important of the National Learning scholars, Motoori was heavily indebted to his predecessors. He insisted that a student should revere learning more than his teacher (the opposite of the Confucian ideal) and that a disciple should not be overawed by his teacher's explanations. Furthermore, he argued that secret teachings and oral traditions had no meaning for proper scholarship. National Learning he saw as bringing together four areas of study, namely, national morality (kokumin-dōtoku-ron), national history (koku-shi), national literature (koku-bungaku), and Shinto studies of the Ancient Way (shin-dō) concept of the body politic (kokutai no kodō). His thought in this regard is more rounded and more clearly focused than that of his predecessors.

Motoori was born during the era of the eighth Shogun Yoshimune, the son of a cotton wholesaler who lived in Matsuzaka City in Ise Province. He received a classical literary education typical in merchant families in the Kyoto-Osaka area and subsequently studied in Kyoto to become a physician and a Confucian scholar. At the age of twenty-eight he returned to Matsuzaka, where he practiced medicine as a pediatrician and lectured on poetry. His life and influence was strongest in the Kansai area, where his academy was located and which he rarely left except for occasional trips to Wakayama and Nagoya. He died sixty-six years before the Meiji Restoration, leaving a full half-century for his ideas to be developed and for the conditions to emerge that made the Restoration possible.

Motoori's meeting with Mabuchi at Matsuzaka at age thirty-four made him Mabuchi's disciple after only that one meeting, at which he probably received inspiration rather than instruction. Until Mabuchi died in 1769 they exchanged letters regularly, arguing about texts and clarifying ideas. Mabuchi's death was a great trauma for Motoori, which indicates the degree of influence he had received. The two things in particular that he received from Mabuchi were his idealism and his doctrine of simplicity. He praised Mabuchi but recognized that he had some limitations, which made it possible for Motoori to take Kokugaku ideas further. He spoke of Mabuchi as opening up the Way of Ancient Learning. His limitations included the fact that because he devoted so much time and energy to the Manyōshū, he was unable to spend much time on the Kojiki and the Nihongi. Therefore he was unable to define the Way in detail because he had not probed the texts thoroughly enough. Also because of this, the Chinese spirit (particularly Taoism) remained influential in his mind; evidence of it can be found in spite of his strong Japanism.

It was to the removal of the last traces of Chinese thought and to the exposition of the purest form of the Ancient Way that Motoori dedicated all his scholastic efforts. Although he was heavily dependent upon Mabuchi, he did not pursue Mabuchi's philosophical route because he was also influenced by Keichū. It was Keichū, he said, who had awakened him from the torpor of dogmatism, acting as his "eye opener" (this is analogous to the manner in which the thought of the Scottish empiricist David Hume awakened Immanuel Kant from what he called his "dogmatic slumber"). Motoori first encouraged the ideas of Keichū while studying in Kyoto. Keichū's method was more coldly analytical and scientific than Mabuchi's, whose poetic and inspirational style also appealed to Motoori. He first turned to the study of Heian learning, from which he developed his notion of *mono no aware* ("sensitivity to things," implying an aesthetic perception of reality). The meaning of Heian literature was not accessible to rational scrutiny but is seen in its feeling and beauty. He formulated and maintained to his death the principle that *ninjō shugi* (human feeling) was the essence of human nature. This explained the ideal of culture and morality in terms of the development and harmony of emotion.

Mabuchi's influence was responsible for Motoori's study of the Ancient Way beginning with the Nara classics, especially the *Kojiki*, although he had begun looking at the Shinto classics in Kyoto. He had relatives in priestly Shinto families near Ise and had retained an interest in Shinto since his youth. During his days in Kyoto he wrote of a "natural *kami* way," an ancient way that was not influenced by Buddhism or Confucianism.

One way to understand Motoori is to see his thought as a combination of the work of Keichū and Kamo Mabuchi, through which he gave *Kokugaku* a distinctive character. His own expository work, especially on the *Kojiki*, gave his ideas an independent basis, because his predecessors had concentrated heavily on the *Manyōshū*. The manner of combination in his later work was part of his unique process of thought.

His writings unfold the development of his conception of *Kokugaku*. In 1771 he produced *Naobi no Mitama* (The Spirit of Straightening) as a general introduction to the Ancient Way. In 1786 he completed his commentary on the *Kami-yo* of the *Kojiki*. By 1786 he had also completed the first volume of his *Kojiki Den* as well as the *Tamaboko Hyakushu* (One Hundred Poems on the Way), a basic and straightforward exposition of the way, and the *Tama Kushige* (Jeweled Comb Box). The year 1786 seems to mark the most developed stage of his thought.

The Ancient Way, as he saw it, consisted of action itself that had been transmitted and maintained by the Imperial ancestral *kami* (*mioya no kami*). Although it was called a "Way," it was not a way in the sense of Taoism or Confucianism. The Way was the creation of the two *kami*, Izanami and Izanagi, through the two creating *kami*, Taka-mi-musubi and Kami-musubi. It was then completed by the *kami* of the sun, Amaterasu; transmitted by successive Emperors; and then reverently observed by the people. Because Japan was the place where the Way came into being, its possession of the Way distinguished it from all the nations of the world throughout history, symbolized most clearly by the single-line descent of the Imperial Family throughout all the ages.

Not only was this true of Japan's past, but it would also be true of Japan's future. The people were expected to reverence the Imperial ancestral *kami* by showing absolute loyalty to the Emperors, who in turn were to be benevolent to their subjects. Children must learn filial piety but along with wives and servants, must be treated compassionately. This is to follow the Way. Motoori claimed that ancient Japan was an ideal age compared, for example, with China. Because Chinese morality was not consistent with the Japanese spirit, he wished to see all traces of Chinese influence eliminated from Japanese society and culture. Only the Ancient Learning could be used to remove such influences. The key to his approach lay in seeking the vestiges of the age of the *kami*, which would be a norm for how things should be. He felt that his studies of the *Kojiki* confirmed that it was the source of the details of that era. Each legend of the age, explained philosophically, could reveal reality as it was, an astonishing hermeneutic and philosophy of history. He claimed to be setting forth in an objective way the consciousness of the ancient Japanese. This was the approach that produced the *Kojiki den*.

Motoori took at face value the account of Izanami and Izanagi giving birth to land. He considered *Takamagahara* to mean the sky, and he regarded the *kami* of the sun as the sun and at the same time as an Imperial *kami*. The doctrine of the sun *kami* becomes the center of his thought, treated in his view "objectively" but in reality with similar literalism to that of a Biblical or Islamic fundamentalist. Motoori was both an expositor of the Ancient Way and a deep believer in its truth. The kind of philosophical critique that Mabuchi might have applied to the *Kojiki* was not possible on the basis of Motoori's reverence for the texts. He could not read the Shinto classics symbolically, which would have been a concession to Chinese influence. He judged Mabuchi's reference to the unbroken Imperial line to be his deepest insight into the spirit of the ancient past and a symbol of the principle of his philosophy of nature. He was a devout believer in the ancient legends; therefore he argued that they should not be subjected to criticism, almost a unique stance in the history of Japanese literature.

This attitude stemmed from his belief that everything was a gift of the *kami* and that the highest form of attitude was that of the sincere heart (*magokoro*), a humanistic ideal far removed from Mabuchi's vision of manliness. In contrast to the more radical Mabuchi, Motoori's ideas tend to be restrained, conservative, and gradual in their development. He was, however, deeply influenced by the optimism he found in the *Kojiki*, namely, that in the matter of the coexistence of good and evil, life and death, life and goodness always prevail. This probably accounts for his lack of radical temperament. His deep religious faith may be traced to the combined influences of Dazai Learning, Pure Land Buddhism, and Suiga Shinto, each of which was characterized by fervent religious sentiments. Motoori was undoubtedly a complex albeit emotional thinker whose influence led him to be revered virtually as a *kami* in his own lifetime. Yet he had enormous intellectual prowess and a basic honesty, as illustrated by his exposition of the controversial passage of the *Engishiki* liturgy for the *Ōbarae* relating to the *kunitsu tsumi*. The earthly offenses (or, in older English, abominations) listed in the *norito* are usually translated as follows: "albinism, skin excrescences, the *tsumi* of violating one's own mother, the *tsumi* of violating one's own child, the *tsumi* of a mother violating her own child, the *tsumi* of a child's violating its mother, and the *tsumi* of transgression with animals."

Earlier commentators had avoided discussing these entirely. Confucian-influenced scholars referred to them as the "mother and child matters of the five elements" (*gogyō*), explaining it in terms of Chinese logic and metaphysics. Others treated them in terms of Confucian ethics. Violation meant not showing filial piety. Watarai Nobuyoshi (1615–1690) took them at face value and declared them to be prohibitions on sexual acts. Yamazaki Ansai (1618–1682) also accepted this view and rejected Urabe and those who treated them as analogies or metaphors. In his *Norito Ko*, *Kamo Mabuchi* did not like the Chinese approach either, but he inherited from Kada a different way of seeing meaning in some of the terms. *Shirobito* (literally, "white person" albinism) he took as a distortion of *shiragi-bito* (people of the Kingdom of Silla in Korea) and *kokuri-bito* (people of the Korean Kingdom of Koguryo). He therefore defined the *tsumi* as wrongs committed by Korean immigrants.

With what must have been startling originality, Motoori rejected all these in favor of the simple view that in antiquity these forms of *tsumi* existed, and that other explanations were far-fetched and unjustifiable. He declared that Mabuchi was mistaken in substituting the character *rai* for *mi* in his study and in interpreting the "*tsumi* of violating one's own mother" as the *tsumi* of the people of Silla and Koguryo. He pointed out that in the *Jokan* code (859–877), the term *kokumi* is written with three different characters but the reading is still *kokumi*. He thought it unlikely that the third character was a mistake for *rai*. In the Ise text of the *Engishiki* (901–923), the earthly *tsumi* are listed in a different order: "cutting living flesh, cutting dead flesh, violating one's mother, violating one's child, transgressions with animals, albinism, skin excrescences, drowning, and burning." Mabuchi's interpretation does not fit the fact that "violating one's mother" comes ahead of *shirobito* and *kokumi*. Violating one's mother has no apparent grammatical relationship to *shirobito* and *kokumi*. His further statement that sexual relations between mother and child were unheard of in the Imperial Court is irrelevant. Motoori declared that it could not be argued that such things did not occur among ordinary people simply because there are no references to them in the *Nihongi* and other ancient texts. They were written to report official matters and would not include references to the habits of ordinary people. He pointed to later and contemporary references concerning persons violating their own daughters. That such happened in the past can be confirmed by the listing of *tsumi* in the Great Purification

Prayer. There is reference in the *Kojiki* to a Great Purification held during the reign of Emperor Chuai. The phrase "sexual intercourse between a parent and a child" is included. It would thus be absurd to say that this referred to acts by immigrants from Silla and Koyuryo, because Korean immigration had not then commenced. This is a good instance of the directness of Motoori's methodology. Not only could he challenge the past, but with logic and philology he could also strengthen his own argument.

To conclude this brief summary of aspects of Motoori's thought that are relevant to the development of Shinto thought during the Edo period, it may be best to mention the work he completed in October 1798, *Uiyamabumi* (First Hike in the Mountains). This was composed three months after he had completed his commentary on the *Kojiki*. It is an exposition of his scholastic method and as such is an excellent introduction to both his work and the *Kokugaku* movement. He never actually used the term *Kokugaku*, preferring to speak of Imperial Country Learning (*mikunimanabi*), Imperial Learning (*kochogaku*), and Ancient Learning (*kogaku*). The work commences by explaining the essentials of Imperial Country Learning, which is four parts: (1) *Kami* study or *Michi* (way) study, which was based on the *kami-yo*, the earlier parts of the *Kojiki* and the *Nihongi*; (2) Antiquarian study (*yusokugaku*), which deals with government offices, ceremonies, and laws together with the study of ancient customs, costumes, and furniture; (3) Historical study, which commences with the study of the six national histories and other ancient works as well as books of later times; (4) Poetic studies, which include both poetry and prose together with the interpretation of poetic and prose works and the study of the origins and usages of the Japanese language.

Motoori considered part 1 to be the most important, the ancient way of the sun *kami* by which the Emperor rules the land, the true Way for the four seas and the nations of the world, which has been handed down only in the Imperial Country. It is based on evidence about the age of the *kami* recorded in the *Kojiki* and the *Nihongi*. Ancient Learning he defined as the study without influence of later ideas that disclose the origins of things in ancient times as recorded in the classics, which in effect equates it with Imperial Country Learning. He carefully explains his research methods, and points out omissions of earlier scholars, especially the distinction between exegetical or expository (*setsumei-gaku*) and normative study (*kihan-gaku*).

Setsumei-gaku is the exposition of the ancient texts. It begins with the clear rejection of Buddhist philosophical theories and Confucian moralistic explanations of human nature in favor of the traditions of the *kami* found in the *Nihongi* and the *Kojiki*. The purpose was to recreate the simplicity of ancient thought by distinguishing it from the influences that had overlaid it in later days. The ancient mind must be disclosed as it was then and followed. The only way to achieve full appreciation of the ancient poetic writing is by trying to compose poems modeled on that style.

Kihan-gaku is demonstrated in his effort to produce an exposition of the Ancient Way in terms of the *Kojiki* only. Motoori assigned greater importance to the *Kojiki* than to the *Nihongi*, which was contrary to the convention of his day. The *Nihongi* he judged to be overlaid by philosophy and morality, whereas the *Kojiki* remained a simpler and purer text. National Learning (which aimed at grasping the ancient mind through the ancient texts) was thus the study of the Ancient Way. It was not simply academic but had tremendous practical implications for both Japan and the world. The purpose of scholarship is to follow the way. The Japanese he considered as fortunate to have been born in the Imperial Country, where the true way, superior to all others on earth or in heaven, had been transmitted.

He applied the distinction between *setsumei-gaku* and *kihan-gaku* to poetry, claiming that although composing poetry modeled on the *Manyōshū* was a beginning for the study of the classic age, the text of the *Shinkokin shu* was the aesthetic ideal. More generally stated, along with exegetical annotation of poems, literary values can be derived from the ideal of *mono no aware*. This point raises the enormous and open question of how the Ancient Way and its study were related in the mind of Motoori to National Learning. A complex personality as well as an original thinker, he left a powerful legacy for Hirata in terms of both ideology and methodology.

Hirata Atsutane (1776–1843)

Hirata was the last of the four most prominent figures of the *Kokugaku* movement.[43] He developed a combination of theological and political concepts that became a valuable support to the goals of the Meiji Restoration. He transcended the thought of Motoori in three important respects, each of which was partly ideological in its import.

First, he carried the interpretation of the mythology much farther than Motoori and more in the direction of an ontological and substantive definition of *kami*. In discussing Motoori's account of the *Kami-yo* in the *Kojiki-Den*, Hirata argued that Ame-no-minaka-nushi-o-kami was a personified *kami* who existed before heaven and earth.

Second, with regard to life after death, he affirmed the existence of a world of souls (the "concealed" world) different from the interpretations of *Yomi-no-kuni* as Motoori lifted the idea from the *Kojiki*. The idea of a concealed world was based upon the separation of powers of the concealed and the manifest referred to in the myth of O-kuni-nushi-no-kami, who yielded his territory to Amaterasu (the manifest world) in return for the concealed world. This interpretation introduced a novel moralistic and life-after-death aspect to Shinto thought through transforming the Ancient Way of the manifold *kami* into something monotheistic and transcendent. The present thus became ephemeral, and the future became real. This all but stood Shinto on its head.

Third, Hirata tried to centralize Japanese ancestral reverence round the worship of the ancestral *kami* of the Imperial Family through arguments from the classics. Shinto as a national ancestral *kami* cult can trace its roots to this development. In this view of Shinto, Hirata held that the *kami* of Japan were world *kami* and that Shinto was therefore the basis of all world religion. In this way Hirata also stood on its head the idea of *honji-suijaku* of the Heian period. The *kami* had finally replaced the Buddha in prominence.

Philosophically, the second point is interesting because the distinction between manifest and concealed creates a dualism between the concealed and revealed (*yugen*) and the hidden and manifest (*inken*) in a way that introduced an element of dualism that brought Shinto closer to the basic tendencies of Western thought. Hirata's disciple, Nanri Yurin (1812–1864),[44] developed this, believing that there was unity in the highest levels of spirituality. In the *kami* nature of Ame-no-Mi-naka-nushi-no-kami he saw a return to this, which was manifest in the existence of an immortal spiritual realm. The essence of Shinto lay in the mind, not in words and deeds. Shinto was a doctrine of the spirit. Man was endowed with a *kami* nature; by perfecting conscience and performing good deeds, this nature could be restored. He could commune with the *kami* and become one with them. He could also bring prosperity and avert disaster. Although this is true in theory, in practice people are not like this; therefore, by enlightenment (*godō*) alone they cannot be in touch with the *kami* principle (*shin-ri*). Faith and dependence upon the *kami* are needed. Faith and sincerity would be rewarded. Therefore, prayer and purification are necessary.

Most important from the viewpoint of the development of Shinto thought, the potential for Imperialism in Motoori was cultivated by Hirata to become a powerful element in the political background to the Meiji Restoration.

Hirata Shinto and National Ideology during the Meiji Restoration

There were many intellectual aspects of the Meiji Restoration, but the influence of Hirata Shinto was one of the most decisive for the direction that Meiji Restoration ideology took. Numerous like-minded thinkers were involved, such as Hirata Kanetane (1790–1880) in Kyoto and Tamamatsu Misao (1810–1872, a student of Okuni Takamasa), who assisted Iwakura Tomomi in strongly advocating the restoration of Imperial Rule. In July 1867, Hirata Kanetake argued strongly with Iwakura for the revival of a Department of Shinto Affairs, insisting that the government should plan the elimination of Buddhism and commence with the removal of all Buddhist ceremonies from the Imperial Court. By December 1867 the policy of *saisei itchi* (unity of worship and administration), centered on Shinto, had been defined by Yano Harumichi (1823–1887) in his work *Kenkin sengo*.

Some of these developments have been discussed in this book in the sections on history and in the account of Shinto Taikyō. Points noted here are especially relevant to Hirata's influence. The restoration of Imperial Rule was proclaimed on 3 January 1868; by February, the Office of Shinto Affairs (*Jingi Jimukyoku*) was re-established. A *Dajōkan* statement of March 13 read: "Whereas the restoration of Imperial Rule is founded upon the achievements initiated by Emperor Jimmu, and whereas the nation is being restored to a polity of general renewal and unity of worship and administration, it is ordered that first of all, the Department of Shinto Affairs shall be revived and further that rites and sacrifices shall thereafter be performed." This was the first of a number of edicts and rules designed to destroy the *jingū-ji* through the clear separation of Buddhism and Shinto. "Shrine monks" of these establishments were ordered back to secular life, thereby purging shrines of Buddhist influences. Shinto had in effect been declared the state religion.

In 1869, the replaced *Jimukyoku* was elevated to the status of ministry, becoming the *Jingikan* as in the Nara age. Missionaries (*senkyō-shi*) of Shinto were sent nationwide; in this, followers of Hirata Shinto were extremely active in promoting the Great Teaching (*Taikyō*)[45] and the Great Way of Kami (*Kannagara no daidō*). Not only was Buddhism attacked but also Christianity, which showed signs of revival in Kyushu. The Ministry of Shinto Affairs was replaced by the Ministry of Religion (*Kyobushō*), in which the Office of Religious Instruction (*Kyodōshoku*) and the Institute of the Great Teaching (*Taikyōin*) carried out the task of re-indoctrinating the people. Buddhist priests were now welcomed to the indoctrination pressures exerted on Christian groups.

The Ministry of Religion promulgated the *Sanjo Kyōken*, three fundamental principles of instruction, on 28 April 1872:

Principle 1: Compliance with the spirit of reverence for *kami* and love of country

Principle 2: Clarification of the "Principle of Heaven" and the "Way of Man"

Principle 3: Exalting the Emperor and obeying the Imperial Court.

Shinto and Buddhist priests were appointed *kyōsei* (instructors) and placed in charge of religious instruction. Konoe Tadafusa (1838–1873), Director of Ceremonies at Ise Grand Shrine, and Senge Takatomi (1845–1917), Great High Priest (*Daigūji*) of Izumo, were selected for this work along with twenty-one Buddhist priests. The Buddhists included Koson of the *Higashi Hongan-ji* and Kosho of the *Nishi Hongan-ji*, receiving the opportunity to train their own instructors (although in fact Shinto priests were also included). The new organization was made into an educational institution for all officials engaged in religious instruction. It came to be known as the Great Teaching Institute (*Taikyō-in*). It was established in Kojimachi in Tokyo but later moved to the *Zojo-ji* temple in Shiba. Middle and small institutes were also set up, known as *chukyo-in* and *shokyo-in*, respectively. "Eleven Themes" and "Seventeen Themes" were drawn up for the training of the officials of religious instruction, to be topics for sermons and teaching.[46]

The Eleven Themes proclaimed by the Ministry of Shinto Affairs included basic themes from Hirata Shinto, including the following points: (1) *Kami* virtue and Imperial favor; (2) Immortality of the human soul; (3) Creativity of the *Amatsu Kami*; (4) Difference between the worlds of the visible and concealed; (5) Love of country; (6) *Kami* worship; (7) pacification of souls; (8) Lord and Subject; (9) Father and Son; (10) Husband and Wife; (11) *Obarae*.

The Seventeen Themes put forward by the *Taikyō-in* were as follows: (1) Imperial country and body politic (*kokutai*); (2) Renewal of Imperial Rule; (3) Immutability of the Way; (4) Adjusting organizations to the situation of the day; (5) Difference between man and animals; (6) The necessity to teach; (7) The necessity to learn; (8) Intercourse with foreign countries; (9) Rights and duties; (10) The use of mind and body; (11) Political institutions; (12) Civilization and enlightenment (*bunmei-kaika*); (13) Development of law; (14) National and civil law; (15) A strong economy and military (*fukoku-kyōhei*); (16) Taxation and labor levies; (17) Production and control of goods.

Tensions arose over the Buddhist use of the *honji-sujiaku*. They were found problematic because they were tacitly acknowledging the primacy of the *kami* over the Buddha. By 1875, the Buddhists had opted out. Shinto indoctrination as planned in 1868 seemed beyond realization; in the face of popular indifference or scorn, the program was finally abandoned and the *Taikyō-in* was abolished. The Shinto Taikyō did survive and continues to exist as a sect. But its power effectively vanished after 1875.

Buddhists began their own campaigns, and within the fragmented world of Shinto many problems began to emerge. There was the *Kanetane* school (originally associated with Hirata), the *Ōkuni* (*Takamasa*) school, and the *Dai-jinja* (*Izumo Taisha*) and Ise schools. Shinto also included Kurozumi-kyō and other Kyōha sects that boasted of historical founders. Although a *Shinto Jimukyoku* had been formed and the *Shinto Daikyō-in* had been established, the system was unworkable in practice. The *Kurozumi* and *Shusei* sects received independent recognition, and in 1888 Tenri-kyō was founded. Unable to deal with these changes, the Ministry of Religion was abolished and the Office of Shinto Affairs (*Shinto Jimukyoku*) was transferred to the Ministry of Home Affairs (*Naimushō*). The practice of Shinto priests serving as indoctrinators was abolished in January 1882.

Why did the Shinto indoctrination program fail in spite of its seeming potential? One explanation is that the program was not fully consistent with the needs of Japan at the time, namely, "civilization and enlightenment." Fukuzawa Yukichi (1834–1901), the leading academic of the era, argued in his famous *Bunmei ron no gairyaku* (An Outline of the Theory of Civilization, written in 1875) that Japan was behind the West and had a lot of catching up to do. He argued further that Shinto was unsuited to achieve the kind of modernization necessary to be on equal terms with Western nations. His views had a softening effect on the attack on Christianity, and his own contempt for Shinto had major implications in academic circles for attempts to use Shinto ideologically. Fukuzawa was typical of a body of thought that showed considerable disdain for numerous aspects of the Japanese tradition, Shinto being one.

A second reason may have been that Shrine Shinto in 1868 was itself too immature (having been only just separated from Buddhism) and intellectually inadequate as a religion to deal with the problems facing the Meiji government. Hirata Shinto was the only real academic base from which an ideology could be developed; and although Hirata's thought was quite well formulated, it was still evolving. It lacked clearly defined concepts that addressed the entire range of ideas to be covered by a local ideology, so little could be achieved. The influence of Hirata Shinto as an ideology was limited to its early appeal because it was not substantial enough to become a complete ideological tool.

A third possible reason was that within Shrine Shinto itself there was controversy and disagreement. Several particularly difficult areas obstructed a unified approach. For example, there were problems regarding the understanding of the Japanese classics and some of Hirata's interpretations of the myths about the origins of heaven and earth. The opening expression "*ametsuchi no hajime no toki*" ("at the time of the beginning of heaven and earth") was interpreted, for example, by Motoori to mean that Ame-no-mi-naka-nushi-no-kami and the two *kami* under him had existed before heaven and earth as creator *Kami*. He developed this into a doctrine in his *Koshi Seibun* (A Composition of Ancient History), in which he argued that the three *kami* were central creators. The Department of Shinto Affairs (1869) accepted Hirata's view, which was included in the first article of the Five-Article Regulations on the Compilation of Religious Books issued by the *Taikyō-in* in July 1873:

That portion of the *Kojiki* dealing with the first seven generations of the *kami* and the Age of the Kami book in the *Nihongi* down to the phrase: *Kami* were born in Heaven and Earth, enable us to understand clearly the *kami* principle of the creation of Heaven and Earth and the evolution of the myriad things. Since they are the foundation stones of the fundamental doctrine of the Imperial Way, not one word is to be deleted from or added to those passages.

These kinds of controversies highlighted a second area of disagreement, namely, the natural incompatibility between conservative and progressive tendencies. Hirata Shinto thinkers such as Okuni Yakamasa did display progressive and somewhat liberal ideas. They also supported the ideals of "civilization and enlightenment" but were opposed by more conservative restorationists. Fukuba Bisei (1831–1907), Assistant Director of the Mission Board, was on the progressive side; although he was in charge of Shinto missionaries, he also advocated the incorporation of useful foreign ideas. For this he was relieved of his duties both in the Department of Shinto Affairs and in the Board of Shinto Missionaries. The progressive element within Shinto and the missionary leadership were eliminated simultaneously.

A test case that arose illustrated just how widely divergent views existed concerning the question of which *kami* should be revered in the Office of Shinto Affairs.[47] In 1873 the Great Teaching Institute was set up and the three creator *kami* and Amaterasu were enshrined. However, when a new shrine was built in Hibiya in 1875, Senge Takatomi advocated that Okuni-nushi-no-kami be included, because he was not only the *kami* who presided over the "concealed rule" of heaven and ruled over the various *kami* under Heaven, but he was also the *kami* who passed judgment upon the souls of men after death. Tanaka Yoritsune (1836–1897) and others opposed this move on behalf of the Ise Shrine. They argued, among other things, that Okuni-nushi-no-kami was a kind of imitation of Jesus and was in that form inappropriate to be included with the *kami* already enshrined.

This was further complicated by the attack of Ochiai Naoki (1852–1934) in his *Shinto Yosho Ben* (Criticism of the Shinto Yosho) on Senge Takatomi's *Shinto Yosho* (The Essentials of Shinto) written in July 1880. In the Preface to Ochiai's book, Miwata Takafusa writes of Senge as a Great Instructor-Rectifier who claims that Shinto theology is weak because Okuni-nushi-no-kami is not worshipped in the Office of Shrine Affairs. He added that there is something improper about the souls of Emperors being judged after death. Some of Senge's followers had second thoughts on the topic. Finally, an Imperial Edict of 1881 decreed that the *kami* and Imperial Spirits enshrined in the Imperial Palace would be worshipped in the Office of Shinto Affairs, which in effect separated mainline Shinto and made way for State Shinto.

Perhaps the major reason for the failure of the proposed program of religious indoctrination envisaged by the Meiji government was the implicit attack on religious freedom, an issue that by then had become as sensitive in Japan as it was in the West. The Christian question in early Meiji times illustrates the point. Although attacks on Christianity were not of the brutal kind used in the early 16th century under the Tokugawa government, greater coercive power was used to discourage Christianity. International reactions to this situation during the Iwakura Mission to Europe threatened to destroy its work, and this finally led to the repeal of the edict against Christianity. However, the claims of Shinto as expounded by the followers of Hirata—that it was indeed a religion with teachings about an afterlife, purification for the remission of sins, and other elements of theology—were criticized by many within Japan who argued that the government's Three Principles of Instruction[48] were artificial. Fukuda Gyokai (1806–1888), a leading priest of the Jōdo sect, in his book *Sanjo no Guben* (Humble Appraisal of the Three Principles of Instruction) declared that after chanting the name of Buddha for almost eighty years, he could not suddenly change and chant *kami* and love of country instead. Most of the strong criticisms came from Western-trained minds. Nakamura Masano (1832–1891),[49] after receiving an education in the United Kingdom, returned to Japan in 1868 and became professor in the Shizuoka *Gakumonjō* (Center for Learning). He wrote in August 1871 in reply to a question raised by Mita Hoko, the official in charge of the Board of Shinto Missionaries in the Shizuoka Han: "I am unhappy about the phrase 'one oath for government and religion.' Government is one thing and religion another; and they should be kept apart. The phrase is Chinese, not European."

Mori Arinori (1847–1889)[50] wrote a book entitled *Religious Freedom of Japan* in 1872 while he was studying in the United States. He argued that among cultured nations, freedom of conscience and freedom of religion are essential for progress. They are not merely right. He condemned the Ministry of Religious Affairs and the idea of forcing an artificial fusion of religion on people. He judged the entire project as incomprehensible as he found it reprehensible.

In addition to these problems within Shinto, attacks from Buddhists were increasing.[51] On the matter of the interpretation of the classics, they argued forcibly that the new Shinto ideas were totally inconsistent with older received doctrines. They insisted that the *Kojiki* was obscure in any case and noted perceptively and cleverly that Hirata's views appeared to have the flavor of Christianity, which implied that they were, in principle, dangerous. Buddhists also attacked the forced separation of Buddhism from Shinto and had some initial success in restricting the religious influence of Shinto.

Buddhists reacted even more aggressively (as many still do) to any attempt at bringing religion under government control, claiming that it was unreasonable to establish political control over religious affairs and religious beliefs. Shimaji Mokurai (1838–1911) was a leading intellectual of the Jōdo-Shin sect. He argued for the separation of religion and government. He offered thorough and detailed criticisms of the Three Principles of Instruction, echoing sentiments that they were artificial and not derived from genuine religious beliefs or feelings. Other Western-trained minds added their weight. By the time the Iwakura Mission encountered criticism in Europe of Japan's backward attitude toward religious freedom, the movement for religious indoctrination was coming to an end.

These factors, among others, led the government to formulate a view of Shinto that lifted it from the purview of religion and identified it as a cultural system that was simply an ancillary to citizenship. It was claimed that it had no impact on personal religious beliefs, provided they did not conflict with the proper duties of a citizen of the Japanese state. Consequently, although Hirata's thought did play a role in the Meiji Restoration, the policy that was finally developed represented a compromise of conflicting interests. This resulted in the emergence of State Shinto, and with it the demise of any possible intellectual and religious developments in mainline Shinto. These circumstances remained until long after 1946.

Hirata's Thought and Christianity

The limitations of Hirata's thought are further underlined by the misty and exceedingly complicated relationship between Hirata and Christianity.[52] Numerous scholars pointed to Christian influences within Hirata's ideas. During the Meiji period, these were identified in a more general way and were used to discredit him. Two areas were highlighted.

First, his views of creation were severely attacked as "neo-Christian" by the scholar Sasaki Yucho. In numerous writings Sasaki drew attention to a number of points. In *Tama no mihashira* (True Pillar of the Soul) and the *Kodō taii* (Outline of the Ancient Way), Hirata's alleged Christian views were identified and discussed. Sasaki took one example from the opening lines of the *Kojiki*. He claimed that in translating "*Ametsuchi hajime no toki*" as "in the beginning of Heaven and Earth," Hirata's reading of *hajime* as "beginning" (as Motoori did) avoided the idea of "creation" but still imposed an alien meaning. The word simply meant "parting," which was proved by another phrase in the preface to the *Kojiki*: "Heaven and Earth first parted and the three *kami* initiated creation." Sasaki was arguing that the native Japanese tradition did not think in terms of a doctrine of creation, but rather in terms of a cycle of birth and coming into being akin to Buddhist cosmology. The story of the moon *kami* (told in the Emperor Kenzo era of the *Nihongi*) includes the phrase that Taka-mi-musubi-no-kami "molded Heaven and Earth." Sasaki argued that the meaning was simply "molding and hardening" and in no way could be used to support a doctrine of creation. Consequently, he claimed that Hirata was following misinterpretations he had acquired from Motoori, which were the result of Christian influences.

Sasaki's argument, which begged the entire question of a Buddhist (Chinese) versus non-Buddhist reading of the Japanese classics, was controversial enough to be damaging to Hirata Shinto. Motoori had argued that embedded in the Japanese classics there was a different and non-Chinese view of the origins of the universe that could be called the native Japanese view, and he had devoted himself to defining it. Sasaki made an issue of the fact that the basic texts of the Japanese tradition were not specific in meaning or consistent in content, and that to define a doctrine based on those early passages (as Hirata tried to do) was bound to be controversial.

In his *Jūichi kendai roku hyo* (Criticism of the Eleven Themes) Sasaki further claimed that the term *Heaven* was intentionally dropped from the July 1873 proclamation of the *Taikyō-in*, in contradiction to the mythology that refers to "Heaven and Earth" as one. These lines of argument, as well as others, gave adequate grounds for the ironic claim that in trying to create a theology out of the Japanese classics, Hirata was guilty of confusing *kami* with barbarians. These contentions were sufficient to undermine attempts to make Hirata Shinto orthodox Shinto teaching.

Hirata was also attacked for his views on the idea of life after death. It was claimed that his understanding of "concealed and the mysterious" had developed under the influence of Christian ideas, and that these—along with the creator *kami* idea—constituted the basic thought of his school, both of which were alien to the Japanese tradition. Hence the destiny or fate of the soul after death also became controversial. Within the Hirata school, this issue was far from settled. The idea of judgment after death was more explicitly Christian in origin (although Hirata was not totally uninfluenced by Buddhism). This tended to support Hirata's claim about the primacy of *O-kuni-nushi-no-kami* over other *kami*. Although Buddhists had little to say on this, it raised problems within Shinto itself. The Senge family of Izumo supported this position, but it met with fierce opposition from the authorities at Ise.

The Meiji government had failed to assess the complexity of the problem. The problems were legion. Desperate to establish the orthodoxy of Motoori and Hirata, in its *Kyōsho henshū taii* (editorial guide for the preparation of religious textbooks) it had declared that the teachings of Motoori and Hirata would be considered definitive of orthodox Shinto. Not only was there no clear consistency and agreement between them, but in many areas there were huge differences of interpretation. In the face of the disarray and disagreement of the Shinto camp and the opposition of the Buddhists and other groups, the government was forced to retreat, eventually settling for the approach that Shinto was not a religion but a folk way that all citizens could be required to follow without impugning their freedom of religion. It solved the impasse for the Meiji government but set back the spiritual development of Shinto to a degree that has taken over a century to reverse.

More recent studies[53] have demonstrated that Hirata did draw upon Christian sources explicitly, but they have highlighted the issue of why he chose to do so. This seems potentially even more controversial. Professor Richard Devine published a valuable and interesting article in the *Monumenta Nipponica* (Spring 1981) on the question of what sources Hirata used and how they influenced his thought. He illustrates the point well by showing parallel texts. The deep question is whether Hirata was influenced by the Christian ideas or whether he was using them to express ideas that he already held. According to Devine, the religious teachings of Hirata survive today in the rituals of the *Yasukuni Jinja*. There is no doubt that aspects of Hirata Shinto were used effectively during the early Meiji era and that their use prevented any further development of the line of thought that Hirata himself may have wished to follow. His thought was frozen for the purposes of the emerging State Shinto, therefore many of his ideas were left only partly developed. This is, of course, only one view.

Arguments have issued from both sides (Christian and non-Christian) to argue the merits and defects of Hirata's thought. In either case, the conclusions are unhappy if the purposes are propagandist. If Hirata was drawing upon Christian sources, then Christianity could be held responsible for certain aspects of Hirata's nationalistic tendencies. If he was simply using Christian sources to express his own ideas, he was less than a Shinto purist. In either case, the result is useless to the party advancing the claim. It seems, based on historical evidence, that he was aware of Christian writings and that he made use of them (perhaps as other Japanese thinkers did with other Western sources) to suit his own purposes. The stated objectives of his thought would be the best instrument to assess his reasons for making use of these sources. But because his thought lacks clarity in many respects, the questions of why and how he used Christian sources may have to remain unanswered.

NOTES

1. Nakamura Hajime, *The Ways of Thinking of Eastern Peoples* (East-West Center Press, Honolulu, 1964), pp. 434–449.

2. Tenkai was favored by Tokugawa Ieyasu, for whom he invented the term *Tōshō* (sun deity of the East). The name was used for Ieyasu after his death.

3. For information, see Kageyama Haruki, *Shinto Bijutsu, Nihon no Bijutsu*, Vol. 18 (Shibundo, Tokyo, 1967). English version: *The Arts of Shinto, Arts of Japan*, Vol. 4 (Weatherhill, Tokyo, 1973), Chapter 7, "Art of the Sanno Cult," pp. 104–118.

4. Records of *Yamatohime no Mikoto* date to the Kamakura period.

5. *Katsuragi Hozan-ki* (The Record of the Sacred Mountain of Katsuragi).

6. *Koro Kujitsu-den* (An Account of Truths Orally Transmitted by the Ancients).

7. Watarai Yukitada (1236–1305), *Tenchi Reiki-Ki* (On the Awesome Energy of Heaven and Earth).

8. *Nisho Daijingū Reiki-ki* (On the Awesome Beauty of the Grand Shrines of Ise).

9. Jihen (1795–1869), *Kuji Hongi Gengi* (Secret Meaning of the Kuji Gengi), and *Toyoashirara Jimpu Waki* (Records of the Divine Wind in Japan).

10. Chikafusa's *Gengen-shū* was an account of the origins of Shinto and Ise compiled around 1337.

11. The term *kanjō* was used in connection with the *sokui girei* (Imperial accession rites), specifically of the *sokui kanjō*—a little-studied Buddhist ordination rite that was part of the *sokui no rei*. Kamikawa Michio, "Accession Rituals and Buddhism in Medieval Japan," *Japanese Journal of Religious Studies* 17, no. 2–3 (June–September 1990): 243–280

12. Nichiren coined the expression *kamikaze* (divine wind) in reference to the storms that aborted the attempted Mongol invasion of Japan.

13. Yoshida Kanetoyo, *Miyaji Hiji Kuden* (An Account of the Oral Transmission among the Masters of Ceremonies at the Imperial Palace).

14. Yoshida Kanetomo, *Shinto Taii* (The Basics of Shinto) and *Yuiitsu Shinto Myobo Yoshu* (Collection of Important Passages Relating to the System of Unique Shinto).

15. Yoshida Kanemigi, *Nijūnisha Chushiki* (Notes on the Twenty-Two Shrines).

16. For a discussion of the development of Honji-Suijaku theory in Pure Land thought, see Matsunaga, *The Buddhist Philosophy of Assimilation* (Sophia University, Tokyo, 1969), pp. 274–284.

17. *Tsukai Sankeiki* (records of Tsukai's pilgrimages to the Grand Shrines of Ise, composed around 1287).

18. *Toyoashihara Jimpu Waki.*

19. The *Engishiki* (Procedures or Ceremonies of the Engi era, compiled by order of Emperor Daigo between 905 and 927).

20. The primacy of Ise was established later by the popular *Okagemairi*, which brought millions to Ise.

21. *Daijingū Shozoji-ki* (Record of Major Incidents Related to Ise Shrine, between 5 B.C. and 1069 C.E.).

22. See my discussion of the Nara period in "Nara Period Shinto (710–794)" in Chapter 1 of this book.

23. From: Mufu Dogyo (1226–1312) of the Rinzai sect of Zen in his *Shaseiki-shu*, a collection of sayings that point to the truth of Buddhism, composed in 1283.

24. *Zo Ise Nisho Daijingū Ho Kihon-gi* (a description of the construction of the two Shrines at Ise compiled by a priest of the Outer Shrine).

25. *Shinto Gobushō*: these texts were a Watarai family memoir concerning the origins and practices of the Grand Shrines of Ise. Although the Canon professed to distinguish Shinto from all other cults, it permitted a certain degree of syncretism in order to make its teachings acceptable to ordinary people.

26. Watarai Ieyuki, *Ruiju Jingi Hongen* (Account of the Origins of the Kami). This was a fifteen-volume account of the teachings and traditions of Ise Shrine written in 1320.

27. Fujiwara Seika (1561–1619) was an early neo-Confucian scholar of the Edo period.

28. Hayashi Razan (1583–1657) was a disciple of Fujiwara Seika. The influence of Hayashi's value system remains visible in contemporary Japanese devotion to

the authority of hierarchy. Absolute obedience to company requirements to live away from home and family indefinitely (as in the case of Japan's 250,000 *tanshin-funin*, salaried workers in this category) is hard to explain in any other way.

29. Chu Hsi (Zhu Xi: see Wing-tsit Chan, *Sourcebook of Chinese Philosophy*, Princeton University Press, 1963, for texts) was the greatest of the neo-Confucian thinkers. See Fung Yu-lan, *A Short History of Chinese Philosophy* (Free Press, Glencoe, 1966), pp. 270 ff.

30. Yamaga Sokō (1622–1685) was a Confucian scholar (*Shushigaku*), military scientist, and historian who combined Shinto myths with Confucian cosmology to stress the identity of the Imperial Way with the Way of Heaven.

31. Regarding Wang-Yangming (1472–1529), see Wing-tsit Chan, *Sourcebook*, pp. 654–691.

32. Nakae Toju (1608–1648).

33. Kumazawa Banzan (1619–1691) was a disciple of Nakae.

34. Ito Jinsai (1627–1705) founded the *Kokigaku* (ancient meaning studies) school. See also Yoshikawa Kojiro, *Jinsai, Sorai, Norinaga* (Toho Gakkai Publications Tokyo).

35. F. H. Bradley, *Appearance and Reality* (Allen and Unwin, London, 1983); *Ethical Studies* (Oxford University Press, 1876).

36. J. R. McEwan, *The Political Writings of Ogyū Sorai* (Cambridge University Press, 1962). Ogyū Sorai founded the *Kobunjigaku* (ancient language studies) school.

37. Dazai Jun (1680–1747), *Dokugo* (Solitary Words).

38. Hattori Nankaku (1683–1759) was a scholar, painter, and disciple of Ogyū.

39. Keichū (1640–1701), *Keichū Zenshū*, ed. Sasaki Nobutsana, 9 vols. (Osaka, 1926–1927). Typical of his approach was his rejection of Buddhistic interpretation of the famous poem by Yamanoe no Okura in Section 6 of the *Manyōshū*. Keichū's version read:

Onoko ya mo	Should a man's existence
munashiharubeki	Have proved so meaningless
yorozuyo ni	That he will not have made a name
kataritsugubeki	That will endure
na wa tatezu shite	For a myriad of ages

This was in contrast to the earlier:

Hito nareba	Because I am mortal,
munnashikarubeshi	I must die.

He saw this as a simple ancient response to death without any moral or metaphysical significance being attached to it.

40. Kada Azumamaro (1669–1736), *Shin'yōshū* (1728), *Kada Zenshū* (1928).

41. Kamo Mabuchi (1697–1769). His main works were *Kanji ko jo* (Preface to the Study of Poetic Epithets); *Manyō ko* (Study of the Manyōshū), and *Norito ko jo* (Preface to the Study of Shinto Liturgy), *Kokinshu* (Anthology of Ancient and Modern Times), *Hyakunin Isshu* (One Hundred Poems by One Hundred Poets). He compiled a Japanese dictionary around 935.

References in the discussion are to the following sources: *Manyōshū kai tsushaku narabi shakurei jo* (Preface to General Interpretation of the Manyōshū with Examples) (*Kamo Mabuchi Zenshū* IV, pp. 495–496); *Manyōshū ko jo, hitotsu* (Zenshū XII, p. 48; X, pp. 311, 361); *Manyō ko* (Study of the Manyōshū), Preface to Scroll 6 (*Zenshū* XII, p. 54); *Manyō ko jo*, Vol. 1 (*Zenshu* XII, p. 49); *Koku-i ko* (*Zenshū* X, p. 375); *Agatai shugen roku* (Collected Utterances at Agatai) or the *Koku-i to* (On the Spirit of the Nation).

42. Sources include the following: Matsuoka Tsunetsugu, *Motoori Norinaga* (Okayama Shōten, Tokyo, 1911); Kobayashi Hideo, *Motoori Norinaga* (Shinchosha, Tokyo, 1965); Tahara Tsuguo, *Motoori Norinaga* (Kodansha, Tokyo, 1968); Matsumoto Shigeru, *Motoori Norinaga* (Harvard University Press, 1970). He should not be considered as Murdoch portrayed him in his history of Japan, as a cynical manipulator of public sentiments through a nihilistic philosophy in which no reasonable person could believe simply because he wanted to reject Buddhism and Confucianism.

Texts referred to include: *Tama katsuna* (Jeweled Wicker Basket), *Motoori Norinaga Zenshu* (Enlarged Edition of the Collected Works of Motoori Norinaga), Vol. 8 (Yoshikawa Kobunkan, Tokyo, 1937–1938), p. 59; *Tama katsuma* (*Motoori Norinaga Zenshu* VII, p. 440). Arguments have been put forward that because the National Learning movement was concerned with Japanese uniqueness, its scholars rejected European styles of analysis (such as they knew) and pioneered something new. National Learning is not unique in its methodology. It is similar to the German *Philologie* of the nineteenth century and the *Form-Geshichte* movement of Biblical scholarship that arose around the same time. They were both concerned with historical origins to understand the *sitz im leben* in which the documents were composed and to understand them linguistically and hermeneutically as a reconstruction of the consciousness of ancient times.

43. Sources include Tahara Tsuguo, *Hirata Atsutane* (Yoshikawa Kyobunkan, Tokyo, 1963); Watanabe Kinzo, *Kirata Atsutane Kenkyū* (Tokyo, 1942); *Hirata Zenshu*, 15 vols. (Hakubunkan, Tokyo, 1911–1918).

44. Nanri Yurin (1812–1864) was a Shinto scholar from Saga Prefecture.

45. See Shinto Taikyō discussion.

46. *Sanjo Kyōken*: for general discussion of these issues, see Tokushige Asakichi, *Ishin seiji shukyo shi kenkyu* (Study of the Political and Religious History of the Restoration) (Isshin Seiji Shukyo-Kenkyū, Tokyo, February 1935). These ideas were expressed in works such as *Shinkoyo yoshi ryakkai* (Brief Explanation of the Essentials of Kami Doctrine) written by Konoe Tadafusa and Senge Takatomi (1873).

47. The *Shinden Saishin Ron* (Debate on the Kami Worshiped in the Shrine of the Office of Shinto Affairs) in the *Gyokuroku* collection of the *Mukyu kai Bunko* is the central source on the issue.

48. *Sanjo taii* (Outline of the Meaning of the Three Principles of Instruction) was written by Yano Harumichi (1875).

49. Jerry K. Fisher, "Nakamura Keiu: The Evangelical Ethic in Asia," in Robert J. Miller, ed., *Religious Ferment in Asia* (1974).

50. Regarding Mori Arinori (1847–1889), see Ivan Parker Hall, *Mori Arinori* (1973).

51. The most severe attacks on Mori Arinori are found in the following texts: (1) *Ketsuja Mondo* (Questions and Answers on Identifying Heresy) in the first issue

of *Kodo sosho* (Collection of Studies on the Way) published in 1870; (2) *Shingaku Benko* (Definition of Kami Learning) by Sasaki Yucho (1870 and 1874); (3) *Juichi Kendai roku hyo* (Criticism of Eleven Themes) by Sasaki Yucho (1874); (4) *Wayo Shinden* (Divine Myths in Japan and the West) by Sasaki Yucho (1875); (5) *Sanjo Bengi* (Analysis of the Three Principles of Instruction) by Shimaji Mokurai (included in the *Hoshi sodan*, 1874–1875).

52. The question of Christian influences on Hirata is a controversial topic. See Ebisawa Aramichi *Christianity in Japan* (International Christian University, 1960–66) in Japanese and Richard Devine, "Hirata Atsutane and Christian Sources," in *Monumenta Nipponica* (Spring 1981) for further reading suggestions.

53. Paradoxically, some Christian thinkers would like to claim that Christian influences were important during the Meiji era and before, and that Hirata had borrowed numerous ideas. Consequently, his thought ceases to be purely Japanese or totally *Kokugaku*. Other thinkers accepted the possibility that the same influences on Hirata were indirectly responsible for the intolerance of Meiji leaders in certain regards and for the ultra-nationalism that has been attributed to them. Could it be that Kokka Shinto was modeled on the idea of the Western "State Church" as found in older European nations? This dilemma illustrates some of the dangers of the loose attribution of cause-and-effect ideas on intellectual history without an adequate theory of the nature of cultural influence.

Hirata was also very likely influenced by Roman Catholic dogma, which was then proscribed in Japan. How ironic it would be if it were proved (as some have suggested) that the worst aspects of State Shinto drew their impetus from the intolerance of Japanese religion on the part of some Roman Catholic missionaries!

Chapter 10

Shinto Ideas and Western Thought

This closing section is a brief discussion of aspects of Shinto presented in Western concepts. I am commencing from the premise that Shinto has within it all the elements found universally in religion and de facto in Western religion; but because many of these are not verbalized, they must be inferred through the study of rituals and their meaning. Therefore, I have tried in an exploratory way to be philosophically and theologically suggestive by conducting the discussion in the traditional categories of ethics and metaphysics. The discussion is presented largely in the form of my own personal observations rather than as completed arguments and fully developed positions. Some of these might suggest ideas worth further research or examination by Western scholars of religion in general and Japanese religions in particular.

Shinto has been judged by many of its critics to be a primitive religion. I have alluded to this in the introduction and elsewhere, and suffice to say I take issue with that view. One of the crucial arguments against it is the two-pronged argument based on the record of two "higher religions" in Japan, Buddhism and Christianity. On the one hand there is the apparent failure of Christianity to edge aside a "primitive religion," which has shown remarkable vitality in the age of artificial intelligence and supersonic travel. On the other hand there is the historical reality regarding Buddhism, which calls for explanation. Why did Buddhism require six centuries to become "naturalized" if it was merely encountering a "primitive religion"? The most successful missionary records of the higher religions have been in cultures where the local traditions were less sophisticated. Consequently, Shinto cannot be classified easily under either of the headings of conventional wisdom. Clearly, Shinto is worthy of the time and effort required for study. Perhaps it is most simply described as the oldest religious tradition of the world's seventh continent!

SHINTO AND ETHICS

One of the most common criticisms of Shinto is that it has no system of ethics similar to those of Judaism or Christianity and that consequently it offers no guidance for life.[1] This is usually used as further evidence of its primitiveness. It is indeed true that there is no written equivalent to the *Pentateuch* or the *Eightfold Path*. However, to claim that there is no ethical content to Shinto whatsoever is to argue simultaneously from an inadequate understanding of Shinto and from a narrow view of the origin and nature of values and ethics.

In the current dialogue of world religions, Shinto representatives are asked from time to time to express views on international issues. When their opinions and idea are expressed, the elements of a system of ethics are made explicit. Such a system is not being created or copied. It is being drawn from the resources of the tradition and formulated to meet the needs of the age. Some preliminary remarks are needed about the nature of ethics in order to set this part of the discussion into perspective.

The Nature of Ethics

Systems of ethics are not like suits of clothes. They cannot be designed, manufactured, and then worn. They evolve and develop with the growth and development of the civilizations they serve.[2] In this regard they do not change rapidly; rather, they adapt slowly to external change or are modified to address new circumstances. Consider the evolution of ethics within the Judaeo-Christian tradition. (1) Primitive Christianity had no value system other than that of Judaism, from which it emerged. Jesus of Nazareth did not add anything new to the values of Judaism. He merely identified strands of the tradition that had been obscured by Pharisaic legalism and re-emphasized them. (2) The Christian Church spent its few centuries dealing with metaphysical issues and did not begin formulating moral rules and ecclesiastical laws until well into the fourth century, largely under the influence of Augustine. (3) The idea that there is a set of "Christian ethics" issued by the founder is untrue both historically and in terms of how value systems develop. Indeed, it is equally arguable that there was a large degree of stoicism integrated into early Christian thought—if Tertullian,[3] an early Christian thinker, is to be considered typical of his age. (4) If the differences in opinion over topics such as birth control are taken into consideration, several systems of ethics can claim the title "Christian": Roman Catholic, Reformed, Protestant, and so forth, and these certainly do not agree on many matters. The cases of Buddhism and Confucianism are more simple. The *Four Noble Truths* and the *Eightfold Path* are the core of Buddhist values; but if the development and expansion of Buddhism are examined carefully, it becomes clear that Buddhism amended many of its precepts and that the development of *Mahayana* and *Tantrayana* made this both necessary and possible. Confucian and neo-Confucian values were not entirely identical, and Japan's adaptation of the neo-Confucian thought of Chu Hsi created yet another variety. But these changes took long decades to complete.

Ethics in the Japanese tradition have been fed from several sources, Buddhism being one, Confucianism being another, but Shinto being the foundation. Shinto provided the idea of purification as the underlying value around which others were organized. The other traditions seemed more concerned with moral issues, although—as our discussion of the worldview of the New Religions demonstrated—ethics and metaphysics are thoroughly integrated. The moral values embedded in Shinto are acquired by imitation and not by memorization, which is the custom of traditional societies. One additional factor must be noted. The Western tradition sees man as created by a God who issues humanity with a moral code. Shinto has clung tenaciously to the idea that humanity is in some way biologically descended from the *kami* and therefore possesses something of a divine awareness. From these ideas, its value system is derived.

Moral Sense Theories and Kannagara

If Shinto ethics were to be classified, it is clear that they would not belong to rationalistic types of Western theory (whether deontological or utilitarian) but rather to a group of theories that would be a minority in the Western tradition, the moral sense theories. These are associated with the names of Francis Hutcheson, David Hume, and Adam Smith (the latter being known better for his innovative writings in the field of political economy). These thinkers held the common view that reason cannot lead human beings to action and that therefore some kind of intervening moral sense is required to lead people to act. This they identified as the moral sense, which was one among various other senses. The idea of a moral sense implies that ethics need not be equated with written codes of rules.

Hutcheson was the first of the three to expound the new theory, which bears a striking resemblance to what Motoori Norinaga said in Japan at roughly the same time. Hutcheson identified several human senses:

Objects, actions or events obtain the name of *good*, or *evil*, according as they are the causes or occasions, mediately or immediately, of a grateful, or ungrateful perception to some sensitive nature.

If we may call every determination of our minds to receive ideas independently on our will, and to have perceptions of pleasure and pain, A SENSE, we shall find many other *senses* beside those commonly explained.

The fourth class (of senses) we may call the *moral sense*, by which "we perceive virtue or vice, in ourselves, or others." This is plainly distinct from the former class of perceptions, since many are strongly affected with the fortunes of others, who seldom reflect upon virtue or vice, in themselves, or others, as an object: as we may find in natural affection, compassion, friendship or even general benevolence to mankind, which connects our happiness or pleasure with that of others, even when we are not reflecting upon our own temper, nor delighted with the perception of our own virtue.[4]

Motoori Norinaga made the following similar observation on ethics:

Human beings having been produced by the spirit of the two creative *kami* are naturally endowed with the knowledge of what they ought to do and what they ought to refrain from. It is unnecessary for them to trouble their heads with systems of morality. . . . If a system of morals were necessary, men would be inferior to animals, all of whom are endowed with the knowledge of what they ought to do, only in an inferior degree to man.[5]

It is interesting to note that after dealing with moral sense, Hutcheson goes on to identify a fifth sense, namely, a sense of honor. Its opposite is a sensation of shame.[6]

This argument differs from the moral sense theory of the West in one significant aspect, which is unique to Shinto. It is assumed that man is a biological descendant of the *kami* and that therefore human beings naturally know good from evil. This position is reminiscent of the Stoics of classical times, who saw the divine spark within men as something to be ignited or revived. Whether the position is similar to moral sense theories or to Stoicism, it can be argued that it is at least akin to recognized forms of moral theory. Arguments that Shinto has no ethics rest upon only one view of the nature of ethics.

In a similar vein, Hirata Atsutane made the observation that the Japanese "have been brought into existence through the creative spirits of the sacred ancestral *kami* and are each and every one, in spontaneous possession of the *kannagara-no-michi*. This means that we are equipped naturally with the virtues of reverence for the *kami* for rulers and parents, with kindness towards wife and children and with the moral principles which in Confucianism are called the five great ethical principles."[7] To follow these in a natural way, he declares, is to conform to the teaching of the *kami*.

There is also the implication that human nature is basically good. In neo-Confucian thought this is the theory of *seizensetsu*. A Japanese proverb puts it this way: "*Honshin ni oite wa akunin wa inai*" ("In their heart of hearts, no one is really evil"). The opposite theory, that human nature is fundamentally evil, is the doctrine of *seiakusetsu*. Doctrines that assume evil in human nature take a different view of the necessity and role of a system of ethics from doctrines that assume good. The Western tradition has been heavily dominated by Augustine's doctrine of original sin. Augustine, it should be remembered, successfully demolished the alternative view put forward by Pelagius and had him declared a heretic through the effective manipulation of ecclesiastical politics.[8] Although moral sense theories in the West do not necessarily posit the inherent goodness of human nature, they do not begin by declaring its innate evil. Modern programs of social reform must assume the opposite of original sin, otherwise they become impossible even to conceptualize. *Kannagara* belongs to this type of theory.

The Shinto Anthropology

Shinto thought has a fairly consistent view of the nature of humanity and the *kami* implied within its rituals and activities. Various doctrines exist about the basic elements of mankind, the soul or *tama* (sometimes *mitama*). In the teaching of *ichi-rei-shi-kon*, four aspects of the soul or four types of soul are seen as coexisting under the control of one spirit. These are usually identified as *ara-tama*, which refers to the wilder and more primal aspects of the soul; *nigi-tama*, the more peaceful and refined aspects of the soul; *saki-tama*, the happy and creative aspects of the soul; and *kushi-tama*, the mysterious and concealed aspects of the soul. The significance of these aspects is reflected in the fact that in different shrines, different aspects of the same *tama* may be enshrined. According to one theory, within the Grand Shrines of Ise there is an *ara-matsuri-no-miya* in which is enshrined the *nigi-tama* of Amaterasu whereas in the *Geku* it is her *ara-tama* that is enshrined.

When Empress Jingu invaded Korea, she was accompanied by the protective *ara-tama* of the *kami* she invoked[9] for her defense, but the *nigi-tama* remained in Japan. There is no doubt that the *ara-tama* was considered to possess special powers and that these were not infrequently associated with the military spirit. Motoori Norinaga identified *saki-tama* and *kushi-tama*. This is usually taken to be reflected in the *mitsu-domoe*, the circle consisting of three equally shaped loops that narrow at one end to meet in the middle.

Closely associated with *tama* is its power or energy, known as *tamashii*. This too has special overtones, as in the expressions *kotodamashii*, the power of the spirit of words; or *Yamato-damashii*, the unique fighting spirit of the Japanese, associated particularly with prewar and war-time moral and political education.

One topic on which the mythology is almost silent is the status of the *tama* after death. In the mythology, *kami* die and later people and Emperors die, yet they continue to be *kami*. The only observation that can be made on this issue is that because Shinto is concerned with development and stages of growth, it views death as simply a stage in a longer process. Certainly there is no Shinto eschatology and little about life after death in the Western sense. Later concepts such as the idea of the Pure Land belong entirely to Buddhism.

Kokoro is also an essential part of the human structure, referring to the heart or the seat of the will and the source of volition and motivation.[10] The *kokoro* was singled out by Ishida Baigan as the place where the training of the spirit can begin, and it became a central concept of the New Religions.

The Moral Vocabulary of Shinto

The subjects discussed in Chapter 6 are germane to this section. Only through the process of comparison can the distinctive character of the ethics of Shinto be made clear. Consider some of the principal terms associated with moral values in Shinto. The most important is *makoto*, translated usually as "sincerity." Kamo no Mabuchi stressed the status of *makoto-no-kokoro*, a sincere heart, as the ideal virtue in Shinto. The term remains extremely important and a generic concept of the tradition. *Junsui*, meaning "pure," is used (in addition to its non-moral usages) to refer to people who are "pure in heart" or pure in the sense of simple, honest, and uncorrupted by the world. Terms related to this are *sei-mei-shin*, the pure heart; *akaki*, which describes brightness with regard to the human heart; and *naoki*, which refers to uprightness of character. All were defined individually by the *Kokugaku* scholars based upon the usages of the *Manyōshū* and the ancient Japanese texts.

Human nature can also be defined in terms of *shinjin goitsu* and *shinjin kiitsu*. The former term refers to the organic unity of human and divine (literally, "*kami*-person-meeting-one") and the latter refers to the restoration of the divine (literally, "*kami*-person-return-one"). Behind this are ideas of the original innocence of human character and its periodic restoration throughout life. Human beings are born with the ability to live in harmony with the divine and with nature, but because of the various forms of impurity that overtake life, purification becomes necessary. Purification effects restoration.

The need for purification is occasioned by the presence of impurities. The Shinto categories of impurity and purification are *kegare*, which means injury or impurity, and *tsumi*, which also refers to impurities and pollution. These are removed by means of *oharai*. The goal to be achieved by the performance of *misogi harai*, purification using water, is the cultivation of *reisei*, the Shinto ideal of spirituality. As the spirit is purified again and again, it can rise to the level of the divine as its spiritual sensitivity is heightened. The repairing and remaking of the *kokoro* is called *tsukuri katamenaosu*.

Kansha, or thanksgiving, is a term used widely in the Japanese language—but especially in Shinto—to express human gratitude for its dependence upon the divine. It frequently appears in statements of corporate philosophy in Japan and carries a neo-religious nuance. People are "thankful" to customers, suppliers, workers, and the invisible powers that bless them; this is fostered as a basic attitude toward society. Individuals are encouraged to express *kansha* in order to maintain a positive outlook, even when things may not be so good.

Related to human effort is *tsui-shin* (hard work), which is praised in Shinto as a virtue. If there is anything that resembles a work ethic in Japan, it is this ideal. It can also be integrated into the thought of the *sankō genri*, the framework of life afforded by the concepts of mission, life, and destiny. *Life* means life in the widest sense of people being within the processes of *Daishizen*, or Great Nature, where they find mission or a clear set of purposes in the form of duties and responsibilities toward society and other people. In fulfilling these, destiny is achieved in the sense of realizing the best and highest of which humanity is capable. In order to keep ideals and the sense of mission alive, purification is necessary. That is the task of Shinto ethics, not a system of ethics that has a moral theology. Shinto ethics may best be classified as an agathistic utilitarianism with a summum bonum as its final end.

SHINTO AND WESTERN METAPHYSICS

Shinto appears from many aspects of its development to be particular rather than universal both in its meaning and application. The late nineteenth-century role of State Shinto appears to strengthen the claim for its particularity. However, this would do less than justice to other aspects of Shinto thinking that stress not the particular and the Japanese, but the universal and the cosmic. Underlying the concept of *kannagara* is the simple idea of following the way of the *kami* within the flow of life in the universe, and this seems capable of wider understanding. It can be viewed as a concept of natural religion, as a way of seeing and experiencing the divine in the midst of life. It has served to keep Shinto true to itself as a way of satisfying the longings and promptings of the human spirit that inspire the human soul to commence the spiritual journey (the history of religion) and that seeks the religious, religious belief, and above all, valid religious experience.

Critics of Shinto would do well to remember the Crusades in the West, the Inquisition, the numerous "holy wars" that have marred Western history, as well as the use of religion to bless weapons of war. Islam retains the concept of *jihad* and the Vatican holds to the doctrine of the "just war," presumably a war that is justified because its own vested interests are threatened. Religion anywhere requires a core of deep, self-correcting spirituality. This can enable it to transcend its own particularity and limitations and discover the universal truths and insights upon which all authentic religion is based and that can act as a guide back to the pathways of original insight when, for any reason, the pathway is not being followed.

Kannagara is the deep core of Shinto in all its many forms; it is another way of expressing that idea.

Beyond this, Shinto is capable of input into the dialogue of world religions because it is the only religious tradition of any sophistication that has grown out of a profound sense of the *immanence* of divinity rather than the *transcendence* of God, the principal feature of the Judaeo-Christian tradition. The latter grew out of the desert wastes of the Middle East, which could see God only as "wholly other" or as the "Beyondness of the Beyond" but not as "within the world." Shinto grew up in an environment blessed with nature in all its plenitude and grace. Shinto can fulfill the role of *complimentarity*[11] by being part of the self-corrective community of truth in which religions supplement each other's limitations and point to the limits of doctrines while seeking to be mutually enriching for the sake of the spiritual development of mankind. I suggest six possible areas:

1. The divine in immanence and transcendence

2. Man and nature in harmony rather than in confrontation

3. The monistic versus the dualistic universe

4. The ultimate reality of presentness

5. The renewing power of purification

6. The metaphysic of process versus the metaphysic of substance

The Divine in Immanence and Transcendence

The Japanese *kami* may be found in all aspects of nature, particularly in special mountains such as Mt. Fuji or deep forests such as the wooded area of Mt. Miksa near the Kasuga shrine in Nara. This sentiment stands in sharp contrast to the Western use (1) in early Christian times of nature as a model of unregenerate man, and (2) in medieval times of the idea that the forest was the abode of demons. People who enjoyed the atmosphere of the forest ran the risk of being accused of witchcraft and consequently of being persecuted and burned at the stake. The divine was thus above nature and nature was an obstacle to divine grace. It could never be the vehicle of the divine. Beauty itself is therefore not a value in the Western system.[12] Values are essentially moral. A "natural" value such as the beauty of a mountain or river could even be considered, at its worst, a form of idolatry. This carries us back to the contrast of "natural religion" and its relation to a "religion of nature."

The Christian tradition has in its more broad-minded forms recognized the significance of natural religion as well as revealed religion, but it has never conceded that a religion of nature might also be a form of natural religion and a means of revelation at the same time. The categories have been widely separated, and under the influence of Barthian theology during the twentieth century they have been completely asseverated. Barth refused an invitation from the Scottish Universities to deliver the famous Gifford Lectures in Natural Theology because he declared himself to be an unequivocal opponent of natural theology in any form. Pope Pius XII called him the greatest theologian since Thomas Aquinas. This has prevented Christian thought from assuming any other than a scientific view of nature, as a result of which it has no basis for an ethic of the environment. This is one of the blind spots of Christian thought that has emerged since the era of environmental concern began in the 1970s. Attempts to suggest that a Christian view of the environment exists are artificial and go against its inherent anthropomorphism and anthropocentrism. Destruction of a man-made work of art, like a landscape painting, will arouse more public indignation than wholesale destruction of nature itself. Any ethic of the environment must begin with a sense of reverence for nature, an attitude of which the Judaeo-Christian tradition is incapable but which Shinto naturally helps to foster.

Man and Nature in Harmony Rather Than in Confrontation

The Western myth of the Garden of Eden is primarily responsible for the image of man struggling with a cruel and relentless natural order, which he must subdue. Adam is told that he will earn his bread by the sweat of his brow and that he will have to battle the elements to survive. The subjugation of nature as a policy can be dated back to the Stoic influences in Roman thought and to the vast works of civil engineering undertaken during Roman times as an expression of Roman ideology. Forests were cleared, marshes drained and settlements established. Tertullian, an early Christian writer, praised this; he thereby married rationalistic Stoicism to Christianity by affirming that the world was made for the benefit of its rational members. Praising Roman civilization, he wrote that "cultivated fields have subdued forests; flocks and herds have expelled wild beasts . . . marshes are drained; and where once were hardly solitary cottages, there are now large cities."[13] He was following the views of Cicero (106–43 B.C.) expressed in his work *Concerning the Nature of the Gods*, in which he argued that the universe existed for the benefit of its rational members, in reply to the Epicurean philosopher Balbus. Later ages never saw fit to challenge this, let alone inquire if it needed to be corrected. In terms of modern environmental thinking, man and nature in harmony is much more significant and relevant. Here Shinto thought may have a contribution to make.

The Monistic versus the Dualistic Universe

Unlike Western religion, which sees the world in terms of good and evil or as an arena in which the conflict of cosmic forces is taking place, Shinto sees the world and man in it as essentially good. From a philosophical point of view, the absence of clear dualism means that Japanese thought tends to be synthetic, uniting and unifying opposites, rather than analytic in the sense of breaking the world down into elements that may express diversity or contradiction. The absence of dualism applied to the realm of ethics also means, for example, that there is no cultural basis for tales about vampires or for movies like *The Exorcist* or *Dracula*. Good and evil are not ultimate opposites that are embodied in God and the Devil, and Heaven and Hell are not rival residences that seek to claim the destiny of the human soul. Human nature is viewed like a mirror that can cease to reflect light because of dust. Once it is washed or polished, it can once again reflect light as it was originally intended. The importance of such monistic thinking as a corrective to some of the influences of dualistic thinking is in its ability to assist the process of integrated holistic thinking. Such broadly lateral thinking is necessary for problem-solving in the complex modern world where conventional approaches have become singularly ineffective.

The implications of monism rather than dualism in culture have been recognized gradually in different areas of academic concern with interesting consequences.[14] Psychology as well as philosophy and theology are affected, as research has shown.

The Ultimate Reality of Presentness

In Shinto, every moment has intrinsic value. The term used to express this is *naka-ima* (literally, "in the middle of the present"). It is a doctrine that affirms the vitality and the significance of *now*. The measured solemnity with which Shinto rituals are performed stresses the importance of every step and every movement in the process of actual performance. In contrast to aspects of modern life that encourage people to rush in a peremptory manner through many activities to get to "essentials" by shortening the "preliminaries," Shinto sees each act as having importance so that the fullness of life and experience can be enjoyed and appreciated in its entirety. *Naka-ima* carries the same nuance as a similar term, *naka-tsu-kuni* (literally, "middle country"), that is, the world as it is or the place in which man's life finds its best environment. It expresses the Shinto ideal that the world is rich in the blessings of the *kami* and that it exists to be appreciated.

Shinto is optimistic about the world, although it may often be a place of suffering and tragedy. But that reflects the short-term view. Human beings are not isolated in their existence, and in their present they unite the past and future. They represent their ancestors in the present and are bringing about the future. The culture and the spirit of past and future meet in the life of the present—which therefore has, in all its moments, intrinsic value and the promise of blessing, which can be received by the power of regular purification. This is a profoundly existential and affirmative idea; it is born of naturalness and rejects the status of means in favor of ends. Everything is equally important because achieving one goal becomes a means to another.

The Renewing Power of Purification

Purification, *harai*, is the means by which *tsumi* is removed and human nature is restored. Its generic form was the act of *misogi* performed by Izanagi after his visit to *Yomi-no-kuni*. Among the ways *misogi* can be practiced, one of the oldest (favored especially by holy men of ancient times and practiced still) is *misogi* performed under a free-standing waterfall. Dressed in a loincloth and headband, participants enter the fall after ritual and physical preparation and invoke the power of the *kami* to purify them and the elements that combine to constitute their existence.

Similarities with the practice of baptism in early Christianity have been pointed out, but there are some significant differences that indicate the distinctive characteristics of *misogi*. First, *misogi* entails instant and total union with nature. The moment of impact when the water and the participant make contact can generate in some a level of cosmic awareness. States of altered consciousness are common among frequent practitioners of *misogi*; these experiences are documented from non-Japanese as well as Japanese who have undertaken *misogi*.

Second *misogi* is a primal, pure, and unmediated experience. It continues to attract people in increasing numbers in a world in which the quality of experience is often measured by what is printed in books or by what experts say that people should experience. The self-discovering process of searching for authentic experience in the world of manmade concrete and plastic has been replaced by the acceptance of much at second hand. In this sense, however, *misogi* defies description. It is an invitation to the purity of authentic experience itself.

Third, *misogi* is not in any sense symbolic. It is actual purification that takes place at a physical and emotional level of which participants are profoundly aware. This may be true of some forms of baptism, but the difference is heightened by the fact that the waterfall is also a *kami*. Furthermore, *misogi* is performed on a regular basis, unlike the "once and for all" character of baptism. Repeated performance itself is a pathway to spirituality for those who have made a discipline out of midnight and morning *misogi*. The therapeutic effects of lowered stress levels and some of the healing side effects have shown that it contains medical as well as spiritual wisdom.[15]

The terms *kiyoshi* (cleansed) and *sayakeshi* (refreshed) are found in the *Manyōshū* over a hundred times, showing how basic the idea was to the earliest literati of Japan. The brightness of the sun and moon are described by these terms, but so is the human spirit once it has been purified and cleansed properly.

Tamamakuze no	Clean precious riverbed
Kiyohi kahra ni	In it do I purify myself
Misogi shite	For the sake of my wife
Iwau inochic wa	
Imoya tame koso	

In this sense, the *Manyōshū* is perhaps the finest guide not only to the outlook of the ancient Japanese but to the mentality of Shinto in the generic sense of the term. *Misogi* and *uranai* (fortune-telling) are closely connected. The purified person is best qualified to discern the times. The *kiyoki* (pure heart) is the origin of *kiyome*, one of the key words in the *misogi* ritual.

The Metaphysic of Process versus the Metaphysic of Substance

The Western intellectual tradition after Aristotle became (and remained) dominated by the concept of substance, which was used in early Christianity to define the relation between Christ and God. This led to the famous "iota of a difference" battle as to whether Christ was of the same substance as the Father or of a like substance to the Father. The theological battle of the Reformation era was over the meaning of the term *transubstantiation*. Did the bread and wine of the Eucharist physically become, as the Roman Church claimed, the body and blood of Christ, or were they merely symbols? The concept of substance has played an important—but from a cultural point of view, sometimes an ambiguous—role in Western thought. Shinto mythology implies an awareness of process as an equally important category for the understanding of life and the world.[16]

The concept of *musubi* as it features in the mythology is understood as the spirit of binding, of birth and becoming. The etymology is usually taken to be from *musubu*, "to grow,"[17] which exists in the tradition close to the idea of embodied creativity. Through the agency of *Takami-musubi-no-kami* and *Kami-musubi-no-kami* the earth comes into being. The role of *musubi-no-kami* also goes further and even includes the creation of some of the clans.

Fujisawa Chikao, a modern exponent of so-called neo-Shinto, claims that the concept of *musubi* can be equated directly and simply with the *élan vital* of Henri Bergson. Western thinkers, too, have in recent times come to see the importance of process. Notable is Alfred North Whitehead (1861–1947), whose ideas have influenced Christian theology in its search for a rapport with Buddhism, for example. In Shinto, life and the world flow like the river and the waterfall. The processes and stages are marked by rituals, and each has value and importance. The waterfall in *misogi* offers the corrective insight that life as well as its purification are ongoing processes. Teilhard de Chardin's idea of the hominization of the universe that leads onward in a teleological way to its divinization seems close in spirit to the approach of Shinto (although of course there are significant differences).

Western parallels to the basic concepts of Shinto are difficult to find because of the dominant influence of revealed religion that suppresses all other routes to the divine. The greatest of the earlier routes is Celtic Christian spirituality, which wed nature and grace in a unique manner. The Celtic dictum that Christ wore two sandals, the Scriptures of the Hebrews and Nature, is the explicit recognition of the other way. Celtic Christian reverence for rocks and stones, mountains and rivers, fire and water united natural and revealed religion. Even ancestral reverence was to some extent preserved in its rituals. The enforced standardization of Christian practices during the seventh century forced its insights into oblivion. Study of the Celtic tradition alongside Shinto would not only be helpful to the comparative understanding of Shinto and its place in the pantheon of world religions but also would assist the Christian tradition in its search for the basis of an ethic of the environment.

Shinto has no more than commenced its dialogue with world religions. In view of the antiquity of its origins and the visible role it plays in Japanese society, as well as the invisible role of its cultural influence, its contribution could prove to be interesting as well as edifying.

NOTES

1. This has been one of the strongest and most dismissive contentions made against Shinto by Christian missionaries. Herbert noted this in *Shinto: The Fountainhead of Japan* (George Allen & Unwin, London, 1967, p. 68). Shinto apologists have not been adept in dealing with it, thereby encouraging the impression that there may be no answer.

For a serious and sympathetic attempt at interpreting the *homo religiosus Japonicus* starting from Shinto concepts, see J. J. Spae, *Shinto Man* (Oriens Institute, Tokyo, 1972). It is the fourth in a series of books that tries to effect a theological meeting between Christianity and Japanese culture.

2. See Stuart Picken, "The Evolution of the Japanese Value-System," *Humanities Journal* 17 (International Christian University, 1983).

3. I have argued elsewhere that although Christianity and Stoicism did engage in head-on collision in the persecutions of Emperor Marcus Aurelius, Christianity eventually adopted more Stoic ideas and values than Christian thinkers might wish to concede. Kant's praise for Stoicism, offered from the viewpoint of the moral consciousness of eighteenth-century Prussian Protestant thought, may be one of the finest pieces of evidence of its long-term influence. That Protestant ethics are deeply imbued with the Stoic ideals of rationality and discipline seems fairly obvious.

4. Francis Hutcheson, *An Essay on the Nature and Conduct of the Passions and Affections* (John Smith, Glasgow, 1728 ed.), pp. 356–357. The entire range of

the relevent members of the group may be sampled in the Oxford University Press two-volume edition of *British Moralists, 1650–1800*, ed. D. D. Raphael (Oxford University Press, 1969).

5. Motoori Norinaga, *Naobi no Mitama* (The Spirit of Rectification) (1771).

6. This puts into a broader perspective the oversimplified dichotomy between "guilt" and "shame" cultures that has often been used to contrast Japan and the West. Perhaps these are not Eastern versus Western values, but rather the preferences of a social system or a way of approaching values.

7. The seat of the emotions in Japanese culture is the *hara* (stomach) in the sense that it was the bowels for the ancient Hebrews. *Hara ga tatsu* (literally, "the stomach is standing") signifies anger. *Haraguroi* ("black stomach") implies "black-hearted." *Hara-gei* ("stomach speaking") refers to the process of non-verbal communication.

8. Mathew Fox was the author of *Original Blessing*. Fox was silenced by the Vatican for one year in 1989 because of his alleged heterodoxical views on creation and spirituality. Pelagius was declared heretical after a debate with Augustine for harboring similar ideas.

9. *Nihongi*, Vol. 1, IX: 8.

10. Regarding Ishida Baigan and his concept of *kokoro*, see Chapter 7 of this book.

11. On complementarity in world religions, see the works of Nolan P. Jacobson. Also relevant is Steve Infantino, "The Principle of Complimentary in World Religions," in Ron Miller and Jim Kelley, eds., *Fireball and the Lotus* (Bear and Co., Santa Fe, 1987).

12. Plato in his earlier years considered beauty on a par with goodness and truth, but later he revised his architectonics of values to eliminate beauty.

13. Tertullian (160–220), *De Anima*, (Garnier, Paris, 1879) *Writings of Tertullian*, Vol. 2.

14. Steve Cousins, "Culture and Self Perception in Japan and the United States," *Journal of Personality and Social Psychology* 56, no. 1 (1989): 124–131. David Loy, *Non-Duality: A Study in Comparative Philosophy* (Yale University Press, 1988).

15. See Yamamoto Yukitaka, *Kami no Michi* (Tsubaki Grand Shrine of America, Stockton, CA, 1987).

16. The application of these ideas has been extremely beneficial to Japan in the area of manufacturing. Process thinking, as in Alfred Whitehead, *Process and Reality* (Macmillan, New York, 1929), or Charles Hartshorne, *Creative Synthesis and Philosophic Method* (Open Court, La Salle, Ill., 1970), is a minority position in the West. See Nolan Pliny Jacobson, *Buddhism and American Philosophy*.

17. *Musubi* and *musu* can be found in the following words, among others: *musuko* (son), *musume* (daughter), *musubi-jo* (a rolled letter tied with string sent by lovers during Japan's medieval age), *musubi-matsu* (a paper expressing a wish tied to a pine tree), and *omusubi* (a ball of rice).

Glossary of Selected Japanese Terms and Expressions

EXPLANATION OF GLOSSARY

1. *Selection of Terms.* The terms compiled are not an exhaustive list of all Shinto names and terms. Terms listed are taken from the main body of the text. The glossary does not contain the names of individual *kami*, nor does it list the names of shrines or notable personalities in *Jinja Shinto* or *Kyoha Shinto*. Some terms used in the Imperial Household are listed because they have appeared in the press over the last twenty years, particularly in connection with the passing of Emperor Showa and the accession of Emperor Heisei. Others are related to the materials in the content.

2. *Chinese Characters.* Verification of the writing of the Chinese characters has been made from several authoritative dictionaries. Reference has been made to the *Kokugo Daijiten, Shinto Jiten,* and *Shin-Shukyo Jiten* as well as to the *Nen-chu Gyoji Jiten.*

3. *Format and Usage.* Parenthesized titles included after explanations indicate the context of usage; usually the sect, the name of the user, the text in which it is found in that form, the Imperial Household, or wherever is appropriate. Where no specific indication is found, it may be assumed that the term is in general usage in the contemporary Japanese language or is an in-use term of *Jinja* Shinto and shrines in general.

4. *Order of Listing.* Terms are arranged alphabetically according to standard English usage based upon the style of romanization of Japanese employed throughout the text. Although there are strong arguments from a scholastic point of view that it would be better to follow the Japanese language format, this would make unnecessary difficulties for the English Language readership for whom this work is intended.

Aidagara 間柄 The dimension of betweenness in a relationship.

Ai-dono 相殿 When several *kami* are enshrined together, the subordinates to the principal are enshrined in *ai-dono* and are known as *ai-do-no-kami*.

Aikidō 合気道 A Japanese self-defense art.

Akaki kiyoki kokoro 明き清き心 Four virtues in Shinto which are conditions of unity with the *kami*; these are also known as *seimei-shin. See Chapter 10.*

Akaki Kokoro 明き心 Bright heart.

Aki-matsuri 秋祭り Autumn Festival of harvest thanksgiving.

Akitsumi-kami 現つみ神 *Kami* in human form, especially the Emperor in the past.

Aku 悪 Evil, not simply in the moral sense but encompassing unhappiness, disaster or misfortune. *See tsumi and kegare.*

Amaterasu Ōkami 天照大神 *Kami* of the sun, principal *kami* of Shinto.

Amatsuhi 天つ日 *Amaterasu* united with the sun.

Amatsu-kami 天つ神 The heavenly *kami* led by Amaterasu.

Amatsu-norigoto 天つ祝詞 Ritual prayer (*Sukyo Mahikari*).

Ame-no-Iwato 天岩戸 The cave in which *Amaterasu* hid herself.

Ame-no-murakumo-no-tsurugi 天叢雲剣 Imperial Sword.

Ame-no-Ukihashi 天浮橋 The Floating Bridge of Heaven.

Ame-tsuchi 天地 An expression meaning "heaven-earth." At creation, the light and pure elements remained in *ame* while the heavier elements remained on *tsuchi*.

Ando 安堵 Ownership rights to land given to the Grand Shrines of Ise.

Anshin Ritsumei 安心立命 Doctrine that teaches people not to worry about daily life concerns, but to pursue their religious goals.

Arahito-gami 現人神 A living, human *kami* (formerly used in reference to the Emperor).

Arimitama 荒魂 Spirit of the *kami* of origins and beginnings.

Asa-gutsu 浅沓 Shoes worn by priests in formal attire made of hollowed paulownia wood and surfaced with black laquer.

Bakufu 幕府 Military Government.

Beppyo Jina 別表神社 A list of the principal 200 shrines nationwide.

Bessha 別社 Independent branch shrine.

Betsu-gū 別宮 Branch shrine.

Bokusen ト占 Divination.

Bon-matsuri 盆祭 Festival celebrated in mid-July to early August to welcome back the souls of ancestors. First a *mukae-bi* (welcoming fire) is lit, and later an *okuri-bi* (sending fire). Buddhist elements are involved, but the festival antedates Buddhism.

Bugaku 舞楽 Ceremonial music and dance.

Bukkyō 仏教 Buddhism (modern term).

Bun-in 分院 Branch of a sect.

Bunkyō-seiji 文教政治 Rule through culture and learning (Edo period ideal).

Bunmei-kaika 文明開化 Civilization and enlightenment (Meiji period).

Bun-rei 分霊 Branch spirit.

Bun-sha 分社 Place of enshrinement of *bun-rei*.

Busha-sai 奉射祭 Arrow-shooting festival celebrated at *Inari Jinja*.

Butsudō 仏道 The Way of the Buddha (ancient form of reference).

Chadō 茶道 The Way of Tea (Tea Ceremony).

Chigi/Katsuogi 千木竪男木 The distinctive gable posts and roof beams on *shimmei-zukuri* shrine roofs. *See Chapter 4.*

Chinju 鎮守 Clan *kami*.

Chinki-shiki 鎮火式 "Fire Calming" ritual in which believers walk bare-footed on hot coals (*Ontake-kyō* and *Shinshū-kyō*).

Chinkon 鎮魂 A ritual to calm the soul (sometimes of the dead).

Chi-no-wa 茅輪 A large ring made of twisted miscanthus reeds through which people pass on June 30 for purification to avoid misfortune.

Chokusai 勅祭 Festival celebrated in the presence of an Imperial messenger.

Chokushi 勅使 An Imperial messenger at highly ranked festivals.

Chōnin 町人 Townspeople (Edo period).

Chūkogaku 中古学 Heian Studies (Edo period).

Chūnagon 中納言 Second rank at the Heian Court.

Chūshi 中祀 Middle ranked festivals in the Heian period.

Da-gakki 打楽器 The percussion instruments used in *gagaku*.

Daidō 大道 The great way, an old name for Shinto.

Dai-Gūji 大宮司 Special title of the High Priest of the Ise Jingū.

Daijō-sai 大嘗祭 Festival at which a newly installed Emperor offers, for the first time, the first fruits of the harvest to Amaterasu. Thereafter, in autumn in the *Niiname-sai*, he continues to do so for the entire length of his reign.

Daikoku 大黒 This *kami* was combined with O-kuni-nushi-no-mikoto to become a *kami* of prosperity (and, in Western Japan, of rice fields).

Dainagon 大納言 First rank in the Heian Court.

Dai-Nippon Jingikai 大日本祇会 Pre-War Organization of Shrines.

Daisai 大祭 Annual ritual marking the death of the previous Emperor (Imperial Household).

Daishizen 大自然 Great Nature.

Dajōkan 太政官 Council of State.

Danna 檀那 Disciple of *shugenja* teacher (Heian period).

Dashi 山車 A large wagon pulled at festivals, differently named in various areas as *yatai, hiki-yama, odori-guruma,* or *yama-boko.*

Daizai Shoni 太宰少弐 Provincial Vice-Governor (Heian period).

Dazai Sochi 太宰帥 Provincial Governor (Heian period).

Dōjin 童人 Mythical child attendants of the *kami* in folk religion.

Dōsojin 道祖神 Also known as *sai-no-kami*, Dosojin are worshipped on village borders or mountain passes to protect travelers.

Dōtaku 銅鐸 Ancient bell-like objects found in parts of Japan.

Dōzoku-shin 同族神 Kinship-*kami*, meaning the *kami* of a family or group with strong kinship ties in a common ancestor.

Ebisu 恵比須 In cities the *kami* of merchants; in rural areas, of rice-fields.

Eboshi 烏帽子 Head dress for priests.

Eirei 英霊 The War Dead.

Ema 絵馬 Wooden tablets that are offered with special prayers written on them.

E-maki-mono 絵巻物 Picture scrolls from the Heian period depicting the origin and wonders of a shrine.

Engishiki 延喜式 A collection of government regulations drawn up between the seventh and ninth centuries, comprising fifty volumes, the first ten of which deal with Shinto rituals.

Fukensha 府県社 Prefectural shrine.

Fukko Shinto 復古神道 Restoration Shinto.

Fukoku-Kyōhei 富国強兵 A strong economy and a powerful military (Meiji period slogan).

Funa-dama 船玉 A *kami* revered by fishermen to protect ships.

Fundoshi 褌 Loincloth used in purification rituals.

Gagaku 雅楽 Ancient court and shrine music.

Gaki 垣 Shrine fences:
    Ita-gaki 板垣 Outer fence.
    Mizu-gaki 水垣 Third inner fence.
    Soto-gaki 外垣 First inner fence.
    Uchi-gaki 内垣 Second inner fence.

Gakuha Shinto 学派神道 Academic Shinto.

Gashō 我象 Sufferings and misfortunes as divine warnings, now referred to as *mishirase* (PL Kyodan).

Gasshō 合掌 Ritual of *Seicho no Ie*.

Gekū 外宮 Outer Shrine of Ise.

Gembuku 元服 Coming of age (Imperial Household).

Gengō 元号 System of naming Imperial eras.

Genkai 現界 Material world (*Sekai Kyūsei-kyō*).

Genreigaku 言霊学 Science of interpreting words by their spirit (*Mahikari*).

Genshi-sai 元始祭 Festival of origins, January 3 (Imperial Household).

Gion 祇園 Susa-no-o-no-mikoto is enshrined in the Yasaka Jinja in Kyoto. The *Gion Matsuri* is celebrated there as one of Japan's major festivals.

Gishiki 儀式 General term for a ritual.

Gishiki-den 儀式殿 A shrine building for special ceremonies.

Go-hei 御幣 Paper or cloth *heihaku* (paper offered to a *kami*) attached to a stick.

Gokoku Jinja 護国神社 Shrine for the protection of the State.

Goma 護摩 Fire ceremony of purification (originally from Shingon Buddhism).

Gongen 権現 "Incarnation" style of shrine buildings.

Gon-Gūji 権宮司 Assistant High Priest of a shrine.

Gorikai 御理解 Sacred scriptures of *Konkō-kyō*.

Goryō-e 御霊会 Ritual to calm angry souls (Heian period).

Goryō-sha 御霊社 Shrine for the War Dead.

Goseigen 御誓言 Sacred text of *Sukyo Mahikari*.

Gosha 郷社 Village shrine.

Goshiki-ban 五色板 Five colored sets of ribbons hung in shrines in the altar area: *kuro* (black) or *murasaki* (purple) are accompanied by *ao* (green), *aka* (red), *shiro* (white) and *kiro* (yellow).

Goshinetsu 御親閲 Report at *Kotai Jingū* by an Emperor on his Accession.

Goshinsui 御神水 Offering water charged with divine power (*Shinrei-kyō*).

Go-shintai 御神体 Symbol of the enshrined *kami* kept in the innermost part of the *Honden*. Also called *mi-tama-shiro* in older Japanese form.

Gūji 宮司 High Priest of a shrine.

Gyōji 行事 One of a shrine's annual fixed rituals, or a personal discipline.

Gyoki 澆季 The age of attenuation (Edo period idea).

Hachimaki 鉢巻 Headband tied on for performing purification rituals.

Hachiman 八幡 Of obscure origins, including being the protective *kami* of copper miners in Kyushu, Hachiman is revered principally as a *kami* of battle.

Hafuri 祝 Shrine estates.

Hagoromo 羽衣 Mythological heavenly female person wearing a robe of swan feathers.

Haibutsu-kishaku 廃仏毀釈 Meiji period anti-Buddhist slogan

Haidatsu 攞脱 Ladle used for washing hands and mouth upon entering the precincts of a shrine.

Haiden 拝殿 Worship hall in a shrine.

Hairei 拝礼 The formal manner of showing reverence to a *kami*.

Hakama 袴 The lower part of the priestly costume.

Haniwa 埴輪 Clay figurines used as funerary offerings.

Happyō-kai 発表会 Meeting (in *Shinrei-kyō*) to report miracles.

Harae-do 祓戸 A building (or area) provided for purification of body and mind prior to participation in religious ceremonies.

Harai 祓い Ritual purification.

Harai-gushi 祓串 A wooden stick with paper streamers used in *oharai* rituals.

Haru-matsuri 春祭 Spring festival to pray for protection of crops.

Hashira 柱 Pillar in a shrine building. The different types are:

    Daikoku-hashira 大黒柱 Throne pillar.

    Futa-hashira 二柱 Two pillars through the veranda.

    Kokoro-no-hashira 心の柱 Heart pillar in the center.

    Mune-mochi-hashira 棟持柱 Ridge-supporting pillar.

    Osa-hashira 狭柱 Small "in-between" pillar.

    Shin-no-mihashira 心の御柱 Same as *kokoro-no-hashira*.

Hashiramoto-goma 柱源護摩 *Goma* (fire purification ceremony) performed with piles of wood introduced into Japan by Shingon Buddhism.

Hatsu-hi-node 初日出 First sunrise of the New Year.

Hatsu-miya-mairi 初宮参 First shrine visit of children to be accepted as parishioners; boys, 32nd day and girls, 33rd day.

Hatsu-mōde 初詣 First shrine visit of the New Year made by over 80 million Japanese during the first two or three days of the New Year.

Haya Okikai 早起会 Ritual of *Jissen Rinri Kosekai*.

Heihaku 幣帛 Pieces of paper and cloth hung as offerings to a *kami*.

Heisei 平成 Era of Emperor Akihito.

Hijiri 聖 Holy man, ascetic.

Hi-machi 日待 Waiting for the sun on the 15th night of the first, fifth and ninth months of the old calendar. Meeting in each other's homes, believers would pass the night talking until the act of devotion could be performed as the sun rose.

Hi-matsuri 火祭 A fire festival performed as an act of purification or divination. Some shrines, such as the one at Nachi, have famous festivals involving fire.

Himorogi 神籬 A sacred space marked off by a rope.

Hi-no-kami 火神 The *kami* of fire.

Hinokishin ひのきしん Daily service in *Tenri-kyō*.

Hitogara 人柄 Moral elegance of personality.

Hiwada 檜 Bark of Japanese cypress.

Hō 袍 The outer priestly garment, also known as *sokutai, ikan,* or *saifuku.*

Hōgyo 崩御 Honorific form to describe the passing away of an Emperor or *kami.*

Hōhon-hanshi 報本反始 Indebtedness to ancestors and return to beginnings (Edo period popular idea).

Hokke Shinto 法華神道 Combination of Tendai Shinto and Yoshida Shinto.

Hōmotsu-den 宝物殿 Repository for sacred articles.

Honden 本殿 Shrine building containing *goshintai.*

Hongu 本宮 The central shrine for the worship of a particular *kami.*

Honjaku Engi Shinto 本迹縁起神道 Shinto of true essence and manifestation.

Honji-suijaku-setsu 本地垂迹説 The principle of noumenal (*honji*) and phenomenal (*suijaku*) aspects of Buddhism and Shinto that enabled the one to be a manifestation of the other, making possible an explanation of the relationship between Buddha and *kami.* Originally, the Buddha was the *honji* and the *kami* were *suijaku.* Later the view was reversed by Shinto thinkers in the theory of *han-honji-suijaku-setsu,* or *shimpon-butsuju-setsu.*

Honso 本宗 Source or root.

Honzan-ha 本山派 Sect of *Shugendo* (Heian period).

Honzen-no-sei 本然の性 Primary nature (Chu Hsi).

Hoshi-no-tama 星の玉 "Star-ball" ornament found in many shrines.

Hotoku 報徳 "Repayment of Virtue" philosophy of Ninomiya Sontoku, which taught four virtues:

Shisei 至誠 Sincerity of mind.

Kinrō 勤労 Industrious labor.

Bundo 分度 Planned economy.

Suijō 推譲 Yielding to others.

Ibuki 息吹 Breathing exercises performed before *misogi harai*.

Ibuki-hō 息吹考 Deep breathing as performed in *Ontake-kyō*.

Ichi-no-miya 一宮 The formally acknowledged and designated oldest shrine of a district (Heian period).

Imi 忌 Avoidance as a form of purification.

Inari 稲荷 The protective *kami* of rice cultivation as well as the five basic grain cereals, popular among the merchant classes of Edo.

In-en-ga 因縁果 Cause-and-effect cycle that affects human destiny (*Shinrei-kyō*).

Innen 因縁 The Buddhist doctrine of Reincarnation.

Inzei 院政 Cloistered retired Emperor.

Ise Shinto 伊勢神道 The teaching of the Ise Shrines.

Itsuki no hime miko 斎姫王 Imperial Princess serving at a shrine.

Iwakura 磐座 A rocky crag or crevice considered to be the seat of a *kami*.

Iwasaka 磐境 A place where the *kami* is worshipped in the open.

Jiba 地場 Sacred place of *Tenri-kyō*.

Jichinsai 地鎮祭 Ground breaking ceremony.

Jingi-in 神祇院 College of the *kami* as in 1940.

Jingikan 神祇官 The ancient government department of Shinto worship.

Jingiryō 神祇令 Government budget for shrines (Heian period).

Jingishō 神祇省 Department of Shinto Affairs.

Jingū 神宮 Shrine with Imperial connections.

Jingū Hōsaika 神宮奉斎会 Association of supporters of Ise Jingu.

Jinja 神社 Sacred place where a *kami* is present and is revered.

Jinja Gappei 神社合併 Enforced shrine mergers, also called *Jinja Seirei*, or "shrine consolidation."

Jinja-Honchō 神社本庁 Association of Shinto Shrines created after 1945.

Jinja Kyoku 神社局 Ministry of the Interior (*Naimushō*) department handling Shinto affairs (1900).

Jinja Shaden 神社社殿 Shrine buildings.

Jisha Bugyō 神社奉行 Edo period magistrate in charge of shrines and temples.

Jisha-hatsuin-no-gi 輀車発引の儀 Transport of Imperial hearse to the funeral site.

Jishuku 自粛 Period of self-restraint.

Jo-ē 浄衣 Priestly head dress.

Jokogaku 上古学 Nara studies (Edo period).

Jōmon 縄文 Earliest period of Japanese civilization.

Jōrei 浄霊 Ritual to cleanse the body of impurities (*Sekai Kyūsei-kyō*).

Jotai 浄体 Cleansing of the body (*Sekai Kyūsei-kyō*).

Junpai/Junrei 巡礼 Pilgrimage through a circuit of sacred places.

Kagura 神楽 Ceremonial dance to please the *kami*.

Kagura zutome 神楽努 Salvation Dance (*Tenri-kyō*).

Kai-i 階位 Four ranks of priests awarded by the *Jinja Honchō*.

Kairiginu 狩衣 Priestly robes, especially the outer garment which originated as a hunting garment of the nobility of the Heian period.

Kairō 回廊 Veranda around a shrine building.

Kairyū-den 廻立殿 Place where the Emperor and Empress change clothes during the accession rituals.

Kaji 加侍 Prayer or ritual in Esoteric Buddhism.

Kakuri-yo 幽り世 Hidden world of the *kami* as opposed to the *utsushi-yo* (visible world).

Kamado-gami 竈神 *Kami* of the hearth, fire and family protection.

Kame-ura 亀卜 Divination by tortoise shell (*Ontake-kyō*).

Kami 神 The object of reverence in Shinto.

Kami-arisai 神有祭 Festival of *Izumo Taisha*.

Kami-dana 神棚 Family altar (shelf) for reverencing tutelary and family *kami*.

Kami-goto o saki to suru 神事を先とする Putting Shinto matters first.

Kami-kaze 神風 Divine winds.

Kami no Michi 神の道 Way of the *kami*.

Kami-yobi-uta 招神歌 Songs invoking the *kami* (*Seicho-no-Ie*).

Kampeisha 官幣社 Highly ranked government shrine.

Kanbe 神戸 Estates that provided shrine revenues.

Kanchō 管長 Title of the president of *Shinto Taikyō*.

Kandokoro 神所 Shrine lands (sixth century).

Kanjo 勧請 Invitation and proposal for the enshrinement of a *kami*.

Kankoku-Heisha 官国幣社 Government and National Shrines.

Kanmuri 冠 Priestly head wear.

Kannagara 惟神 Following the will and way of the *kami*.

Kannamesai 神嘗祭 Autumn Festival.

Kannushi 神主 Older term for a priest. Ranks are as follows:
    Chokkai 直階 "Uprightness," fourth rank.
    Jōkai 浄階 "Purity," first rank.
    Meikai 明階 "Brightness," second rank.
    Seikai 正階 "Righteousness," third rank.

Kanrodai Sekai 甘露台世界 Perfect divine kingdom (*Tenri-kyō*).

Kanrodai Zutome 甘露台努 Salvation Dance.

Kansha 感謝 Gratitude.

Kanyo 寛容 Tolerance.

Kanzukasa 神司 Central agency for selected ceremonies (sixth century).

Kashikodokoro 賢所 Shrine in the Imperial Palace enshrining past Emperors.

Kashikomu 畏む Attitude of respect toward a *kami*.

Kashimono-karimono 貸物借物 "Things borrowed, things lent" (*Tenri-kyō*).

Kashiwade 拍手 Ritual clapping (in *Kurozumi-kyō*) when the founder's words are quoted.

Kasumi 霞 Area of authority of leading *shugenja* (Heian period).

Kegare 穢 Impurity or injury.

Keiba 競馬 Horse races.

Kenkokusai 建国祭 Constitution Day (after 1945) to replace National Founding Day, *Kigensetsu*.

Kensen-no-gi 献饌の儀 Dedication of offerings.

Kessai 潔斎 Purification or priests.

Kibuku 忌服 Mourning.

Kihan-gaku 規範学 Evaluative study of ancient texts (Motoori Norinaga).

Kigan 祈願 Prayer to the *kami* in whom the individual believes.

Kigensetsu 紀元節 The commemoration day of the mythical accession of Emperor Jimmu in 661 b.c.

Kimotosai 木本祭 Ceremony related to the reconstruction of the Grand Shrines of Ise.

Kinryū-den 金龍殿 Golden Dragon Pavilion, sacred place of *Omoto-kyō*.

Kisei Shūkyō 既成宗教 Older established religions (Jinja Shinto, Buddhism) in contrast to New Religions and sects.

Kishitsu-no-sei 気質の性 Physical nature (Chu Hsi)

Kitsune-mochi 狐持 Possession of fox power.

Kitsune-tsukai 狐使 Use of fox power.

Kitsune-tsuki 狐憑 Being possessed by a fox.

Kiyoki-no-kokoro 清きの心 Purified heart.

Kiyome-no-ike 清めの池 Purification pond.

Kiyoshi 清し Cleansed (*Manyōshū*).

Ko 講 A meeting for religious ceremonies or spiritual guidance.

Kobunjigaku 古文辞学 Ancient Rhetoric School (Ogyu Sorai).

Kōchōgaku 皇朝学 Imperial Learning (Motoori Norinaga)

Kodo 古道 The ancient way, an old name for Shinto.

Kofun 古墳 Ancient Imperial burial mounds.

Kogaku 古学 Ancient Learning (Motoori Norinaga).

Kogigaku 古義学 Ancient Meaning School (Ito Jinsai).

Kokka Shinto 国家神道 State Shinto (Meiji period).

Koku 石 Rice Measure (Edo period).

Koku-bungaku 国文学 National literature (Motoori Norinaga).

Kokugaku Shinto 国学神道 National Learning Shinto.

Koku-Heisha 国幣社 National shrines.

Kokumin-dotoku-ron 国民道徳論 National morality (Motoori Norinaga).

Koku-shi 国史 National history (Motoori Norinaga).

Kokutai 国体 Body politic.

Kokutai-no-kodo 国体の行動 Way of the body politic (Motoori Norinaga).

Koma-inu 狛犬 A pair of sculptured lion-dogs placed at the entrance of a shrine as protective symbols.

Kōreiden 皇霊殿 Sacred pavilion within the Imperial Palace.

Kōrinkaku 光輪閣 Sacred place of enshrinment of the founder of *Shinrei-kyō*.

Koshin-no-gi 貢進の儀 Alighting of a *kami* on a *sakaki*.

Koshitsu-saishi 皇室祭祀 Shinto ceremonies of the Imperial Household.

Koshitsu-Saishierei 皇室祭祀令 Ordinance of 1900 governing Imperial Household ceremonies.

Koto-dama 言霊 Pleasant-sounding words thought to please the *kami*.

Kotsu anzen harai 交通安全祓い Purification for road safety.

Kugatachi-shiki 誓湯式 Subduing hot elements shown by pouring boiling water on the body without harm (*Ontake-kyo, Shinshū-kyō*).

Kumori 曇 Roots of unhappiness (*Sekai Kyūseikyo*).

Kunaicho 宮内庁 The Imperial Household Agency.

Kunigara 国柄 National character.

Kunitsu no kami 国つ神 The *kami* of earth, head of whom is Sarutahiko-Okami.

Kura 蔵 State Storehouse.

Kushimitama 奇し御魂 Soul of life and creativity.

Kyōbushō 教部省 Ministry of Religious Instruction (Meiji period).

Kyodoshoku 郷土色 System of Shinto Instructors (Meiji period).

Kyōha Shinto Rengokai 教派神道連合会 Association of Sect Shinto groups.

Kyo-ichi-nichi-shugi 今日一日主義 One day at a time (*Jissen Rinri Koseikai*).

Kyōha Shinto 教派神道 Sect Shinto (specifically the thirteen sects approved during the late Edo and early Meiji periods).

Kyōkai 教会 Church, used of groups in some sects of Shinto.

Kyoken-Jikkajo 教憲十ケ条 The Ten Precepts of *Shinshū-kyō*.

Kyōku 局 Administrative ward in *Kurozumi-kyō*.

Kyokun 教訓 Lessons for today (*Shinri-kyō*).

Kyōshin-to 教信徒 Learner/believer in *Shinri-kyō*.

Kyōshu 教主 The head of *Misogi-kyō*.

Kyōsosama 教祖様 Founder of a religion (used especially in reference to New Religions).

Kyūchū Sanden 宮中三殿 Three shrines within the Imperial Palace.

Magokoro 真心 Sincere heart (*Manyoshu*).

Mahikari no Waza 真光の業 Light from the hand (*Mahikari*).

Majinai 禁厭 Healing through infusion of *Nippai* (*Kurozumi-kyō*).

Makoto no kokoro 真の心 Sincere heart.

Mappō 末法 The doctrine of an apocalyptic evil age in Buddhism.

Marebito 賓人 Visiting *kami* in disguise.

Massha 末社 Subordinate shrine.

Matsuri 祭 Festival.

Matsuri-goto 祭事 Government (ancient name).

Megumi 恵 Bestowing of grace.

Meishusama 明主様 Enlightened Master (*Sekai Kyūsei-kyō* founder).

Michi 道 Way.

Michi no Kami 道の神 *Kami* of the road.

Michizure 道連れ Follower (*Kurozumi-kyō*).

Mifune-no-Iwakura 御船の磐座 Landing place of *Ninigi-no-Mikoto*.

Mikagurauta 御神楽歌 Sacred writing by founder of *Tenri-kyō*.

Miki 神酒 Rice wine offered to a *kami*.

Miko 巫女 Shrine maiden or supplementary priestess.

Mikoshi 御輿 Portable shrine for carrying *kami* through the community.

Mikoto 御言 The command of a kami, or a title of respect.

Mikoto 命 Suffix denoting a divine being.

Mikoto 尊 An Imperial prince in Japanese mythology.

Mikunimanabi 御国学び Imperial Country Learning (Motoori Norinaga).

Minkan Shinto 民間信仰 Folk beliefs.

Minsha 民社 Local folk shrine.

Miroku-Ōkami 大光明真神 *Kami* revealed to founder of *Sekai Kyūsei-kyō*.

Misasagi 陵 Imperial mausolea.

Misogi Harai 禊祓 Purification by immersion in a river, the sea or under a waterfall.

Misogi Shuhō 禊修法 *Misogi harai* as a discipline.

Mitarashi 御手洗 Water provided for washing hands and mouth before taking part in a religious ceremony. *See Te-mizu-ya.*

Mitegura 幣 Other name for *gohei*.

Miyabika 雅 Refined elegance (Kamo no Mabuchi).

Miya-za 宮座 Organization that oversees shrine ceremonies.

Mono 物 Object.

Mono-imi-hō 物忌法 Abstinence from food and drink (*Shinshū-kyō*).

Mono no aware 物の哀れ The pity or sadness of things, aesthetic sensitivity.

Mushūkyō 無宗教 No denominational allegience.

Musubi 産霊 The spirit of birth and becoming.

Naidōjō 内道場 Buddhist court rank modelled on practices of T'ang Dynasty China.

Naiku 内宮 Inner Shrine of Ise.

Naitei 内廷 Part of the Imperial Household Budget.

Nakaima 中今 Doctrine that the present moment is the best moment.

Nakatomi 中臣 Ancient family that undertook Shinto rituals.

Naka-tsu-kuni 中つ国 Similar idea to *nakaima*.

Naobi-no-kami 直日神 *Kami* of purification.

Naoki kokoro 直き心 Straight heart.

Naorai 直会 Communing with a *kami* after a ritual, which includes drinking *sake*.

Natsu-matsuri 夏祭 Summer Festival.

Negi 禰宣 Senior Priest of a shrine under whom is a *Gon-negi*.

Nembutsu 念仏 Ritual invocation of the Buddha.

Nenchū-gyōji 年中行事 The annual cycle of shrine festivals and rituals.

Niiname-sai 新嘗祭 Autumn Festival.

Nigimitama 和御魂 Spirit of integrating power.

Ni-jū-ni-sha 二十二社 The principal twenty-two shrines of the Heian period.

Nikkū 日供 Prayers offered on behalf of those unable to attend daily worship (*Kurozumi-kyō*).

Ninja 忍者 Martial arts specialist.

Ninjō-shugi 人情主義 Principle of human feeling as the essence of humanity (Motoori Norinaga).

Ni-Ō 仁王 Guardians at the entrance of a Buddhist temple, corresponding to the *Ya-daijin* at some shrines.

Nippai 日拝 Inhaling the sun (*Kurozumi-kyō*).

Nissan 日参 Recitation of the *Obarae no Kotoba* (*Kurozumi-kyō*).

Nittoku 日徳 The sun virtue of Amaterasu.

Noh 能 Religious drama.

Norito 祝詞 Words addressed by a priest to the *kami* in traditional style.

Ōbarae-no-kotoba 大祓詞 Words of ritual purification as compiled in the Heian period. *See Chapter 3.*

Oboe 覚 Things to be learned and remembered (*Shinri-kyō*).

Ofuda 御札 An amulet bearing the name of a *kami* kept by believers.

Ofudesaki 御筆先 Sacred scriptures of *Tenri-kyō*.

Oharai 御祓 Purification in any of its forms. *See harai and Chapter 3.*

Okagemairi 御蔭参 Thanksgiving shrine visits every sixty years (Edo period).

Okumotsu 御供物 Sacred food offerings (*Shinrei-kyō*) charged with divine power that believers take home.

Okura 御蔵 National Treasury.

Omairi 御参 Going to a shrine to offer worship.

Omamori 御守 Protective talisman from a shrine that may be for travel, health, road safety or good fortune.

Omikuji 御御籤 Divination by lots.

Ominuki 御身抜 Release of spirit from body to receive the words of the *kami* (*Jikkō-kyō*).

Omochi 御餅 Rice cakes.

Oni 鬼 A near human form of a spirit with frightening appearance.

Onogorojima 石殷馭慮島 The archipelago of Japan (or the

planet Earth) in the mythology.

Onsashiha 御翳 A canopy to conceal the sacred, used in processions.

Osazuke 授け Gift of the divine to an aspiring teacher of *Tenri-kyō*.

Oshi 御師 A highly ranked *Shugendō* teacher (Heian period).

Oshoku 御職 Leading master guide in *Shugendō*.

Oyagami 親神 Parent *kami* (*Tenri-kyō*).

Rei 霊 Spirit.

Reikai 霊界 Spiritual realm (*Sekai Kyūsei-kyō*).

Reisai 例祭 The principal festival of any shrine performed once or twice a year depending on local custom.

Reisei 霊性 Spirituality.

Reitai 霊体 Spiritual part of human beings (*Sukyō Mahikari*).

Rigaku Shinto 理学神道 Confucian Shinto.

Rikkyo Shinden 立教神伝 Divine call to Akazawa Bunji in 1859 (*Konkō-kyō*).

Rokkon-sho-jo 六根清浄 Purification of the six elements of existence, a term used in *misogi* and in mountain climbing for purification.

Ryōbu Shinto 両部神道 Dual Shinto based on the two Shingon mandalas.

Renso-tojitsu-hinkyusai 斂葬当日殯宮祭 Funerary ritual preceding burial (Imperial Household).

Ryosho-no-gi 陵所の儀 Ceremony of entombment (Imperial Household).

Sachimitama 幸魂 Spirit of harmony and expansion.

Sadaijin 左大臣 Highly ranked official (Heian Court).

Saifuku 祭服 Priestly vestments.

Saigū 斎宮 Imperial Princess serving at at a shrine (also *Saiō*).

Saijitsu 祭日 The day on which a festival is celebrated.

Saikan 斎館 Purification of priests.

Saikigu 祭器具 Utensils used in Shinto rituals, including:

Hassoku-an	八足案	Eight-legged table set up to bear offerings.
Heihaku	幣帛	Offerings.
Oshiki	折敷	Four-sided tray.
Sambō	三方	Offerings tray.
Shinsen	神饌	Food offerings.
Takatsuki	高杯	Sacred utensil for carrying offerings, *kaku-takatsuki* (square) and *maru-takatsuki* (round).

Tamagushi　玉串　*Sakaki* branch.

Saisei-itchi　祭政一致　Unity of Worship and Government.

Saisen　賽銭　Money offered during shrine visits.

Saitansai　歳旦祭　New Year's Day ceremony in the Imperial Household.

Sakaki　榊　A Japanese evergreen used in Shinto rituals.

Sakoku Jidai　鎖国時代　Era of the closed country (Edo period).

Sampai　参拝　Offering worship at a shrine.

Sangaku Shinko　山岳信仰　Mountain cult of spirit worship.

Sankan　三管　"Three reeds," wind instruments used in rituals:

    Fue　笛　Six-holed flute.

    Hichikiri　篥　Nine-holed flageolet.

    Shō　笙　Seventeen bamboo-tubed instrument.

Sanko　三鼓　Three drums used in ritual music:

    Kakko　羯鼓　Small drum for time-keeping.

    Shōko　小鼓　Small accompanying drum.

    Taiko　太鼓　Large drum used in most rituals.

Sanko-genri　三光源理　Cosmic diagram based on three principles. *See Chapter 6.*

Sannō　山王　"Mountain King," another name for *Hie Jinja.*

Sannō-Ichijitsu-Shinto　山王一実神道　Tendai Shinto.

Sanshu-no-Shinki　三種神器　The Imperial Regalia.

Sasara　簓　Wooden clappers.

Sayakeshi　清けし　Refreshed (*Manyōshū*).

Sei-aku-setsu　性悪説　Doctrine of inherent evil in human nature (Confucian concept).

Seikyō　聖教　Teaching of the sages.

Seikyō Bunri　政教分離　Separation of religion and politics.

Seikyō Shinto　聖教神道　Confucian Shinto (Edo period).

Seimei　清明　Purity and brightness of heart.

Seimei-shin　清明心　Same as *akaki kiyoki kokoro.*

Seishiki Sampai　正式参拝　Formal worship at a shrine by offering a *tamagushi.*

Seishinteki bunmei　精神的文明　Spiritual civilization (*Shinrei-kyō*).

Seiza　正座　Reverential posture in *Seicho-no-Ie.*

Sei-zen-setsu　性善説　Doctrine of inherent goodness of human nature (Confucian concept).

Sendatsu　先達　Name for the *Shugenja* of Kumano.

Sengoku Jidai　戦国時代　Era of the civil wars.

Sengu　遷宮　The ceremonial removal of a *kami* to a new shrine building.

Senkyoshi　宣教師　Meiji period Shinto missionary in Japan.

Sen-nichi-kai-hō-gyō 千日回峰行　Mountain ascetic discipline of *Tendai-shu* that takes 1,000 days to complete over a period of seven years.

Senshūryaku 千秋楽　Last day of a *Sumo* tournament.

Senso 践祚　Imperial Accession Rites.

Seppuku 切腹　Ritual suicide (Edo period).

Sessha 摂社　Embraced shrine.

Setsubun-sai 節分祭　Equinox festival.

Setsumei-gaku 説明学　Exposition of ancient texts (Motoori Norinaga).

Shaden 社殿　General name for shrine buildings.

Shaku 笏　A scepter-like stick carried by courtiers and by priests.

Shamushō 社務所　Shrine office.

Shichi-go-san 七五三　Rites of passage festival for children aged three, five and seven years.

Shichi-fuku-jin 七福神　Seven folk *kami* of good fortune.

Shihohai 四方拝　Ritual of showing reverence to north, south, east, and west as an act of reverence toward nature.

Shikinen-sengū 式年遷宮　Removal of *kami* to a new building after a prescribed number of years.

Shikiten kaishi 式典開始　Formal entry of a priest to perform a ceremony.

Shimbu-shiki 神舞式　Sacred dance ritual(*Ontake-kyō*).

Shimenawa 標縄　The rope set up to mark a sacred area or object.

Shinboku 神木　A sacred tree within shrine precincts.

Shinbutsu-bunri 神仏分離　Meiji period separation of Shinto and Buddhism.

Shinbutsu-shūgo 神仏習合　Integration of *kami* and Buddha (Heian period).

Shinden 神殿 One of the three shrines inside the Imperial Palace grounds.

Shindensai 神殿祭　Festival at the *Shinden*.

Shingaku 神学　The study of *kami* in Shinto belief and ritual (theology).

Shingaku 心学　The "Heart Learning" movement founded by Ishida Baigan.

Shinja 信者　Believer.

Shinji-hō 神事法 Divine possession (*Shinshū-kyō*).

Shinjin-gōitsu 神人合一　Organic unity of human and *kami*.

Shinjin-kiitsu 神人帰一　Restoration of the divine to the human.

Shin-koku 神国　Land of the *kami*.

Shinkō-shiki 神幸式 Bearing a *kami* around the community and fields.

Shinkō-shūkyō 新興宗教 New Religions.

Shinmon 神門 "*Kami* gate," general name for shrine gate:

    Kara-mon 唐門 Kamakura period Chinese-style gate.

    Rōmon 楼門 General name and name for gate used by *Chokushi*.

    Sōmon 総門 Outer or first after outer gate.

    Yatsu-ashi-mon 八脚門 "Eight pillars" gate.

    Yotsu-ashi-mon 四脚門 "Four pillars" gate.

    Zuijin-mon 随身門 Gate style that enshrines guardian *kami* of the gate

Shinrei-no-Ōkami 神霊大神 *Kami* of *Shinrei-kyō*.

Shinri-kyō 神理教 Teaching of the Divine Principle (*Kyōha Shinto*) sect.

Shinsen 神饌 Food offerings to the *kami*:

    Jukusen 熟饌 Cooked food.

    Seisen 生饌 Raw food.

    Sosen 素饌 Vegetarian food.

Shinsen-den 神饌殿 Kitchen in which *Shinsen* are prepared.

Shinshoku 神職 Shinto priest.

Shin-shūkyō 新宗教 New Religions.

Shinsōkan 神想観 Meditation (*Seicho-no-Ie*).

Shinten 神典 Sacred writings about Shinto.

Shinto Honkyoku 神道本局 Meiji period Office of Shinto affairs.

Shinto Taikyō 神道大教 Sect of *Kyōha Shinto* that teaches the following:

    Tentoku 天徳 Cosmic world.

    Chion 地恩 The creation of the world.

    Shōjō 清浄 The phenomenal realm.

    Kōmyō 光明 How to live life.

Shinza 神座 *Tatami*-matted reclining throne used in the *Daijosai*.

Shinzen kekkon 神前結婚 Wedding ceremony at a shrine.

Shinzō 神像 Shinto statuary.

Shishi koma inu 獅子狛犬 Same as *Koma-inu*.

Shishi-mai 獅子舞 Ritual lion dance.

Shizen 自然 Nature.

Shōgatsu 正月 New Year.

Sho-gūji 少宮司 The special rank of Associate High Priest at *Ise Jingu*.

Shodō 書道 Japanese calligraphy.

Shōkonsha 招魂歌 Shrine for the War Dead.

Shōshin-no-gi 昇神の儀 Ascent of a *kami* after a ritual.

Shūbatsu 修祓 Self-purification of priests before a ceremony.

Shugendō 修験道 Mountain cult combining Buddhism and Shinto.

Shugenja 修験者 Practitioner of *Shugendō*.

Shuin-ryō 朱印領 Vermilion seal money, shrine grants (Edo period).

Shūki Kōreisai 秋期皇霊祭 Spring Equinox (Imperial Household).

Shūkyō Hōjin 宗教法人 Legally incorporated religious body (post-1946).

Shunki Shindensai 春期神殿祭 Major Spring Festival (Imperial Household).

Shūri-kōsei 修理佼成 "Strengthen and secure," meaning to observe the moral law as understood in *Shusei-ha*.

Sofuku 喪服 Uniform worn by guards of the Imperial bier.

Sojōden-no-gi 喪場殿の儀 Funeral Hall Ceremony (Imperial Household).

Sokaren 葱花輦 Palanquin bearing an Imperial coffin.

Sokui-kanjō 即位灌頂 Traditional Buddhist element in Imperial accession rites purged in the Meiji period.

Sokui-no-rei 即位の礼 Imperial accession proclamation ceremony.

Sonnō-joi 尊王攘夷 Meiji period ideological slogan of anti-foreign groups: "Revere the Emperor, Expel the Barbarians."

Sonnō-shugi 尊王主義 Principle of reverence for the Emperor (Yamazaki Ansai).

Suki-den 主基殿 One of the two halls used in the *Daijō-sai*.

Sonsha 村社 Village shrine.

Sōri Daijin 総理大臣 Chief Minister of State (Prime Minister).

Sosai 総裁 Funeral ceremonies according to Shinto belief and practice.

Sosha 総社 Joint shrine.

Suiga Shinto 垂加神道 Shinto of "divine blessing" (Edo period).

Suijin 水神 *Kami* of water.

Sukei 崇敬 Worship at a shrine.

Sukeisha 崇敬者 "Worshipper" at a shrine.

Suki-den 主基殿 One of the two halls used in the *Daijō-sai*.

Suki-den-kyosen-no-gi 主基殿供饌の儀 Ritual performed in the *Suki-den*.

Sukuinushi-sama 救主様 Master of salvation (*Mahikari*).

Sumō 相撲 Japanese style wrestling that originated as a form of harvest divination and later became a popular sport and the

Imperial sport.

Suzu 鈴 A tambourine-like instrument with bells.

Ta-asobi 田遊 A ritual pantomime of the year's rice cycle performed at the first full moon of the New Year to ensure a good harvest.

Tadashiki kokoro 正しき心 Correct and upright disposition.

Taihō-ryō 大宝令 Law of Taiho era.

Taiko 太鼓 Drums used in Shinto rituals.

Taiko-bashi 太鼓橋 High-arched round bridge found at many shrines resembling the shape of a drum.

Taikyoku 太極 The supra-rational metaphysical Absolute (Chu Hsi).

Taikyō Senpu 大教宣布 Teachings of Emperor Meiji.

Taisai 大祭 The highest ranked festivals of the year nation wide.

Taishi Ryū Shinto 太子流神道 The Shinto of Shotoku Taishi.

Taishō Tennosai 大正天皇祭 Festival for Emperor Taisho (Imperial Household).

Taisō-no-rei 大喪の礼 State funeral (Imperial Household).

Takakuya 高久屋 Primitive "High House" shrine building.

Takama-no-hara 高天原 The Plain of High Heaven.

Tama 玉 Jewel.

Tama-gaki 玉垣 A fence surrounding the buildings of a shrine.

Tama-gushi 玉串 Offering branch of *sakaki* with strips of paper (*shide*).

Tama-gushi-no-hoten-no-gi 玉串奉奠の儀 Offering a sacred branch to a *kami*.

Tamashii 魂 The human soul.

Tanka 短歌 Japanese poetic form.

Ta-no-kami 田の神 *Kami* of the rice fields.

Taru 樽 Barrel-shaped *sake* container.

Tatari 崇 Misfortune.

Te-azekura て校倉 Ancient style of shrine construction.

Teidō 帝道 Imperial Way, an old name for Shinto.

Te-mizu-ya 手水屋 Ablution pavilion for hand and mouth washing at the entrance to a shrine.

Tempon 點本 Japanese readings (of the *Manyōshu* by Kamo no Mabuchi).

Tenchi-gongen 天地権現 Primitive "heaven-earth" style of shrine building.

Tenchi kakitsuke 天地書附 Heaven and Earth reminders (*Konkō-kyō*).

Tenchi Kane no Kami 天地金乃神 *Kami* of *Konkō-kyō*.

Tengu 天狗 Mountain spirit.

Tenjin 天神 The *tamashi* of Suguawara Michizane (*kami* of learning).

Tenmei 天命 Mandate of Heaven.

Tenmei-jikiju 天命直受 Receipt of the Heavenly Mission by Munetada Kurozumi.

Tennōsei 天皇制 The Imperial lineage.

Tokoyo 常世 The world in which the purfied spirits of the dead reside.

Tōkyō-Jutsu 東教術 Doctrine of improving human instincts through observing the Oriental Zodiac (*Taisei-kyō*).

Tomoe 巴 Logo of a circle divided by three curved lines emanating from the centre seen at many shrines.

Torii 鳥居 Gateway to shrine precincts. Styles are as follows:

Chūren	注連	Two posts joined by a *shimenawa*.
Daiwa	台輪	Same as *Inari*.
Gashhō	合掌	"Peaked top" same as *Sannō*.
Gongen	権現	Same as *Ryōbu*.
Hachiman	八幡	Upper beams are cut with a slant
Hie	日吉	Same as *Sannō*.
Inari	稲荷	Usually set up in large numbers and painted bright red at *Inari* shrines.
Ise	伊勢	Similar to *Shinmei* with a pentagonal *kasagi*. (*See "elements" that follow*).
Karahafu	唐破風	Style influenced by Chinese ideas.
Kashima	鹿島	Style associated with *Kashima Jingu*.
Kasuga	春日	First style to be painted red and with a *shimagi*.
Komochi	子持	Same as *Miwa*.
Kuroki	黒木	"Wild cherry," using undressed wood.
Mibashira	三柱	"Three-legged" style.
Miwa	三輪	Twelfth century triple-beamed style seen with and without doors.
Munetada	宗忠	Old style using straight lines.
Myōjin	明神	"Gracious *kami*" style, which uses a low stone base.
Naikū-gen	内宮	Similar to *Ise* with octagonal *hashira*.
Nakayama	中山	Local style from Ichinomiya in Okayama.
Nemaki	根巻	"Wrapping the foot" so called because of wooden covers at the base of the

posts to prevent decay.

Ryōbu	両部	Distinctive because of supports in front of and behind *hashira*.
Sanchū	三柱	Same as *Mibashira*.
Sanko	三光	"Three lights," same as *Miwa*.
Sankyaku	三脚	Same as *Mibashira*.
Sannō	山王	Recognised by its *gashho* (peaked top).
Shikyaku	四脚	"Four legged," same as *Ryōbu*.
Shimenawa	注連	Same as *Chūren*.
Shinmei	神明	"Divine brightness"
Shinmon	神門	"*Kami* gate," shrine gates.
Sode	袖	"Sleeve," same as *Ryōbu*.
Sogo	総合	"Synthetic," same as *Sannō*.
Tohafu	唐破風	Same as *Karahafu*.
Waki	脇	"Side," same as *Miwa*.
Waku	輪枠	"Framed," same as *Ryōbu*
Sumiyoshi	住吉	Distinguished by its square *hashira*.

Elements:

Daiwa	台輪	Upper cross-beam rest.
Gakuzuka	額束	Inscription holder.
Hashira	柱	Vertical beams.
Kamebara	亀腹	Vertical beam supports.
Kasagi	笠木	Upper cross-beam.
Kusabi	楔	Lower cross-beam wedges.
Nuki	貫	Lower cross-beam.
Shimagi	島木	Upper cross-beam.

Toritsugi 取次 Meditation (*Konkō-kyō*).

Tōrō 灯籠 Lantern.

Toshi-gami 年神 *Kami* of the New Year.

Toshigoi no matsuri 年越の祭 Festival for a good harvest.

Tōya 頭屋 Group of laypersons who oversee the affairs of a shrine that has no resident priest. *See also Miya-za.*

Tsuka 塚 Sacred mounds used for worship or other ritual purposes.

Tsukinami-sai 月次祭 Main festival of *Shūsei-ha*.

Tsumi 罪 Impurity, misfortune, which can be removed by means of *oharai*.

Tsustushimi 慎み A circumspect attitude.

Tsutome 努め Worship in *Tenri-kyō*.

Ubasoku-zenji 優婆塞 Wandering ascetics.

Uchi-mono 打物 Percussion instruments used in ritual music.

Ugadama 食魂 Food spirit.

Uji-bito 氏人 Clan member.

Uji-gami 氏神 The ancestral kami of a family or house.

Uji-gawa 宇治川 Izu River in Ise.

Uji-ko 氏子 Parishioners living under the protection of a shrine.

Uji-ko-kai 氏子会 Organizing committee of *uji-ko*.

Uji-ko-sōdai 氏子総代 Same as *uji-ko-kai*.

Ushitora-no-Konjin 丑寅の金神 *Kami* of *Ōmoto-kyō*.

Wa 和 Harmony.

Wagaku 和学 Japanese learning (Keichu).

Waka 和歌 Japanese poetic form.

Wakamiya 若宮 Young (newly formed branch) shrine.

Wakon-Yosai 和魂洋才 Western learning, Japanese spirit.

Wazawai 災い Disaster understood as a form of *tsumi*.

Yabusame 流鏑馬 Heian period horse-backed archery contest using three targets.

Yakubarai 厄払い Purification to calm a troubled *kami*.

Yakudoshi 厄年 The years of misfortune, traditionally thirty-three for women and forty-two for men.

Yamaguchi-sai 山口祭 Ceremony relating to the reconstruction of the Grand Shrines of Ise.

Yamamiya 山宮 Mountain shrine.

Yama-no-kami 山の神 *Kami* of the mountains revered in traditional *Sangaku Shinko*, or the cult of the mountains.

Yamato 大和 Ancient name for Japan.

Yamato damashii 大和魂 Unique martial spirit of the Japanese race.

Yamato kotoba 大和詞 Ancient Japanese language before Chinese influences entered Japan.

Yao-yorozu-no-kami 八百万の神 The myriads of *kami*.

Yasaka nin no magatama 八尺瓊の曲玉 The Jewel in the Imperial Regalia.

Yashiki-gami 屋敷神 The *kami* enshrined in the corner of a dwelling, or *yashiki*.

Yasurakeku 安らけく Serenity (Kamo no Mabuchi).

Yatagarasu 八咫烏 The crow that guided *Ninigi-no-mikoto*.

Yatai 屋台 Large wagon pulled in festivals.

Yata no Kagami 八咫の鏡 Mirror of the Imperial Regalia.

Yatsu no hokori 八つの埃 The eight kinds of dust (impurities), the source of unhappiness (*Tenri-kyō*).

Yoki 陽気 Essence of the *kami* (*Kurozumi-kyō*).

Yokigurashi 良き苦らし Happiness and freedom from suffering as the goal of life (*Tenri-kyō*).

Yōmei-Gaku 陽明学 Yang-Ming Confucianism.
Yomi 黄泉 The land of pollution.
Yorishiro 依り代 Rock piles used to mark sacred places in ancient times.
Yoshida Shinto 吉田神道 Shinto thought of Yoshida Kanetomo.
Yudate 湯立 Purification ritual using sprinklings of boiled water.
Yuishō 由緒 Historical lineage of shrine and its *kami*.
Yuiitsu Gempon Sogen Shinto 唯一原本宗源神道 Original true-essence Shinto of Yoshida Kanetomo (*Yuitsu Shinto*).
Yuki-den 悠紀殿 One of the buildings used in the *Daijo-sai*.
Yuki-den-kyosen-no-gi 悠紀殿供饌の儀 Imperial ritual performed in the *Yuki-den*.
Yū-shide 木綿四手 Paper streamers hung on straw ropes (*shimenawa*) at shrines. Same as *gohei*.
Yūsokugaku 有識学 Antiquarian study (Motoori Norinaga).
Za 座 Committee of laypersons supervising a shrine.
Zen 善 The good, happiness and sometimes the superiority of an object.
Zoka Sanshin 造化三神 The three central *kami* of creation.
Zukuri 造 General term for styles of shrine architecture:

Aidono-zukuri	相殿造	"Joint enshrinement" modification of *Shinmei*.
Asama-zukuri	浅間造	"Two-storied" style.
Gion-zukuri	祇園造	Style modeled on homes of the ninth century rich and aristocratic.
Gongen-zukuri	権現造	"Incarnation" style noted for its Buddhist temple-shaped roof.
Hachiman-zukuri	八幡造	Three-building style with connecting roofs associated with *Hachiman kami*.
Hie-zukuri	日吉造	Combined Buddhist, Chinese, and Japanese style.
Hiyoku-irimoya	比翼入母屋	"Wings abreast" (double roof) *Iromoya* style.
Hōden zukuri	寶殿造	General name for the architectural style of the *Honden* of a shrine.
Irimoya-zukuri	入母屋造	Large gabled roof with small sloping roof marked by the absence of *chigi* and *katsuogi*.
Ishi-no-ma-zukuri	石の間造	Same as *Yatsumune* style.

Kashii-zukuri	香椎造	Local style from northern Kyushu.
Kasuga-zukuri	春日造	Chinese influenced sweeping roof style using Japanese cypress bark.
Kibitsu-zukuri	吉備津造	Rare style unique for its enormous size.
Nagare-zukuri	流造	Flowing roof style.
Ōtori-zukuri	大鳥造	Modification of *Sumiyoshi*.
Shinmei-zukuri	神明造	"Divine brightness" style.
Sumiyoshi-zukuri	住吉造	Style based on buildings erected for festivals.
Taisha-zukuri	大社造	"Great palace" style.
Yatsumune-zukuri	八つ棟造	"Eight roof" style meaning many roofs.

Selected Bibliography and Research Resources in English

PRINCIPAL CLASSICAL WRITINGS AND ANCIENT SOURCES

Engishiki. Tr. F. Bock, Books 6–10 (Sophia University, Tokyo, 1972).
Kojiki. Tr. B. H. Chamberlain (Tuttle, Tokyo, 1982).
———. Tr. D. Philippi (University of Tokyo Press, Tokyo, 1968).
Manyōshū. Tr. H. H. Honda (Hokuseido Press, Tokyo, 1967).
Nihongi. Tr. W. G. Aston (Tuttle, Tokyo, 1972).
Norito. Tr. D. L. Philippi, *A New Translation of the Ancient Japanese Ritual Prayers* (Tokyo, 1959).
Shoku Nihongi. Tr. Snellen, "Shoku Nihongi: Chronicles of Japan Continued from 697–779." TASJ, Second Series, 11 (1934): 151–239; and 14 (1937): 209–279.

GENERAL STUDIES IN JAPANESE CULTURE AND RELIGION

Anesaki, Masaharu. *Art, Life and Nature in Japan* (Boston, 1932).
———. *History of Japanese Religion* (London, 1930).
———. *Religious Life of the Japanese People* (Tokyo, 1970).
Ashida, K. "Japan." *Encyclopaedia of Religion and Ethics*, ed. James Hastings, vol. 7 (Edinburgh, 1914), pp. 481–489.
Bellah, Robert. *Tokugawa Religion* (Glencoe, Il., 1957).
Blacker, Carmen. *The Catalpa Bow* (London, 1975).
Bunce, William. *Religions in Japan* (Tokyo, 1973), Chapter 6–8.
Chamberlain, Basil Hall. *Things Japanese* (London, 1905).
Cousins, Steve. "Culture and Self Perception in Japan and the United States." *Journal of Personality and Social Psychology* 56, no. 1 (1989): 124–131.

Note: TASJ stands for Transactions of the Asiatic Society of Japan.

Dorson, Richard M. *Folk Legends of Japan* (Tokyo, 1962).

Earhart, H. Byron. *Japanese Religion: Unity and Diversity* (Wadsworth, CA, 1974).

———. *Religion in the Japanese Experience: Sources and Interpretations* (Wadsworth, CA., 1974).

Earl, David. *Emperor and Nation in Japan: Political Thinkers of the Tokugawa Period* (Seattle, 1964).

Fisher, Jerry T. "Nakamura Keiu: The Evangelical Ethic in Asia." *Religious Ferment in Asia*, ed. Robert J. Miller (1974).

Fung Yu-lan. *A Short History of Chinese Philosophy* (Glencoe, 1966).

Griffis, William Elliot. *The Religions of Japan: From the Dawn of History to the Era of Meiji* (New York, 1901).

Hakeda, Yoshito S. *Kukai: Major Works* (New York, 1972).

Hase, Akihasa. *Japan's Modern Culture and Its Roots* (Tokyo, 1982).

Havens, T. R. *Farm and Nation in Modern Japan: Agrarian Nationalism* (Tokyo, 1974).

Hearn, Lafcadio. *Japan: An Attempt at Interpretation* (New York, 1904).

———. *Kokoro: Hints and Echoes of Japanese Inner Life* (Boston, 1927).

Heaslett, Samuel. *The Mind of Japan and the Religions of the Japanese*. Religions of the East Series, No. 1 (London, 1947).

Keene, Donald (Ed.). *Anthology of Japanese Literature: From the Earliest Era to the Mid-Nineteenth Century* (New York, 1955).

Kindaichi, Haruhiko. *The Japanese Language*, tr. Hirano Umeyo (Tokyo, 1978).

Kishimoto, Hideo (Ed.) *Japanese Religion in the Meiji Era*, tr. John F. Howes (Tokyo, 1956).

Kitagawa, Joseph. "The Contemporary Religious Situation in Japan." *Japanese Religions* (Kyoto) 2, no. 2–3 (May 1961): 24–42.

———. "Japan: Religion." *Encyclopaedia Britannica*, vol. 12 (, 1962), pp. 899–904.

———. "Japanese Religion." In Charles J. Adams, ed., *A Reader's Guide to the Great Religions* (New York, 1965).

———. *Religion in Japanese History* (New York, 1966).

———. "Religious and Cultural Ethos of Modern Japan." *Asian Studies* 2, no. 3 (December 1964): 334–352.

Knox, George William. *The Development of Religion in Japan* (New York, 1907).

Latourette, K. S. *History of Japan* (New York, 1957).

Longford, Joseph H. "Note on Ninomiya Sontoku." *TASJ* 22, pt. 1 (1894): 103–108.

Loy, David. *Non-Duality: A Study in Comparative Philosophy* (New Haven, 1988).

McEwan, J. R. *The Political Writings of Ogyu Sorai* (Cambridge, 1962).

Ministry of Education. *Religions in Japan* (Tokyo, 1963).

Morioka, Kiyomi. *Religion in Changing Japanese Society* (Tokyo, 1975).

Morris, Ivan. *Nationalism and the Right Wing in Japan: A Study of Post-War Trends* (London and New York, 1960).

———. *The Nobility of Failure* (New York, 1975).

Murakami, Shigeyoshi. *Japanese Religion in the Modern Century* (Tokyo, 1980).

Nakamura, Hajime. *Development of Japanese Thought* (Tokyo, 1971).

———. *Ways of Thinking of Eastern Peoples* (Honolulu, 1973).

Nielsen, Niels C. *Religion and Philosophy in Contemporary Japan*. Rice Institute

Pamphlets 43, no. 4 (Houston, 1957).

Nitobe, Inazo. *Bushido: The Soul of Japan* (New York, 1905).

Nivison, David S., and Arthur Wright (Eds.). *Confucianism in Action* (Stanford, 1959).

Norbeck, Edward. *Religion and Society in Modern Japan.* Rice University Studies 56, no. 1 (Houston, 1970).

Nozaki, Kiyoshi. *Kitsune* (Tokyo, 1961).

Ohe, Seizo. "Sontoku Renaissance." *Humanities* 11 (ICU, 1978): 211–215.

Okakura, Kakuzo, *The Book of Tea* (Edinburgh, 1919).

Okubo, Genji. *The Problems of the Emperor System in Postwar Japan* (Tokyo, 1948).

Picken, Stuart D. B. *Buddhism: Japan's Cultural Identity* (Tokyo, 1981).

———. *Christianity and Japan: Meeting—Conflict—Hope* (Tokyo, 1982).

———. "Japanese Religions and the 21st Century: Problems and Prospects." Japan Foundation Orientation Seminar 24 (Tokyo, 1987).

———. "Jesus, Kierkegaard and Zen." *Japanese Religions* 8, no. 1 (March 1974): 29–46.

———. "Religiosity and Irreligiosity in Japan: Aspects of *mu-shukyo.*" *Japanese Religions* 11 (December 1979): 51–67.

———. "The Understanding of Death in Japanese in Japanese Religion." *Japanese Religions* 9, no. 4 (July 1977): 47–59.

Ponsonby-Fane, R.A.B. *History of the Imperial House of Japan* (Kyoto, 1959).

———. *Sovereign and Subject* (Kyoto, 1960).

Reischauer, A. K. *Studies in Japanese Buddhism* (New York, 1917).

Reischauer, E. O. *Japan: Past and Present* (New York, 1946).

Reischauer, R. K. *Early Japanese History*, 2 vol. (Princeton, 1937).

Sansom, Sir George. *History of Japan.* 3 vols., new ed. (Tokyo, 1979).

———. *Japan: A Short Cultural History* (New York, 1951).

Smith, Robert J. *Ancestor Worship in Contemporary Japan* (Stanford, 1974).

Smith, Robert J., and Richard K. Beardsley (Eds.). *Japanese Culture: Its Development and Characteristics* (Chicago, 1962).

Smith, Warren W., Jr. *Confucianism in Contemporary Japan: A Study of Conservatism in Japanese Intellectual History* (Tokyo, 1959).

Spae, Joseph. *Japanese Religiosity* (Tokyo, 1971).

Stevens, John. *Marathon Monks of Mt. Hie* (Boston, 1988).

Tsunoda, Ryusaku; William. Theodore de Bary; and Donald Keene. *Sources of the Japanese Tradition* (New York, 1958).

Yanaihara, Tadao. *Religion and Democracy in Modern Japan* (Tokyo, 1948).

STUDIES IN SHINTO

Aichi Prefectural Shinto Youth Association. *An Explanation of Shinto for People of Foreign Lands*, eds. Handa Shigeru et al (1985).

Akiyama, Aisaburo. *Shinto and Its Architecture* (Kyoto, 1936).

Anesaki, Masaharu. *Japanese Mythology. The Mythology of All Races*, vol. 8 (Boston, 1928).

Anzu, Motohiko. "The Concept of 'Kami.' " Proceedings of the Ninth International Congress for the History of Religions (Tokyo, 1962), pp. 218–222.

Aston, W. R. *Shinto: The Way of the Gods* (London, 1905).

Ballou, Robert O. *Shinto, the Unconquered Enemy* (New York, 1945).

Bender, Ross. "The Hachiman Cult and the Dokyo Incident." *Monumenta Nipponica* 31, no. 2 (Summer 1979): 125–153.

Buchanan, Daniel C. "Inari, Its Origin, Development and Nature." Asiatic Society of Japan, no. 12 (Tokyo, 1935), pp. 1–191.

Bukkyo Dendo Kyokai. *The World of Shinto* (Tokyo, 1985). An anthology of Shinto Texts.

Creemers, Wilhelmus. *Shrine Shinto after World War II* (, 1968).

Devine, Richard. "Hirata Atsutane and Christian Sources." *Monumenta Nipponica* (Spring 1981).

Dumoulin, Heinrich. *Kamo Mabuchi (1697–1769): Ein Betrag zur japanischen Religions—und Geistesgeschichte* (Tokyo, 1943).

Earhart, H. Byron. *A Religious Study of the Mount Haguoro Sect of Shugendo* (Tokyo, 1970).

Florenz, Karl. "Der Shintoismus." *Die Orientalischen Religionen*. Die Kultur der Gegenwart, Teil I, Ableitung III, 1 (Berlin and Leipzig, 1906), pp. 194–220.

―――. *Die Historischen Quellen der Shinto-Religionen aus dem Altjapanischen und Chinesischen Ubersezt und Erklart* (Gottingen, 1919).

Fridell, Wilbur. *Japanese Shrine Mergers 1906–1912* (Tokyo, 1973).

Fujisawa, Chikao. *Concrete Universality of the Japanese Way of Thinking* (Tokyo, 1958).

―――. *Zen and Shinto: The Story of Japanese Philosophy* (Westport, CT, 1971).

Garfias, Robert. *Gagaku: The Music and Dances of the Japanese Imperial Household* (New York, 1959).

Gluck, Carol N. *Japan's Modern Myth: Ideology in the Late Meiji Period* (Princeton, 1985).

Grapard, Allan. "Shinto." *Kodansha Encyclopaedia of Japan* (Tokyo, 1983), pp. 125–132.

Grapard, Allan. *The Protocol of the Gods* (Berkeley, 1992).

Gundert, Wilhelm. *Der Shintoismus im Japanischen No-Drama* (Tokyo, 1926).

Harada, Toshiaki. "The Development of Matsuri." *Philosophical Studies of Japan*, Japanese National Commission for UNESCO, vol. 2 (Tokyo, 1961).

―――. "The Origin of Community Worship." *Religious Studies in Japan* (Tokyo, 1959), pp. 213–218.

Hardacre, Helen. *Shinto and the State: 1869–1989* (Princeton, 1989).

Hearn, Lafcadio. *Japan's Religions: Shinto and Buddhism* (New York, 1966).

Herbert, Jean. *Shinto: The Fountainhead of Japan* (London, 1967).

Hibino, Yutaka. *Nippon Shindo Ron, c⸱ the National Ideals of the Japanese People*, tr. A. P. McKenzie (Cambridge, 1928).

Hirai, Naofusa. *The Concept of Man in Shinto*. Master's thesis: University of Chicago, 1954.

―――. "Fundamental Problems of Present Shinto." *Proceedings of the Ninth International Congress for the History of Religions* (Tokyo, 1960), pp. 303–306.

Holtom, D. C. *The Japanese Enthronement Ceremonies* (Tokyo, 1928).

―――. "The Meaning of Kami." *Monumenta Nipponica* 3, no. 12 (1949): 1–27; 3, no. 2 (1940): 32–53; and 4, no. 2 (1941): 25–68.

————. *Modern Japan and Shinto Nationalism* (Chicago, 1943).

————. *The National Faith of Japan* (New York, 1938).

————. "Shinto in the Postwar World." *Far Eastern Survey*, no. 14 (February 14, 1945): 29–33.

————. "Shintoism." *The Great Religions of the Modern World*, ed. Edward J. Jurji (Princeton, 1946), pp. 141–177.

Hori, Ichiro. "Mountains and Their Importance for the Idea of the Other World in Japanese Folk Religion." *Japanese Religions* 6, no. 1 (August 1966): 1–23.

————. "On the Concept of Hijiri (Holy Man)." *Numen* 5, no. 2 (April 1958): 128–160; and 5, no. 3 (September 1958): 199–232.

Iro, Nobuo. "Shinto Architecture." *Kodansha Encyclopaedia of Japan* (Tokyo, 1983), pp. 132–134.

Ishida, Eiichiro, "Mother-Son Deities." *History of Religions* 4, no. 1 (Summer 1964): 30–52.

Ishida, Takeshi. "Popular Attitudes toward the Japanese Emperor." *Asian Survey* 2, no. 2 (April 1956): 29–39.

Iwamoto, Tokuichi. "Shinto Rites." *Kodansha Encyclopaedia of Japan* (Tokyo, 1983), pp. 136–139.

Jinja Honcho. *Basic Terms of Shinto* (Tokyo, 1958).

————. *Jinja Shinto Shrines and Festivals* (Tokyo, March 1970).

————. *An Outline of Shinto Teachings* (Tokyo, 1958).

Kageyama, Haruki. *The Arts of Shinto* (Tokyo, 1973).

Kageyama, Haruki, and Christine G. Kanda. *Shinto Arts: Nature, Gods and Man in Japan* (Tokyo, 1976).

Kanda, Christine G. "Shinto Art." *Kodansha Encyclopaedia of Japan* (Tokyo, 1983), pp. 134–136.

Kato, Genchi. *A Historical Study of the Religious Development of Shinto*, tr. Hanayama Shoyu (Tokyo, 1973).

————. "Shinto Worship of Living Human Gods in the Religious History of Japan." Seventeenth International Congress of Orientalists (Oxford, 1928).

————. "Shinto's Terra Incognita To Be Explored Yet." Paper for private circulation (Gotemba, 1958).

————. *A Study of Shinto* (Tokyo, 1926).

————. *What Is Shinto?* (Tokyo, 1935).

Kato, Genchi, with Karl Reitz and Wilhelm Schiffer. *A Bibliography of Shinto in Western Languages from the Oldest Times till 1952* (Tokyo, 1953).

Kawazoe, Noboru. "The Ise Shrine." *Japan Quarterly* 9, no. 3 (July–September 1962): 285–292.

Kidder, J. E., Jr. *Japan before Buddhism* (London, 1959).

————. "Reconstruction of the 'Pre-Pottery' Culture of Japan." *Artibus Asia* 17 (1954): 135–143.

Kitgawa, Joseph. "Shinto." *Encyclopaedia Britannica*, vol. 21 (Chicago, 1962).

Lange, R. "Die Japaner, II Der Shintoismus." *Lehrbuch der Religionsgeschichte*, vol. 1 (Tubingen, 1905): pp. 141–171.

Lokowandt, Ernest. "The Revival of State Shinto." Asiatic Society of Japan lecture (Tokyo, 1982).

Lowell, Percival. *Occult Japan or the Way of the Gods* (New York, 1895).

Mason, J.W.T. *The Meaning of Shinto: The Primaeval Foundation of Creative Spirit in Modern Japan* (New York, 1935).

————. *The Spirit of Shinto Mythology* (Tokyo, 1939).

Matsumoto, Shigeru. *Motoori Norinaga* (Cambridge, MA., 1970).

Matsunaga, Alica. *The Buddhist Philosophy of Assimilation* (Tokyo, 1969).

Ministry of Education. *Kokutai no Hongi: Cardinal Principles of the National Entity of Japan*, tr. John Owen Gauntlett (Cambridge, 1949).

Miyagawa, Munenori. "The Status Quo of Shinto Shrines." *Shinto Bulletin* 1 (March 1953): 4–6.

Morris, J. "A Pilgrimage to Ise." *Transactions of the Japan Society of London* (1905–1906): 248–262.

Muraoka, Tsunetsugu. *Studies in Shinto Thought*, tr. Delmer M. Brown and James T. Araki (Tokyo, 1964).

Nishitsunoi, Masayoshi. "Social and Religious Groups in Shinto." *Religious Studies in Japan* (Tokyo, 1959), pp. 219–228.

Nosco, Peter (Ed.). "The Emperor System and Religion in Japan." *Japanese Journal of Religions* 17, no. 2–3 (June–September 1990). A collection of articles about the Imperial accession rites and the Emperor System, including some interesting translated papers by Japanese scholars.

Numazawa, Franz Kiichi. "The Fertility Festival at Toyota Shinto Shrine, Aichi Prefecture, Japan." *Acta Tropica*, Supplement 16, no. 3 (1959): 197–217.

Ono, Sokyo. "The Contribution to Japan of Shrine Shinto." *Proceedings of the Ninth International Congress for the History of Religions* (Tokyo, 1960), pp. 387–392.

————. *Shinto: The Kami Way* (Tokyo, 1962).

Paine, R. T., and Alexander Soper. *The Art and Architecture of Japan* (Harmendsworth, Eng., 1975).

Picken, Stuart D. B. *Handbook of Shinto* (Stockton, 1987).

————. "The Place of Shinto in Japanese Culture." *Institute of Korean Humanistic Sciences International Cultural Symposium* (Seoul, 1986).

————. "Shinto." *Oxford Dictionary of Politics* (New York, 1993).

————. "Shinto and the Beginnings of Modernization in Japan." *Transactions of the International Conference of Orientalists in Japan* 22 (1977): 37–43.

————. *Shinto: Japan's Spiritual Roots* (Tokyo, 1980).

Piggot, Joan R. "Sacral Kingship and Confederacy in Early Izumo." *Monumenta Nipponica* 44, no. 1 (Spring 1989).

Ponsonby-Fane, R.A.B. *Studies in Shinto and Shinto Shrines* (Kyoto, 1942).

————. *The Vicissitudes of Shinto* (Kyoto, 1963).

Price, Willar. *Son of Heaven* (London, 1945).

Revon, Michel. *Le Shintoisme* (Paris, 1907).

Ross, Floyd H. *Shinto: The Way of Japan* (Boston, 1965).

Sakamaki, Shunzo. "Shinto: Japanese Ethnocentrism." *The Japanese Mind*, ed. Moore (Honolulu, 1967), pp. 24–33.

Satow, E. M. "Ancient Japanese Rituals." *TASJ* 7 (1879): 97–132; and 9 (1881): 182–211.

————. "The Mythology and Religious Worship of the Ancient Japanese." *Westminster and Foreign Quarterly Review* (1878): 25–57.

————. "The Revival of Pure Shin-tau." *TASJ* 3 (1875): 1–87.

————. "The Shinto Shrines of Ise." *TASJ* 1 (1874): 99–121.

Saunders, E. Dale. "Japanese Mythlogy." *Mythologies of the Ancient World*, ed. Samuel Noah Kramer (Garden City, 1961), pp. 409–442.

Schurhammer, Georg. *Shin-To, the Way of the Gods in Japan (According to the Printed and Unprinted Reports of the Jesuit Missionaries in the Sixteenth and Seventeenth Centuries)* (Leipzig, 1923).

Schwartz, W. L. "The Great Shrine of Idzumo." *TASJ* 41, no. 4 (October 1913): 493–681.

Smyers, Karen A. "Of Foxes, Buddhas, and Shinto Kami: The Syncretic Nature of Inari Beliefs." *Japanese Religions* 16, no. 3 (January 1991): 60–75.

Spae, Joseph. *Shinto Man* (Tokyo, 1967).

Supreme Commander for the Allied Powers (SCAP). *Religions in Japan* (Washington, DC, 1948).

Swanson, Paul L. "*Shugendo* and the Yoshino-Kumano Pilgrimage." *Monumenta Nipponnica* 36, no. 1 (Spring 1981): 58–84.

Tange, Kenzo, and Noboru Kawazoe. *Ise: Prototype of Japanese Architecture* (Tokyo, 1965).

Toda, Yoshio. "Traditional Tendency of Shintoism and Its New Theoretical Developments." *Religious Studies in Japan* (Tokyo, 1959), pp. 229–232.

Tyler, Susan E. *The Cult of Kasuga through Its Art* (University of Michigan, 1992).

————. "Is There a Religion Called Shinto?" *Rethinking Japan* 11, no. 30 (Kent, England, 1990), pp. 261–270.

Umehara, Suyeji. "Ancient Mirrors and Their Relationship to Early Japanese Culture." *Acta Asiatica*, no. 4 (Tokyo, 1963): 70–79.

Underwood, A. C. *Shintoism: The Indigenous Religion of Japan* (London, 1934).

Watanabe, Yasutada. *Shinto Art: Ise and Izumo Shrines* (Tokyo, 1974).

Wheeler, Post. *The Sacred Scriptures of the Japanese* (New York, 1952).

Yamamoto, Yukitata. *The Kami Way* (1985).

SECT SHINTO AND NEW RELIGIONS

General

Earhart, H. Byron. *The New Religions of Japan: A Bibliography of Western-Language Materials* (Tokyo, 1983).

Hammer, Raymond. *Japan's Religious Ferment* (New York, 1962).

Iwamoto, Tokuichi. "Present State of Sectarian Shinto." *Research Papers*, Ninth International Congress for the History of Religions (Tokyo, 1958).

Neill, MacFarland. "The New Religions of Japan." *Perkins School of Theology Journal* 12, no. 1 (Fall 1958): 3–21.

————. *The Rush Hour of the Gods* (Macmillan, 1967).

Offner, Clark B., and Henry van Straelen. *Modern Japanese Religions* (Tokyo, 1963).

Schiffer, Wilhelm. "New Religions in Postwar Japan." *Monumenta Nipponica* 11, no. 1 (April 1955): 1–14.

Thomsen, Harry. *The New Religions of Japan* (Tokyo and Rutland, 1963).

Kurozumi-kyō

Hardacre, Helen. *Kurozumi-kyo* (Princeton, 1986).
Hepner, Charles William. *The Kurozumi Sect of Shinto* (Tokyo, 1935).
Stoesz, William. *Kurozumi Shinto: An American Dialogue* (Chambersburg, Pa., 1989).

Konko-kyō

Konkokyo: A New Religion of Japan (Konko-machi, 1958).
Fujii, Kineo. *Hitowa Mina Kaminoko* (Konko-machi, 1984).
Matsui, Fumio. *Konko Daijin: A Biography* (Konko-machi, 1972).
Schneider, Delwin B. *Konkokyo: A Japanese Religion* (Tokyo, 1962).
Yasuda, Kozo. *Konkokyo Scriptures* (Konko-machi, 1983).

Tenri-kyō

A Short History of Tenrikyo (Kyoto, 1960).
Masuno, Michioki. *Tenrikyo* (Tenri City, 1928).
Van Straelen, Henry. *Religion of Divine Wisdom* (Kyoto, 1957).

Omoto-kyō

The Oomoto Movement, Its Origin, Aims and Objects (Kameoka, 1950).
Deguchi, Nao. *Scripture of Omoto* (Kameoka-shi, Kyoto-fu, 1957).
Deguchu, Kyotaro. *The Great Onisaburo* (Tokyo, 1973).
Franck, Frederick. *An Encounter with Oomoto* (New York, 1975).
Tucker, Beverley D. "Christian Worship with Ōmoto-kyō." *Japanese Religions* 9, no. 4 (July 1977): 60–63.
Young, Richard Fox. "Jesus, the 'Christ' and Deguchi Onisaburo." *Japanese Religions* 15, no. 4 (1989): 26–49.

Mahikari

Tebecis, A. K. *Mahikari: Thank God for All the Answers* (Tokyo, 1982).

PL Kyodan

Yuasa, Tatsuki. "PL (Perfect Liberty.)" *Contemporary Religions in Japan* 1, no. 3 (September 1960): 20–29.

Shinrei-kyō

Light from the East (Tokyo, 1986).
Towards the Dawning World (Tokyo, 1981).

Tensho-Kotai-Jingū-Kyō

Guidance to God's Kingdom (Tabuse, 1956).
Tensho-Kotai-Jingū-kyo: The Prophets of Tabuse (Tabuse, 1954).

VISUAL AIDS

1. Japan Society of the United States, (New York), *Shinto: Nature, Gods and Man in Japan* (movie by Peter Grilli).
2. Various shrines have movies of their own festivals and buildings, especially the Grand Shrines of Ise and Tsubaki Grand Shrine in Mie Prefecture. *Jinja Honcho* (Harajuku, Tokyo) can provide more detailed information.
3. The *Nihon Minsozku Bunka Eizo Kenkyujo* (Japan AV Research Institute for Folk Culture) (Shinjuku, Tokyo) has excellent Japanese-language materials.

Index

400 • Index

About the Author

STUART D.B. PICKEN is Professor of Philosophy at International Christian University in Tokyo, where he specializes in ethics and Japanese thought. He is also an adviser on international affairs for the High Priest of the Tsubaki Grand Shrine, and was formerly Director of the Centre for Japanese Studies and Visiting Professor of Japanese Thought at the University of Stirling. He has published more than half a dozen books and some 130 articles and papers.